T0270607

SKY WARRIORS

Also by Saul David

SKY WARRIORS

British Airborne Forces
in the Second World War

SAUL DAVID

**WILLIAM
COLLINS**

William Collins
An imprint of HarperCollins*Publishers*
1 London Bridge Street
London SE1 9GF

WilliamCollinsBooks.com

HarperCollins*Publishers*
Macken House
39/40 Mayor Street Upper
Dublin 1
DO1 C9W8
Ireland

First published in Great Britain in 2024 by William Collins

1

Copyright © Saul David 2024

Saul David asserts the moral right to be identified
as the author of this work in accordance with the
Copyright, Designs and Patents Act 1988

A catalogue record for this book is available from the British Library

HB ISBN 978-0-00-852216-2
TPB ISBN 978-0-00-852217-9

All rights reserved. No part of this publication may be reproduced,
stored in a retrieval system, or transmitted, in any form or by any
means, electronic, mechanical, photocopying, recording or otherwise,
without the prior permission of the publishers.

This book is sold subject to the condition that it shall not, by way of trade
or otherwise, be lent, re-sold, hired out or otherwise circulated without
the publisher's prior consent in any form of binding or cover other than
that in which it is published and without a similar condition including
this condition being imposed on the subsequent purchaser.

All plate section images are taken from the public domain

Typeset in Bembo MT Pro by
Palimpsest Book Production Ltd, Falkirk, Stirlingshire

Printed and Bound in the UK using 100% Renewable Electricity
at CPI Group (UK) Ltd

This book contains FSC™ certified paper and other controlled
sources to ensure responsible forest management.

For more information visit: www.harpercollins.co.uk/green

To Barbette

Contents

Maps

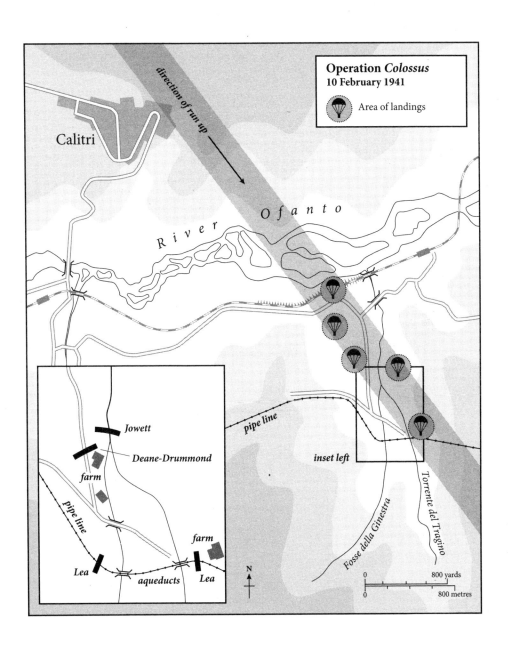

Calitri

direction of run up

River Ofanto

Operation *Colossus*
10 February 1941

Area of landings

pipe line

inset left

Jowett

Deane-Drummond

farm

pipe line

farm

Lea

aqueducts

Lea

Fosse della Ginestra

Torrente del Tragino

N

0   800 yards
0   800 metres

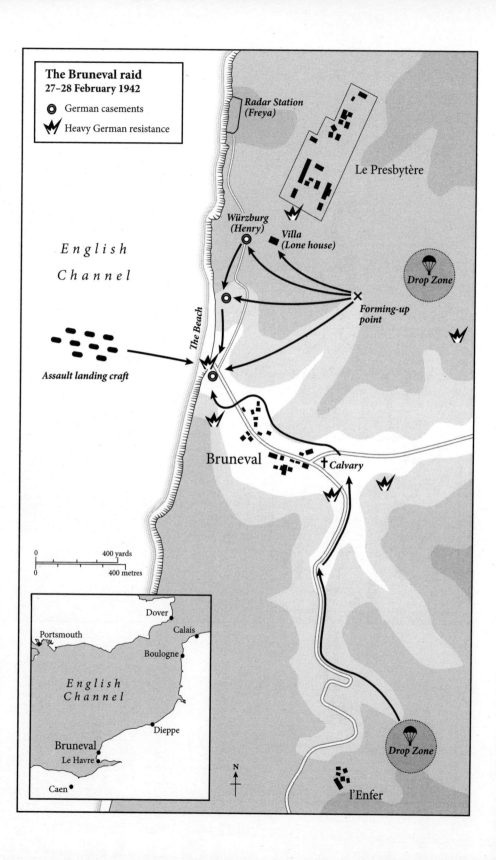

The Bruneval raid
27–28 February 1942

◎ German casements

🔱 Heavy German resistance

Radar Station
(Freya)

Le Presbytère

English
Channel

Würzburg
(Henry)

Villa
(Lone house)

Drop Zone

Forming-up
point

The Beach

Assault landing craft

Bruneval

✝ *Calvary*

0   400 yards

0   400 metres

Dover

Portsmouth

Calais

Boulogne

English
Channel

Dieppe

Bruneval

Le Havre

Drop Zone

Caen

N

l'Enfer

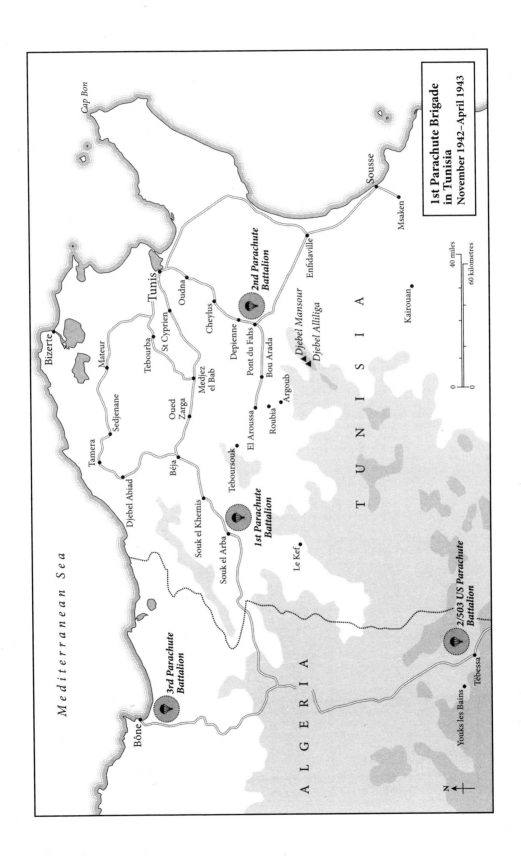

**1st Parachute Brigade
in Tunisia
November 1942–April 1943**

Mediterranean Sea

Cap Bon

Bizerte

Bône

Tunis

Sousse

Msaken

Enfidaville

Kairouan

Mateur

Tebourba

St Cyprien

Oudna

Cheylus

Depienne

Pont du Fahs

Djebel Mansour

Djebel Alliliga

Sedjenane

Medjez
el Bab

Bou Arada

Tamera

Oued
Zarga

Argoub

Roubia

Djebel Abiad

Béja

El Aroussa

Teboursouk

Souk el Khemis

Le Kef

Souk el Arba

Youks les Bains

Tébessa

**2nd Parachute
Battalion**

**1st Parachute
Battalion**

**3rd Parachute
Battalion**

**2/503 US Parachute
Battalion**

T U N I S I A

A L G E R I A

N

40 miles

60 kilometres

0

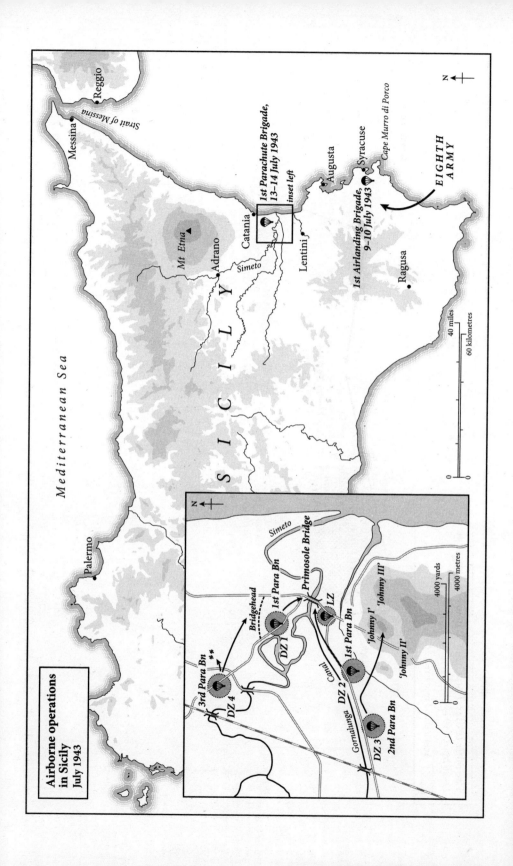

Airborne operations
in Sicily
July 1943

Mediterranean Sea

Reggio

Strait of Messina

Messina

S I C I L Y

Palermo

Mt Etna ▲

Adrano

Simeto

Catania

1st Parachute Brigade,
13–14 July 1943
inset left

Lentini

Augusta

Syracuse

Cape Murro di Porco

1st Airlanding Brigade,
9–10 July 1943

Ragusa

*EIGHTH
ARMY*

N

40 miles

60 kilometres

0

0

N

Simeto

Primosole Bridge

1st Para Bn

Bridgehead

1st Para Bn

LZ

'Johnny I'

'Johnny III'

'Johnny II'

DZ 1

3rd Para Bn

DZ 4

Canal

Gornalunga

1st Para Bn

DZ 2

2nd Para Bn

DZ 3

4000 yards

4000 metres

0

0

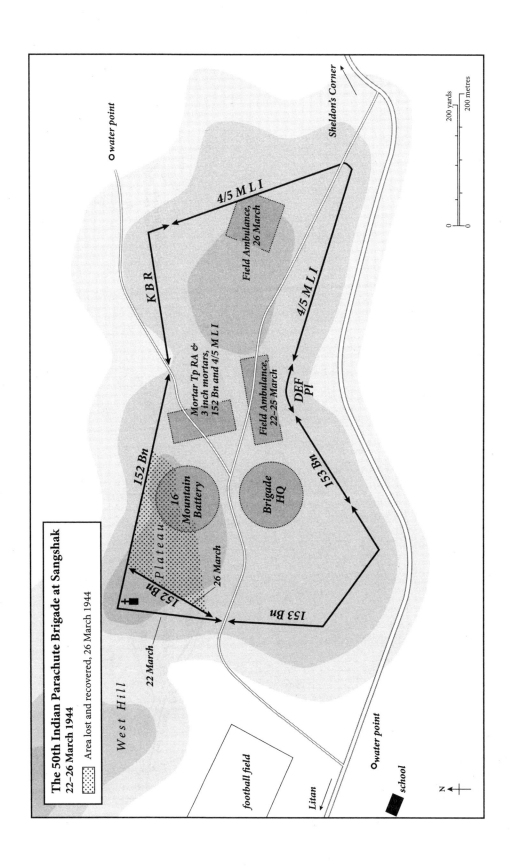

The 50th Indian Parachute Brigade at Sangshak
22–26 March 1944

Area lost and recovered, 26 March 1944

water point

4/5 M L I

Field Ambulance,
26 March

K B R

Mortar Tp RA &
3 inch mortars,
152 Bn and 4/5 M L I

4/5 M L I

Field Ambulance,
22–25 March

DEF
Pl

152 Bn

16
Mountain
Battery

Brigade
HQ

153 Bn

Plateau

26 March

152 Bn

153 Bn

West Hill

22 March

Sheldon's Corner

football field

Litan

water point

school

N

0   200 yards
0   200 metres

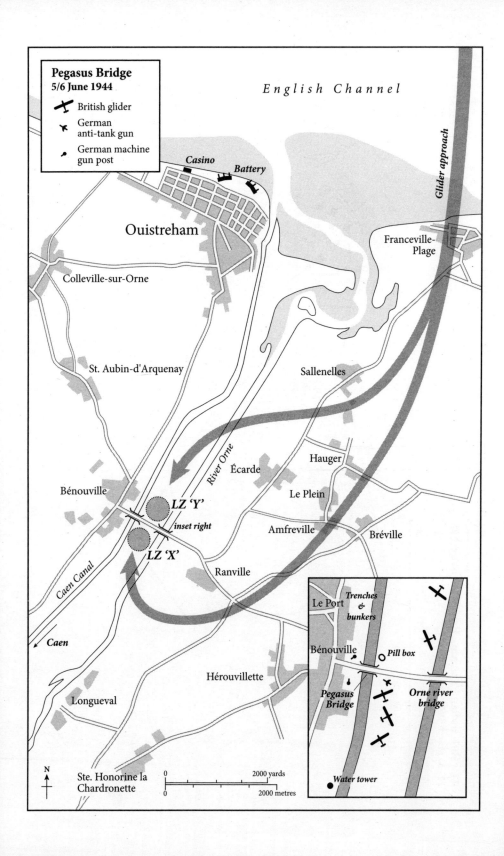

Pegasus Bridge
5/6 June 1944

✈ British glider

✄ German anti-tank gun

✦ German machine gun post

English Channel

Casino

Battery

Ouistreham

Franceville-Plage

Glider approach

Colleville-sur-Orne

St. Aubin-d'Arquenay

Sallenelles

River Orne

Hauger

Écarde

Le Plein

Bénouville

LZ 'Y'

inset right

Amfreville

Bréville

LZ 'X'

Ranville

Caen Canal

Caen

Hérouvillette

Longueval

N

Ste. Honorine la Chardronette

0   2000 yards

0   2000 metres

Le Port

Trenches & bunkers

Bénouville

Pill box

Pegasus Bridge

Orne river bridge

Water tower

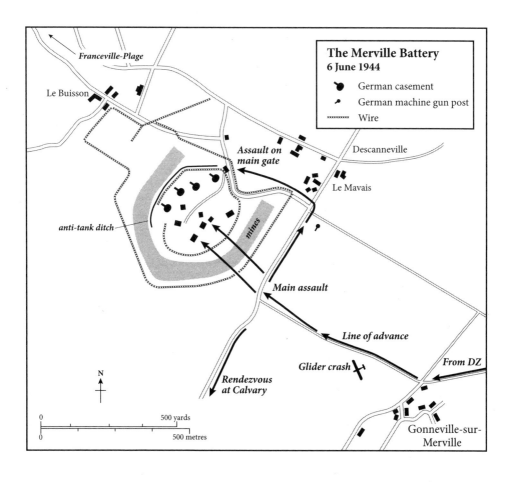

The Merville Battery
6 June 1944

- 🖤 German casement
- ✎ German machine gun post
- ┈┈┈ Wire

Franceville-Plage

Le Buisson

Assault on
main gate

Descanneville

Le Mavais

anti-tank ditch

mines

Main assault

Line of advance

Glider crash

From DZ

N

Rendezvous
at Calvary

500 yards

500 metres

Gonneville-sur-
Merville

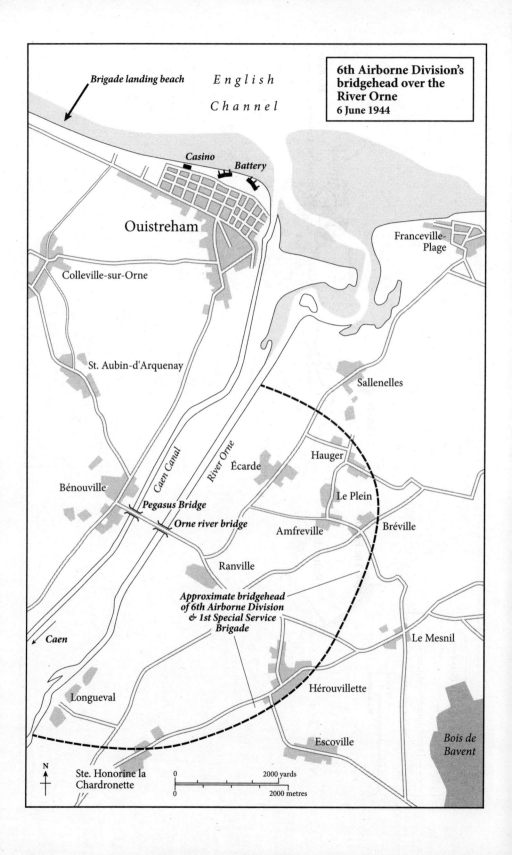

6th Airborne Division's bridgehead over the River Orne
6 June 1944

Brigade landing beach

English Channel

Casino

Battery

Ouistreham

Franceville-Plage

Colleville-sur-Orne

St. Aubin-d'Arquenay

Sallenelles

Caen Canal

River Orne

Écarde

Hauger

Bénouville

Le Plein

Pegasus Bridge

Orne river bridge

Amfreville

Bréville

Ranville

Approximate bridgehead of 6th Airborne Division & 1st Special Service Brigade

Le Mesnil

Caen

Hérouvillette

Longueval

Escoville

Bois de Bavent

N

Ste. Honorine la Chardronette

0   2000 yards

0   2000 metres

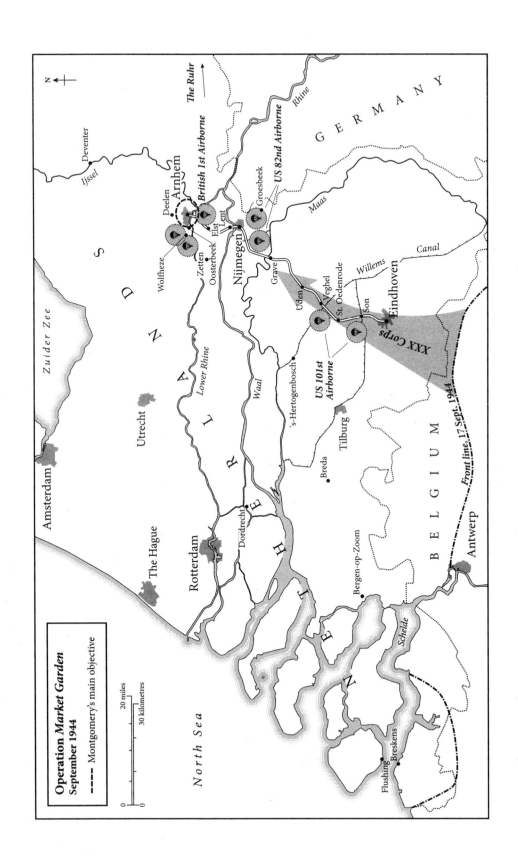

Operation *Market Garden*
September 1944

— · — · — Montgomery's main objective

20 miles

30 kilometres

0

North Sea

Zuider Zee

Amsterdam

The Hague

Utrecht

Rotterdam

Dordrecht

N E T H E R L A N D S

Breda

Tilburg

's-Hertogenbosch

Bergen-op-Zoom

Breskens

Flushing

Schelde

BELGIUM

Antwerp

Front line, 17 Sept. 1944

Eindhoven

XXX Corps

Son

St. Oedenrode

Veghel

Uden

US 101st Airborne

Willems

Canal

Grave

Nijmegen

Groesbeek

US 82nd Airborne

Lent

Elst

Oosterbeek

Zetten

Wolfheze

Deelen

Arnhem

British 1st Airborne

GERMANY

The Ruhr

Rhine

Maas

Waal

Lower Rhine

Ijssel

Deventer

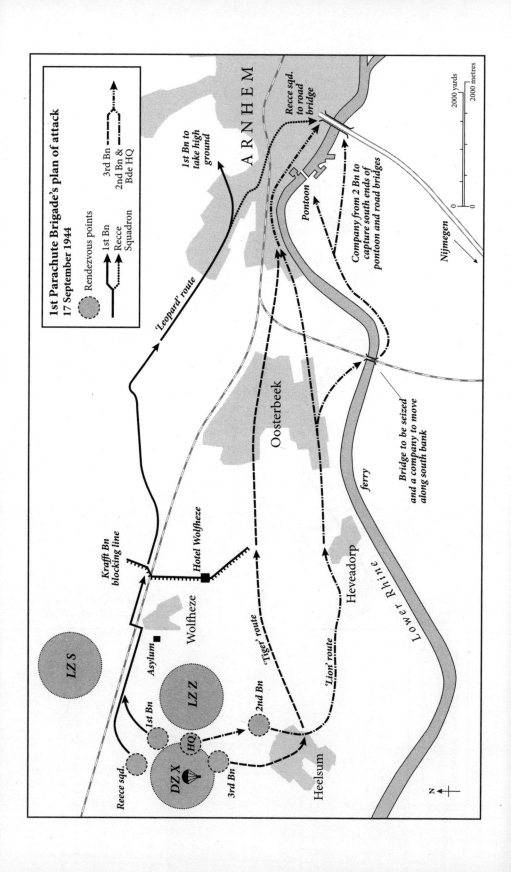

1st Parachute Brigade's plan of attack
17 September 1944

Rendezvous points
1st Bn
Recce Squadron
3rd Bn
2nd Bn & Bde HQ

ARNHEM

Recce sqd. to road bridge

1st Bn to take high ground

Pontoon

Company from 2 Bn to capture south ends of pontoon and road bridges

'Leopard' route

Oosterbeek

Nijmegen

Krafft Bn blocking line

Hotel Wolfheze

Bridge to be seized and a company to move along south bank

ferry

Wolfheze

Heveadorp

Lower Rhine

Asylum

'Tiger' route

LZ S

LZ Z

2nd Bn

'Lion' route

Reece sqd.

1st Bn

HQ

DZ X

3rd Bn

Heelsum

N

2000 yards

2000 metres

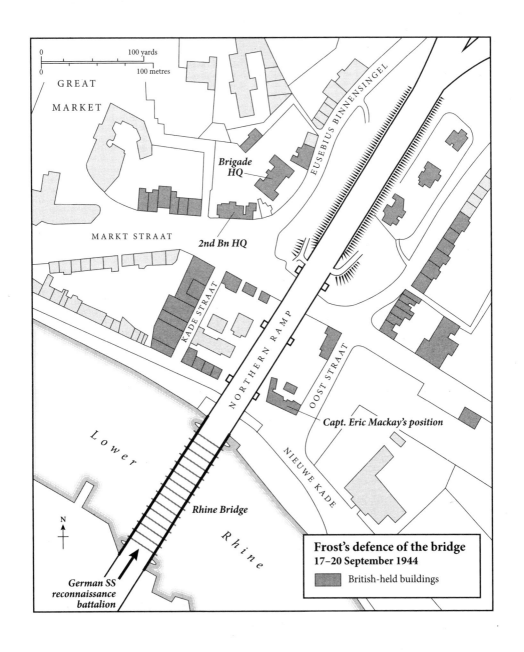

0
100 yards
0
100 metres

GREAT
MARKET

EUSEBIUS BINNENSINGEL

*Brigade
HQ*

MARKT STRAAT

2nd Bn HQ

KADE STRAAT

NORTHERN RAMP

OOST STRAAT

Capt. Eric Mackay's position

NIEUWE KADE

L o w e r

R h i n e

Rhine Bridge

N

*German SS
reconnaissance
battalion*

**Frost's defence of the bridge
17–20 September 1944**

British-held buildings

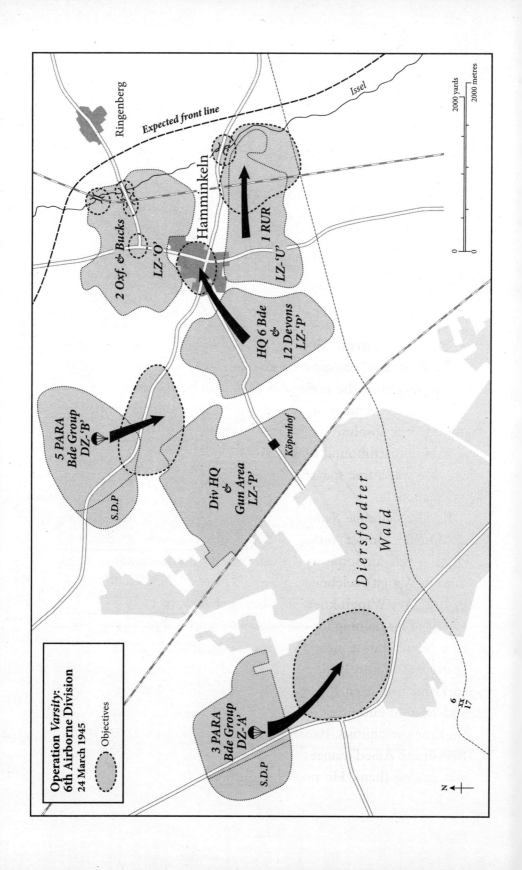

Operation *Varsity:*
6th Airborne Division
24 March 1945

‑ ‑ ‑ Objectives

Ringenberg

Issel

2000 yards
2000 metres

Expected front line

Hamminkeln

2 Oxf. & Bucks

LZ-'O'

1 RUR

LZ-'U'

HQ 6 Bde
&
12 Devons
LZ-'P'

5 PARA
Bde Group
DZ-'B'

S.D.P

Köpenhof

Div HQ
&
Gun Area
LZ-'P'

*Diersfordter
Wald*

3 PARA
Bde Group
DZ-'A'

S.D.P

6
xx
17

N

Introduction

'GUY JUMPED. FOR A second, as the rush of air hit him, he lost consciousness. Then he came to himself, his senses purged of the noise and smell and throb of the machine. The hazy November sun enveloped him in golden light. His solitude was absolute . . . He experienced rapture, something as near as his earthbound soul could reach to a foretaste of paradise . . . He was a free spirit in an element as fresh as on the day of its creation.'[1]

In *Unconditional Surrender*, Evelyn Waugh captures perfectly the intense, almost 'out of body' spiritual experience that parachuting was for some of the airborne pioneers. The novel, the third in Waugh's celebrated *Sword of Honour* trilogy, was published in 1952. Yet Waugh knew of what he wrote. In December 1943, as part of his training for the SAS, he attended a parachute course at a 'secret house near Ringway' airfield in Manchester. The house was Tatton Hall, a neo-classical mansion whose extensive parkland had been loaned to the RAF by its eccentric owner and aviation enthusiast, the 4th Baron Egerton, to train Britain's wartime parachutists. Between 1940 and early 1946, almost 60,000 British and Allied trainees made their first drops at Tatton. Waugh was among them. He noted in his diary:

We did two jumps. The first was the keenest pleasure I remember. The aeroplane noisy, dark, crowded; the harness and parachute irksome. From this one stepped into perfect silence and solitude and apparent immobility in bright sunshine above the treetops. We were dropping at 700 feet only, so that the pleasure was brief. All too soon the ground seemed to be getting suddenly nearer and then, before one had time to do all one had been told, one landed with a great blow.[2]

Waugh's first drop went well enough. He told his wife Laura that he had 'felt absolutely no reluctance to jump – less than in taking a cold bath'. But on the second, he landed awkwardly and cracked the fibula in his left leg, preventing him from completing the course and earning his 'wings'. The same fate befalls his fictional alter ego in *Sword of Honour*, Guy Crouchback, who injures himself on his first drop. Then 39 years old, Waugh never completed a combat jump and saw out the conflict writing *Brideshead Revisited* and acting as a liaison between the British Army and Tito's partisans in Yugoslavia.

But thousands of other British airborne pioneers did go to war by parachute and glider and, in the process, helped to realise what American diplomat Benjamin Franklin had envisaged as early as 1783: 'ten thousand men descending from the clouds' in balloons to attack an enemy's 'third flank', his relatively undefended rear area. Franklin's ideas had long been dismissed as science fiction. Yet in just a few short years in the early 1940s they became a reality.[3]

Britain came late to the airborne party. In the 1930s, when many of Europe's powers – Italy, Soviet Russia, Germany, Spain, Poland and France – were developing a parachute and airlanding capability, Britain confined its airborne efforts to troop resupply and transportation. Only after defeat in Belgium and France, and the miracle of the Dunkirk evacuation, did Winston Churchill call on 5 June 1940 for the raising of 'parachute troops on a scale equal to 5,000' as one way of taking the fight to Nazi Germany's 'Fortress Europe'.⁴

Certainly, fear of the exact opposite – an invasion of Britain by German parachutists – was something that preoccupied government and civilians for much of the war. The alarm was first raised in the House of Commons on 13 May 1940 – just three days into Germany's blitzkrieg campaign – when a concerned MP asked Anthony Eden, the Secretary of State for War, whether, 'in order to meet the imminent danger of enemy parachute landings in this country', he would consider raising a 'voluntary corps composed of older, responsible men to be armed with rifles and Bren guns and trained for instant action in their own localities'.

Eden said yes. The matter had been 'receiving urgent attention in the light of recent events', and he hoped to make an announcement 'at a very early date'. He was as good as his word. On 14 May 1940, Eden appealed on BBC radio for people to join the newly raised Local Defence Volunteers – later renamed the Home Guard (and depicted on British television in the 1970s in the popular sitcom *Dad's Army*) – and within six days more than 250,000 people had answered the call. One of their key roles, Eden's deputy Sir John Grigg told the House of Commons on 22 May, was to act as 'parashootists' who would 'deal with small enemy parties landing from the air'.

On 4 June – as part of his rousing 'We shall fight on the beaches' speech – Churchill warned of the dangers of enemy 'parachute landings'. A couple of weeks later, the Ministry of Information issued every household with a pamphlet entitled, 'If the Invader comes – what to do and how to do it.'⁵

But even as the invasion threat receded with defeat for Germany in the aerial Battle of Britain in 1940, the War Ministry was responding to Churchill's call by creating its own airborne capability. These forces – the legendary 'Red Devils' – were some of the finest combat troops of the Second World War. They began as a single parachute battalion of 500 men and grew into three 10,000-strong airborne divisions: the 1st, 6th and 44th Indian, each composed of parachutists and glider-borne troops. Wearing their distinctive maroon berets, steel helmets and Dennison smocks, they served with distinction in every major theatre of the conflict – including North Africa, Sicily, mainland Europe and the Far East – and played a starring role in some of the most iconic airborne operations in history: the Bruneval Raid of February 1942; the capture of the Primosole, Pegasus and Arnhem Bridges in July 1943, June 1944 and September 1944 respectively; and Operation Varsity, the biggest single-day parachute drop in history, near Wesel in Germany in March 1945.

The difference between parachutists and glider troops was stark. The former leapt from planes at altitudes as low as 400 feet, and oscillated towards terra firma beneath a flimsy silk canopy. The latter effectively crash-landed in a large box of steel, plywood and fabric that was 'not unlike a section of the London Tube railway in miniature'. Both methods of insertion were extremely hazardous, but few of the Para Boys would have swapped places with the Glider Lads, and vice versa. John Howard, the hero of Pegasus Bridge, was genuinely surprised when a fellow officer moved from gliders to parachutes because he could imagine few worse situations than jumping out of an aircraft, praying his canopy would open and unsure where he would land. It was, in his view, infinitely preferable to arrive by glider with a pilot in charge. The Para Boys felt just as strongly that they didn't want to 'prang into action'.

Their rivalry was enhanced by the fact that parachutists received more risk money than glider lads: two extra shillings a day, compared to a single shilling, the cause of much ill feeling among the glider troops. The one thing they all had in common was that they had volunteered for highly dangerous duty: the sooner the better.[6]

A parachutist was free to choose what he took with him, as long as he kept within the load quota. Company Sergeant Major Jack Harries of Merville Battery fame, for example, jumped bearing a Sten gun and four magazines, two Mark 36 Mills grenades, a phosphorus grenade, three Gammon bombs, gas cape, camouflage net, knife, ground-to-air recognition triangle, mess tin, 24-hour ration pack, map, message pad, entrenching tool, bootlaces, spare socks, singlets and briefs, small towel, washing and shaving kit, pay book, handkerchiefs, writing paper and envelopes, binoculars, torch, French money, shell dressing, pack of contraceptives, toilet paper, toggle rope, boiled sweets, boot polish and brush and comb. He also had an escape kit which included a compass hidden in a brass button, a four-inch metal file, silk maps sewn into his trousers and smock, and half a bottle of brandy. Most also had a kit bag containing up to another 65 pounds of equipment that, once they had jumped, would dangle beneath them on a rope.[7]

Handicapped during its early years by inter-service rivalry and a chronic lack of suitable aircraft and equipment, Britain's airborne force gradually expanded, learned from its mistakes, and developed a number of roles that included small-scale raids (Colossus, Biting and Freshman), fighting like traditional infantry (North Africa and India) and, its favoured option, dropping behind enemy lines to secure vital ground and infrastructure in conjunction with a ground offensive (Ladbroke, Fustian, Tonga, Market and Varsity). It was in this latter role that Britain's airborne forces made their most significant contribution to Allied victory during D-Day and the Crossing of the Rhine; even at Arnhem, where they ultimately came up short, their superhuman fighting qualities meant a flawed operation almost succeeded in shortening the war.

Along the way, guns were pulled on American pilots, mistakes were made, lives were lost and taken. Yet all the time the airborne force was learning from its mistakes and finessing its equipment and tactics. It ended the war with a fearsome reputation. But that was as good as it got: the development of helicopters in the 1950s meant that mass paratroop drops and glider landings were soon a thing of the past.

This is the first book to join up the dots and tell the story of Airborne across the whole war, drawing on multiple archives, published memoirs, unpublished diaries and letters, and interviews with participants. Since the publication of *The Red Beret* by Hilary St George Saunders in 1950, and T. B. H. Otway's official history of *Airborne Forces of the Second World War* a year later, fragments of the story have been told by, among others, Cornelius Ryan, W. F. Buckingham, Antony Beevor, Lloyd Clark and Mark Urban. But *Sky Warriors* is the first book to knit all those stories together into a single continuous narrative, told in the words of those who were there.

PART I

Beginnings, 1940–42

I

Operation Colossus – Southern Italy, 10–12 February 1941

'FIFTEEN MINUTES TO TARGET,' came the word from the cockpit. Sergeant 'Taff' Lawley woke the men and there was a burst of activity as equipment was checked, parachute static lines sorted out and the plywood exit doors unbolted.

After what seemed to Lieutenant Tony Deane-Drummond a very long quarter of an hour, the tail-gunner appeared from his perch and shouted: 'You are due to drop in under a minute. Get cracking.'

The intercom had failed and for about 10 seconds there was pandemonium as the plywood doors were hauled open and the first two paratroopers swung their legs over the edge of the hole. Through it, they could see the lights of Calitri flash by. Then the red light came on, signalling five seconds to go. Random thoughts flashed through Deane-Drummond's mind. *This is unreal. What am I doing sitting over a hole looking down at Italy?* He glanced at his men and wondered what they were thinking. They 'looked cheerful but pale'.

Operation Colossus was the first British airborne mission of the war. The assault on the Apulian aqueduct in southern Italy by X Troop of the 11th SAS Battalion (later the 1st Parachute

Battalion) in January 1941 had the hopelessly ambitious strategic objective of preventing Italy from fighting a war on two fronts. Yet, if X Troop could blow up the aqueduct and sever the water supply in Apulia for a time, it would achieve a propaganda victory to boost British morale and spread fear among the Italians. Crucially, it would prove – after much investment and exhaustive training – that Britain's fledgling airborne forces really could make a difference.

The River Ofanto flashed by in the pale moonlight. It could not be long now. The red light changed to green. 'Number One!' shouted Lawley. The first paratrooper dropped through the hole. Numbers Two and Three followed. Lawley then pressed the release switch for the containers and their coloured parachutes which fell from the bomb bay. After a slight pause, he counted out Numbers Four and Five. The latter was Deane-Drummond. He remembered a 'tearing gale, a slight jerk', and then 'swinging gently in blissful silence a few hundred feet above the ground'.

Dropped at 500 feet, it took Deane-Drummond just 15 seconds to reach terra firma. He landed perfectly in a ploughed field barely 100 yards from the aqueduct which 'stretched below and in front of him across the steep little ravine of the Torrente Tragino, the bottom of which was covered with scrub and small trees, and led up to a small hill beyond'. Over the brow of the hill was a second aqueduct crossing another stream, the Fosse della Ginestra. On Deane-Drummond's left the mountainside 'rose steeply with a group of farm buildings 50 feet above him'. Across the ravine to his right, 'a track led away from the farthest pier of the aqueduct, dipped over the hill in front, came into view again by some farm buildings on the other side of the Ginestra and ran along the slopes of the valley past the confluence of the two streams down towards the main road, the railway and the River Ofanto'.[1] *Well done the pilot*, he thought to himself.

The containers had dropped nearby and, having opened them

and distributed the weapons, he divided his section into two and ordered them to search the two clusters of farm buildings and bring the occupants back to the aqueduct where he would be waiting. It was deathly quiet. His plane had been due to drop third, but there was no sign of anybody else. Had they lost their way? If so, and he and his men were on their own, they would have to do the best they could with the explosives they had brought. But the chances of doing any serious damage were not good.

By 10 p.m., his men had returned with the Italian peasants from the farm buildings: 12 men and another 12 women and children. Five minutes later, to his intense relief, he heard more planes overhead. They were Whitleys that, one after the other, turned for a run in over Calitri and dropped their loads. As the parachutes floated down, the Italian peasants grouped near the aqueduct 'continually crossed themselves in amazement', while their children leapt in the air and clapped their hands. '*Angeli, angeli!*' they shouted.

A short while later, hearing a 'loud crashing' through the bushes and thorn ash in the valley below, Deane-Drummond's men prepared to fire. But when the trees parted out came Major 'Tag' Pritchard, 'a little out of breath, as his plane load had been landed about a mile away down by the river'. Pritchard was accompanied by Sergeant 'Clem' Clements, the first man out of the plane, who had almost dropped in the wrong place. But the pilot realised his error in time and switched the light back from green to red, causing Clements to be grabbed by his colleagues and held with his feet dangling through the hole until the plane had made another circuit. They were still dropped too close to the Ofanto, causing Lance Corporal Harry Boulter of the North Staffordshire Regiment to land awkwardly on rocks and break his ankle. He was being helped along by two of his comrades.

Following soon after were the parties led by Captain Lea and Second Lieutenants Paterson and Jowett. All had been dropped late, between a half and three-quarters of a mile below the target, because the signalling lights in their planes had malfunctioned. There was no sign of Captain Daly and his section of sappers. Even more worrying was the news that some of the planes had failed to drop their containers, giving Paterson and the remaining sappers only a third of the explosives that had been allocated for the mission.*

With time getting on, Pritchard gave out his orders: Daly, Jowett and Deane-Drummond's sections were to take up covering positions in a semi-circle to the north and downstream of the target, and also covering the approaches to both aqueducts; the Italian peasants were to be used to collect the heavy 50-pound boxes of guncotton, a request they readily agreed to as it 'would give them something to talk about for the rest of their lives'; and Paterson, now the senior sapper, was to make a quick survey of the aqueduct and decide how best to destroy it. Everyone was to assemble at the far end of the Ginestra aqueduct when the job was done.

Paterson found the aqueduct much as he had been led to expect from his study of the intelligence – in the form of a written description, photographs and diagrams – but with two important exceptions. The central pier 'was in the middle of the stream and 30 feet high, not squat as shown in the diagram'; and the piers were made not from masonry, as in the description, but reinforced concrete which required six times more explosive to destroy. Short of explosives, and unable to attack either the centre pier or the conduit itself (the planned alternative if the piers were indeed made of reinforced concrete), the young

---

* This would not have been a problem if the piers had been constructed of masonry, as expected, because the allocation of explosives had been more than double what was required.

Canadian 'decided to concentrate on the western pier, which was most easily reached'.

He therefore piled 640 pounds of explosive against the base of the western pier 'at ground level on the uphill side and tamped with earth and stones'. He also placed 'two necklace charges' weighing 160 pounds on the upper part of the pier, one on the top under the water way and one on the ledge at the top of the base. This took time because 'mud had to be pressed in behind the guncotton slaps to make good contact'.

Just before midnight, once Paterson had collected enough explosives to blow the western pier, Pritchard sent a runner to Deane-Drummond, who was on watch on the track that led from the Ginestra to the road that ran parallel to the Ofanto, to stop the carrying parties. He intercepted the last porter who was carrying two boxes on his shoulders. 'It seemed such a pity to waste it,' recalled Deane-Drummond, 'so I put it under one end of a small bridge carrying the track which led to the main aqueduct. This would delay the repair work.'[2]

At 12.15 a.m. on 11 February, with the main charges on the aqueduct in place, the sappers withdrew to the far end of the Ginestra aqueduct. At the same time the local men were taken back to the farm buildings 'where two or three were trussed up to encourage the others, warned by the interpreter that the sentry outside the door would shoot to kill, and locked in with the women and children'. There was no sentry.

Shortly before 12.30 a.m., Paterson 'fired a one pound guncotton slab, the warning signal that the main charge was to be blown a minute later and that the protective parties were to join the sappers'. Paterson and Pritchard lit the fuses and ran for cover over the brow of the hill towards the Ginestra. At the same time, Deane-Drummond ordered Corporal Watson of the Royal Engineers to fire the charge at the little bridge. Once he had done so, the pair ran to safety.

Boom! A huge explosion rocked the aqueduct followed, 30 seconds later, by a *Whoomf!* at the small bridge.[3] It had gone up in a 'cloud of flying concrete, rails and bits of masonry'. The civilians in the cottages started to wail, and a woman ran out of the house with a baby in her arms when the bits started thudding down on the roof. The small bridge had been 'neatly cut and one end lay in the bed of the stream'.

Pritchard and Paterson went back to inspect the aqueduct, and found the western pier collapsed and the water way broken in two. 'The two halves,' read the official report, 'were sloping up to the abutment and the centre pier, with the broken ends in the bed of the torrent. Water was flooding down the ravine.'

The others were waiting impatiently at the Ginestra aqueduct. When Pritchard and Paterson appeared with grim faces, Deane-Drummond and the others feared the worst. Surely 700 pounds of guncotton had been enough?

Pritchard put up his hand to still the babble of voices and said: 'Listen.'

They strained their ears and, sure enough, could hear the sound of a great waterfall. The aqueduct had been cut. They cheered spontaneously, ignoring the fact that they were in enemy country and their noise 'must have been heard a good mile or two away'.

Operation Colossus had, against all odds, succeeded.[4]

Now came the problem – intrinsic to parachuting behind enemy lines – of how to get out. As agreed beforehand, 'Tag' Pritchard now split his force into three small parties to give it the best chance of making the rendezvous with the submarine at the mouth of the Sele river on the night of 15/16 February, a distance of 50 miles.* He and Tony Deane-Drummond would lead the first party

---

* At first, the only people who knew about the plan of escape were Pritchard

14

(which also included the Italian speakers Fortunato Picchi and Private Nastri), Christopher Lea and 'Pat' Patterson the second, and George Jowett and Flight Lieutenant Lucky the third.

Lucky, who wore 'ribbons from the 14–18 War', was one of three Italian speakers in the party. The other two were Private Nicola Nastri of 11th SAS Battalion, who would travel under the pseudonym Private John Tristan to protect him from Italian reprisals, and a 44-year-old civilian called Fortunato Picchi, a former head waiter at the Savoy Hotel 'who was fanatical both in his hatred of [Mussolini's Fascists] and his love of Italy'. Picchi was, at face value, an odd choice to take on such a dangerous mission. A 'suave polite little man', with a bald top to his head and 'slight middle-aged spread', he had no military experience.[5] He was selected because he had volunteered to return to his homeland as an SOE agent. His SOE report stated: 'non-politically minded, but anti-fascist. An idealist, an excellent worker and organiser who cannot allow failure. Wants above all things for everyone to be treated fairly.'

What role the SOE envisaged for Picchi is unknown. But, in line with SOE operations elsewhere, it is likely that he was being sent back to Italy to coordinate fellow resisters to Mussolini's rule and provide vital intelligence for future British/Allied operations. To protect his identity, Picchi used the alias of a Free Frenchman called 'Private Pierre Dupont'.[6] For security reasons, this was all kept from the men of X Troop who assumed Picchi would return with them.

Before departing, the men were ordered to lighten their loads by ditching their heavier weapons, including Brens and tommy guns. This still left each man carrying 'a 30-pound pack

_____

and Deane-Drummond. The other officers were let in on the secret at the aerodrome in Malta, and the sergeants after the aqueduct was severed. The junior ranks were never told.

containing five days' rations, mess tin, water bottle and miniature primus stove'. For arms they kept only their Colt automatic pistols and their two hand grenades.

Their plan was to climb the mountain behind the aqueduct and then follow the contours until they reached the highest point of the pass over the Apennines 'before moving down the north side of the Sele valley towards the Mediterranean'. Lance Corporal Harry Boulter, however, would be left behind: having broken his ankle on landing, it would be impossible for him to keep up. Pritchard and Deane-Drummond both shook his hand and wished him luck, with the latter trying to convey by expression rather than words how important it was that Boulter did not crack under questioning. The lance corporal responded: 'On your way, you lot. Don't waste time on me. I'm the lucky one. I've got out of that bloody long march over the mountains.'

As they set off, dogs began to bark. 'It seemed impossible,' noted Deane-Drummond, 'that we would not have all Italy on our heels by the morning. This was going to be no easy walk over the Scottish moors. We bent our backs and laboured slowly through the mud and up the hills.'[7] With their rubber-soled jump boots slipping on the slick ground, it was heavy going and they stopped every three-quarters of an hour to munch chocolate or sip a little water until they were 'sufficiently recovered to continue'. On and on they tramped, pulling themselves up the sides of the steep little gorges by their hands and then slithering down the other side on their bottoms.

At 7 a.m. they found a 'nice, sheltered little ravine in which to lie up during the day'. There was a stream nearby and plenty of cover, so they took off their equipment and tried to sleep. They had walked for about six miles, but were still only three and a half miles from the aqueduct, as the crow flies, and would have to double their mileage on future nights if they were to reach the coast in time.

After a 'wonderful three hours' rest', they were woken at 10 a.m. by the sound of a low-flying plane that was obviously looking for them. They kept perfectly still, their faces to the ground, until the plane flew away. Soon after, they pulled Primus stoves from their packs and boiled water to make sweet tea or a greasy porridge of biscuits and pemmican. The latter, made from meat extract with added fat, was an old polar explorers' standby that tasted like 'concentrated greasy Bovril'. Deane-Drummond found it 'quite nauseating', though it assuaged his hunger.

From their hiding place they could see peasants at work in the fields and, beyond them, the village of Calitri perched on the side of the mountain. The sun was shining and a light breeze 'brought the delicate smell of wild thyme, mint and rosemary' wafting over them, though they were in 'no position to appreciate such muted pleasures'. Deane-Drummond's chief concern was a 300-foot-high cliff, a quarter of a mile ahead, that they would have to scale that evening.

When night fell, they donned their packs and, having crossed a fast-flowing stream, set off up the cliff using a goat track that 'Tag' Pritchard had spotted earlier that day. 'With some difficulty we pulled ourselves up the slope of mud and shingle,' noted Deane-Drummond, 'using every bit of scrub or long grass as we scrambled up to the top. All our reserves of energy had been used up to climb that hill and we were to feel it later on.'[8]

No one felt the strain more than Fortunato Picchi, the middle-aged former Savoy waiter, who 'appeared to be suffering from some chest disorder and coughed continuously'. Yet he was determined to keep pace with the others and managed to do so.[9]

They crept slowly on in single file 'with ears strained for any unusual sound'. They could see a few cottages against the skyline, and assumed they must be the outskirts of the village of

Pescopagano. Before them stretched mile after mile of wild and seemingly impassable country, every natural hillock and glade distorted by the moonlight into 'grotesque and weird shapes'. Few landmarks could be picked out, so they decided to march by compass to a large crossroads near the source of the River Sele. They were always walking 'either up or down along the side of a hill', but did manage to find a small road.

Deciding it was too risky to walk along the road, they kept it a quarter of a mile below them as a guide, 'trying to avoid the scattered little farmhouses which were becoming more numerous'. At every brook they threw themselves flat to drink the ice-cold water. With some of the men close to exhaustion, Pritchard ordered a halt for a brew. The hot sweet tea was 'like nectar'.

At 1 a.m. on 12 February, having not seen any traffic for some time, they took to the road and 'damn the risk'. Five or six miles later they came to a crossroads that, they reckoned, was the highest point of their route to the coast. It was now down-hill all the way and their only concern was to find a place to hide up before dawn. Looking down into the valley, they could see it 'stretching for miles in the moonlight, with rugged culti-vated sides', dotted with innumerable farmhouses, and it seemed unlikely that 'things would continue so well'.

A light clopping of hooves on the road ahead brought them out of their reverie. They were too tired, and there was too little cover, to make a run for it, so Pritchard formed them into single file and told Private Nastri to call the step in Italian. A pony cart laden with vegetables came into view. Fortunately, its female peasant driver was fast asleep. With this mini-crisis averted, they left the road. Deane-Drummond's 'feet ached as they had never ached before', and his whole body was 'limp with exhaustion'.

With dawn approaching, they needed a hiding place. The maps indicated that a nearby hilltop was covered with woods, so they headed for it, climbing steadily through ploughed fields. Shivering and exhausted, they were kept going by the fear of being discovered in the open at dawn. But the woods failed to materialise. Pritchard and Deane-Drummond climbed a little higher and found a cluster of boulders and juniper bushes that would have to do. It was far from ideal, but they were 'unable to move another step from sheer exhaustion'.

They soon fell asleep in their makeshift hideout. When Deane-Drummond woke at dawn, an hour later, it felt as if every bone in his body ached and shivered; his clothes were 'soured with sweat' and his teeth could 'not stop chattering'. He looked out and saw, barely 100 yards away, an Italian peasant looking intently in his direction. As the peasant began to walk away, Pritchard sent Fortunato Picchi after him to tell him they were a party of Italian and German troops on an exercise. When Picchi returned, he said he thought he had convinced the farmer, but that there were a lot of women and children who had also seen the fugitives. Some of them had run off down the hill to a nearby village, possibly to alert the *carabinieri*.

Pritchard was in a quandary. If he ordered the men to move, it might attract more attention. So they remained where they were, in acute suspense. Some 'half naked and filthy Italian children with a few mongrel dogs' were the first to appear. They sat down 100 yards away, sucking their thumbs and gazing at the paratroopers as if they were 'men from the moon'. A minute or two later, a man came over the hill behind them, accompanied by two pointers and holding a shotgun. 'He seemed very frightened,' wrote Deane-Drummond, 'as he pointed his shotgun straight at Tag and kept up a running commentary, which of course was unintelligible to us.'

Gradually more people arrived, 'typical Italian peasants with nut-brown faces and long dirty black dresses'. Picchi tried to convince the man with the shotgun that they meant no harm, but he was having none of it. He waved his gun aggressively, insisting that they lay down their arms. Pritchard consulted with Deane-Drummond, telling him that he was minded to give the order. When the lieutenant disagreed, Pritchard said: 'All right, Tony, you throw a grenade at those people on the right and I will throw mine over there.'

Deane-Drummond knew he could never do that. Men, women and children were everywhere and there were bound to be casualties among them if they tried to fight their way out. The best they could hope for was 'a few extra hours of freedom at the price of a particularly odious and inglorious action'. Reluctantly he agreed with Pritchard who told the men. There was a shocked silence, followed by an incredulous voice: 'Aren't we going to make a fight of it, sir?'

Pritchard's face betrayed his anguish. 'I'm sorry,' he replied, 'but we have to give in.'

As soon as they dropped their pistols, the peasants came surging up to them and took all their equipment, much to Deane-Drummond's 'chagrin and disgust'. The date was 12 February 1941. He wrote later: 'I have never felt so ashamed before or since, that we should have surrendered to a lot of practically unarmed Italian peasants.'[10]

2

'Are you ready for the fight?' – UK, June–July 1940

EIGHT MONTHS EARLIER – on 22 June 1940 – a small parade was held at Cambrai Barracks in Perham Down, Hampshire, to mark the formation of Britain's first airborne unit. The day was unusually cool and overcast for midsummer – a contrast to the previous few weeks of exceptionally fine weather – and the seven officers and 55 men were wearing a variety of uniforms and cap badges from units and corps across the British armed forces: gunners, sappers, Royal Ordnance Corps, Royal Army Service Corps, Royal Armoured Corps, light infantry, line infantry and the Royal Tank Regiment.[1] All had answered the call, first issued on 12 June, for 'volunteers for special service who are willing to join a parachute unit'.[2]

Addressing the men of C and D Troops of the newly raised No. 2 (Parachute) Commando★ was their commanding officer, Major Ivor Jackson. Commissioned into the Royal Tank Corps (later Regiment) in 1925, Jackson had spent two long stints on

---

★ The 500-strong No. 2 Commando was eventually raised by volunteers from all the British Army's regional commands: C and D Troops from the Southern Command; A and B Troops from the Northern Command; E and F Troops from the Eastern Command; G and H Troops from the Western Command; J Troop from the Scottish Command and K Troop from Northern Ireland District.

secondment to the RAF. This personal knowledge of the air arm had convinced the War Office that he was ideally suited to command airborne infantry. Yet Jackson had no combat experience and would later be criticised by some of his officers as out of his depth. What he did not lack, however, was enthusiasm. 'He was very keen about the whole thing,' noted Corporal Ernie Chinnery, one of those on parade. 'He was a firm man, but not harsh, then aged about 37 who had been trained by the RAF as a pilot.'

A long-serving member of the 17/21st Lancers★ – the famous 'Death or Glory' cavalry regiment that had only switched from horses to armoured cars in 1938 – Chinnery had recently been posted to Perham Down as an instructor in the 54th Armoured Training Regiment. Piqued, he immediately volunteered for the parachute Commando. 'I'd been in the Army for 12 years,' he recalled, 'so I wasn't prepared to spend the next few years in a training unit . . . I went and put my name down.'

It helped that Chinnery was supremely fit and itching to see action. 'Are you ready for a fight?' he was asked at his interview.

'Any time.'

He had never seen an aircraft, let alone ridden in one, but he would 'sooner go and fight overseas than let those buggers come over here'.[3]

The raising of these airborne pioneers was a direct – and, some might argue, desperate – response to the recent defeat of Allied forces on the continent, prompting the chaotic evacuation of the British Expeditionary Force from Dunkirk. On 3 June, with the heroic rescue all but complete, Prime Minister Winston

---

★ Formed in 1922 by an amalgamation of the 17th Lancers and 21st Lancers. The 17th had taken part in the infamous charge of the Light Brigade at Balaklava in 1854; while the 21st, with a young subaltern called Winston Churchill, charged at Omdurman in the Sudan in 1898.

Churchill wrote to Major General Hastings 'Pug' Ismay, military secretary to the War Cabinet (and the link between the prime minister and his chiefs of staff), warning of possible German air and sea landings on British soil. He specifically demanded the raising of 'self-contained, thoroughly equipped units of say 1,000 up to not less than 10,000 [men]' to tie up enemy troops by raiding the German-held coastline of Europe. 'How wonderful it would be,' wrote Churchill, 'if the Germans could be made to wonder where we were going to strike next instead of forcing us to try to wall in the island and roof it over. An effort must be made to shake off the mental and moral prostration to the will and initiative of the enemy from which we suffer.'4

Two days later, Churchill sent Ismay a second and more detailed minute on the subject. 'We have got to get out of our minds,' he warned, 'the idea that the Channel ports and all the country between them are enemy territory. They must become "no man's land" . . . Enterprises must be prepared, with specially trained troops of the hunter class who can develop a reign of terror down these coasts, first of all on the "butcher and bolt" policy; but later on, or perhaps as soon as we are organised, we should surprise Calais or Boulogne, kill and capture the Hun garrison, and hold the place until all the preparations to reduce it by siege or heavy storm have been made, and then away.'

It was imperative, he continued, to end the 'passive resistance war'. The Chiefs of Staff must come up with measures for a 'vigorous, enterprising, and ceaseless offensive against the whole German occupied coast-line'. He envisaged sending tanks across the Channel in 'flat-bottomed boats' for raids deep inland that would 'leave a trail of German corpses behind them'. The lives of 'ordinary' German troops – those left to guard the coastline – 'must be made an intense torment'. To that end, he expected to hear proposals for organising and transporting the 'striking' forces; a 'proper system of espionage and intelligence'; the use of 15-inch guns on railway mountings to fire across the Channel; and the 'development of parachute troops on a scale equal to 5,000'.[5] Having hinted at the creation of an airborne force in his 3 June memo, Churchill was now, two days later, effectively ordering his military chiefs to make it happen.

On 9 June, the War Office responded by asking the British Army's Southern and Northern Commands to collect the names of up to 40 officers and 1,000 other ranks who were prepared to join a 'special force of volunteers for independent mobile operations'.

Known as 'Commandos' – a nod to the Afrikaans horsemen who had given the British so much trouble during the Anglo-Boer War of 1899–1902 – they would be composed of fit young men who could swim and were immune to sea-sickness. Particularly sought after were men who had seen active service and could drive a motor vehicle. Officers were expected to have 'personality, tactical ability and imagination', while the men sought were those of 'intelligence and independence', who could 'behave without supervision'.[6] Most of the Commandos were to operate as amphibious troops and carry out coastal raids, hence the concern about sea-sickness. But, thanks to Churchill, one Commando – No. 2 – would have a parachute capability.

The prime minister's interest in airborne matters went back to 1912, when he began to take flying lessons himself. In 1917, as Minister of Munitions, he had first suggested the deployment of troops from the air. Almost two decades later, he warned against parachute landings in the north-west of England in a 1936 paper entitled 'Invasion by Air', reissuing it after Dunkirk. But the trigger for Churchill's 5 June 1940 directive for the raising of 5,000 British parachutists was the enemy's largely successful use of airborne troops in the recent Norway and Low Countries campaigns.[7]

The theory of using a skyborne force to attack an enemy's

open rear flank went back to the late 18th century, when Benjamin Franklin, American ambassador to France and one of the Founding Fathers of the United States, witnessed one of the Montgolfier brothers' manned hot-air balloon flights in Paris in 1783.'Five thousand balloons capable of raising two men each, could not cost more than five ships of the line . . . And where is the Prince who can afford so to cover his country with troops for its defense, as that 10,000 men descending from the clouds might not in many places do an infinite deal of mischief before a force could be brought together to repel them,' he wrote.[8]

Hot-air balloons, of course, were too vulnerable to enemy fire and adverse weather conditions to be a viable option for military operations. The game-changer was the invention of a working aeroplane by the Wright brothers in 1903, and its subsequent adoption by the military for reconnaissance, air-to-air combat and bombing missions during the Great War. By the 1920s, most of the great powers possessed multi-engined planes of sufficient size and power to make air transportation possible.

The irony was that it had been the British who had pioneered the use of planes to transport troops and supplies in the interwar years, using parachutes, for example, to replenish forces in Kurdistan in 1923. Since then, however, it had lagged behind, leaving other military powers to adapt air transport for a direct battlefield role.

It was the Italians who were the first to use parachutes to deliver soldiers from the air straight into combat – or, at least, that was the theory. In 1927, using the static-line Salvatori parachute (a canopy and suspension lines in a bag stitched to the back of a modified jacket), they established the world's first military parachute-training course near Milan. Though development slowed thereafter – partly because of the death of the new arm's commander in a training accident – the Italian armed forces contained several parachute battalions by the late 1930s. They would not make their active service debut, however, until the capture of the Greek island of Cephalonia in April 1941.[9]

Long before then, the Italians had been overtaken in airborne development by both Soviet Russia and Germany. In 1928, an aviation detachment of the Red Army carried out an 'air-landing assault' on guerrillas in Turkestan. By 1934, Soviet air-landing units were more than 10,000 strong, backed by a 'dedicated training organisation and a coherent operational doctrine'. Following trials in 1930, the Red Army had also embraced the parachute as a means of troop delivery. In March 1936, Minister for War Duff Cooper told the House of Commons that 'the invention of flying . . . has worked a tremendous change in every form of human activity and especially in all questions of defence', citing as evidence the Russian Army's 'very interesting experiment' near Kiev of the summer before, recorded on film, in which 'one could see 1,200 men descending simultaneously by parachute, and such heavy weapons as tanks, not to mention machine guns, being conveyed simultaneously with the men to the scene of battle'.

Another MP, Major-General Knox, questioned the Soviet film as 'excellent propaganda but nothing else'. Later in 1936, however, the future British field marshal Lord Wavell witnessed with his own eyes a similar feat near Minsk: more than 1,200 Soviet paratroopers, flown 100 miles and dropped in 'enemy' rear areas to seize bridges and an airfield, into which an entire infantry division was air landed.

Some combat experience was gained by Red Army paratroopers who dropped during the Winter War with Finland (1939/40) and the occupation of Bessarabia in June 1940. A year later, the Soviets claimed to possess 15 airborne brigades, totalling 100,000 men.*[10]

---

* Apart from the odd diversionary raid, the majority of Soviet airborne troops would be deployed against the invading Germans in 1941 in a conventional infantry role.

In the 1930s, inspired by the Soviet example, the Spanish, French and Poles would all experiment with different types of airborne troops, although the French had inexplicably disbanded their two-company *Infanterie de l'Air* by the outbreak of war. The British, meanwhile, confined their airborne efforts to troop resupply and transportation. Part of the problem was doctrinal: while the British Army was trying to mechanise its ground troops, the RAF was preoccupied with aerial bombing and, to a lesser extent, imperial policing. This left neither service committed to airborne innovation. There was also the issue of inter-service rivalry and funding. 'The RAF may have possessed the necessary transport aircraft,' wrote William F. Buckingham in *Paras: The Birth of British Airborne Forces*, 'but parachutes and all their ancillary training and storage equipment were expensive.'[11] Who would pay – the RAF or the British Army?

This left the field clear for the Germans who were to make, after the Soviets, the greatest advances in airborne warfare in the 1930s. Hermann Göring, the future Reichsmarschall and head of the Luftwaffe (Air Force), set up the first German parachute unit in April 1935. Originally part of the Prussian paramilitary police, it was integrated into the Luftwaffe in October 1935 as the parachute wing of the Herman Göring Regiment. By early 1936, the Luftwaffe parachute-training school had opened at Stendahl in eastern Germany, and the term *Fallschirmschützen* (parachute soldiers) had been superseded by *Fallschirmjäger* (parachute hunters), after the formation of the 1st Jäger Battalion in January 1936.

At around the same time, the Heer (German Army) set up its own parachute capability. Perhaps inevitably, the two services disagreed over the size and employment of airborne troops: the Luftwaffe wanted to deploy small teams of parachutists as saboteurs, whereas the Heer 'leaned towards Soviet practice and saw parachute troops as a spearhead for large-scale air-landing operations in support of ground forces'. A third school of thought, proposed by Kurt Student, head of the Luftwaffe's training schools, was the creation of a self-sufficient airborne force with integral transport aircraft, close air support and artillery. It would operate under a tactical doctrine that Student dubbed the 'drops of oil' method: seizing multiple landing zones behind enemy lines which would expand and link up, 'first with each other and then with advancing ground forces'. German airborne doctrine would contain elements of all three ideas.[12]

The opportunity to put these ideas into practice came in May 1940 when Hitler insisted that the German assault on the Low Countries be spearheaded by elements of the Luftwaffe's 7. Flieger-Division* (paratroopers) and the army's 22. Luftlande-Division (air-landing, or glider, troops). For the most part, these operations in Holland and Belgium had a considerable impact on the campaign as the German airborne troops seized vital airfields, road and rail bridges, and, in the case of glider troops from 'Assault Battalion Koch', the strategic Belgian fortress of Eben Emael and three nearby crossings over the Albert Canal. The only setback was the failure to capture airfields in central Holland, costing Group North 90 per cent of its aircraft and a high proportion of officers and men captured or killed. Some of the captives – both the Luftwaffe's *Fallschirmjäger* and Heer air-landing troops – were shipped by the Dutch to British POW camps, and their pictures appeared in *The Times* on 20 May and 21 June 1940. It was, therefore, no coincidence that the original British parachute troops of 2nd Commando wore the same step-in cotton duck jump smocks and high-leg, side-laced boots favoured by the Germans.[13]

---

* The name *Flieger* or 'Air' was used to mask the fact that the division was composed of paratroopers (*Fallschirmjägers*). In 1943, it reverted to its proper name: the 1. Fallschirmjäger-Division.

On 4 June, as the last of 338,000 British and French troops were being rescued from Dunkirk,* and with the success of German airborne operations fresh in mind, Frederick Cocks, MP for Nottingham Broxtowe, asked Secretary of State for War Anthony Eden if he intended to organise a British corps of parachutists and gliders. Eden's response was evasive, yet that same day the War Office issued an internal memorandum entitled 'Creation of a Parachute Corps'. 'The idea,' it noted, 'has real possibilities at the present time. The objection will come from the RAF e.g. provision of special equipment and troop carrying aircraft. Will you make a short preliminary investigation into the possibilities of putting it into effect.'[14] A day later, Churchill wrote to Ismay, demanding action on his earlier recommendation to raise 'hunter class' raiding units, and specifically the 'deployment of parachute troops on a scale equal to 5,000'.[15]

Churchill was under enormous pressure as he attempted to square support for metropolitan France – locked in an unequal fight with Nazi Germany and, from 10 June, Mussolini's Italy – with, as he put it, 'the need to create an effective army at home and to fortify the island'. The immediate priority was the re-forming and re-equipping of the BEF, while simultaneously arming and organising the population, and bringing home from the Empire 'whatever forces could be gathered'.[16] But he was also determined to take the initiative, hence his demand for the creation of Commando and airborne units.

On 22 June – as the first elements of Jackson's No. 2 (Parachute) Commando paraded at Perham Down and, more significantly, the French government signed the armistice with Germany that

---

* Despite the relative success of the ad hoc evacuation, the British Expeditionary Force (BEF) left behind 68,111 personnel (killed, wounded and missing), and the vast majority of its weapons and supplies: 2,400 artillery pieces, 63,000 vehicles, 76,000 tons of ammunition, and almost 200,000 tons of stores and fuel.

left Britain to fight on alone – Churchill reminded Ismay of his earlier request:

> We ought to have a corps of at least 5,000 parachute troops, including a proportion of Australians, New Zealanders and Canadians, together with some trustworthy people from Norway and France . . . I hear something is being done already to form such a corps, but only I believe on a very small scale. Advantage must be taken of the summer to train these forces, who can, none the less, play their part meanwhile as shock troops in home defences. Pray let me have a note from the War Office on the subject.[17]

Ismay reassured the prime minister that Lieutenant General Alan Bourne, newly appointed Director of Combined Operations (with responsibility for training the Commandos and planning their operations), had the matter in hand. 'His proposals,' wrote Ismay, 'include the organisation and training of 5,000 parachute troops.'[18]

This was not true, and Ismay was either being deliberately obtuse or had confused the total number of commandos with parachutists. The real situation was revealed at a meeting in the War Office on 20 June at which Brigadier Otto Lund, the Deputy Director of Military Operations, explained that just one of the 11 Commando units being raised – each numbering 500 men – would have a parachute capability. 'Only one parachute Commando can be raised at present,' said Lund, 'as the RAF cannot train more, but other Commandos might be converted to parachute units at a later date.'[19]

The RAF's reticence was regrettable but not surprising. Still fixated on strategic bombing, and soon to be fighting the desperate air battle for Britain's survival,* it was unwilling to

---

* The Battle of Britain, the struggle for control of British airspace that was the vital precursor to a German invasion, lasted from 10 July to 31 October 1940,

devote more than a few of its precious resources to training paratroopers. Yet the Air Ministry did agree to provide RAF Ringway, near Manchester, as the location for its new parachute training facility.[20] Known as the Central Landing School (CLS), it would be run by a dozen instructors – six officers and six NCOs – led by 48-year-old Squadron Leader Louis Strange. A decorated Royal Flying Corps aviator of the Great War – awarded the DSO, MC and DFC – Strange had been recalled for active service in December 1939 with the lowly rank of acting Pilot Officer, and was awarded a Bar to his DFC in late May 1940 for flying a patched-up and unarmed Hurricane fighter from an abandoned airfield in France to RAF Manston, avoiding pursuers 'with a near suicidal display of low flying' and landing his 'badly shot-up machine safely'.

Strange only got the opportunity to command the CLS when the squadron leader originally chosen by the Air Ministry broke his leg in a parachute training accident. His appointment, wrote one historian, was both 'whimsical and serendipitous, as he was an extremely capable military maverick with a long-standing habit of bending or simply ignoring rules and regulations if he thought it necessary'. He was, therefore, the 'right man in the right place at the right time for the establishment of a British airborne force, and he swiftly embarked upon his new task in his own inimitable style'.[21]

Inevitably, Strange's task of setting up the parachute school at Ringway was ad hoc and rushed. 'Aircraft, parachutes and training staff are assembling as soon as they are available,' wrote Group Captain Geoffrey Bowman of the Air Staff to Lieutenant General Bourne on 29 June. 'No definite date can yet be given when instruction can commence, owing to the impossibility of forecasting the date by which aircraft can be modified for parachute

---

and ended in defeat for the Luftwaffe.

dropping and when sufficient training type parachutes can be produced.'

Possessing no specialist aircraft to carry paratroopers, the RAF had decided to convert the Mark II Armstrong Whitworth A38 Whitley, a 30,000-pound twin-engined medium bomber nicknamed 'the Elephant'. One had been 'modified completely and [was] awaiting dropping tests', explained Bowman. The remaining five would come through 'more quickly', one every three days. As for parachutes, the first 100 would be delivered 'by the end of the week', during which time the instructional staff, Army and RAF would draw up a syllabus of instruction.[22]

Bowman's letter was followed by one to Bourne on 4 July from Air Commodore Jack Slessor, the Air Staff's director of plans. 'I am rather uneasy about the air side of the development of parachute troops,' wrote Slessor, 'and am afraid if we are not careful that it will be a case of more haste less speed. I am also a bit afraid that if we go too fast we may have unnecessary training casualties which will be a set-back . . .' He added:

> The fact is that, until two or three weeks ago when the Prime Minister told us to develop the 5,000 parachute troops, we had, rightly or wrongly, not made any preparations, either in the sphere of aircraft or personnel, to raise any parachute troops at all. That may show lamentable lack of foresight on the part of the Air and General Staffs in the past, but we need not worry about that now. The point is that the development of what amounts to a completely new arm of the Service required a technique which we have never considered, material which we have never thought of providing, and a special personnel whom we have never thought of training, is not a thing that can be done in the twinkling of an eye; and I am rather afraid that we have tried to go ahead too fast in aiming to start the first course at the Parachute Training Centre so soon.

We have only just got the first aircraft of the six which we are modifying for this purpose. We have no instructors with any experience of this particular work – the parachute training in the Air Force has hitherto been entirely confined to the use of the parachute as a means of saving life.

It was Slessor's understanding that the first 100 volunteers – C and D Troops of Major Jackson's No. 2 Commando – were due to report to Ringway to begin their parachute course on Monday 8 July. He would, he told Bourne, 'very much rather put that off for a week so as to give the newly appointed Commandant and his staff some time to get the thing organised, and incidentally to train some instructors'. He ended the letter by acknowledging the 'necessity for getting on with this as fast as possible'. Yet it had 'taken the Germans three or four years to create a parachute corps', and he was 'anxious not to prejudice the success of the new organisation by trying to rush it unduly at the beginning, especially as morale and confidence are such an important factor in this respect'.[23]

Bourne's response on 5 July acknowledged Slessor's concerns, but at the same time, he could 'foresee a very important role for parachutists in bringing the war home to the Germans – after the blitzkrieg and when we have reasonable air proportions – and so helping to end the war'. He was, as a result, 'anxious for the development of the parachute arm'.

He also made the point that the first 100 men from Jackson's No. 2 Commando were available for parachute training now, with others coming forward 'at the rate of 100 every fortnight', and he did 'not want to keep them in suspense longer than can be helped'. He therefore agreed to delay the start of the course until 15 July, but wanted to move the No. 2 Commando volunteers up to the Ringway area before that 'to get settled in and do some ground training', adding: 'Will this be a nuisance to you?'[24]

3

'I'm afraid I've got some bad news'
– UK, July–September 1940

O N 5 JULY 1940, Major Jackson's C and D Troops were moved north to the village of Benchhill, south of Manchester, and billeted on a large housing estate. They had spent their first 10 days at Perham Down 'doing all sorts of training, mostly map reading and going out in twos and threes on initiative tests, getting to rendezvous points all over Salisbury Plain'. Volunteers were expected to weigh no more than 250 pounds 'when fully clothed and lightly equipped', to be capable of passing 'comfortably through a circular aperture, 3 ft in diameter when wearing equipment and parachute', and to possess 'no physical disabilities which might render them unsuitable for parachute work', such as 'thin skulls and weak ankles'.[1]

Each troop was brought up to war establishment strength of 3 officers and 47 men. Ernie Chinnery's C Troop was commanded by a gunner, Captain J. M. Bayley, with two sappers – Second Lieutenants George 'Pat' Paterson and Ivor Davies – as section leaders. Raised in the Canadian city of Kelowna, British Columbia, the 21-year-old Paterson had been studying forestry at Edinburgh University when the war broke out. He immediately enlisted in the Royal Engineers and in June 1940, a month after receiving his commission, volunteered for special service. Tall and strikingly handsome, with blue eyes and brown hair, Paterson was 'exceptionally popular with officers, NCOs and the men'.[2]

D Troop had a Royal Marine in charge, Captain R. G. Parks-Smith, and subalterns from the Royal Fusiliers (Lieutenant R. H. Gardner), and the Royal Army Service Corps (Second Lieutenant I. C. D. Smith). Each troop, in addition, was composed of 24 NCOs and 23 privates.[3]

On 6 July, after parading in the car park of the Sharston Hotel, the two troops were marched three miles to Ringway airfield. 'It was a historic moment for us,' recalled Chinnery. 'We were the very first parachute unit, although we hadn't jumped yet. All the time we were wondering what the jumping was going to be like, but we didn't do any for a few days, just bags of PT. Then we were split up into groups of six each. They took us over to an aeroplane and said, "We're going to give you some flights to get you used to flying."'[4]

Meanwhile, Squadron Leader Strange and his staff – including an adjutant, intelligence officer, chief flying instructor, three pilots (all, oddly, unqualified on the Whitley), a chief and assistant chief landing instructor, a chief PT instructor and Major John Rock, RE, the official representative of the War Office – were putting the finishing touches to the training syllabus, including the best way to exit the modified Whitley. There were two options. One was the so-called 'pull-off' method, by which the parachutist jumped from the plane's open tail, from which the rear gun turret had been removed. One airborne pioneer recalled: 'My God, that first jump. We crawled into the fuselage of a Whitley . . . and so to the rear turret, where the victim squatted in prayer and trepidation gripping a cross-bar. You pulled the ripcord and the silk and rigging lines niggled at your back. Like the crack of a hunting whip, you were yanked from the perch, and saw the aircraft tail departing below as you started the pendulum swing towards terra firma.'[5]

The alternative was to drop through a three-foot diameter hole in the fuselage, created by the removal of the dorsal gun turret, using a modified static-line parachute that opened automatically. Both versions – the 'pull-off' and the aperture jump – were used during the first 'live' parachute demonstration by Strange and some of his CLS staff on 13 July, 'witnessed by a large crowd of civilian onlookers despite supposed secrecy'. Having taken off from RAF Ringway, they dropped over Tatton Park, a large area of pasture (dotted with the occasional lake) five miles to the south-west that had been owned by the Egerton family since the 16th century. More test jumps were made by RAF and Army instructors over the next few days, prompting the decision to concentrate on the aperture method: it was thought to be safer and quicker.[6]

The first live jumps by the trainees were scheduled for the morning of 22 July. To prepare them, the jump instructors created a mock-up of the Whitley bomber which was 'merely a platform with a hole in the middle'. They would sit on the edge with a parachute on their back, and practise jumping through the hole without hitting the other side. They also jumped from different heights 'to get used to shock, and to show us how to fall properly'. The motto of the instructors was 'Knowledge Dispels Fear', which Chinnery thought was 'very true'. He found them a 'nice bunch, very helpful, and their experience rubbed off onto us'.

The evening before their maiden jump, they were taken into the hangar and kitted out. This included the issue of pads to protect every part of their body, including a jock-strap for their 'wedding tackle', but nothing for their heads apart from 'aircrew helmets'. They were also given an unpacked parachute and had to take it to a table where they watched while it was packed. 'This took a bit under 10 minutes,' noted Chinnery, 'and all the time the chaps were showing us and telling us what they were doing. This gave you a bit more confidence; you knew what was going to happen when you jumped.'[7]

For most trainee paratroopers, the first jump was an exhilarating, if nerve-racking experience. One volunteer had 'never been in an aeroplane, let alone jumped out of one, so it was with a sense of awe, bewilderment and apprehension' that he climbed into the fuselage of a 'long, dark, noisy, smelly Whitley bomber'. It took off for the seven-minute flight to Tatton Park and circled while they looked down through the round hole at the scenery below. The first to go was ordered to swing his legs over the hole and wait for the signal.

Suddenly the light went green and the instructor shouted 'Go!' as his hand fell in a chopping motion. 'I jumped into space,' noted the volunteer, 'and possible oblivion. Almost before I could draw a breath, I felt a jerk on my back, and, as if by magic, I saw above me the reassuring canopy of silk opened out and I began to float gently to earth.' Relieved to be out of the noisy, coffin-shaped aeroplane, the trainee felt at peace and was just beginning to enjoy himself when he noticed the ground fast approaching. He could see the reassuring figures of the medical officer and the attractive FANY ambulance driver on the drop zone. Someone shouted: 'Keep your feet together! Feet together, you clot!'

He did so, and 'bumped the ground without injury'.[8]

Ernie Chinnery's first three jumps were also 'fine', but for his fourth, on 25 July, he went up with a stick of eight men from C Troop that included Bombardier Jim Bushnell, attached from the Royal Artillery, and Welsh-born Driver Ralph Evans of the Royal Army Service Corps. 'Two or three men dropped with no problems,' recalled Chinnery, 'and then Evans, who was in front of me, left the aircraft and we circled round whilst I got into position. But before I could jump, the aircrew said we'd got a red light [flare] from the ground; the last chap had been injured and we were going back to Ringway.'

Once on the ground, they were addressed by Squadron Leader Strange. 'I'm afraid I've got some bad news. The last man, Driver Evans, was killed. All jumps will be suspended until we've worked out what went wrong.'[9]

The cause of death, it transpired, was the hurried adaptation of the RAF's training parachute – made by US firm Irvin – for use with a static line. This meant attaching a length of woven tape to the manual rip-cord handle and clipping the other end to a strongpoint in the aircraft, so that the parachute was automatically deployed as the jumper fell away. The parachute canopy was designed to emerge first from the pack, followed by the rigging lines that linked it to the jumper's harness. This was not a problem in free fall or pull-off jumps because the parachutist's velocity or plane slipstream would inflate the canopy before the rigging lines appeared. But in static-line drops the slower speed might cause the rigging lines to emerge and become tangled with the canopy before the latter was fully deployed, a mishap known as a 'Roman candle'.

To be certain that Driver Evans' death was a systematic fault rather than a freak accident, eight sandbag dummies were dropped by static line the following day. When three suffered the same malfunction that had killed Evans, the modified Irvin training parachute was removed from service and sent to Raymond Quilter of the GQ Parachute Company for a remedy. By redesigning the Irvin's parachute pack as a simpler system, with a less severe opening shock, Quilter hugely reduced the risk of rigging lines fouling the canopy.* On 2 August, Quilter delivered 150 of these hybrid Irvin/GQ parachutes – known as the X-type – to Ringway. Six days later, the new 'chutes had completed 500 dummy test drops without incident.

---

* Quilter's modified parachute would be used by British airborne forces throughout the Second World War and on into the 1960s.

Improving the parachutes, however, solved only one problem. There was also the unsuitability of the Whitley bomber as a transport for paratroopers, an issue raised by Air Commodore Slessor after the accident. In an internal Air Staff memo on 12 August, he admitted the Whitley was 'far from ideal technically' in that the men had 'to leave the fuselage by a hole in the floor, which is an exceedingly unpleasant performance and has some dangers'. Moreover, there was a tactical consequence in that the 'relatively slow rate of leaving the fuselage' meant that men would be 'dropped over a considerable area of ground'.

The solution, of course, was to use an aircraft with a side door. Yet most had doors that were either 'too small or too far aft', noted Slessor. The exceptions were the Bristol Bombay and the Douglas DC-3 civil airliner. The Bombay was 'suitable', but no longer in production and only three of the available aircraft had engines.★ The Douglas – the military version of which would be known as the C-47 Dakota transport plane – also ticked a number of boxes, yet there were only five in the country and all were owned by the Dutch firm KLM. 'As they are suitable for tropical use,' wrote Slessor, 'we are extremely anxious to get the use of them for the Trans-Africa route, which is of great military importance.' However, the Under-Secretary of State for Air would examine the possibility of getting 'substantial numbers' of DC-3s when he visited America in the near future.

In the meantime, concluded Slessor, 'we have either to use the Whitley, accepting a somewhat high casualty rate, or give up for the time being the idea of parachute troops'. It was an issue that would have to be resolved with the DCO and the War Office. Yet he and the directorate of plans had their doubts:

★ While the Whitley was grounded, a single Bombay was used at Ringway to drop more than 130 parachutists from 6 to 14 August 1940. (Buckingham, *Paras*, pp. 101–2.)

We are beginning to incline to the view that dropping troops from the air by parachute is a clumsy and obsolescent method and that there are far more important possibilities in gliders. The Germans made excellent use of their parachute troops in the Low Countries by exploiting surprise, and by virtue of the fact that they had practically no opposition. But it seems to us at least possible that this may be the last time that parachute troops are used on a serious scale in major operations.

We are pressing ahead with the development of gliders, and have made good progress . . . We have already got a suitable glider for carrying a number of troops, and they can be put into production quickly, easily and cheaply.

It is, however, a little early to say whether they are really going to be practicable for the carriage of troops in any considerable numbers, and we shall have to have further technical and tactical trials before we can go nap on them.[10]

One man in no doubt that parachutists were needed was Winston Churchill. Told by Lieutenant Colonel Ian Jacob, 'Pug' Ismay's assistant, that the 'present limitations' of training equipment and aircraft made it impossible 'for the time being to go beyond the first 500', the prime minister kept asking when the original figure of 5,000 parachute troops *would* be ready for action.[11]

Wing Commander Guy Knocker, the assistant director of Combined Operations (Air), responded on 23 August that para-chutists were being trained at Ringway at the rate of 100 per week, which meant a force of 5,000 would not be available for at least a year. Another hindrance was the fact that the Whitley bomber was 'the only aircraft available or likely to be available at present'. Even to drop 600 or 700 parachutists 'would absorb all the aircraft' in the Whitley group. There was some hope, said Knocker, that the Douglas DC-3 might be suitable, but it was unlikely to be 'available in any numbers'. The Air Ministry, he added, were 'not prepared to divert aircraft and personnel in order to increase this rate of production' unless they could point to 'some definite operation which will call for it'.[12]

In fact, there was another aircraft suitable for parachutists in the form of the Handley Page Harrow bomber transport, with more than 100 in service by 1937. The Harrow could lift 20 fully laden troops, or 9,500 pounds of cargo, and had a starboard side-door. But it was never mentioned as an alternative because the Air Ministry did not want bomber production capacity to be diverted toward transport planes like the Bombay and the Harrow. 'The Air Ministry failure to supply Ringway with sufficient aircraft was deliberate,' notes one historian, 'and was intended to hamstring the project and draw out development until Churchill lost interest.' The Air Ministry's support for a glider force – as set out in Slessor's memo of 12 August – was also an attempt, the historian believes, to avoid the diversion of bombers from their primary purpose.[13]

Churchill had his own suspicions, telling Ismay on 1 September that if the glider scheme 'is better than parachutes, we should pursue it, but is it being seriously taken up?' Were they not, he asked, 'in danger of being fobbed off with one doubtful and experimental policy and losing the other which has already been proved?' He wanted to see a full report of what had 'been done about gliders'.[14]

At the prime minister's prompting, a high-level inter-service conference was held at the Air Ministry on 5 September to formulate a unified airborne policy with the War Office and Combined Operations. In attendance were no fewer than 24 officers – 17 from the RAF and seven from the Army – including Air Marshal Sir Richard Pierse and Lieutenant General Robert Haining, vice chiefs of the Air Staff and the Imperial General Staff respectively, Lieutenant General Bourne (now deputy DCO since his supersession by Admiral of the Fleet Sir Roger Keyes,

hero of the 1918 Zeebrugge Raid, in July), Air Commodore
Slessor, and Wing Commander Knocker.

True to form, the RAF – in the form of Group Captain
R. V. Goddard, the Air Staff's deputy director of Plans – tried
to downplay the potential effectiveness of airborne forces by
insisting that the recent 'success' of German airborne operations
in the Low Countries was 'primarily due to the absence of
opposition'. Where even minor forces had been encountered,
'notably in Holland', said Goddard, 'very heavy' losses were
suffered by both aircraft and parachutists. The best use of mass
jumps, in his view, was to secure a landing zone for gliders.
They would need, moreover, air superiority and the element of
surprise, and both 'would be almost impossible' to achieve in
the European theatre 'for some time to come'.

After a heated discussion, Lieutenant Colonel Dudley Clarke,
commanding MO9 (the department set up to oversee continental
raids) and the man who had come up with the name 'Commando',
set out the War Office's position that there were three scenarios
for possible airborne operations:

(a) A raid by airborne troops at a selected position to be
     followed by an evacuation of the raiding force by air.
(b) A raid by airborne troops to be followed by evacuation by
     sea.
(c) An operation for which airborne troops would form the
     spearhead and would be followed by strong supporting
     forces on land, similar to the tactics employed by the
     Germans in Holland.

He was backed by Lieutenant General Bourne who reminded
the conference that if a raid on German soil 'were possible, the
moral effect would be considerable'. But Lieutenant General
Haining, the VCIGS, did not hold out much hope that 'an

isolated airborne invasion anywhere in Europe, at any rate next year', had much chance of success because the 'effort devoted to such an enterprise would be likely to be ill-rewarded'.

The meeting did, however, reach a number of general conclusions: a large-scale airborne operation would require both air superiority and surprise; there might, as a result, be greater opportunities for operations by airborne forces in the Middle East than in Europe; the use of parachutists 'as saboteurs pure and simple should not be lost sight of'; and to prepare for their ultimate task spearheading a large-scale operation in which they were supported by ground forces, airborne troops should carry out 'minor operations such as raids and sabotage'.

Despite the short-term plan to concentrate on relatively small-scale operations in the immediate future, the conference agreed to raise and train an airborne force of 3,000 men by the spring of 1941 to cover potential losses. The majority – 90 per cent, or 2,700 men – would be carried in gliders, with only 10 per cent (300 men) assigned as parachutists. A further 200 parachutists would be given special training as saboteurs, making 500 in total.

The outcome of the conference, therefore, was a victory for the Air Ministry in that it won the argument to concentrate on glider-borne troops, which required the commitment of fewer existing bombers as tugs than parachutists needed for transport. It was agreed that 360 glider pilots and gliders would be needed to transport the 2,700 men, and that in future larger gliders needed to be obtained that could carry 'light tanks, guns and heavy equipment'. Already, noted the assistant chief of Air Staff, orders had been placed for 12 gliders capable of carrying eight men, while the manufacturing capacity to produce 700 more was being arranged.

The Air Ministry was not successful, however, in its attempt to mirror the German model and organise the parachutists as a branch of the RAF. The main function of parachutists was 'to fight as soldiers', insisted the representatives of the War Office, and already 350 had been recruited from the British Army. That system would remain. Their training as parachutists, however, would be an RAF responsibility, as would the flight training of glider pilots. It was also agreed that Combined Operations would continue to advise on the air training and transport of an airborne force, but that its principal function would be to plan and carry out raids.[15]

4

11th Special Air Service Battalion – UK, July–December 1940

IN LATE JULY 1940, with all jumps at Tatton Park suspended after the 'Roman candle' debacle, Sergeant Ernie Chinnery and his colleagues were sent up to Torcastle, near Fort William in Scotland, for two weeks' Commando training. As the rain fell in sheets, C and D Troops were taught close combat, pistol-shooting and knife-fighting techniques by William Fairburn and Eric Sykes, two former Shanghai municipal policemen who would go on to design the double-edged Commando fighting knife that bears their name.* They were, remembered Chinnery, 'bloody smashing blokes' who used to say: 'You don't need a weapon, all you need is your hands and feet.'

The trainee parachutists also learned the art of stalking from the dashing and hardy Lord Lovat who took them out into the hills until they were up to their necks in heather. Try as they might, they failed to spot the approach of Lovat's ghillies until they were within a few yards. Fishing was easier. 'We'd lob a

---

* The first batch of 50 Fairburn-Sykes fighting knives was produced by Wilkinson Sword Ltd in January 1941 after the two men had travelled to its factory to discuss the design in late 1940. An initial order of 1,500 was placed, later rising to 38,000 of the second (revised) pattern.

grenade into a stream,' said Chinnery, 'and all the fish would float to the surface. We'd spear them out with bayonets and feast on fish for a couple of days.'

They returned to new civvy billets in Knutsford, near Ringway, in time for the recommencement of parachute training on 15 August. Also in residence were the newly arrived A and B Troops – recruited by the British Army's Northern Command – bringing No. 2 Commando's total strength up to 200 men. 'There was a really smashing spirit among the lads,' recalled Chinnery, 'and we did a lot of drinking at our "headquarters" – the White Bear at Knutsford. We thought we'd be sent over the other side and sabotage Germany, especially when C Troop went to a place called Horwich, where they gave us explosives training and even taught us how to drive trains.'[1]

By September, with three separate and overlapping courses underway, a total of 464 parachute jumps had been made and a 10-week training syllabus drawn up. Henceforth the trainees would spend the first four weeks on fitness, weapons, sabotage and map-reading training. This would be followed by a three-week parachuting course at Ringway: week one was ground training and a single jump from 800 feet; week two included two jumps, this time in pairs from 500 feet; week three was two more jumps, with equipment and weapon containers, in a stick of four and eight respectively. Trainees would then spend the final three weeks on tactical training at Tatton Park, to include at least one group descent. Only then would they be considered fully qualified parachutists.[2]

On 1 October, having finally completed the course, C and D Troops were presented with their GQ parachute qualification badges. The forerunner to the famous cloth 'wings' – which were worn on the shoulder and first issued in December 1940 – the metal badge was a similar design with a silver canopy and black enamel rigging lines surmounted on a pair of orange enamel wings. At the base of the canopy was a tiny suspended parachutist, topped by the maker's name 'GQ' in black enamel.★ Receiving the badge was a proud moment for Chinnery and the other airborne pioneers. 'You stuck that on your chest,' he recalled, 'which expanded to about 10 times its normal size.'[3]

Despite the improved X-type parachute, fatal accidents were an ever-present danger. On 27 August, Trooper Stanley Watts of the Royal Horse Guards had been killed when his parachute failed to open. This time, Raymond Quilter identified a fault with the packing design and changes were quickly incorporated into the GQ production line. A few weeks later, 25-year-old Corporal Hugh Carter from Newport in Wales plummeted to his death when the snap hook that connected his parachute pack to the static line was forced open after it caught on the edge of the Whitley's jumping hole. Witnessing this horrific scene was former actress Cicely Paget-Bowman who, having volunteered for the First Aid Nursing Yeomanry (FANY) after the fall of France, was posted to Tatton Park to drive the ambulance for the medical officer. As the last man came out, she could see two hands feeling for the rigging 'but it wasn't there – the parachute had failed to open'.

The other parachutists were 'so young and keen that they managed to throw it off', but for Paget-Bowman, it was a shocking reminder of the risks these young men took, even before they met the enemy. As the only female on the staff, she had been taken under the wing of the 'wonderfully friendly' trainees. They called this ambulance driver their mascot – 'Miss Bowman and her blood tub' – and played endless games of darts and drank beer with her at the George pub in Knutsford. 'Oh,'

★ The US firm Irvin issued a similar parachute qualification badge. It had a white parachute and blue rigging lines surmounted on a pair of golden wings. At the base of the parachute was the maker's name, 'Irvin'.

she remembered, 'they were a wonderful lot. Everything from Dons to gaol-birds – an incredible crowd . . . They were so different from ordinary soldiers; they had to be special to get in, and they trained very hard, but they still retained their great individuality.' It would have been easy to fall in love with one of them: but some instinct – maybe self-preservation – made her hold back. 'I love them all,' she wrote. 'We all shared a fine sense of comradeship. In those early days we really had a marvellous time; we laughed an enormous amount at a time when there wasn't all that much to laugh about.'[4]

Fortunately, Carter's death was not in vain as it prompted Wing Commander Buxton's Technical Unit to devise a simple remedy: attaching a locking safety pin to the static-line hook to prevent an accidental opening. An obvious safety precaution would have been to issue all jumpers with a reserve parachute, the practice of all US airborne units after their first test platoon was formed in June 1940. But it was rejected in Britain on the grounds of expense. 'Throughout the war we only had one parachute, no reserves were carried,' recalled Lieutenant Tony Deane-Drummond, who was 23 years old when he joined No. 2 Commando in July. 'The decision would save the Treasury a lot of money. We thought it rather sissy much later on when we saw American parachute troops with two parachutes.'

Just nine when his parents separated, Deane-Drummond and his two sisters had been brought up by their mother in a comfortable former vicarage in the Cotswolds. Considered 'backward and delicate', he was sent to Marlborough College – rather than the more demanding Eton or Winchester – and was fortunate to be taught by the inspirational A. R. Pepin who told him: 'Put your heart and soul – as well as brains – into anything you do at school or after you leave here and you will get to the top.'

It was good advice. In 1937, after 18 months at the Royal Military Academy, Woolwich, he was commissioned into the

Royal Signals, and, while on a course at Catterick, realised a childhood ambition by learning to fly with the Yorkshire Gliding Club. He was a quick learner and, having completed the necessary distance (40 miles), height (3,300 feet) and duration (five hours) qualifications, he was awarded the Silver C Badge, 'whose issue was controlled by the Germans, who were the acknowledged leaders of the sport'. Deane-Drummond was 'hooked' and, though the war soon intervened, dreamed 'of once again soaring over the lovely English countryside and perhaps doing better than my peers'.

Rescued from Dunkirk with men of the 3rd Divisional Signals in early June 1940, he was stationed in Lincolnshire awaiting the seemingly inevitable German invasion when he saw the notice for volunteers for special service. Determined to avenge the defeat on the continent, and 'to do something more active', he put his name forward and was surprised when he was the only officer accepted. He joined No. 2 Commando at Ringway and completed his first jump from a Bristol Bombay. 'It had a side-opening door,' he remembered, 'which, when open, could be lifted off the two vertical pins on which the door swung. My static line cord, which automatically opened the parachute, was tied to one of the pins with two half-hitches. Such a procedure would horrify modern safety standards, but it shows how urgently everybody worked to produce an answer to Churchill's requirements.'

He completed the jump without a problem and, like the other airborne pioneers, took the 'occasional tragic failure' in his stride. Most jumpers reasoned that the low likelihood of an accident – around one in 5,000 – meant that it 'would never happen' to them.[5]

Another officer who joined No. 2 Commando after narrowly escaping from Dunkirk – and who, like Deane-Drummond, was destined to play a prominent role in the story of Britain's airborne forces – was 23-year-old Lieutenant Tony Hibbert. The son of a Malaya rubber planter who had flown with the RFC during the First World War (in which he had won three Military Crosses and a Distinguished Flying Cross), Hibbert joined the Royal Artillery in 1938 and fought with a half-battery of anti-aircraft guns at Dunkirk before he and his men were rescued in the water and ferried home in a Thames tug.[6] 'We had been defeated,' he noted, 'but they gave us a hero's welcome in Ramsgate. In due course, we reformed at Aberystwyth, but since we had no weapons, there was little to do except march up and down the sea front.'

He and his men started to apply for any unit 'that looked like it might have some weapons' and get them 'back into the fight again'.* Much to his amazement – given that both his eardrums had been ruptured at Dunkirk and he 'practically had to go round with an ear trumpet' – he was accepted as a troop leader in No. 2 Commando and sent to Ringway for jump training. [7] There he tried to stir up a competitive spirit by clocking up as many jumps as he could. One evening he jumped from the balloon in his full mess kit, complete with spurs. 'It wasn't bravado,' he insisted, 'but it raised a laugh and perhaps helped to make parachuting seem a bit less intimidating.'[8]

Witnessing Hibbert's drunken bravado was Cecily Paget-Bowman. Suddenly she was grabbed by Hibbert's friends and dragged towards the balloon. 'Now, come on,' said one, 'you're going to jump.' Luckily, she managed to break free. 'I don't regret refusing to jump,' she said. 'I would have broken both my legs.'

Paget-Bowman knew the risks, having treated 'lots of scrapes

---

* Hibbert was one of three subalterns who applied to leave the battery: one joined the RAF and became the commander of a famous squadron of rocket-firing Typhoons; the other, Peter Porteous, joined No. 4 Commando and won a Victoria Cross during the infamous Dieppe Raid.

and bangs and broken limbs'. One afternoon they had to call in the fire brigade to rescue a parachutist who was stuck in a tree. He could have got down, but was paralysed with fright and had to be treated for shock.[9]

Once the men were parachute qualified, they concentrated on 'night-attack exercises, weapons training and unarmed combat – sticking knives into the backs of sentries, that sort of thing'. Hibbert wrote: 'We found it exciting, but it probably wasn't very realistic; our commanding officer, Colonel Jackson, was a Tank Corps man. There were very few of us with any experience of commando or special force fighting, and we really weren't sure what we were supposed to be doing.'[10] Hibbert did not have a high opinion of Jackson.[11]

On 21 November, to better reflect its true purpose, Jackson's No. 2 Commando was renamed the 11th Special Air Service (SAS) Battalion. It was scheduled to complete its advanced group parachute training by February 1941, at which point the 500-strong battalion would be available for operations. But this was complicated by the fact that many of the men needed to learn basic infantry skills, and it was not until Christmas Eve 1940 that all ranks had passed the individual parachute course.[12]

Meanwhile, the more experienced troops in the battalion – A, B, C and D – gave the first parachute demonstration – part of a larger exercise on Salisbury Plain on 3 December – for Lieutenant General Sir Bernard Montgomery and the staff of his 3rd Infantry Division. It was followed by a larger combined parachute and glider assault at Tatton Park on 13 December, witnessed by General Sir John Dill, the Chief of the Imperial General Staff. Both went well. But as the Air Ministry continued to question the relevance of the airborne project, the need for a successful operation became ever more pressing: 'to demonstrate that the airborne idea merited further development'; and, given the 'gloomy strategic background' of Britain continuing to face

Germany and Italy alone, to provide 'a propaganda success for domestic and international consumption'.[13]

Under the circumstances, Operation Colossus – the first British parachute mission – was a godsend.

5

'A pity, a damned pity'
– UK and Malta, December 1940–February 1941

THE SEEDS OF OPERATION Colossus had been sown two
months earlier when the Air Ministry received confidential
information from a Mr Ardley of the London engineering firm
George Kent & Sons. Ardley's company had helped to build a
130-mile-long aqueduct – known as the Acquedotto Pugliese
– in southern Italy to divert the water from the head-waters of
the River Sele, which flowed west to the Mediterranean, back
through the Apennine mountains to the towns on the south-east
coast. It had become, as a result, the 'only source of pure water'
for the whole province of Apulia, including the vital naval ports
of Taranto, Brindisi and Bari. If that water supply was severed
for even just a month, an area of two million inhabitants, 'many
engaged in important industries', would have to rely on local
reservoirs whose maximum capacity might be limited to 30
gallons a head. Those reserves would not last long, and the
subsequent lack of drinking water was bound to disrupt the flow
of supplies and reinforcements from the ports to Italian armies
fighting in North Africa and Albania, and might even persuade
Mussolini's government that one or both campaigns needed to
be brought to 'an abrupt end'.[1]

The Air Ministry was intrigued. The aqueduct was, on the

face of it, a hugely tempting target, the destruction of which might change the course of the war. But how best to do the job? The first consideration was aerial bombing. But that was quickly rejected on the grounds that the recommended target – a bridge carrying the pipeline over the River Tragino, 'in wild and mountainous country' 40 miles from the west coast – would be impossible for the RAF to pinpoint. It was also not a mission that the Special Operations Executive (SOE) – set up by Churchill to coordinate resistance in occupied Europe – was prepared to take on. Finally, the task was passed to the planning staff of Combined Operations who concluded that 'the only practical method is to drop a British demolition party by parachute at night from aircraft, the party to consist of sappers and a covering force'. Once the bridge had been blown, the party would make their way over the mountains to the west coast 'where a submarine would take them off'. To help the planes locate the target, the operation was scheduled for the full moon period of 9–19 February 1941.[2]

On 8 January, once the Chiefs of Staff had agreed to the operation in principle, the Central Landing Establishment (as the Central Landing School at Ringway had been renamed) was ordered to select the parachutists from Jackson's 11th SAS Battalion and begin their training.[3] Designated 'X' Troop, the raiding force eventually numbered 36 men: two officers and 16 sappers to blow the bridge; a covering force of four officers and 12 men; and two Italian interpreters (one in the uniform of an RAF flight lieutenant). The force commander was 29-year-old Major Trevor 'Tag' Pritchard, Jackson's deputy, a regular with the Royal Welch Fusiliers who had volunteered for airborne duties to get out of running a transit camp (or 'hotel duties' as he put it). 'In fact,' remembered Tony Deane-Drummond, 'he was rather heavy for a parachutist, having been a good heavyweight boxer in his younger days. Despite a rather gruff and inarticulate manner, there could not have been a more likeable or a more loyal commander officer.'[4]

Pritchard had typically put himself forward for the job and, once appointed, had selected the five officers to accompany him. They all came from the first four troops to be raised in No. 2 Commando: A, B, C and D. The two sapper officers were Captain Gerry Daly, 'short and studious, but very knowledgeable', and Second Lieutenant George Paterson, the young Canadian from C Troop. The remaining officers were: Captain Christopher Lea of the Lancashire Fusiliers, 'lanky and languid, but this concealed a highly professional and very energetic person underneath'; Second Lieutenant Geoff Jowett, another Canadian who was 'small and stocky with a nearly bald head and a large mustache', and who 'wore his emotions on his sleeve and prided himself on being more aggressive and bloodthirsty than anyone else; and, lastly, Lieutenant Tony Deane-Drummond.[5]

All delighted to be on the list, the officers picked in turn a senior NCO and five men from their sections. Pritchard's right-hand man was Sergeant Percy 'Clem' Clements, a fine sportsman who had joined the Leicestershire Regiment in 1928. After lengthy service with the 1st Battalion in India, he returned to England in 1939 to help train new recruits. A year later, keen to do his bit, he joined No. 2 Commando under the impression that the requirement to able to fit through a circular hole, three feet in diameter, meant he would serve on submarines. He was surprised to discover that the hole was in fact in the floor of a Whitley bomber, and that he would be dropping through it with a parachute.[6]

Deane-Drummond's senior NCO was 35-year-old Sergeant Arthur 'Taff' Lawley, an ex-coal miner who had served with the South Wales Borderers in Egypt and Palestine during the inter-war years. When his time expired, Lawley became a London bus driver, but was recalled to the Colours at the start of the war and in 1940, in search of a new challenge, volunteered for 'special service'. Deane-Drummond thought him 'a superb soldier with a tangy wit' and together they picked the remaining men. The composite 'X' Troop was then quarantined from the rest of 11th SAS Battalion to prepare for the mission.[7]

Anyone not on the list was hugely disappointed. 'We all wanted to be involved,' remembered Eric Chinnery, but priority was given to men with 'experience in demolition'.[8]

Despite X Troop's isolation, Tony Hibbert and some of the other officers got wind of what was happening and used any means, fair or foul, to get little chits to 'Tag' Pritchard, pointing out that the operation would be a 'total and utter waste of time' unless they were involved. Needless to say, their approaches were ignored.[9]

Having left their comfortable billets in Knutsford for a secure camp at Ringway, X Troop trained hard for the mission. Their daily schedule included three-mile runs followed by 30 minutes of PT before breakfast, and usually a 12- to 15-mile march after it. Wearing full parachute marching order, they were expected to keep up a pace of 5-6 miles per hour. In the afternoon they practised on a wooden mock-up of the bridge that had been built at Tatton Park. 'As we trained,' noted Deane-Drummond, 'so our efficiency improved and eventually we found we could place the half ton or so of explosive in position in just over half an hour.' For the final dress rehearsal on 1 February they concentrated on a fast exit from the Whitleys so they would all land as close together as possible. It did not go to plan. 'The night was cloudy,' remembered Deane-Drummond, 'the wind was strong. Half the aircraft dropped their sticks in the wrong place so that many landed in trees and had to face the ignominy of being helped down by the local fire brigade.'[10]

The official report noted, 'Dress rehearsal successfully completed at CLE in a 35 mph wind and a time of 2 hours. 2 men broke their legs but the result was satisfactory.'[11]

Soon after, having been let into the secret that X Troop's

mission was to blow up the Tragino aqueduct in southern Italy, Deane-Drummond left with the advance party for Malta. He was followed on 7 February by Major 'Tag' Pritchard and the rest of X Troop. Before departing in eight Whitleys★ from RAF Mildenhall in Suffolk at 10 p.m., they were given a pep talk by Admiral Sir Roger Keyes, director of Combined Operations. A celebrated First World War naval commander who had planned and led the daring Zeebrugge Raid of April 1918, the 68-year-old Keyes had been brought back from retirement by Churchill to breathe life into Combined Operations which, up to this point, had launched only a couple of minor and largely ineffective Commando raids in the Channel.†

Having spoken to each member of X Troop individually, Keyes addressed the group.

'You are setting off on a very important job,' he told them, 'and I should like you to know that I have been assured no better, fitter or braver men could have been selected than you to play this very vital role. I know that you will tackle this job with determination and enthusiasm, and with a bit of luck I am sure you will pull it off. We shall be waiting to hear how you have got on; waiting to learn what British paratroopers can do. I decided that I just couldn't let you go without coming here to say goodbye to you.'

Keyes then saluted, a dramatic gesture that caught them

★ All of the latest type and commanded by Flight Lieutenant J. B. Tait DFC 'who was later to become famous for bombing the *Tirpitz*' battleship in Norway fjord in 1944. (Deane-Drummond, *Return Ticket*, p. 17)

† Operation Collar (24/25 June), a minor propaganda victory when 200 men of No. 11 Independent Company (forerunners of the Commandos) landed near Boulogne and killed two German soldiers; and Operation Ambassador (14/15 July), a botched attempt by men of No. 3 Commando to bring prisoners back from the Channel Island of Guernsey, thanks to hasty planning, navigational errors and mechanical breakdown.

unawares. They responded in ones and twos 'until finally the whole parade was stiffly at the salute'.

The admiral knew all too well that the likelihood of anyone returning from such a mission was virtually nil. As he turned away, he muttered under his breath: 'A pity, a damned pity.'[12]

By the time the eight Whitleys carrying X Troop touched down in Malta at 9 a.m. on 8 February – having flown the 1,400 miles from England 'with a following wind' and in 'record time' – Deane-Drummond had gathered together the explosives and supplies that were needed for the operation. They included six days' rations for 36 men, and more than 2,300 pounds of guncotton explosive,* fuses and detonators.[13]

At 4 p.m. on 10 February, with the planes loaded and ready, 'Tag' Pritchard briefed X Troop on its 'actual object' and the hoped-for result. 'Only now,' he told the men, 'can I let you into the big secret of this trip. The job on which you are embarking is an experiment to see what you can do. We are to jump right into the middle of Mussolini's Italy and blow up an aqueduct which takes water to a large military area. After we have done the job – and we shall see to it that we do – the only way out will be across the mountainous country to the coast.'

He paused to let the news sink in. The men's expressions were mostly of excitement and anticipation. They had been led to believe that their destination was Abyssinia. Now that it was confirmed as Italy, they cheered. 'Quite simple and straightforward,' concluded Pritchard, 'and I should like to wish you all the best of luck.'

---

* Developed by the Swiss-German scientist Christian Friedrich Schönbein in 1846, guncotton or nitrocellulose was a mixture of nitric and sulphuric acid and cotton (later wood pulp). It was practically smokeless and had six times the explosive power of gunpowder.

Maps were then handed out and final instructions issued. The blowing up of the bridge had been 'practised and rehearsed at Tatton Park in the minutest detail', remembered Deane-Drummond, but the 'subsequent orders to get to the coast were necessarily vague'.[14] They would split up into several parties and rendezvous at the submarine pick-up point on the coast, close to the mouth of the Sele river, five days later. That night they would flash a recognition signal out to sea and the submarine, having acknowledged it, would send dinghies in to pick them up. Anyone who did not arrive that night, but was known to have got away, would be picked up four days later.[15]

At 5 p.m. the weather reports indicated light winds and good visibility. The mission was on. The men gulped down a final meal of hot tea and boiled eggs, though few had much of an appetite. 'Our fingers twitched with nervous excitement as we dressed,' wrote Deane-Drummond, 'ending with the parachute which we checked with each other. It would not be long now. A truck waiting outside took us to our plane and we squeezed laboriously down the narrow tunnel of the Whitley. We all had a Li-Lo mattress to lie on to insulate us from the cold in the unheated plane.'[16]

Each man was wearing battledress – or BD, a short jacket and trousers made of wool serge – over a shirt and pullover, and topped by a loose gaberdine jacket. They were also clad in rubber-soled parachute boots, woollen gloves, balaclavas and flying helmets. In their pockets were two grenades, a clasp knife, a field dressing, a box of matches, chewing gum and some toilet paper. Their two haversacks contained a groundsheet, spare pair of socks, mess tin, enamel mug, five days' special rations and a torch. They were all armed with a .32 Colt automatic pistol and 18 rounds of ammunition, and two hand grenades. Some, in addition, had .303 Bren light machine guns and .45 Thompson sub-machine guns ('tommy guns'). All officers and NCOs wore compasses and watches, while the former also had field glasses and maps.[17]

Six of the Whitley bombers were loaded with paratroopers – six to a plane – and the containers that held their weapons, ammunition and explosives. The other two would create a diversion by bombing Foggia railway station. At 5.40 p.m., they started their engines and took off, one after the other, and headed on a north-westerly bearing. The plan was to skirt the west coast of Sicily – and therefore avoid its plentiful anti-aircraft batteries – before moving in a north-easterly direction across open sea to mainland Italy. Striking the coast near the Gulf of Salerno, the planes were to follow a road through the Apennines to the region of the objective which, it was hoped, would be clearly identifiable in good moonlight. It was a total flying distance of 450 miles.[18]

'Quite soon,' remembered Deane-Drummond, 'we were flying at 10,000 feet over Sicily and were rocked a little by anti-aircraft fire as we passed over the northern coastline. My word it was cold. But soon after crossing the Italian coast which showed up clearly in the bright moonlight, the aircraft began a slow descent towards our target area.'

The aqueduct itself was awkward to get at because it was astride the Tragino, a small tributary of the Ofanto river that flowed from the Apennines to the Adriatic. Little villages were perched on both sides of the valley, and 'connected to each other by twisting roads which wound their way up in a series of hairpins'. The plan was to fly low over the village of Calitri, turn half-right and drop the men between the main river at the bottom of the valley and the line of the tributary leading up to the bridge. The planes would then turn left to avoid hitting the mountains directly ahead. Operation Colossus was, as Deane-Drummond put it, 'quite a challenge for a "first" operation'.[19]

6

'Viva Carabinieri! Viva Duce!' – Italy, February 1941

THIRTY-SIX HOURS LATER, WITH the bridge blown but still 35 miles short of the coast, X Troop commander 'Tag' Pritchard and his men were led down the hill by their grinning captors and handed over first to 'a number of creatures in army uniform' and then to carabinieri, who combined the duties of civil and military police. Commanded by a fat little sergeant who was sweating with exertion, the carabinieri all 'wore navy-blue serge jackets and knickerbockers of the same colour, which had a thin red stripe down the outside'. They were armed with pistols and small rifles, which they cocked ostentatiously as they approached. Having searched the captives, and tied them together in parties of three or four – with only Pritchard spared this igno-miny – they were taken down a narrow winding track to the nearby village of Teora where they were met by a small crowd.

'*Viva Carabinieri! Viva Duce!*' shouted one or two, as if either had played any part in the capture of the paratroopers.

Escorted to the local police station, they were locked in a whitewashed cell with a 'cold red-tiled floor', its window looking out 'through heavy one-inch bars' on to the green hillside down which they had just come. They tried to look cheerful, but inside were 'mighty depressed'.

After an impromptu meal of bully beef and bread, they were questioned by a tiny, self-important general who wanted to know how many more of them there were. They refused to answer. The two Italian speakers, Nastri and Picchi, were then interrogated by a blackshirted officer who told them that they would all be shot at dawn the next day, so they might as well tell him everything. They laughed in response.

That evening, they were driven by lorry to Calitri railway station and held overnight in an 'evil-smelling' waiting room. Gradually they dozed off and in the morning were reunited with the other two parties who had been captured nearby. In attempting to get away, one of Geoff Jowett's party had fired a tommy gun (kept in spite of Pritchard's instructions), killing an Italian officer and two peasants. Not surprisingly the entire group were 'roughly handled' when they were captured soon after.

At 10 a.m., surrounded by so many guards it was 'laughable', they were put on a train for Naples and arrived an hour after sunset. During the journey, 'Pat' Patterson became so exasperated by the guards' disgusting habit of clearing their throats and spitting, that he swore at them 'in as loud and offensive a tone as possible and pointed to the *non sputare* notice in the compartment'. This had the effect of reducing the rate of spitting to 'about one an hour', with some even leaving the compartment to 'humour the mad Englishman'.

At Naples, where Mount Vesuvius 'glowed red against the stars', they were taken to the military prison and thrown into tiny cells, 10 feet by 5 wide, with straw for a bed and a smelly hole in the ground to use as a lavatory. In the morning, after a bowl of ersatz coffee and a small piece of dried fig, they were lined up in the corridor outside their cells and interrogated one by one. Deane-Drummond noticed that Picchi was looking thoroughly depressed, and tried to cheer him up.

'It's no good,' responded Picchi. 'They'll find out who I am.

I don't see how they can fail. So I'm going to tell them and they will understand. I know nobody likes the Fascists. They will see that I am a true lover of Italy, but at the same time a hater of the Fascist regime.'

This alarmed Deane-Drummond. 'You mustn't talk like that,' he insisted. 'They won't find out who you are if you stick like glue to the official story – that you're a Free Frenchman in the British Army. I really don't think they can prove a thing. To say who you are is very dangerous.'

Picchi looked unconvinced. He was eventually led off for questioning and did not return.

The others were questioned in two separate rooms. The story told to the men was that 'they had been caught making war on the civilian population by committing acts of sabotage, and in Italy that is punishable by death'. Only by cooperating could they avoid execution.

Fortunately, the sergeants calmed their fears. 'It's a face,' they said. 'It's just a ploy to try and make us talk.'

A different tactic was used on the officers who were questioned by a civilian flanked by two blackshirted fascists. 'I am the Commandant of the camp you are going to,' he told them, 'and all I want are a few details for the Red Cross.'

This was a lie, of course, designed to put them at their ease. It did not work. 'My number is 71076,' said the Royal Signals officer, 'my rank is Lieutenant and my name is Deane-Drummond and you can expect nothing else.'

Having refused to answer all other questions, he was returned to his cell and a 'tolerably good lunch', followed by a shave from a local barber.

Later the officers were moved to a local aerodrome where they 'ate too much, took too little exercise but could see no way out'.[1] They were joined there by Captain Gerry Daly whose 'missing' stick of sappers had been dropped two miles north of the aqueduct in the wrong gorge, and two hours late, after their plane lost its way. Hearing explosions an hour later, and guessing the aqueduct had been blown, they made for the coast and might have arrived on time but for encountering a snow storm on the night of the 13th that caused them to travel in a circle. By dawn on the 16th, still 18 miles from the rendezvous (scheduled for 10 p.m. that evening), Daly decided that they had to risk walking by day and they were captured by 'a mixture of soldiers, carabinieri and civilians at 11 a.m'.

They almost persuaded their captors that they were 'German airmen on special duty carrying despatches and had to be in Naples by 1400hrs'. A car was provided to speed them on the way. But their cover story collapsed when the local mayor appeared and demanded to see their papers. Taken to a civilian jail, Daly escaped by forcing a corroded lock. But he was recaptured the following morning as he tried to board a train, and sent to join the other officers at the aerodrome.[2]

Even if Daly and his men had got to the coast on time, they would have waited in vain. The submarine HMS *Triumph* had been ordered not to make the rendezvous by Admiral of the Fleet Sir Dudley Pound, the First Sea Lord and Chief of the Naval Staff, because of an apparent breach of security by the pilot of one of the diversionary Whitleys. Developing engine trouble over the sea between Sicily and Italy, he had ordered his crew to bale out. But before he crash-landed his aircraft, he had sent a message in a simple code in the hope that he could be picked up from the mouth of the Sele. He insisted later that he did not know the arrangements for the rescue of the Colossus parties, and that his choice of the same location was a complete coincidence. But it was enough to convince Pound that the 'security of the place of embarkation' had been compromised.[3]

When Admiral Sir Roger Keyes learned of Pound's decision, he did everything in his power 'to get the recall of HMS *Triumph* cancelled' on the grounds that the submarine 'would not have run risks which could not be accepted'. But he failed, and later admitted to both Group Captain Harvey and Lieutenant Colonel Jackson, commanding the Central Landing Establishment (CLE) and 11th SAS Battalion respectively, that it had been a matter of 'great regret' to him 'that the Naval arrangements to rescue the Colossus troops were not carried out'.[4]

The first information that Sir Roger Keyes and the staff of Combined Operations received of Operation Colossus was an Italian High Command communiqué of 14 February. It claimed that British parachute troops had been dropped in southern Italy with the intention of using dynamite to interrupt communications and destroy hydro works. Thanks to the 'immediate intervention' of Italy's Home Guard, however, they had all been 'captured before they could carry out their plans'.

This was followed three days later by a *Times* 'Special Correspondent at the Italian Frontier' who wrote that the region for the parachute mission was 'well chosen for an experiment, because it is wild, lonely and thinly populated, but ill-suited for sabotage, as objectives are few'.

There was no indication as to whether the mission had been a success until another report of 25 February, from an American source, claimed that the Italians were 'much disturbed by recent landing of parachutists in Southern Italy'. It added: 'Italian authorities much concerned as to whether or not they had all been rounded up. At least one bridge had been put out of action by parachutists.'

Confirmation that all but six – Captain Daly's stick – of the 36-strong Colossus party had been captured was provided by the British military attaché in Berne on 26 February. He had received the information from the Vatican. This message prompted Keyes to ask MI9 – the War Office's escape and evasion department, set up by Major Norman Crockatt in September 1939 – to send the following coded message to the Colossus captives on 1 March:

(a) Was any success obtained?
(b) If not, what prevented?
(c) Are any German soldiers in the country?

While Keyes awaited the response, he was informed on 15 March that a report had been sent to the Foreign Office by a correspondent of the *Chicago Daily News* who had recently been expelled from Rome. It stated:

> The Apulian Aqueduct which was recently blown up by our [sic] parachutists was repaired in 2½ days. These parachutists were visited by American [military attaché]. Their morale was 'terrific' and they told him that they intended to escape at the first opportunity. They said they had blown up a railway bridge besides damaging aqueduct. Local inhabitants carried their dynamite for them under the impression that they were Germans.[5]

Three weeks later, on 6 April 1941, came news of the first casualty when the BBC carried a Rome wireless report that a certain Fortunato Picchi 'had been taken prisoner, recognised, denounced and shot as a traitor'.*

There was still no definite word on the success of the mission until MI9 received on 18 April a secret communication from Flight Lieutenant Lucky who, with the other officers, had been

---

* A similar report was read in the Italian newspaper *Messagero* by Deane-Drummond and the other Colossus captives (who were unaware of Picchi's work for SOE). 'We all felt sad at his passing,' recalled Deane-Drummond. 'The job he had been given had been so small compared with the risks he had taken. He was a great little man.' (Deane-Drummond, *Return Ticket*, p. 46)

moved to Campo PG 78, a prisoner-of-war camp near Sulmona in central Italy. He wrote: 'Full success. Other prisoners report great scarcity water Southern Italy. Will try make a break for it from next concentration camp.'

This was followed, during the next two to three months, by messages from Captain Lea, Major Pritchard and Second Lieutenant Jowett (all dated April 1941), that confirmed they had blown the aqueduct's west pier, that all parties had been captured, and that in future the release of containers should be 'fool-proof', and the men's parachutes needed to be coloured so they could not be seen by moonlight.

Finally, on 4 October, Keyes received through 'devious channels' a note from 'Tag' Pritchard that read:

> The light which should light up when aircraft drop equipment did not function in three aircraft. The 6th dropped equipment in the wrong valley; light did not show up. Only half the dynamite arrived . . . Only one box of arms arrived.
>
> All parachutists, one wounded, were captured, but the Italians do not know this.
>
> Aqueduct was blown and BRINDISI cut off for 10 days. The bankseats and one column were destroyed.

Pritchard's message was, noted Keyes' staff, the 'first definite and reliable information as to damage achieved'.[6]

The operation had been costly – all 36 participants had been captured and one, the gallant Fortunato Picchi, executed – and its hopelessly optimistic strategic objective of discouraging Italy from fighting a war on two fronts was never likely to be achieved. Yet it could still be regarded a tactical and moral victory. On 23 February 1941, long before the full results were known, Air Chief Marshal Portal, the Chief of the Air Staff, wrote to Group Captain Harvey to convey his appreciation and thanks for the care with which the operation was prepared 'and the skill and gallantry of the Army and Air Force personnel who took part'. He added: 'We must remember that material results are not the only measure of success and that the moral effect of such boldness upon both our friends and enemies must be considerable.'[7]

A War Office report on Operation Colossus – based on information supplied by Deane-Drummond – made the same point:

> There is no doubt of the effect on morale. The sudden and unexpected descent of parachute troops who had succeeded in blowing up an important aqueduct caused widespread alarm. An organisation akin to the Home Guard was formed [in Italy] to watch important points and air raid precautions were improved. One may suppose that, in particular, the blackout at Calitri was tightened up. The destroyed aqueduct was, [the POWs] had heard, replaced by a syphon within a month, but of interruption to the water supply they had heard but vague rumours. Other sources reported that Bari was without water for a few days.

Therefore, concluded the War Office report, while the mission had had a 'negligible effect on the war in Albania', it 'did spread great alarm in Southern Italy and caused a large amount of serious effort to be wasted on more stringent air raid precautions and on unnecessary guards'. This was a 'lasting effect'.[8]

It had also played a vital role in proving the worth of Britain's fledgling airborne forces. Colossus had shown, noted Group Captain Harvey, that it was 'possible to land a party of paratroops fully armed and with a considerable quantity of equipment and explosives close to a given point providing that no serious ground opposition is encountered'. To ensure future success, more training needed to be given 'to air crews as well as to paratroops' and full scale rehearsals needed to be 'practised over country, if possible, similar to the actual target'.

Harvey also recommended that suitable aircraft were 'made available in ample time to allow preparatory work to be carried out properly'; that the CLE was allowed to carry out 'detailed planning' before any future operations were given the green light; that targets were selected with 'great care and the fullest possible information'; and that future paratroop operations that included demolition work should be undertaken by a high proportion of sapper-trained officers and men.

He ended his report by observing that the landing of para-troopers in 'bright moonlight' was 'practically as easy as in daylight'; that the wooden mock-up of the target was of such assistance to the air crew and the paratroopers that 'similar models should be made for all future operations'; and that the 'morale and enthusiasm' of the paratroopers was 'very high' and did not require drugs like Benzedrine★ to keep them going.[9]

As none of the Colossus party managed to evade capture, it was difficult to justify the award of gallantry medals. The exception was Squadron Leader James 'Willie' Tait DFC, the 24-year-old commander of the eight Whitley bombers, who in April was awarded the Distinguished Service Order (DSO)† for leading the night mission.[10] This prompted Lieutenant Colonel John Rock, the senior army officer at Ringway, to ask Admiral Keyes on 16 June if it might be possible to give the same award to Major 'Tag' Pritchard. Rock added: 'Pritchard was a born leader. He put his heart and soul into the job, organised the expedition

---

★ An amphetamine-based stimulant that was widely taken by combat soldiers in the Second World War.

† The DSO was, after the Victoria Cross, the second-highest award for gallantry that could be given to British and Commonwealth officers. The third-highest award for gallantry for army officers was the Military Cross (MC). Its navy and air force equivalents were the Distinguished Service Cross (DSC) and the Distinguished Flying Cross (DFC).

excellently and brought the men to the highest pitch of enthusiasm. I have little doubt that his leadership and handling of the situation after landing were equally good.'[11]

Keyes agreed and on 24 November 1941, by which time more details about the mission had emerged, Pritchard's award was confirmed by the *London Gazette*. Part of the citation read: 'The success of the operation, as a result of which the aqueduct to Brindisi was blown up, the bankseats and one column destroyed, and the town cut off for 10 days, was due to his leadership and inspiration. Major Pritchard had a reasonable chance to escape if arrangements had gone according to plan. The fact that they did not and that he was captured, was due to no error of judgement on his part.'★[12]

★ Other members of the Colossus party were decorated for gallantry. But in most cases the award was chiefly for escaping from Italian captivity, operating with local partisans, or providing vital intelligence from POW camps. The medals included an MBE for Major Pritchard; MCs for Captain Lea, Lieutenant Tony Deane-Drummond and Second Lieutenants George Paterson and Geoff Jowett; a Distinguished Service Medal (DCM) for Sergeant Percy Clements; and Military Medals for Sergeants 'Taff' Lawley and E. W. Durrie, Lance Corporals Robert Watson and Harry Boulter, and Private James Parker.

7

'A whole year has been lost' – UK, January–July 1941

E VEN AS OPERATION COLOSSUS was being planned, the Air Ministry and War Office continued to argue about the future use of Britain's airborne force. The RAF, worried about a diversion of resources, was keen to restrict the force to a small mostly glider-borne capability that would carry out raids and minor operations. The British Army, on the other hand, wanted more paratroopers and an expanded role that included strategic targets. On 10 January 1941, for example, it suggested the creation of two parachute 'Aerodrome Capture Groups' that would also be capable of seizing small tactical features or similarly sized bridgeheads. They were to be 500 strong and capable of operating for a maximum of 36 hours within a 500-mile radius of their launch point. They could also act as a spearhead for two air-portable (glider-borne) 'Invasion Corps', consisting of four infantry battalions with light armour and artillery support. This would increase Britain's airborne force to around 5,000 troops, the number originally envisaged by Churchill, and double the existing establishment.

Needless to say, the proposal was backed by the CLE which wanted, in addition, engineers and anti-tank forces to accompany the Invasion Corps. The RAF, on the other hand, was sharply opposed to such an expansion because it would have to provide the transport.

The impasse might have been broken anyway as the Air Ministry and War Office moved slowly towards a compromise. But the process was certainly speeded up by Winston Churchill after his visit to Ringway on 26 April 1941 with 'Pug' Ismay and Air Marshal Sir Arthur Barratt, the head of the RAF/Army Co-operation Command. Aware that the deadlock between the War Office and the Air Ministry might even result in the abandonment of the Airborne project, the CLE 'pulled out all the stops and indulged in some shameless stage-managing'. This included an inspection of 400 paratroopers, a demonstration of ground training, and a mock assault on Ringway's control tower by 44 Free French trainees and their instructors using the five available Whitleys. Churchill was delighted with the enthusiasm shown by the airborne troops, but less so by the progress that had been made in creating a fully functioning force.[1]

Back in London, he demanded to see the paper trail that had caused his original force of 5,000 paratroopers to be reduced to just 500. He also wanted 'all the present proposals for increasing the Parachute and Glider force together with a timetable of expected results'.[2] On 27 May 1941, having spent a month digesting this mountain of reports, memoranda and papers, Churchill wrote to Ismay:

> This is a sad story, and I feel myself greatly to blame for allowing myself to be overborne by the resistance which was offered. One can see how wrongly based these resistances were . . . in light of what is happening in Crete,* and may soon be happening in Cyprus and in Syria.

---

* On 20 May 1941, the Germans launched Operation Mercury, an airborne attack on the British-held island of Crete by 8,000 paratroopers and 14,000 men of the 5. Gebirgs-Division. Despite very heavy casualties – 4,000 killed and 2,500 wounded – the Germans eventually overwhelmed the numerically superior British garrison of 42,000 men. The successful operation confirmed for Churchill the value of airborne troops.

See also my minute on gliders . . . The gliders have been produced on the smallest possible scale, and so we have practically now neither parachutists nor the gliders except those 500.

Thus we are always behind-hand the enemy. We ought to have 5,000 parachutists and an Air-borne division on the German model, with any improvements which might suggest themselves from experience. We ought also to have a number of carrier aircraft. These will all be necessary in the Mediterranean fighting of 1942, or earlier if possible. We shall have to try to retake those islands that are being occupied by the enemy . . . A whole year has been lost, and I now invite the chiefs of staff, so far as is possible, to repair the misfortune.[3]

On 31 May, the Chiefs of Staff responded to Churchill's note with a joint paper: it made a number of important recommendations that would transform Britain's airborne force from a small ad hoc organisation into something much more powerful and flexible. The key change was in the size and balance of the force: it would expand massively from 3,000 to 10,000 men; and it would be divided equally between parachutists and glider-borne troops (whereas before it had been dominated by the latter). Both components, moreover, would be made up of two brigades (roughly 2,400 men each), one based in the UK and the other in the Middle East. Sufficient transport aircraft, tugs and gliders would be provided. Tests had been done on Wellington bombers and, in future, all these planes would be 'modified for parachuting'. The bulk of air-landing troops would be carried by a new 25-seater operational glider (later dubbed the 'Horsa'), which could also carry support weapons and light vehicles, and was scheduled to be in production by January 1942.[4]

Once Churchill had approved the Chiefs of Staff paper, the War Office thrashed out some of the details in a conference chaired by Brigadier Nye on 23 July 1941. It agreed to raise three new parachute battalions by 1 March 1942, using the existing volunteer system but without the Commando cash subsistence and option to Return to Unit after six months. This would be offset by a new parachute pay allowance – of four shillings a day for officers, and two for other ranks (the same paid to Commandos), payable after three parachute jumps – which would also act as a recruiting inducement; airlanding troops, by contrast, would only receive 'danger' money of just one extra shilling a day. In addition, a 1st Parachute Brigade HQ would be formed, a parachute War Establishment drawn upon the standard infantry battalion template, and a cadre of volunteer officers and NCOs raised and trained in small batches before the rank and file. The new battalions were to be based at Hardwick Hall in Derbyshire – the beautiful Elizabethan mansion, 'more glass than wall', owned by the dukes of Devonshire – and parachute training at Ringway with the assistance of instructors drawn from the 11th SAS Battalion. Lastly, the Royal Engineers would provide an 'Air Troop' for airborne service.[5]

★

While the future of Britain's airborne force was being thrashed out at the highest level, 11th SAS Battalion was busy trying to recruit and train new paratroopers. It helped, of course, that Italian reporting of Operation Colossus had been widely quoted in the British press. Suddenly the public was aware that Britain possessed a parachute capability, and this was a 'useful fillip for 11 SAS Battalion, which was experiencing difficulty attracting new volunteers and retaining those it already had'.[6]

Among the latter was 20-year-old Lance Corporal Reg 'Lofty' Curtis from Catford, south-east London. Curtis had left school at 14 to work as an apprentice at an engineering firm in Lewisham. But, disgusted by a series of strikes, he left after three years and joined the Grenadier Guards for which his strapping size – six feet two inches, and 14 stone – made him eminently suitable. His long-term plan was to join the police, but war intervened and, after service with the 3rd Grenadier Guards in France and Belgium (providing, at one point, covering fire for Lance Corporal Harry Nicholls who won a Victoria Cross as he led his section in a counter-attack against overwhelming German forces near the River Escaut on 21 May 1940), he was rescued from Dunkirk by a minesweeper.

Like many other Dunkirk veterans, Curtis was eager for a chance to strike back at the enemy and volunteered for the paratroopers after his family home was destroyed in a German bombing raid. Formed with other Guards volunteers into L Troop, under Captain Bromley Martin, Curtis did his preliminary training at Ringway before being sent up to Scotland for the Commando endurance course at Achnacarry in the Highlands. 'For everyone,' he remembered, 'it was a test of strength, coordinated with guts, sheer cunning, and determination to win through. I didn't know it at the time, but here we were being used as guinea pigs, testing out new methods of roughing it, in the way of food, clothing and stamina, in readiness for later training for the process of building up a new and unique way of delivering a soldier to the place of battle.'

Returning to Ringway, he made his first parachute jump from a barrage balloon. Only one recruit refused to jump, and was promptly returned to his unit. Curtis was elated that he had got through unscathed. 'I felt bloody good. I was part way to becoming a real Parachutist.'

Towards the end of January 1941, he jumped for real from a Whitley bomber – as part of No. 3 Advanced Training Course at Ringway – and, as he did so, managed to bang his nose (or 'ring the bell') on the side of the aperture. That aside, he loved the feeling of weightlessness as he floated down and knew he 'was going to like parachuting'. He completed his remaining six jumps in just a week, and could not have been prouder to sew on to the shoulder of his tunic the famous parachute insignia – an open white parachute flanked by a pair of light blue wings – which had replaced the metal parachute qualification badge in December 1940. 'It was rather odd,' wrote Curtis, 'to see men walking around [the nearby suburb of] Wythenshawe and Manchester, with the winged shoulder slightly forward of the rest of the body. Civilians were saying, along with other non-Para soldiers, "Who are these blokes with wings up? Some sort of secret unit?" I think that we were something special!'

Curtis and his troop – L – carried out a number of practice drops and exercises, including one to capture Norwich Castle in February 1941. He and his section commandeered a bus as transport – 'turfing off a very reluctant bus driver and conductor who had to be forcibly removed' – and lying low on the floor to disguise their intention. For the final approach to the castle they made their way on foot 'through back alleys, gardens and side roads', and piled on to an ambulance for the last half mile or so. Joining up with the rest of L Troop, under Captain Bromley-Martin, they stormed through the castle gates and took possession, a job well done.

When Churchill visited Ringway in late April 1941, Curtis was a member of the unarmed combat demonstration. The plan was for a friend 'to throw me after a lunge with a knife. He obliged the Prime Minister with the best throw anyone had carried out for ages. I felt the after-effects for days, after being flung unceremoniously on my back with my right arm taking my 14 stone.'[7]

Inspired by what he had seen, Churchill was spotted 'ferociously attacking an imaginary enemy with a Fairburn-Sykes fighting knife in an unguarded moment'.[8] The FS knife was highly prized by the parachutists who kept it 'in perfect working order', and used it to prepare meals and kill and gut animals 'for food to replenish army issue'. Each man had a favourite place of concealment: fixed either to the leg or belt, inside the sleeve of the airborne smock, or between the neck of the smock and the battledress blouse.[9]

A change that many of the early members of 11th SAS Battalion thought was long overdue was the sacking in June 1941 of the commanding officer, Lieutenant Colonel Ivor Jackson. He was replaced by 39-year-old Major Ernest ('Eric') Down, a no-nonsense Cornishman who had considered a job as an economist before choosing the army instead. Down's career since had been solid if unspectacular, including service with the Dorsetshire Regiment in the Sudan, a six-year attachment to the Royal West African Frontier Force, and a spell in Jamaica with the King's Shropshire Light Infantry. In 1940 he attended Staff College, a necessary step for any ambitious officer, and was working for the War Office on the future use of parachute troops when Jackson's fate was decided. Having made no secret of the fact that he preferred leading men to staff duties, Down was given the job.[10]

Before taking command of 11th SAS Battalion at Ringway, he felt he ought to qualify as a parachutist. But with no time to complete a course in the conventional manner, he borrowed an instructor and within a few hours had completed the requisite number of jumps. It was extraordinarily brave – some might say foolhardy – but left no one in any doubt that he meant business.

His first impression of his new command was far from positive, and the feeling was mutual. 'He was a formidable personality,' recalled Tony Hibbert, 'and immediately acquired the nickname of "Dracula" because he looked like death warmed up. He was absolutely appalled by us. He thought we were totally incompetent and thoroughly undisciplined.'[11] In his opening address, Down ruffled feathers by telling the men their 'ballet dancing' days were over. When they booed in response, he laughed.[12]

Sergeant Eric Chinnery recalled: 'Jackson had been a popular sort of bloke. Now we had got an entirely different character. He assembled the whole lot of us in a hall in Knutsford, introduced himself and said, "Your bloody civvy days are over; I'm going to make soldiers out of you." Before he came, the atmosphere was pretty "Ça ne fait rien", but that soon changed.'[13]

Down's main concern was that the battalion had trained only on the basis of individual hit-and-run tactics, yet he knew from his work at the War Office that the long-term plan was to use large numbers of paratroopers and glider-borne troops as a strategic asset, possibly by capturing bridges and airfields until attacking ground forces could relieve them. 'He envisaged us as highly disciplined, superbly trained attacking infantry,' noted Hibbert, 'the only difference being that we would be delivered to the battle by air instead of by sea or by road. This meant that we'd need a totally different course of training and also a different type of recruit: so, sadly, quite a few of those wonderful first chaps who'd been with us for over a year were returned to unit within weeks of Down's arrival. The new intake were rather more regular, infantry-minded people.'

Down at once upped the intensity of the training, marching the men clean off their feet, 'hour after hour, day after day, on the cobbles, all round the streets of Manchester'. Discipline was 'severe' as the men 'were given endless weapon training, firing, platoon tactics, company exercises' and even live manoeuvres behind a creeping artillery barrage. It resulted in one or two casualties, and was very unpopular, but it would pay dividends when the battalion fought in a real battle.

That, of course, lay in the future. To begin with, Down was

universally 'loathed' because, wrote Hibbert, 'he had got rid of so many of our friends whom we thought the world of and he'd broken up the unit that we loved and believed to be efficient and effective'. It got so bad that the officers were 'seriously worried that if we went into action some disgruntled chap might even shoot him in the back he was so detested'.[14]

8

A Tale of Two Brigades
– UK, September–November 1941

WHILE THE 11TH SAS Battalion was being knocked into shape by Down in early September 1941, the War Office set up the headquarters of the newly formed 1st Parachute Brigade at Hardwick Hall Camp, and put 45-year-old Brigadier Richard 'Windy' Gale in command. Six feet four inches tall, with slicked-back dark hair, a bushy moustache and a ruddy face, he was an imposing figure who, but for the coincidence of the Great War, might never have become a soldier.

Born in London in 1896, and raised for much of the first 10 years of his life in Australia and New Zealand, Gale was a mediocre student who loved the Classics and found, in Homer's *Iliad*, 'a type of beauty and adventure that had a strong appeal'. On leaving Aldenham School in 1913, he wanted to join the Royal Artillery. But he lacked the necessary grades to gain entry to the Royal Military Academy, Woolwich, and got a job in the City as an insurance agent instead. When war broke out a year later, he volunteered for the Territorials but failed the medical. He was finally accepted into Sandhurst in the summer of 1915 and was commissioned into the Worcestershire Regiment. He soon switched to the Machine Gun Corps, and fought as part of the 55th Division at both the Somme and in the Ypres Salient.

In March 1918, he narrowly escaped capture when his company was almost cut off during the Ludendorff Offensive.

Despite these and other close shaves – at the Somme, for example, he was spattered with the blood and human remains of comrades killed by a shell – Gale chose to remain in the military after the war and served many years in India until, following a spell at Staff College at Quetta, he worked at the War Office on training manuals and war plans. But he tired of life as a 'Whitehall Warrior' and in January 1941 took command of 2/5th Leicesters. Nine months later, he was promoted to brigadier and given the task of raising Britain's first parachute brigade.[1] His instinct was to start from scratch by disbanding Down's 11th SAS Battalion and distributing those men who were willing into four new parachute battalions. But after inspecting the unit, and discussing its future with General Sir Alan Brooke, commanding Home Forces, he decided to keep the 11th and rename it the 1st Parachute Battalion. The changeover took place on 15 September. Also, to make it easier to absorb and train the extra volunteers, Brooke and Gale decided that only two new parachute battalions – the 2nd and 3rd – would be raised at first, making three in total, and leaving the fourth for a later date.[2]

Already, volunteers for the new battalions were coming in from infantry units across the UK. Candidates had to be between 20 and 32 years old (with exceptions for officers and NCOs who met the physical standards), A1 fit with 6/12 vision in both eyes and acuity to at least Army Hearing Standard Two, a minimum of eight sound teeth, and weighing no more than 196 pounds. Signal and mortar officers were especially sought after, and captains were to be company command-qualified. Only 10 soldiers per unit were permitted to volunteer, to avoid depleting existing battalions.

Ground training was to be carried out by Gale's brigade staff at Hardwick Hall, while Ringway continued with live parachute training. The former practice of billeting the Ringway trainees with locals was to be discontinued and a permanent Army camp constructed. But, in the meantime, trainees would commute from Hardwick to Ringway where they would complete a two-week qualification course of two balloon and four aircraft jumps in groups of 200.

By early October, the 1st Parachute Brigade was composed of a headquarters and three battalions. Each battalion was sub-divided into three rifle companies, nine platoons and twenty-seven 10-man sections. The sections were now commanded by a sergeant rather than a corporal to counteract the tendency for paratroopers to disperse on landing. There was, in addition, a 64-strong troop of Royal Engineers and a skeletal brigade signal section.[3]

Even as the two new parachute battalions were being formed, Eric Down was not above poaching the best candidates for his own unit, the 1st Battalion. A prime example was 25-year-old Major Alastair Pearson, a 'rugged Scot who, through sheer personality, became one of the great fighting commanders of the Second World War, a man who probably more than anyone else set the standards expected of a parachute soldier in battle'.[4] The son of a Glasgow grain merchant, Pearson was a nervous youth with a thick Scottish brogue who struggled to pronounce the letters 'L' and 'R': his favourite expletive 'blast' would come out as 'bwast'.* But having left Kelvinside Academy for the austere Sedbergh School in Cumbria at the age of 14, he blossomed into a 'confident and robust young man'. He was not a diligent student, however, and left school without any academic qualifications to become an apprentice in his uncle's bakery. But he

---

* Later, fighting in North Africa, Pearson would refer to the German commander Erwin Rommel as 'Wommel'.

had gained his Officer Training Corps' Certificate A at school, and was able to join the local Territorial battalion, the 6th Highland Light Infantry,★ as a second lieutenant.

Called up in September 1939, Pearson and his company spent much of the 'Phoney War' – the name given to the eight-month period of virtual inactivity on the Western Front – guarding vital infrastructure. In early June 1940, as the original BEF was being evacuated from Dunkirk, Pearson's battalion was sent as part of the 52nd (Lowland) Division to the continent to encourage the French to continue the fight. It was a hopeless mission that could have resulted in the capture of the whole division – as indeed the bulk of its sister formation, the 51st (Highland) Division, was forced to surrender at St Valery-en-Caux on 12 June. Fortunately, the commander of the second BEF, Lieutenant General Alan Brooke, managed to persuade Winston Churchill that further resistance was futile and, after some minor skirmishing – during which Pearson's men almost shot the commanding officer of the neighbouring battalion – the 52nd Division was evacuated from Cherbourg on 17 June. Given the job of disabling the battalion transport, Pearson followed on a few hours later in a tramp steamer.

Frustrated when his battalion was given defensive duties in Scotland, Pearson eventually applied for 'Special Service' and was surprised to be told that it would involve parachuting. Undaunted, he set off to join the newly raised 2nd Parachute Battalion at Hardwick Hall, as second-in-command to Lieutenant Colonel Edwin ('Ted') Flavell. He had only been there a week when he was approached by Eric Down, the commander of the 1st Parachute Battalion, and asked why he was with the 2nd.

'I was posted here, sir,' he replied.

★ During the Great War, the 6th HLI had been commanded by his uncle who won both the DSO and MC.

'You're supposed to be 2 i/c [second-in-command] of my battalion,' said Down. 'How long will it take you to pack and put your kit in my car?'

'About 15 minutes.'

'Right. Go and pack while I sort out your posting order.'

The following day, having carried out some practice jumps through the hole of a mock Whitley fuselage at Ringway, Pearson was taken up in a plane to do it for real. 'He floated down,' noted his biographer, 'landing like a sack of potatoes, but was able to stand up. As he picked himself off the ground, there was a photographer from *Picture Post* recording the moment.'[5]

On 10 October, a month after the creation of its parachute equivalent, the 1st Airlanding Brigade was formed by the conversion of the mountain-warfare trained 31st (Independent) Infantry Brigade to a glider role. Commanded by Brigadier George 'Hoppy' Hopkinson, the brigade was comprised of four infantry battalions: the 1st Border Regiment, the 2nd South Staffordshire Regiment, the 2nd Oxfordshire and Buckinghamshire Light Infantry and the 1st Royal Ulster Rifles. The support units included a signal section, an anti-tank battery, two anti-aircraft batteries, a company of sappers and medical and supply detachments. Any men from the original brigade deemed to be unsuitable for airborne warfare were replaced by volunteers from other units. The decision to adapt existing units – rather than create units from scratch with volunteers – had been taken to speed up the process, and would be used for future parachute battalions.

Though the Chiefs of Staff paper of 31 May had stipulated the creation of a glider-borne brigade, this one was closer to its German equivalent in that it was designed to be transported into battle by two methods: in engine-less gliders that had been towed close to their landing zones in planes known as 'tugs'; and in transport planes landing on airfields. Its potential roles included the capture of vital enemy communication centres; attacking enemy field formations behind the front lines, having linked up with advancing ground troops; capturing airfields; and subsidiary operations in conjunction with amphibious landings. Like the paratroopers, its men were expected to operate up to 500 miles from their home airfields against both small-arms fire and tanks and armoured cars. Typically, the brigade would fight as a self-contained unit for up to three days, though on occasion this period of isolation might be longer and require resupply from the air. Ideally, it would operate in conjunction with paratroopers who acted as pathfinders and secured the landing zone.[6]

The sticking point, at this stage, was securing enough transport planes and gliders to fly the brigade into battle. As early as September 1940, an order had been placed for 400 GAL48 Hotspur Gliders, designed and built by the British company General Aircraft Ltd. Thirty-nine feet in length, and with a wingspan of 62 feet, the Hotspur was designed to carry eight men and a cargo of 1,880 pounds. But even as the initial batch of gliders were being produced, this payload was found to be inadequate because it had been decided that glider-borne troops needed to be landed in as large a group as possible.

It was agreed, therefore, to develop several other types of military glider, including a 25-seater which would become the Airspeed Horsa and a tank-carrying glider known as the General Aircraft Hamilcar. The Hotspur remained in production as a training aircraft and a stop-gap in case the other programmes were unsuccessful. In February 1941, an order was placed with Airspeed for 400 Horsa gliders, though most of these would not be delivered until 1942. In its final form, the Horsa was 'a high-winged monoplane with a tricycle undercarriage' which would be jettisoned in favour of a central skid. It was, at 67 feet in length and with a wingspan of 88 feet, much larger than the

Hotspur. It was capable of carrying up to 28 fully equipped
soldiers and two pilots; or 6,500 pounds of equipment, which
might include an anti-tank gun, a 3.7-inch howitzer or a small
vehicle.

Inside, it looked 'not unlike a section of the London Tube
railway in miniature, the fuselage being circular and made of a
skin of plywood attached to numerous circular ribs of stouter
wood'. The seats ran down the length of each side and were
'also of light wood, each being provided with a safety harness
fitting over the shoulders of the wearer, while a belt encircles
his waist'. The floor was corrugated 'to prevent slipping'. There
were two entrances: one on the left, or port side, near the nose;
the other on the right, or starboard, near the stern. The doors
opened vertically upwards, though the whole tail could be
detached 'to enable the quick unloading of Jeeps, anti-tank guns
and other heavy material'. In an emergency, the tail could be
blown off by means of a dynamite cartridge.[7]

The Horsa made its maiden flight at Heathrow in September
1941, but attaining mass production was difficult because it was
competing for space and raw material with other wooden aircraft,
including the Avro Anson trainer, and the Armstrong Whitworth
Albemarle and De Havilland Mosquito bombers. There was also
the cost, estimated by the Treasury in April 1941 to be in excess
of £8 million.

Another major obstacle facing the No. 1 Glider Training
School – which had relocated from Ringway to RAF Thame
near Aylesbury in early 1941 – was getting enough trained pilots.
At first, to ring-fence its own personnel, the Air Ministry had
insisted that the pilots were provided by the army; it then changed
its mind and stipulated that they all needed to be fully trained
RAF bomber pilots. But when it realised that the estimated 800
pilots for the two projected air-landing brigades would have to
be taken from existing bomber crews, the Air Ministry pivoted

again in August 1941 by recommending that glider pilots should be Army officers and NCOs, fully trained for ground combat, and temporarily seconded to the RAF for flight training. The War Office agreed and, henceforth, 'glider pilots would conform to the mental and physical standards of RAF aircrews and would be interviewed by combined Air Force/Army selection boards'. From the army's perspective, the glider pilot would be a 'total soldier' who 'could fly and also fight on the ground with any weapon with which airborne troops were armed', and who was also a trained signaller and liaison officer.

The arrangement was formalised in January 1942 with the formation of the Glider Pilot Regiment (GPR), under the airborne pioneer Lieutenant Colonel John Rock.* The trainees would spend 12 weeks at RAF Elementary Flying Training School, learning to fly a light aircraft. Then another 12 weeks at Glider Training School with Hotspurs. And, finally, six weeks at a glider Operational Training Unit with Horsas. Those who qualified would receive the Army Flying Badge.[8]

---

* After Rock's death conducting glider experimental work in October 1942, Lieutenant Colonel George Chatterton took command of the GPR.

9

Mr du Maurier
– UK, October 1941–February 1942

O N 29 OCTOBER 1941, Major General Frederick 'Boy' Browning was appointed 'Commander of Para-Troops and Airborne Troops'. As, at this stage, it had not been definitely agreed that airborne forces would operate in formations larger than brigades, Browning's job was to coordinate the development and training of airborne forces. Yet General Sir Alan Brooke, the Commander-in-Chief, Home Forces (and soon to replace General Dill as Chief of the Imperial General Staff), was keen for Browning to have a 'more definite operational responsibility' than envisaged by the War Office. He got his way in November 1941 when Browning's command was re-designated the Airborne Division, and ultimately the 1st Airborne Division. It was a turning point in the history of airborne forces because Browning was far-sighted enough to realise that, used in large numbers and in coordination with ground troops, they could change the course of a battle and even a campaign.

Browning's headquarters was located in the lower basement of King Charles Street, Mayfair, with its original members – including Wing Commander Sir Nigel Norman as air advisor – known as the 'Dungeon Party'. Under Browning's command were the 1st Parachute Brigade, the 1st Airlanding Brigade and

the glider pilots. Even at this early stage, it was Brooke's intention, and also that of Major General John Kennedy, the War
Office's director of Military Operations, that Browning's men
would eventually be employed 'as a complete division'.[1]

Born in December 1896, the son of a London wine merchant,
Browning had been educated at Eton and Sandhurst, and won a
DSO as a young lieutenant in the 2nd Grenadier Guards at the
Battle of Cambrai in 1917. 'He took command of three companies whose officers had all become casualties,' noted his citation,
'reorganised them and proceeded to consolidate. Exposing himself
to very heavy machine-gun and rifle fire, in two hours he had
placed the front line in a strong state of defence.' He acquired
the nickname 'Boy' because of his youthful appearance.

Tall and 'devilishly good looking, in spite of a rather long
hooked nose', Browning dressed beautifully and had a passion
for classical music, particularly the ballet. He was also a fine
sailor and athlete – winning the English hurdling championship
on three occasions and competing in the 1928 Winter Olympics
as a member of the British bobsleigh team – and married the
novelist Daphne du Maurier after meeting her on a boating
holiday to Cornwall in 1932. His wife, then 25 years old, was
just starting out on her writing career; as she gained an international reputation for a string of bestselling novels – including
Jamaica Inn (1936) and *Rebecca* (1938) – her increasingly overshadowed husband was sometimes referred to as 'Mr du Maurier'.
His military career between the wars included a spell as resident
captain of the Guards Depot, adjutant of Sandhurst, and
commanding officer of his old battalion in Egypt. Promoted to
brigadier in May 1940, Browning was in England during the
BEF's ill-fated Low Countries campaign, and missed the Dunkirk
evacuation. But a subsequent spell as commander of the 24th
Guards Brigade, defending London from attack, preceded his
appointment as airborne supremo.[2]

Exactly why Browning was selected is unclear. He had no experience of airborne operations and had never commanded a formation in battle larger than a company. Yet his work with the 24th Guards Brigade had impressed Brooke who noted in his diary on 24 October 1941: '[Watched] a demonstration by Browning of attacks on tanks. A first class show very well staged and full of useful lessons. I am arranging to have it made into an instructional film which ought to be useful. Also informed Browning that he had been selected for command of the Airborne Division, and what I wanted him to do about it.'[3]

However it came about, Browning's appointment ensured that Britain's growing airborne capability would not be frittered away in what he called 'penny-packets'. 'Browning was convinced,' wrote one of his officers, 'that a handful of parachute troops could not affect the course of a battle and that, as with ordinary infantry, the lowest formation must be a self-supporting division . . . He was well aware that time was a vital factor. Aircrews required experience in dropping parachutists and towing gliders and without training and practice the results could be disastrous – as in some cases they proved to be.'[4]

But before Browning could provide proof that a properly trained airborne division could achieve strategic results, another smaller mission landed on his desk: Operation Biting. It had come about through a combination of hard work and good fortune. 'During the winter of 1941,' wrote Winston Churchill in his epic (if at times self-serving) history of the Second World War, 'our Intelligence suspected that the Germans were using a new Radar apparatus for giving the direction and range of our planes to their anti-aircraft guns. This apparatus was believed to look like a large electric bowl fire. Our secret agents, our listening devices and air photographs, soon found out that a chain of stations stretched along the northern coast of Europe, and that one of them, probably containing the new equipment, was established at Bruneval, on Cap d'Antifer, not far from [Le] Havre.'

On 5 December, having learnt of the suspicions of British intelligence, a squadron leader of the Photograph Reconnaissance Unit had made a personal decision to fly over the Normandy village of Bruneval and take a 'brilliant and successful' picture of the radar apparatus. 'Although the station was at the top of a 400-foot cliff,' noted Churchill, 'a shelving beach near by provided a possible landing-place, and a Commando raid was planned accordingly.'[5]

The target of the raid was the new Würzburg early-warning radar system. Given that RAF Bomber Command was losing an average of four planes to every 100 sent on raids over occupied Europe, negating the Würzburg radar – which had a range of 25 miles and could control flak and searchlights, as well as spot incoming planes – was a priority. To do that, they needed to 'capture as much of the equipment as possible, and a few of the personnel', to help them 'examine enemy technique, and to look for weak points' and possible counter-measures.[6]

Combined Operations – now commanded by Commodore Lord Louis Mountbatten, the king's dashing 41-year-old cousin – was given the job of planning the operation with Major General Browning's Airborne Division. They used photo-intelligence and information from the French resistance to build up an accurate picture of the location of the radar and its defences. The radar station itself (built near a lonely clifftop villa) was manned by 30 signallers and guards; at Le Presbytère, a cluster of buildings in woods nearby, were another 100 or so reserve signallers and coastal defence troops; and 40 men were guarding the nearest village, Bruneval, and its adjacent beach.[7] The average age of the garrison was thought to be 35 to 40 years old, and they possessed no specialised training. The nearest infantry reinforcements, moreover, were five miles away at Etretat, while a reconnaissance battalion was stationed at Yebleron, 16 miles from Bruneval. Both would take at least an hour to arrive on the scene.[8]

The plan was to drop a company of parachutists, some sappers and a specially trained RAF fitter – 120 men in all – in fields half a mile inland of the radar in three main parties, starting at 12.15 a.m. The job had been given to C Company of the 2nd Parachute Battalion, rather than the much more experienced men of Down's 1st Battalion, because Brigadier Gale wanted 'to prove that his whole Brigade was ready for action at any time'. This caused a certain amount of bad feeling and jealousy. But in the long run it was a wise decision.[9]

The man chosen to command this vital mission was Major John Frost, the 29-year-old son of a general, who had been serving with the Iraq Levies★ when Hitler invaded the Low Countries in May 1940. Frost immediately applied to rejoin his parent regiment, the Cameronians (Scottish Rifles), and eventually got his way. Back in England, he was posted to a battalion defending the Suffolk coast. This was not the heroic role he had envisaged and, on the verge of applying for the Staff College, he saw a War Office letter soliciting volunteers for special air service battalions. Unsure what they were, he applied nonetheless, assuming it would be 'something in the Commando line and just what the doctor ordered'.

When he discovered that special air service involved parachuting, he was shocked. 'At the time,' he wrote, 'I knew that some Commandos had been trained in this role, but the subject was still very secret, and my knowledge of parachutes and

---

★ Established when Iraq became a British mandate in 1919, the Levies was a 'force of Assyrian, Kurdish and Arab tribesmen, organised into rifle companies, with a small support weapons and signals element', based at RAF Habbaniya. Its role was to guard RAF airfields and keep open lines of communication with Jordan. (Frost, *A Drop Too Many*, p. 1)

parachuting consisted solely of accounts of what the Germans had achieved by this method of moving into action . . . On the whole the press had rather scoffed at the effectiveness of the new arm and I found it difficult to take seriously the threat of German parachutists landing behind our own defences in Britain.'

His commanding officer was also far from convinced. 'I can't imagine,' he told Frost, 'any sensible person choosing to be a parachutist. You ought to keep your feet firmly on the ground.'

But Frost was determined to pursue his application and his colonel, a kindly soul, agreed not to stand in his way. Despite a poor interview, he was assigned to the 2nd Parachute Battalion at Hardwick Hall Camp, commanded by Lieutenant Colonel Edwin 'Ted' Flavell, the 43-year-old son of a commercial clerk who had won a Military Cross and two Bars as a machine-gunner in the Great War, serving in 'Windy' Gale's company in 1918. Flavell made Frost his adjutant, the officer responsible for administration and discipline.[10]

Swamped by paperwork, it was not until December 1941 that Frost and his commanding officer found time to do their qualifying jumps at Tatton Park. They began with a jump from the basket of a tethered observation balloon at a height of 600 feet. 'The Colonel went first and I soon followed,' remembered Frost. 'The first sensation of falling drew the breath from my lungs till a crackling sound from above and a sudden pull on my harness told me that the parachute was open, and the rest of it was heavenly. I had a very gentle landing and the Colonel likewise, so we decided to do another one right away.'

Over-confident now, Frost ignored the cries from the ground to keep his legs together, and landed with his feet apart and all his weight on his left leg. He felt a 'savage wrench in that knee and lay on the ground for a few seconds before being able to get up'. It was a bad injury that required an operation to remove fluid from the knee. As he recovered in hospital, surrounded by other injured parachutists from Poland, Holland, France and Belgium, he assumed that his time in the 2nd Battalion was over. But Flavell assured him that that was not the case.

In early January 1942, soon after he was promoted to major and given command of C Company – composed entirely of men from Scottish regiments – Frost was told his unit had been earmarked for special training at Tilshead on Salisbury Plain, prior to giving a demonstration to the War Cabinet. But first he had to complete his jump training at Ringway. Frustratingly he spent the first 36 hours grounded because of fog, completing his first two jumps from a plane during the afternoon of the second day. He much preferred it to leaping from a balloon, and found the 'noise and harsh movement of the one was definitely reassuring after the silence and sickening sway of the other'. Two days later, having completed the remaining two jumps, he had earned his wings.

Frost went straight to Tilshead to rejoin his men. After 'Boy' Browning had inspected the company – telling Frost that 'you've got a good lot of men but I have never seen such a dirty company in all my life!' – a liaison officer appeared with detailed instructions about their demonstration for the War Cabinet. 'We were to practise landing by night behind the imaginary enemy defences,' remembered Frost, 'the destruction of an enemy headquarters, followed by a move down a gulley between cliffs to the beach from which we were to be evacuated by small naval craft.' But when told that the company would be split into five parties, dropped at separate intervals, and each with a special task, Frost complained that it was unworkable as he, the company commander, would have no overall control.

The upshot was that the liaison officer returned the following day and, having bound Frost to 'absolute secrecy', told him the story about the demonstration to the War Cabinet was a cover for the fact they would be 'required to carry out a raid on the coast of enemy-occupied France' in late February, accompanied by a party of Royal Engineers who would 'dismantle and bring back to England the essential parts of the latest enemy radiolocation apparatus'. The plan had been specially devised to deal with the enemy defences; if Frost still did not like it, the officer would find somebody who did.

Frost dropped his objections.[11] It was just as well, for he was the right man to lead this daring raid: untested in combat but a natural leader, charismatic, determined and confident, possessed of both moral and physical courage, and one who cared deeply for his men. He was, noted a brother officer, tall and heavily built, with eyes that 'twinkled behind heavy lids', though they could, at times, 'flash with impatience if not anger'. He grew a bushy moustache 'which he had a habit of pulling and twisting' as he tried to solve a problem. He was 'sentimental, sometimes ruthless when he had to be, sometimes aloof, but always calm'. If he ever felt fear, he never let it show.

He laughed easily, and was a modest man, even shy. On the other hand, if he disagreed with a proposed plan of action, he was quick to challenge his superiors 'with an authority and a conviction which was almost divine!'[12]

The plan was to capture part of the German early-warning Würzburg radar station at Bruneval in Normandy. Frost divided C Company into five parties, each named after a famous admiral. There was 'Nelson' party, 40 men under John Ross and Euen Charteris, whose task was to capture the beach defences from the rear, so that the raiders could be evacuated from the beach; three assault parties, called 'Jellicoe', 'Hardy' and 'Drake', whose job was to capture the lonely villa and the radar equipment; and finally a reserve party called 'Rodney' that would block any approach of the enemy while the radar was being dismantled.[13]

They used an accurate five-feet square model of the clifftop radar station and its defences – including 'full details of houses, woods, paths, fissures in cliffs, etc' – to prepare for any eventuality.[14] The hope was to achieve complete surprise so that everyone was in position to carry out their tasks before the alarm was raised. The signal would be a blast from Frost's whistle. Only the officers, at this stage, were told where they were going.

Their training included a trip up to Loch Fyne in Scotland to practise with the landing-craft that would take them off the beach. They enjoyed good weather and a change of scenery, but were a 'little disconcerted to find the business of embarking in the dark' was not quite as simple as they had imagined. While there, they received a visit from Lord Louis Mountbatten who gave all ranks, naval and military, the first inkling of what they were about to do.

Before leaving Scotland, a young German Jew called Peter Nagel was attached to Frost's party as 'Private Newman'. His job was to interpret. Concerned that an 'unknown, untried man might become a liability if things went wrong', Frost told Mountbatten that he would prefer to do without him. But he was told to take him anyway because he would find his language skills invaluable during the raid.[15]

By now, the excitement and enthusiasm felt by officers and men alike had reached 'fever pitch'. Here, finally, 'in the dreary, depressing days of early 1942', noted 22-year-old Lieutenant Peter Young, commanding the 'Jellicoe' party, 'was actually a chance to hit back.'[16] That Britain needed some good news was not in doubt. The surprise Japanese attack on the US Navy's Pacific Fleet in Pearl Harbor, Hawaii, on 7 December 1941 had brought America into the war on the Allied side. But, since then, one disaster had followed another. First, on 10 December, the battleship *Prince of Wales* and the battle cruiser *Repulse* were sunk by Japanese planes off Malaya. Then the Japanese advance into southeast Asia – launched on 8 December – resulted in the fall of Hong Kong on Christmas Day 1941, and the fortress island of Singapore, at the tip of the Malayan Peninsula, on 15 February 1942, with the loss of its 85,000-strong garrison (causing Churchill to lament that the numerically superior defenders 'should have done better').[17]

The first window of opportunity for the Bruneval raid, when the moon was full and tidal conditions favourable, was 24 to 26 February. Failing that, they would have to wait a month for similar conditions.[18] On the 24th, Frost and his men packed their containers and sent them off to Thruxton aerodrome. Then they waited impatiently for the signal to go. Yet that day, and the following two, brought news of a 24-hour postponement because of bad weather. It seemed as if the window had passed.

The next morning, Frost was 'expecting to be told to pack up or go on leave' when a staff officer arrived with the news that, if all went well, they could go that night. 'Once again,' he recalled, 'we went through the routine of inspections, tidying up, sending the containers to the aerodrome and so on, but this time perhaps rather listlessly and without much enthusiasm.' Only Gerry Strachan, Frost's experienced and efficient company sergeant major, formerly of the Black Watch, was optimistic that Friday the 27th was the day.

He was right. At 3 p.m., the Airborne Division HQ received the signal it had been waiting for: 'Carry out Operation Biting tonight.'

'Boy' Browning hurried over to Tilshead to inform Frost that they were 'really going at last'.[19]

10

The Bruneval Raid
– UK and France, February 1942

A FTER DINNER ON 27 February 1942, John Frost dressed in his parachutist rig – camouflaged airborne smock, steel helmet, rubber-soled boots, fighting knife, .45 automatic pistol and two grenades – and was driven by staff car to Thruxton aerodrome.[1] The company was already dispersed in huts around the airfield perimeter and he visited each little party in turn. 'Some were fitting their parachutes,' he recalled, 'some having tea, others standing talking, and one little party singing. It was a lovely clear night, no wind or noise from above.' It was only now that he told the men their destination.

Soon after, Frost received a call from Group Captain Sir Nigel Norman who had planned the air side of the operation. 'Good luck,' said Norman. 'The latest news is that there is snow on the other side and I'm afraid the flak seems to be lively.'

Frost was annoyed that the German 'hive' had been disturbed and fretted that they should have been issued with white smocks to move about in the snow. But it was too late to do anything about it now.

At 9.40 p.m., to the sound of Piper Ewing's bagpipes, they marched out in little parties to board the 12 Whitley bombers – each carrying 10 paratroopers – that would take them to France.

Frost was in the sixth plane and, shortly before boarding, he shared a flask of tea laced with rum with his 10-man stick, including Company Sergeant Major Gerry Strachan and Flight Sergeant Cox. He was interrupted by Wing Commander Charles Pickard, leading the Whitleys and the 'survivor of countless bombing raids', who drew him aside to apologise for taking him on such a high-risk mission. 'I feel,' he told Frost, 'like a bloody murderer!'

Once inside the belly of the Whitley – which he found 'draughty, uncomfortable, cold' – Frost had time to mull over the prospect of going to war by air. To him and his men, the Germans were a 'terrible people' who, despite recent reverses near Moscow, were formidable in battle. Many things could go wrong on the mission, but Frost's greatest fear was that the Germans knew they were coming. He almost 'longed for a last minute cancellation' and, as the aircraft began to move and bump along the perimeter track, he felt anxiety gnawing his stomach. But as the aircraft accelerated along the runway, these doubts disappeared. It was 10.30 p.m.

The first four planes, carrying Lieutenant John Ross and the 'Nelson' party, had departed 15 minutes earlier. Sitting side-by-side on the ribbed aluminium floor, their legs covered with army blankets, Frost and his men sang to keep their spirits up, though it was hard to hear their voices above the noise and vibration of the plane. A few played cards, chiefly pontoon and rummy. Like Frost, the officers and senior NCOs were armed with fighting knives and pistols, while a few had the new Sten, a light and simply designed sub-machine gun with a folding stock and a side-mounted magazine that held 32 9mm bullets. It was a useful weapon at close quarters, but prone to stoppages. The men were carrying knives and hand grenades. In one container in the bomb bay were their rifles, one Bren gun per section and spare ammunition; in the other containers were No. 38 wireless sets, demolition charges and mine detectors.[2]

Warned that they were getting close, Frost and his men removed the cover from the jumping 'hole' and saw, 600 feet below, the water of the Channel 'moving gently in the moonlight'. With the temperature dropping, they pulled their blankets more tightly around them and began to count the minutes.

Suddenly, the pilots took evasive action to avoid the incoming flak from anti-aircraft batteries at Le Havre, the orange and red tracers reminding Frost of 'a pleasant firework show'. The sudden change of direction was enough to confuse the navigators of the first two planes, and as a result their sticks were dropped two and a half miles short of the correct location. 'This was unfortunate,' noted Frost, 'for it halved the strength of the party detailed to overcome the beach defences, i.e. 40 men.'

'Action stations!' warned Strachan.

Blankets, sleeping bags and other comforts were hurriedly stowed. The No. 1 jumper dangled his legs in the hole as the plane's engines 'abated to a gentle humming'.

The green light came on. 'No. 1 Go!'

He disappeared, followed soon after by No. 2. Frost jumped third. As he descended, he could see in the bright moonlight that the terrain was exactly as it had been depicted in the model.

He landed softly in the snow. There was no wind and all was silent apart from the noise of the aircraft 'stealing away into the night'. His first act was to unbutton his flies and urinate on the ground. 'It was not good drill,' he acknowledged later, 'for now was the time when a stick of parachutists are most vulnerable and one's first concern should be to make for the weapon containers. However, it had become essential and was also an act of defiance.'

Quickly locating the containers, which had also landed in the right place, Frost and his men armed themselves before heading to the rendezvous nearby where the other parties were gathering.

They left Flight Sergeant Cox and the sappers to assemble the canvas trolleys that would be used to carry the radar apparatus.

'We collected at the rendezvous,' remembered Frost, 'and in about 10 minutes we were ready to move off. Just as we started towards the coast the next lot of aircraft came in and we could see some of "Nelson" landing safely.'

Frost led 15 'Hardy' men towards the isolated villa, while Second Lieutenant Peter Young and the 'Jellicoe' party made for the radar set. Once his men had surrounded the villa, Frost approached the front door, pistol in hand. 'It was open,' he wrote, 'and I nearly forgot to blow my whistle before going in. As soon as I blew it explosions, yells and the sound of automatic fire came from the proximity of the radar set and my party rushed into the house.'

Finding the ground floor rooms empty, Frost led four of his men upstairs, shouting, 'Surrender!' and 'Hände Hoch!' They discovered only a single German firing from a window at the party attacking the dugouts surrounding the radar set. He was shot and killed with a Sten gun.[3]

Meanwhile, Second Lieutenant Peter Young and the 'Jellicoe' party had headed straight for the 'radiolocation set' where, as they negotiated the knee-high barbed wire, they spotted groups of Germans 'wearing overcoats over pyjamas' climbing slowly up from dugouts. They stood, hands in pockets, just watching the paratroopers. None was armed, and it later transpired that they thought Young and his men were German soldiers on manoeuvres. Suddenly firing could be heard from the house and the nearby farm, causing the Germans to scramble back into their dugouts for their weapons. But they were too late. 'In a few minutes,' noted Young, 'we had captured the set and the defenders were dead.'[4]

What Young failed to mention is that, in line with his orders, five Germans had been killed in cold blood. This was discovered by Frost when, having left most of his men in the villa, he ran over to reinforce the party at the radar set. 'Our orders,' he wrote in his report, 'were to take only the experts prisoner and to kill the remainder. It was Lieutenant Young in command of the party who had killed all these Germans, and his sergeant remonstrated with him on the grounds of cruelty, saying, "You are a cruel bastard."' Young could legitimately claim that he was only following orders. Clearly, though, not all orders *should* be carried out.

Two prisoners had in fact been taken, one a non-expert. The first was Johannes Tewes, a radar operator, who had 'slipped and fallen over the cliff' in an attempt to escape. Fortunately, he only fell 10 feet before he grabbed hold of a rocky outcrop. He was captured as he climbed back up the cliff.[5] The second was a telephone orderly, George Schmidt, who was on the phone to his battalion commander when paratroopers 'burst in, firing tommy guns'. He put his hands up.[6]

Frost got Peter Nagel (aka 'Private Newman'), the interpreter, to ask the prisoners how many of their comrades were in the vicinity. 'A thousand,' replied Tewes.

Knowing this was a lie, Sergeant Gregor McKenzie – who had reproached Young for killing the Germans – 'hit the Hun a hell of a belt on the jaw'. This brought him to his senses and he admitted the actual number was only a hundred.

By now they were coming under fire from the woods and buildings known as Le Presbytère, 400 yards to the rear. Frost ran back to collect the men from the villa, and as they were leaving a Private McIntyre was shot and killed.

Frost had instructed Lieutenant Vernon, Flight Sergeant Cox and the sappers to hang back until the radar set and the villa were secure. They now appeared and quickly got to work, photographing the radar apparatus, dismantling it, and stashing the pieces into special canvas trolleys that they had brought with them.[7]

The radar set, as Cox recalled, 'was housed in a kind of pit in the ground, with a two-foot wall running round it above ground level. The wall was made of turf and roofed with duck boards. The whole thing looked very much like a searchlight, except for a little cabin . . . on the side.' They began by cutting the radio element and the cable from the aerial to the box. Then they removed the transmitter, a 'box with cathode rays in it and then two more boxes'. Some of it had to be ripped out by 'sheer force'.

As they worked, the incoming fire from the edge of Le Presbytère increased in intensity. Two bullets struck the apparatus, but most went high. This was fortunate, remembered Frost, because Cox and the sappers were 'standing up round the set, which above ground consisted mostly of an instrument like an old-fashioned gramophone loudspeaker.'

Spotting vehicles coming up the track, Frost told Vernon that it was time to go. With none of the Type 38 wireless sets working, he had 'no idea how the other parties had fared' and began to 'feel the lack of a proper Company Headquarters organisation'. Leaving the fatality behind, they headed for the embarkation beach, 600 yards to the south. They knew there was a German strongpoint on the shoulder of the cliff as it sloped down towards the beach, but suspected – correctly – that it was not manned. When they reached it, a voice from the beach shouted, 'The boats are here. It's all right. Come on down.'

But as they began to descend, a machine gun opened up from the opposite shoulder. 'Its fire was close and accurate,' remembered Cox, 'for I saw little bits of grass trembling at the impact of the bullets almost at my feet. Some bullets went through the trolley and one through part of the apparatus in my hand.' Two men were hit. Company Sergeant Major Gerry Strachan was just five yards behind Frost when he 'stopped seven bullets, three in the abdomen'. Frost ran back, pulled Strachan into some dead ground and gave him an injection of morphine to dull the pain.

It was now that Captain John Ross, Frost's second-in-command, shouted up from the beach: 'Don't come down. The beach has not yet been taken.'[8]

Unable to get to the beach, Frost's carefully timed operation was beginning to unravel. 'The German defenders were fighting from secure pill boxes,' noted Young, 'and our beach party were pinned down. Furthermore, flares and distress signals were going up from German positions all around and inland we heard the ominous sounds of engines being started up and the menacing rattle of tank tracks. An all-out attack on the beach was vital.'

Frost ordered Young and his men to help Ross knock out the beach pillboxes and defences. 'After shouted agreement,' recalled Young, 'our party and the beach assault party moved in to the attack. As we did so we heard heavy firing and cheering coming from the other side of the German positions. The two lost planeloads under Lieutenant Charteris had literally "Marched to the sound of the guns" and had arrived just at the crucial moment.'[9]

Having been dropped 2½ miles short by, of all people, Wing Commander Pickard, 20-year-old Second Lieutenant Euen Charteris had led his 'Nelson' section, and one from 'Rodney' that had also come down in the wrong place, north towards the target, suffering one casualty, a Private Sutherland shot in the shoulder, south of the village of Bruneval. 'We went through some scrubby and difficult country,' noted Charteris, 'and presently reached the edge of the Bruneval village into which we plunged making a lot of noise. I was sure, however, that speed was more important than silence. At the bottom of the valley there was a road with some open ground on each side. I put a Bren gun team to cover us while we doubled across the open ground. While climbing up the other side of the valley we were again fired on.'

Losing touch with four of his men, who had taken cover in

a wood, Charteris pressed on 'at a fast lollop of between six and seven miles an hour' and eventually fell in with the rest of the covering 'Rodney' party under 27-year-old Lieutenant John 'Tim' Timothy, a former private in the Grenadier Guards. Timothy told Charteris 'that the Germans still held the beach' and that one of the 'Nelson' sections 'was held up at the bottom of the valley approaching the beach'.

Charteris moved forward and met Major Frost who was surprised to see him because Charteris should, by then, have been on the beach. Unsure what was happening in the valley, and mindful that time was running out, Frost ordered Charteris' party to attack downhill. The young officer led from the front, feeling 'naked as a baby' as he advanced down a gully just 70 yards from the house on the beach that was held by the enemy. Between his party and the house was a sunken road and some barbed wire. Lying down in front of the wire, they threw two volleys of hand grenades onto the balcony of the house. Then they charged across the sunken road and entered the house. 'If Jerry had had the wit or the guts to put up a good resistance,' noted Charteris, 'he must have done us great damage for all he had to do was to lob a grenade into us when we were in the sunken road. He did not, however, do so.'

Inside the house, Charteris found a single German called Schmidt with his hands up, and relieved him of his weapon. Having cleared a neighbouring dugout, he worked round towards the beach and placed his men in defensive positions, facing inland, to cover the beach behind them.[10]

It was a joint effort, but the arrival of Charteris' party had tipped the balance. 'Attacked with volleys of grenades from three sides,' wrote Second Lieutenant Young, 'by men who knew their lives depended upon gaining the beach, the Germans broke and the beach was ours! In no time at all, a semi-circle of determined men were guarding the beach approaches while the signallers started tapping out the "Come in" call to the Navy. German fire increased and a few shells started whistling over. It was an anxious time.'[11]

It was now about 2.45 a.m. and, with the beach secure, Frost moved the wounded, prisoners, and captured radar apparatus down to the edge of the water. The badly wounded Strachan was shivering with cold so Timothy gave him a cricket sweater he had brought along to keep warm during the flight.

Everyone was anxious to get away. But with the signallers unable to contact the Navy by either radio or infra-red beacon, Frost ordered the emergency signal – two green Very lights – to be fired several times from both ends of the beach.

There was no response. 'With a sinking heart', wrote Frost, 'I moved off the beach with my officers to rearrange our defences in the entrance to the village and on the shoulders of the cliff. It looked as though we were going to be left high and dry and the thought was hard to bear.'

Suddenly, a voice shouted: 'Sir, the boats are coming in! The boats are here! God bless the ruddy Navy, sir!'

As several dark shapes glided across the water towards the beach, Frost ordered the men to prepare for embarkation. The plan had been for two landing craft to come in at a time, but all six appeared at once. The wounded, prisoners and captured radar parts were taken off first. Flight Sergeant Cox and the sappers had to wade through thigh-deep water carrying their booty. As the first landing craft was being pushed off, a German machine gun opened up from the cliff above, and was answered by Bren guns from all the other craft. 'The noise,' remembered Frost, 'was indescribable and I could not make myself heard.'

All order was lost and the officers herded their men on to the closest craft. Frost got on board with the last party. 'We had to wade out about five or ten yards,' he reported. 'One boat – the one in which I was – remained a short while behind to see if anyone was left on the beach, then we all hurried out to meet the MGBs [motor gun boats].' In the chaos, some of the men guarding the perimeter were left behind, among them three from Charteris' party 'who had been prevented from reaching the beach by the heavy fire from the Landing Support Craft'.

When Frost realised, he asked Commander Cook, the flotilla commander, if he could take a boat back to look for them. Cook refused. He had narrowly avoided two German destroyers and two E-boats (fast-attack craft armed with torpedos and machine guns), and, to ensure the safety of the whole party, 'it was essential to clear out quickly'. In worrying about the unfortunate few, Frost had almost forgotten that they had achieved their objective and that no operation goes entirely to plan. 'We were considerably cheered therefore,' he wrote, 'to get a message from the ship which carried the captured radar equipment to say that we had managed to get practically everything that was wanted.'

The gunboat with the booty returned independently at high speed and reached Portsmouth at 10 a.m. on the 28th. The rest of the flotilla, composed of gunboats towing the landing craft, had a much slower journey through choppy seas. As daylight came, a squadron of Spitfires arrived overhead to deter enemy planes. Later the flotilla was escorted by two destroyers and, arriving in Portsmouth, was met with the strains of 'Rule Britannia' ringing out from loud hailers on the shore. Transferred to the *Prins Albert*, a Belgian cross-Channel ferry requisitioned by the Royal Navy in 1940, they were welcomed by Charles Pickard and his pilots. 'The ship,' wrote Frost, 'was crowded with staff officers, photographers, reporters and all who had taken part in the raid. The limelight was strange after weeks of secrecy and stealth. All we really wanted was dry clothes, bed and oblivion; but before that there was some serious drinking to be done.'[12]

★

In the evening after his return to Tilshead, Major John Frost was about to take a well-deserved bath when an officer hammered on the door and shouted: 'You have to get up to London right away because the Prime Minister wants to know the details. Division are sending a staff car and the driver will know where to take you.'

He was dropped off on Birdcage Walk, Whitehall, and taken to an underground room that contained the briefing model for Operation Biting. Before long, Clement Attlee, leader of the Labour Party and Deputy Prime Minister in the coalition government, arrived and asked Frost to tell him about the mission.

Frost had not been talking long when Attlee interrupted. 'How do you know all this?'

'Because I was there.'

'You mean you were actually on the raid?'

'Yes, and I have been sent up here to tell the Prime Minister all about it.'

'Good heavens,' said Attlee, with a look of puzzlement. 'Well, perhaps we had better wait to hear the whole story from the start.'

Soon they had been joined by the rest of the War Cabinet, the Chiefs of Staff, Major General Browning and Lord Louis Mountbatten who 'came up and said nice things'. Finally the prime minster appeared, 'siren-suited and with outsize cigar'. He went straight up to Frost, conspicuous in the uniform of a Cameronian major, and said: 'Bravo, bravo, and now we must hear all about it.'

Nervous about speaking in such exalted company, Frost was relieved when Mountbatten, who had digested all the details of the raid, took over from him and told a 'most exciting and unusual tale'. Just as Mountbatten was getting into his stride, a 'mumble of diversionary conversation' could be heard coming from a corner of the room where Anthony Eden, the Foreign Secretary, was huddled with Air Secretary Archibald Sinclair.

Churchill frowned, held up his hand to halt Mountbatten, and turned slowly to face the miscreants. 'Come over here, you two,' he said, as if addressing two naughty schoolboys, 'and listen to this, for then you might learn something for once in your lives.'

With sheepish looks, and their hands behind their backs, they 'skipped across to take their places near the model'. Churchill then signalled for Mountbatten to continue, but stopped him soon afterwards to ask Frost whether the intelligence had been accurate.

'Yes, Prime Minister,' said Frost. 'It was correct in every detail, even down to the name of the German sergeant in command.'

When Mountbatten had finished, Churchill asked: 'What did we get out of all of this?'

Air Chief Marshal Sir Charles Portal, the Chief of the Air Staff, began to describe the possible benefits in language that was far too technical for the prime minister.

'Now just stop all that nonsense, Portal,' Churchill said, 'and put it into language that ordinary normal mortals can understand.'

Unabashed by the put-down, Portal said: 'We now have every hope of not only being able to improve our own radar, but that at some future date of our own choosing we will be able to jam the whole of the enemy radar advanced warning system.'

This pleased Churchill who walked up to the model and ran his fingers up the cliffs. 'This is the way they will come,' he said, 'if they come, up and over the cliffs. Just where we least expect them. Now about the raids. There must be more of them. Let there be no doubt about that.'

He then swept out of the room, leaving General Sir Alan Brooke, Mountbatten and Browning to advance on the Chief of the Air Staff, saying: 'More aircraft, more aircraft, more aircraft.'

Portal raised his fists 'in mock defence, and backed slowly and smilingly out of the room'. Once the meeting had broken up, Frost was driven to his London club for his 'much delayed bath'.[13]

Earlier that day, Winston Churchill had been handed a preliminary report that suggested the raid had managed to collect '75% of all the equipment that it was possible to get, and it was hoped that this, together with the prisoner's story, would enable our experts to secure a complete reconstruction of the equipment sufficient to show exactly what it can do and what our counter-measures might be'.[14]

A more detailed scientific report, submitted on 13 July 1942, confirmed this assessment of the raid. 'Judged by the proportion of the major objects achieved,' it noted, 'the raid was very successful. The only failures were the omission to take fuller sketches of the inside of the cabin and to remove the presentation equipment; otherwise, every object was fulfilled, and even the omissions were remedied by a helpful prisoner . . . We now know that the equipment was a type A Würzburg . . . [This is] the normal aircraft reporting Würzburg, and has shown us the quality and policy of German RDF [Radio Direction Finding] construction; this demonstration alone would have justified the raid.'

When the apparatus was examined, 'it took a long time to find a specifically weak point'. But there was a 'possibility that one has now been found which makes the Würzburg apparatus vulnerable to simple radio counter measures, apart from those originally contemplated and whose prospective success has been confirmed'.[15] Those measures were the dropping of metal-strip reflectors (known collectively as 'Window') which, by creating false echoes or reflections in the enemy radar, would conceal the incoming aircraft. Another technical revelation, thanks to the Bruneval Raid, was that German defences were more likely to be overwhelmed by concentrated bomber 'streams', rather than scattered formations.[16]

'We thus became,' wrote Churchill, 'the possessors of vital portions of a key piece of equipment in the German Radar defences and gathered information which greatly helped our air offensive.'[17]

For Churchill, the Bruneval Raid was both a personal vindication of his original demand for an airborne force, and a welcome piece of good news at a desperate time. Depressed by the loss of Hong Kong and Singapore, and further setbacks in Burma – where the capital Rangoon would fall to the Japanese on 7 March – Churchill had suggested to his naval aide, Richard Pim, that it might be time for him to stand down. 'But my God, sir,' responded Pim, 'you cannot do that.'

It is doubtful that Churchill seriously considered resignation. But it was undeniable that, since the start of the war, one defeat had followed another, in Norway, France, Greece, Crete, Libya and now the Far East. Would Britain's warriors ever be able to match their Prime Minister's soaring rhetoric with deeds? His army chief, Sir Alan Brooke, was thinking the same thing. 'If the army cannot fight better than it is doing at present,' noted Brooke in his diary, 'we shall deserve to lose our Empire.'[18]

Now Bruneval, although a minor operation, had shown that Britain's forces could indeed fight both ingeniously and tenaciously. As Frost put it, 'Many people were disgruntled after a long catalogue of failures, and the success of our venture, although it was a mere flea-bite, did have the effect of making people think that we could succeed after all.' It had also helped, wrote Frost, to 'put airborne forces on the map'. Before the mission, Browning had been struggling to persuade senior military figures that airborne forces could 'play a really useful part' in the war. This was down to the 'traditional conservatism of many Service chiefs' and the fact that 'more conventional resources were already strained'. But thanks to Bruneval, Browning 'was able to get some degree of priority and the Prime Minister, who had initiated the formation of our Parachute troops, was encouraged to ensure that we had the necessary support'.[19]

Considering 'the risks involved and the importance of the mission', the casualties had been light: two killed, seven wounded and six missing (later captured). All the wounded made rapid recoveries apart from Company Sergeant Major Gerry Strachan who, Frost wrote, was 'on the danger list for a long time, having received several bullets in the stomach'. But even he slowly got back on his feet and, 'to everyone's amazement was parachuting again a few months later and eventually rejoined the battalion as RSM [regimental sergeant major]'.*[20]

Recognising the publicity value of the raid, and the positive impact it would have on the nation's morale, the Admiralty, War Office and Air Ministry issued a joint communiqué on 28 February and allowed three participants – an officer, an NCO and a private – to speak to the press about their exploits. They were, however, forbidden to mention the fact that radar equipment had been brought back to the UK.[21] The response by William Joyce ('Lord Haw-Haw') – the English traitor and pro-Nazi propagandist who made nightly radio broadcasts from Berlin – was to condemn the parachutists 'as a handful of redskins'.[22]

Amidst all the backslapping, it seems odd that so few awards were given to the participants: Frost and Lieutenant Charteris received the Military Cross; Flight Sergeant Cox and Sergeants Grieve and McKenzie the Military Medal. Lieutenant Young – perhaps as a result of his bloodthirsty killing of Germans at the radar set – had to be content with a paltry mention in

---

* Having survived the war, Strachan died in July 1948 from an obstruction in his bowel, a complication that was described by the coroner as a 'sequel' to the serious injuries he had received at Bruneval. (*Sheffield Star*, July 1948)

despatches. By contrast, no fewer than four Distinguished Service Crosses, a Distinguished Service Medal and seven MiDs were given to naval personnel, none of whom had set foot on hostile territory. Company Sergeant Major Strachan's leadership and bravery was later recognised by the French authorities when they awarded him the *Croix de Guerre*; from the British he received nothing.[23] Nor did Peter Nagel ('Private Newman'), the German Jew who had gone along as a translator, and who faced certain death if caught and identified.* Such an unequal division of spoils between Navy and Army was surely unfair on the parachutists who had taken the greater risk. Yet it followed the pattern of Operation Colossus, when only a single medal was awarded, and would be repeated many times in the future.

Operation Biting – or the Bruneval Raid as it became known – underlined the promise shown by Britain's fledging airborne force the previous year in southern Italy. Unlike Colossus, however, Biting was an unqualified success. At a cost of just 15 casualties, the 2nd Parachute Battalion's C Company had succeeded in bringing back to the UK vital parts of the new German early-warning radar system which, in Churchill's own words, 'greatly helped our air offensive', cheered up the nation at its lowest ebb and convinced senior military figures that airborne forces could, as Frost put it, 'play a really useful part in the war'.[24]

---

* Despite this snub, Nagel bravely volunteered for the follow-up Commando raid – Operation Chariot – to destroy the drydock at St Nazaire by ramming an obsolete destroyer packed with explosives into its gates. The mission succeeded, and henceforth any major German warship requiring repairs would have to return to its homeland via British-controlled waters. The cost was crippling: of the original attacking force of 621 officers and men, 403 were killed and missing (many taken prisoner, including Nagel), and only 218 made it back to Britain. But, in contrast to the parachutists' first two missions, the participants in Chariot were generously rewarded with no fewer than 89 decorations, including five Victoria Crosses. (Churchill, *The Second World War*, IV, p. 178)

11

'Thirsting for action'
– UK, March–September 1942

THE SUCCESS OF THE Bruneval Raid notwithstanding, 'Boy' Browning was convinced that the real value of airborne troops lay in their use on a grander scale: 'to attack the enemy in force' by dropping behind the front line, seizing bridges and other vital infrastructure, and eventually linking up with ground troops who were advancing in a conventional manner. He therefore treated his command as a division-sized striking force which could, at the same time, provide any 'sabotage or raiding parties' that were needed. In the long run, however, he hoped it would be used in a more ambitious way.

In March, to assist with the concentration of the division, the whole of the 1st Parachute Brigade was moved to Bulford Camp on Salisbury Plain. This was followed, in early April, by the formation of 1st Airborne Divisional Signals and its medical component, the 16th Parachute Field Ambulance. Shortly after, Churchill, Lord Louis Mountbatten and the heads of the services visited the 1st Airborne Division at Netheravon to watch a joint parachute/glider demonstration. All available aircraft from the RAF's No. 38 Wing were on show: 12 Whitleys for the parachutists, and nine Hectors towing Hotspur gliders.[1]

The exercise did not go to plan. 'We prepared hard for a

week,' a subaltern of the 1st Parachute Battalion told his family, 'but on the actual day could not jump because of the wind. However we operated from lorries, and everyone was thoroughly satisfied.'[2]

Not quite. On returning to London, Churchill was determined that 'the RAF side of airborne forces should keep pace with that of the Army'. First, he told Air Chief Marshal Portal to increase the number of discarded bombers which could be placed at the disposal of the Airborne Corps, hoping that at least 100 could be found within the next three months. That idea was trumped, however, by the creation of a self-contained force, No. 38 Wing, to consist of four squadrons and a total of 96 aircraft, 'whose primary task would be to train and operate with' the 1st Airborne Division. It was led by Wing Commander Sir Nigel Norman.

In May, Churchill made a special plea to President Franklin D. Roosevelt of the United States for 'an immediate stepping-up of the allocation of transport aircraft, even at the expense of deliveries due later in the year'. Roosevelt replied that all available aircraft had been earmarked for America's rapidly expanding military forces. What he could do, however, was speed up the departure of four transport groups of the United States Army Air Force to Britain. Two arrived in June, and two more a month later, a total of 208 aircraft, mostly Dakota transport planes. Another four groups were due to arrive by November, doubling the number of aircraft, all of which were available 'to assist the British forces in both training and in operations'.[3]

John Frost was present when the first squadron of Dakotas flew into Netheravon. They were, he remembered, 'far superior to anything we had seen before and could carry 20 men instead of the 10 which was all that the Whitley could hold'. After various trials, the 2nd Battalion went up in the Dakotas to jump company by company. Frost was struck by the American pilots' technique of approaching the dropping-zone 'at almost ground level until they were about one mile away when they pulled their aircraft up sharply and suddenly to 700 or 800 feet'. This always brought a cheer from the stick of parachutists who, standing one behind each other, were tilted back as the plane climbed steeply. Then, just before giving the signal to jump, the pilot throttled back and put the aircraft into a shallow dive. As it descended, the men poured out of the rear exit door in a continuous stream.

That was the theory. In practice, however, the 2nd Battalion tragically lost four men killed that day in three accidents. One man suffered a 'Roman candle', while another came down with his parachute unopened after the dog clip which fastened the static line was 'forced open'. The third accident was caused by 'the canopy of one man's parachute becoming entangled with the tail of the aircraft', causing its owner to collide with one of the men following, and both to plummet down 'to lie together like crumpled bundles on the ground'. There were other issues too. The American pilots were only trained in daylight operations and needed to learn to fly and drop paratroopers by night. The Dakotas, moreover, 'were comparatively slow unarmed aircraft' and 'vulnerable to enemy fighters in daylight', unless escorted by Spitfires and Hurricanes. It would take time to train their pilots 'to fly exactly to, and drop loads on, a certain place hundreds of miles from home base'. Any operations in the meantime would have to be undertaken by day.[4]

Shortly after the move of the 1st Parachute Brigade to Bulford in March 1942, the famous 'Pegasus' flash was issued for the first time. Determined to create a powerful, unifying symbol for the airborne forces, Major General Browning had rejected the initial design of lightning flashes as too 'Germanic'. But remembering the myth of the legendary Greek warrior Bellerophon astride the winged horse Pegasus, he asked Major Edward Seago,★ a self-taught artist who was helping to develop camouflage techniques, to submit some designs. The one chosen as the main symbol − Bellerophon about to launch a spear from the back of Pegasus − in Cambridge blue on a claret background, was said to have been the racing colours of Browning and his wife Daphne du Maurier. It was worn on the right shoulder of all airborne soldiers.[5]

In April 1942, much against his wishes, 'Windy' Gale was reassigned to the War Office as head of the new Air Directorate which had been formed 'to look after and sponsor the affairs of the airborne forces and to act as a special link between the War Office and Air Ministry'. Vitally, and for the first time, the airborne forces had a man at the War Office who was working in their interest, and who was able to maintain 'some degree of continuity of policy and co-ordination of requirements'.[6]

Gale was replaced as commander of the 1st Parachute Brigade by Ted Flavell who, in turn, was succeeded as boss of the 2nd Battalion by Lieutenant Colonel Geoffrey Gofton Salmond of the Sherwood Foresters, with Major Geoffrey Pine-Coffin − known by his men as 'Wooden Box' − as his deputy.[7]

In the spring, the War Office agreed to the formation of another parachute brigade, the 2nd, and it was activated on 17 July 1942 with three parachute battalions: the 4th (transferred from the 1st Parachute Brigade), 5th (Scottish) and 6th (Royal Welch). The latter pair had been converted from existing infantry battalions − the 7th Cameron Highlanders and 10th Royal Welch Fusiliers − to speed up the process.

Given command of the 2nd Parachute Brigade was Eric

★ Seago went on to become a favoured artist of the Royal Family, and designed the silver sculpture of St George slaying the dragon that was affixed to any state car in which Queen Elizabeth II travelled.

'Dracula' Down.[8] He had been hugely unpopular when he first took over the 1st Parachute Battalion, but the officers and men, almost to a man, were now sorry to see him go. 'Up until almost the moment he left,' recalled Tony Hibbert, 'he was so unpopular with the troops that I was really convinced that going into battle someone would shoot him. They hated him until that sudden moment when they realised how good he was.' Hibbert had no doubts. Of all the senior officers he knew during the war, Down was the 'one absolute shining light' and the 'most wonderful commander'.

In Hibbert's opinion, part of the secret to Down's success was the ability to choose first-rate officers like Alastair Pearson and James Hill.[9] Having joined the 1st Parachute Battalion as second-in-command in the autumn of 1941, Pearson was Down's natural successor. But, shortly after the 1st Battalion's move to Bulford, he blotted his copybook by enjoying a 'wild night' out in Salisbury with his great pal, Captain Peter Cleasby-Thompson, for which they were given a 'severe dressing-down' by Down and confined to camp for 28 days. Pearson also lost his job as Down's second-in-command.[10]

His replacement was Major James Hill, the 30-year-old son of a general, who had been educated at Marlborough and the Royal Military Academy, Sandhurst, where he was captain of athletics and won the Sword of Honour for the best officer cadet. In 1936, after five years' service with the Royal Fusiliers, Hill transferred to the Supplementary Reserve so that he could marry and join the family's ferry company. He was recalled to the Colours in 1939 and commanded a platoon on the Maginot Line before his appointment as a staff captain at the BEF's General Headquarters. He carried to Calais the dispatches of Lord Gort, the British Commander-in-Chief, and later took charge of the evacuation from La Panne beach, near Dunkirk, for which he was awarded the Military Cross.

Hill would never have answered Churchill's call for volunteer parachutists but for the loss of his excellent batman who had done just that. 'I was then looked after for about six weeks by a [member of the Royal Pioneer Corps],' he recalled, 'which was an uncomfortable experience, so I had absolutely no alternative but to volunteer for parachuting in order to get my batman back! I was very lucky because Eric Down, who was commanding the 1st Parachute Battalion, wanted a second-in-command. I was interviewed by him at Bulford and he gave me the job.' When Down left, Hill took over and reinstated Pearson as second-in-command.[11]

Upset to have missed out on the Bruneval Raid, the men of the 1st Parachute Battalion were delighted to be assigned to the next Combined Operations mission, a large-scale air and sea assault on the port of Dieppe, codenamed Rutter.[12] It had come about because the United States was pushing for a full-scale invasion of continental Europe to distract German resources from hard-pressed Russia. Aware that a premature invasion might end in disaster, the British military was keen to do *something* to appease her allies. Dieppe was the result.

Having landed parachutists to knock out gun batteries and secure the high ground either side of Dieppe, the intention was to storm the town with a frontal attack by infantry and tanks. The long and hopelessly optimistic list of objectives included the capture of 40 invasion barges in the inner harbour, the destruction of local infrastructure and port facilities, and the seizure of radar components and Enigma material to assist the codebreakers of Bletchley Park. But none of this, wrote Patrick Bishop, the author of a recent book on the raid, 'made Dieppe obviously special' or substantiated the post-facto justification made by Mountbatten and others that it was launched as a trial run for the eventual invasion of Europe. What it *was*, with regard to the airborne forces, was a bloodbath avoided.

Though they did not realise it at the time, the men of the
1st Parachute Battalion were immensely fortunate that the original operation – Rutter – was postponed because of high winds
in early July 1942. When it was resurrected a few weeks later,
in the slightly modified form of Operation Jubilee, the airborne
component had been removed.* 'The longer nights of summer
would create more problems as the paras would have to land in
darkness,' writes Bishop. 'A much better option was to use
commandos who would arrive by boat like everyone else. They
could take care of the big [gun] batteries at Berneval and
Varengeville and one area of uncertainty was diminished.'

The raid finally took place on 19 August 1942 but, apart from
a few minor successes (such as Lord Lovat's 4th Commando
knocking out the Hess Battery to the west of Dieppe), it ended
in bloody failure as the gallant troops of the 2nd Canadian
Division came up against 'a near-perfect system of interlocking
arcs of fire that combined to generate a maelstrom of bullets and
shells that, unless preceded by a shattering bombardment, should
stop dead any frontal assault on the town'. They did. Of the
6,000 men who took part, 2,010 were taken prisoner and almost
1,000 were killed. Years later, a survivor railed against 'the absolute needless slaughter . . . the feeling that we had been
bamboozled as guinea pigs'.[13]

This lucky escape did nothing to dampen the spirits of the
1st Parachute Brigade men who, noted John Frost, 'were all
thirsting for action whatever might be the cost'. At Bulford, they
all worked on their physical fitness and were soon able 'to travel
considerable distances without fatigue'. All platoons were required

---

* James Hill remembered: 'We nearly had a mutiny on our hands from our
fellows who had been waiting and training, some of them since 1940, and were
now denied their battle. It was lucky for us in many ways that we didn't take
part, because it appeared a costly failure.' (Hill, in Arthur, *Men of the Red Beret*,
pp. 37–8)

to cover 50 miles in 24 hours, and all battalions to march 30 miles and more for several days in succession. Corporal Reg Curtis remembered feeling 'tired' but 'on top of the world' as he and comrades returned to Bulford 'after a gruelling 100-mile march in three days with full equipment'. Frost wrote: 'These semi-endurance tests resulted in a solid welding together of officers, NCOs and men and it was soon obvious that a very fine instrument of war was being prepared.'

They used live firing exercises, whenever possible, to prepare the men for the sights and sounds of combat. But the one skill they might have practised more was marksmanship. 'We failed to spend quite as much time on the ranges as we should have done,' admitted Frost. 'We were to find out that there is no short cut or substitute for skill-at-arms and without [it] fitness, discipline, enthusiasm and all the rest counted for little when there was a real live enemy to contend with.'

To provide a depot for the increasing number of parachute battalions, the Parachute Regiment was created on 1 August 1942. Henceforth, the 1st Parachute Battalion was known officially as the 1st Battalion, The Parachute Regiment. Like all airborne troops, the parachutists wore on their sleeves the 'Pegasus' shoulder flash, and on their heads the newly issued maroon beret. They also displayed their blue parachute 'wings', while the air-landing troops sported a shoulder flash with the word 'AIRBORNE' in pale blue on a maroon background.

As summer turned to autumn, Reg Curtis remembered strong rumours circulating at Bulford 'of an intended move to an unknown battle front', and that an 'eagerness of getting to grips with the old enemy was the main topic of conversation'. In the NAAFI, washrooms, guard room and barracks, there was endless speculation as to where they might be sent. It always ended with a joyous rendition of the parachutist's favourite song, 'Come sit by my side if you love me',[14] which begins:

Come and sit by my side if you love me,
Do not hasten to bid me adieu,
Just remember the poor parachutist,
And the job he is trying to do.

It ends:

So stand by your glasses steady,
And remember the men from the sky,
Here's to the dead already,
And three cheers for the next man to die.[15]

12

Operation Freshman
– UK and Norway, October–December 1942

PERCHED ON A BROAD shelf of rock, rising sheer from the river bed of a narrow, thickly forested valley in the Westfjordalen area of southern Norway, 80 miles west of Oslo, lies the Vermork hydroelectric power plant. Built by Norsk Hydro in 1911, the plant's original purpose was to fix nitrogen for the production of fertiliser. By the 1930s, however, it was using electrolysis to produce 'heavy water' (deuterium oxide) for nuclear research. When Germany invaded Norway in 1940, the plant's existing stocks of 'heavy water' were sent for safe keeping to France and later the United States. But production soon resumed, under German control, and in 1942 the Allies received word that the Nazi nuclear weapons programme was getting close to developing a nuclear reactor. As this would require a great deal of 'heavy water' to function, the destruction of the Norsk Hydro plant and its stockpile of 'heavy water' became an urgent priority.

Various options were discussed at a series of meetings at Combined Operations HQ – housed in the Regency splendour of No. 1 Richmond Terrace, Whitehall – in October 1942. They included an aerial bombing raid, which was ruled out because of 'the risk of killing large numbers of Norwegians and because it was a difficult target to find'; and an attack by Norwegian saboteurs, again rejected on the grounds that it would be 'too difficult' to provide the necessary 'technical training' and transport the 'quantity of explosive needed'. This left an airborne operation, which became the preferred option.

The question then became: should the troops arrive by flying boat, parachute or glider? The first method required landing on a nearby lake, which would probably give the game away, and could only be done during the October moon period which was too short notice; the second entailed 'low flying in precipitous valleys and would have aroused the populace even if none of the aircraft crashed'; the third promised a relatively silent insertion and the ability to transport a decent quantity of explosives. The glider option was chosen, and the operation was given the codename Freshman.[1]

The key meeting at Combined Operations HQ on 14 October – chaired by Mountbatten's deputy Major General Charles Haydon, and with Major General 'Boy' Browning, Group Captain Sir Nigel Norman, and representatives from SOE present – agreed that it was 'essential to carry out this operation by the end of 1942'; that 'in all probability there could only be one attempt at the FRESHMAN objective and that must be successful'; and that SOE agents needed to be sent ahead to prepare the ground and guide the glider-borne force to the target area.[*][2]

With intelligence suggesting that as few as 40 Austrian troops were in the vicinity of Vermork – while only six were guarding

---

* On 18 October 1942, in an operation codenamed Grouse, an advance party of four Norwegian SOE agents – Jens-Anton Poulsson, Knut Haugland, Claus Helberg and Arne Kjelstrup – had parachuted by night onto the Hardangervidda, a large wilderness to the north-west of Vermork that was avoided by German forces. They then trekked for 15 days towards Møsvatn where they linked up with local sympathisers, selected a suitable glider-landing site and reconnoitred the best line of attack for the raiding force.

the plant itself – it was decided that a force of 30 airborne sappers and four pilots from the Glider Pilot Regiment would be enough to do the job. Skilled in the use of explosives, the sappers were drawn from the 1st Airborne Division's two companies of Royal Engineers. They would travel in two Horsa gliders towed by Halifax bombers from Skitten airfield, near Wick in northern Scotland. The flight would take from three to three and a half hours, with the gliders due to land by moonlight on a 700-yard stretch of level ground on the edge of the Møsvatn Lake, 10 miles to the south-west of the plant. There they would be met by the four Norwegian SOE agents who had earlier marked out the landing zone with flares. If anything happened to one of the gliders, the 17 occupants of the other glider would be enough to do the job.

'On the approach march,' noted the Airborne Division Operation Order, 'the object will be to avoid detection. If they are challenged by an enemy sentry he will be killed and a detachment will be left to cut any telephone wires that appear to leave his post, and rejoin the main body.' The march was expected to take around five to six hours, and, once inside the wire surrounding the plant, the force would be split into three: one group to blow up the 'power house'; one to destroy the electrolysis plant; while the two glider pilots and the force commander headed for the office buildings to 'smash the telephone' and lock the workers into a single room. Preparing the demolitions was expected to take 20 minutes.[3]

Once the job was done, the men would head east on foot in pairs towards the Swedish border, a distance of at least 150 miles over difficult terrain. There were two recommended routes: the northern route, which was less direct and 'therefore less likely to be watched', but entailed a much longer march of 250 miles in very cold temperatures, and required crossing the formidable barrier of the River Glommen; and the shorter southern route through less difficult country, and in weather that would not be 'so severe', but with more German guards and through a narrow bottleneck which might be patrolled.

For the mission they would be armed with Sten guns and carry the explosives, 10 days' iron rations – including preserved meat, cheese, biscuit, tea, sugar and salt – and extra equipment (like gauntlet gloves and Balaclava helmets) in their Bergen rucksacks. They would wear steel helmets, army boots and ordinary battledress over civilian clothes such as white anorak jackets, woollen sweaters and blue ski trousers and army boots. They were to remain in their uniforms for at least the first five miles of their escape route, and then discard them, their arms and accoutrements when opportunity allowed. 'Subsequent behaviour must be that of a Norwegian civilian, and there must be no question of carrying or using arms . . . As the Germans will expect you to go south, the majority of the party should, to begin with, go north.'

Successful escapees would need two main qualities: the guts to 'carry on when your body tells you to give up'; and the ability to bluff others, and convince them, 'by your appearance and manner, that you are a civilian (remember to smile)'. If they were unlucky enough to be captured, they were only to give their name, rank and number. 'Do not,' they were advised, 'invent false particulars. There is nothing a good interrogating officer likes so much as a prisoner of war who tries to be too clever.' Above all, if they had been helped by Norwegians, they were not to admit that.[4]

The raiding force was composed of 30 sapper volunteers from the 1st Airborne Division's two companies of Royal Engineers: the 9th Field and 261st Field Park. Their commander was 24-year-old Lieutenant Alexander Allen, the eldest of four siblings and a keen sportsman who had attended King Edward VI Grammar School in Birmingham. Experienced in bomb disposal,

Allen volunteered for Operation Freshman because he was keen to do his bit for the war effort. Quietly spoken and engaged to the daughter of a vicar, he was a determined character who 'commanded a natural authority and respect among his men'.[5]

Once the 30 men had been selected, the first task was to toughen them up for the harsh terrain and weather of Norway by sending them to Wales for survival training and mountaineering. They were then despatched to North Hertford for explosives training with the SOE, then recces of Port Sunlight on Merseyside and Fort William in Scotland where there were plants similar to the one in Norway. They also trained on large models and mock-ups of the buildings they would have to destroy.[6]

On 17 November, thanks to an injury, the slightly reduced group of two officers and 27 airborne sappers moved to the departure airfield at Skitten, a satellite of Wick in the far north of Scotland. Their earliest departure was scheduled for the night of 19/20 November, when the moon in Norway would be close to full.[7]

While Allen and his men prepared for the mission, the RAF was mulling over the best method to get them to Norway. It was not an enviable assignment. 'The 500-mile tow, to be made during the hours of darkness, was longer than any so far attempted even in daylight,' noted a history of the Glider Pilot Regiment. 'The weather prevailing in that part of the world at the beginning of winter was unpredictable and mostly unfavourable, and it was essential that the glider landings be made during clear conditions.'

Because of the long approach flight, the only aircraft suitable was the four-engined Handley Page Halifax bomber. Yet at this stage of the war, Halifaxes were in extremely short supply. But eventually three aircraft – two for the operation, and one in reserve – were assigned. The two six-man crews chosen were led by Squadron Leader A. B. Wilkinson and Flight Lieutenant Parkinson, assisted by two pilot officers. 'It was fully understood,' noted No. 38 Wing's report,

> that the difficulties of carrying out the operation were tremendous, since it demanded exceptional weather conditions for the carrying out of a glider tow by night far longer than had ever been previously attempted in training, even in daylight; a glider landing in very difficult country on a flare path of the limited nature that can be laid out by agents; the whole of the tugging and the identification of the landing area being carried out by crews of limited experience who would have had only a small amount of training on the four-engined aircraft which they had never previously flown.

Rebecca/Eureka navigational aids were meant to guide the Halifaxes to the correct landing zone. The plan was for the SOE agents to set up the Eureka radio-beacon device on the ground; it would then emit a signal which, with luck, would be picked up by the Rebecca device that had recently been fitted to the aircraft, thus providing it with vital navigational information. But the system was untested in a Halifax and, moreover, had not been used by the scratch crews. Despite all these problems, No. 38 Wing 'accepted full responsibility for mounting the operation in this way in the knowledge that a small team of picked men can, in case of necessity, accomplish things far beyond those contemplated in normal operations'.[8]

The four men chosen to pilot the gliders were Staff Sergeants M. F. D. Strathdee and Peter Doig of the GPR (Glider Pilot Regiment), and Pilot Officer Davies and Sergeant Fraser of the Royal Australian Air Force, the latter pair bomber pilots who had been converted to gliders. Strathdee hailed from Croydon,

London, and had joined the 1st GPR after a stint in the Royal Armoured Corps. Doig was a 25-year-old Glaswegian who had worked as a laboratory assistant at his local university before joining the Cameronians in 1940 and later transferring to the 1st GPR. While both were 'excellent pilots', their glider training to date 'had necessarily been all too brief, certainly not sufficient preparation for the impending operation'. They were both still 'as keen as mustard'.[9]

On 19 November, the first weather report from Norway was 'unfavourable', with a strong westerly airstream over Scotland and the North Sea. But later in the morning it was reported that 'conditions might be possible'. Partial cloud layer was expected for most of the flight, but as long as the target area was reached after 8 p.m. it would be 'cloudless with good visibility and sufficient winds to keep the valleys clear of fog'. This was good enough for the pilots, and Team 'A' – Wilkinson's Halifax towing Strathdee and Doig's glider, with Lieutenant Allen and 14 men on board – took off at 5.55 p.m., slightly delayed because of problems with the intercom between the aircraft and glider. Team 'B' – Flight Lieutenant Parkinson in the Halifax, and Pilot Officer Davies and Sergeant Fraser in the glider, with Lieutenant Methven, and 13 men – followed 30 minutes later.

Despite altering course several times to avoid the cloud layer, which extended to over 5,000 feet, Team 'A' had an uneventful flight across the North Sea until the Rebecca generator failed. Fortunately, the sky cleared as they crossed the southern coast of Norway, which meant they could fix their position and set a course north-west towards the target. But 'despite bright moonlight, no fog in the valleys and only one to two tenths cloud', it was impossible to map read or identify features by sight. A second approach was made, again without success. Without the Rebecca transceiver, it was impossible to pinpoint the correct landing zone.

'By this time,' recalled Group Captain T. B. Cooper DFC, who had accompanied Wilkinson, 'the cloud had increased to about 3/10ths. The target could not be found and as it was then extremely doubtful if there was sufficient petrol to tow back to Scotland, course was set for Peterhead.' Flying at 9,000 feet, they hit more cloud and struggled to climb above it with the weight of the glider. In doing so they collected some ice which made it impossible to maintain height or even speed. They were forced to descend to 7,000 feet with lights ablaze. Cooper wrote:

At this height conditions became extremely bumpy and cloud much thicker, and at 23.11 hours, after two or three very violent surges, the tow rope broke or the glider cast off. An SOS request for position was sent, followed by a . . . message stating 'Released in Sea' which, it was hoped, would be sufficiently non-committal to puzzle the enemy for at least 24 hours. Unfortunately, however, the Wireless Operator subsequently transmitted 'Glider in sea' in plain language, owing to a combination of poor crew procedure and misunderstanding.

A subsequent check by the Navigator showed that, in fact, the glider would have landed well inland in Norway and not in the sea. After the glider had released, the aircraft was able to climb out of the clouds with ease as the icing was only very slight . . . Course was set for Wick and the return was uneventful. Subsequent analysis of the petrol consumption revealed that it might just have been possible to tow back to Peterhead.[10]

After the tow-rope broke, Strathdee and Doig struggled to control their glider and it eventually crash-landed in mountainous terrain at Fylgjesdalen, near Stavanger, in south-west Norway. Both pilots and six sappers were killed in the crash, and four more were severely injured. The casualties were helped by Lieutenant Allen and the other four survivors to a nearby farm which they reached at 1 a.m. 'At the farm,' noted a report by an SOE agent who met some of them in captivity, 'they called in a Norwegian doctor, who immediately telephoned for another doctor, but also told them that the Gestapo were coming. The Gestapo duly arrived and took the men away.'

The agent was taken to see them at Gestapo headquarters in Stavanger because he spoke English. He later told SOE in London that 'four men were in one large cell, and five, who were badly wounded, were in a small cell'. The conditions were 'unsanitary' and the men had 'apparently received no medical attention'. They were happy to give the Germans their 'names and addresses', but 'would not give their objective'. During one of his two visits, the agent witnessed a dispute between the German Wehrmacht (Army) and the Gestapo. The former wanted the men to be treated as prisoners of war, but the Gestapo refused to give them up.[11]

The fate of the captives was sealed by the infamous 'Führer Befehl' or 'Commando Order', issued by Adolf Hitler a month before Operation Freshman on 18 October 1942. It stated: 'From now on all enemies encountered by German troops on so-called Commando expeditions in Europe or Africa whether ostensibly uniformed soldiers or sabotage agents with or without weapons are to be annihilated both in battle and in flight to the last man.'[12] The order, in effect, gave Hitler's security agencies – the Gestapo and the SD (Sicherheitsdienst, the intelligence agency of the SS) – the green light to murder any Allied soldiers that were captured on missions behind enemy lines.

The Freshman captives were the first victims of this appalling breach of the Geneva Conventions. According to an official account – compiled from various sources – the badly wounded men from Allen's party were 'later poisoned by a German doctor [Werner Seeling] and buried at sea'. Allen and the other four lightly injured men received only a temporary reprieve:

moved to Grini concentration camp, they were taken to nearby woods, blindfolded and executed by the Gestapo on 18 January 1943.[13]

Team 'B', meanwhile, had also met with disaster. Both Halifax and glider crashed in a snowstorm in the mountains near Helleland, southern Norway, having crossed the coast at nearby Egersund. All the occupants of the Halifax – Flight Lieutenant Parkinson, his five crew and the lone observer Pilot Officer Howard – were killed, as were three of the 16 men on the glider. But the fact that so many on the glider survived – albeit with injuries, some serious – is an indication that it was able to cast off from the Halifax before it hit the ground.

According to a Norwegian woman who lived near the crash site, the glider came down because the towing plane had 'engine trouble'. Two of the able-bodied British soldiers went to get help. Turned away from one farm, they were invited in to another, but once again the locals tipped off the Germans by telephone. The two soldiers then led a party – including the witness who acted as a 'nurse' – back to help the injured, but there was 'really nothing' for her to do 'because the injured ones had been properly bandaged' and the dead men 'sewn up in a tarpaulin'. She insisted that the British were wearing long jerseys or 'islandinger' on top of their uniforms, and that they were 'all young lads and all in excellent spirit and temper'. A German officer told them that their war was over and they would be interned. As far as she could see, the conduct of the Germans to the prisoners 'was excellent'.

It was not until a few days later that the woman and her husband discovered the 'horrific' fate of the captives. First they were taken to a camp at Slettebø, near Egersund, where they were interrogated by several German SD officers who had arrived by car from Oslo. Then, after just two hours of this, they were taken out one by one and executed in the woods near Slettebø

Camp. One man, who had broken his leg, was 'shot seated on a chair'. Among the victims was the youngest member of the raiding force, 18-year-old Sapper Gerald Williams from Doncaster, a talented carpenter at the local technical high school who had lied about his age so he could join the forces. One of his officers described him as a 'good lad . . . always ready to have a bash' and an 'outstanding soldier for his age'.[14]

A separate source noted that the men who carried out the executions were all volunteers from the 12th Company of the local Wehrmacht battalion, and were commanded by a non-commissioned officer called Wagner. The corpses were taken by lorry to the coast and secretly buried in the sand dunes at Ogna.[15]

Three years later, when the 1st Airborne Division arrived in Norway at the end of the war, the Freshman dead were reburied with full military honours. The five from the first glider were reinterred at the Commonwealth War Graves plot at Vestre Gravlund, near Oslo. The second glider's occupants were reburied at Eiganes churchyard in Stavanger, and the Halifax aircrew at Helleland. The man who had ordered the murders, the head of the Gestapo in Oslo, avoided retribution by committing suicide before he could be apprehended. But others paid the price: SS Dr Werner Seeling and Hauptscharführer Erich Hoffman were both executed for their crimes in 1946, while Unterscharführer Fritz Feuerlein was sentenced to life in prison.[16]

★

Operation Freshman was a costly failure.* None of the key

---

* In February 1943, a second attempt was made to destroy the Vermork plant, codenamed Operation Gunnerside. This time six Norwegian SOE operatives, led by 23-year-old Joachim Ronneberg, were parachuted on to the Hardangervidda where they met up with the original Grouse team. Carrying explosives dropped from the air, they penetrated the beefed-up German security around the plant

objectives – the destruction of the Vermork hydro-electric plant and its stocks of 'heavy water' – had been achieved, and all 31 men on the two gliders, and the six crew and one passenger of the downed Halifax bomber, had lost their lives. The brutal executions of those who survived the crashes caused many in Britain to question the wisdom and morality of such missions. Were they really legitimate combatants or, as the Germans insisted, little better than saboteurs or spies who got what was coming to them? To make a clear distinction between the two, the official report recommended that in future 'parties of this sort' were not given civilian clothing 'to effect their escape'.

After the success of Biting, Freshman was a setback for Browning's 1st Airborne Division. Yet it taught the need, in future, for the 'early report and prediction of changing weather conditions' because they 'may affect the equipment and training of the forces'; and the folly of allowing maps to be carried on which the objective had been marked (as was the case with Freshman). As for the air aspect of the operation, it was felt in retrospect that it was 'unwise to attempt to carry out operationally something which has not been, in fact, frequently done experimentally and in training'. With this in mind, and the fact that towing gliders at night was a 'much more difficult technique than is generally realised', it was thought that the operation

---

by descending into a ravine, fording the icy river and climbing the steep hill on the far side. They then followed a single railway track right into the plant, encountering no guards along the way, and placed explosive charges on the heavy-water electrolysis chambers. These were detonated successfully, several hours later, destroying vital equipment and the entire inventory of heavy water. All of the SOE men evaded capture: five by escaping to Sweden, two to Oslo, and four remaining in the region for further resistance work, including the sinking of the SF *Hydro* as the Germans attempted to transport new stocks of heavy water across Lake Tinn. The Norwegians' successful destruction of the Vermork plant was the subject of the 1965 British war film *Heroes of Telemark*, starring Kirk Douglas and Richard Harris.

would have had a 'bigger chance of success had the Military party been introduced by parachutes'. Lastly, it was felt unwise to place too much reliance on special navigational aids like Eureka/Rebecca because they could, as in this instance, fail.[17]

There were some silver linings. As Group Captain Norman's report for No. 38 Wing noted:

Although the operation was unsuccessful, a great deal of most valuable technical and tactical information has been obtained . . . The manifest difficulties of a glider operation at long range at night as compared with a parachute operation under the same conditions, have been clearly indicated.

The report praised in particular the glider pilots – Strathdee, Doig, Davies and Fraser – who 'accomplished feats of towing unapproached before' and 'embarked upon the operation well knowing the risks it involved for them, not only on the long tow over sea and mountains through doubtful weather but also on the ground'. The report added: 'Their courage, skill and enthusiasm were beyond praise and should serve as a shining example to all who may follow them, the first British glider pilots to take part in an operation against the enemy.'[18]

PART II

Growing Pains, 1942–44

13

'You will hear from me ultimately' – North Africa, November 1942

I N EARLY NOVEMBER 1942, Mrs Alice Clements received a letter from her 23-year-old son Alan, a platoon commander in the 1st Parachute Battalion. 'Dear Mother,' it read, 'I thought I would write you a mid-week letter since it's possible that certain circumstances may prevent my writing at the end of the week. There is in no case any need to worry since you will hear from me ultimately.'[1]

It was the last his parents Alice and Reginald – the manager of Barclays Bank in Holbeach, Lincolnshire – would hear from him until early 1943. In the interim, they could only speculate on where he was and what he was doing. On 25 November, for example, his father wrote:

My dear old boy,
We wonder and we wonder. We spend the greater part of our time wondering . . . We saw in the 'Evening News' yesterday a picture of Parachutists disembarking in Algiers; with the aid of a magnifying glass and a fine tooth comb we finally decided you were not among them. But Mummy still walks around the house with it, and pores over it at intervals. We are longing for your first letter, and do sincerely hope that you are well and happy. May laurelled victory soon sit upon your sword![2]

Their guess that Alan was in North Africa was correct. By late November he had already made his first combat jump into battle – and survived. Not all his colleagues had been so fortunate.

The decision to include the 1st Parachute Brigade in Operation Torch – the Anglo-American air and sea landings in French North Africa – was taken at the last minute. The original plan had been to drop a single battalion of the 503rd US Parachute Regiment to capture airfields near the Algerian port of Oran which, along with Algiers, and Casablanca in Morocco, were the main targets for the amphibious landings on 8 November. But when Major General 'Boy' Browning – in his capacity as British airborne advisor to Allied commanders in all theatres of war – was briefed on Torch in late September, he strongly suggested that more than one para-chute battalion should be used in a campaign that was bound to be fought 'over great distances' and with the probability that in its early stages 'only comparatively light opposition would be encountered'. The War Office agreed and the 1st Parachute Brigade was duly placed under the command of General Dwight D. Eisenhower, the Commander-in-Chief of the Allied Expeditionary Force, and sub-allotted by him to Lieutenant General Kenneth Anderson's British First Army for specific operations.

The sticking point was the Air Ministry's unwillingness to supply enough planes to transport the brigade. This problem was partially solved when the United States Army Air Force (USAAF) offered to assume responsibility for airborne operations in North Africa. To prepare, No. 60 Group of the USAAF's 51 Wing (Dakotas) dropped its first unit of British parachutists in the UK on 9 October, but a series of accidents cost four men their lives. Practice drops were delayed while new jumping techniques were agreed with the unfortunate consequence that a large proportion of the 1st Parachute Brigade was deployed to North Africa without ever having jumped from a Dakota.[3]

Most went by sea, with the main body sailing from Greenock

in Scotland and arriving at Algiers on 12 November, four days after the amphibious landings.* Corporal Reg 'Lofty' Curtis – who was travelling with James Hill, Alastair Pearson, Alan Clements and the rest of the 1st Parachute Battalion on the former cruise ship *Arundel Castle* – kept boredom at bay with endless games of poker, 'Crown and Anchor' or 'Pitch and Toss', watching escort ships 'nipping in between the lines of Merchant Ships, like sheep dogs mustering their flocks', and catching sight of Tangiers with its 'lights blazing away in the clear Mediterranean sky'. At Algiers, they marched 'singing and whistling' from the docks to the aerodrome at Maison-Blanche† where they made sure that 'every detail was in order in the way of rations, arms, field dressings, maps, ammunition'.[4]

The 2nd Parachute Battalion sailed in the same convoy from Greenock commanded by Major John Frost MC, who was only recently back with the unit after a stint as second-in-command of the 3rd Parachute Battalion, swapping with Major Geoffrey Pine-Coffin who moved the other way.[5]

On landing at Algiers, Frost and his men marched to the suburb of Maison Carrée, where they were billeted. 'Although the local French seemed to be friendly,' wrote Frost, 'many were dubious about coming back into the war with us as allies. Moreover most of them were anti-de Gaulle and his Free French movement and so there was the possibility of a difficult emergency suddenly arriving. This made it hard to keep training as rigorously as I would have liked.'[6]

---

* The Allies encountered unexpected resistance and bad weather near Casablanca and Oran, but both were captured after short sieges. They met less opposition at Algiers – partly because the local Vichy commander was in league with the Allies – and the troops were able to push inland and force the French to surrender on the first day. Allied losses were 1,100 killed and 756 wounded; Vichy forces suffered 1,300 killed and almost 2,000 wounded.
† Today it is Algiers' Houari Boumediene International Airport.

Because of a shortage of aircraft, the only parachutists to fly to North Africa were the headquarters and two rifle companies of the 3rd Battalion, under the recently promoted Lieutenant Colonel Pine-Coffin. Delayed by fog, they eventually left RAF St Eval in Cornwall in the early hours of 10 November and arrived at Maison Blanche airfield, outside Algiers, via a refuelling stop at Gibraltar, at 8 a.m. the next day. Briefed by General Anderson himself, Pine-Coffin was given the task of capturing Bône airfield in eastern Algeria, close to the border with Tunisia where Axis troops were beginning to concentrate.

The scion of West Country landowners whose unusual name commemorated the union of two families in the late 18th century, Pine-Coffin had been commissioned into the Devonshire Regiment as a regular in 1928, and later saw action with the 2nd Duke of Cornwall's Light Infantry during the withdrawal to Dunkirk. A pugnacious character who boxed for the army, he quickly tired of garrison duty and in late 1941 volunteered for the airborne forces, switching from the 2nd to the 3rd Parachute Battalion a year later. He was 33, and recently widowed, when he led his men onto Bône airfield at 8.30 a.m. on 12 November. It was Pine-Coffin's first operational drop.[7]

They captured the airfield without opposition, even though the men were scattered over three miles, and took time to recover their containers and head for the target. One man was lost to friendly fire and three more when two Dakotas came down in the sea. The drop was far from perfect, but it was certainly timely in that the Germans, with the same idea, had also just despatched a battalion of *Fallschirmjäger* in Junkers Ju-52 transport planes to occupy the airfield. Arriving too late, they called off their operation and Pine-Coffin was able to consolidate. Three days later, having faced nothing more severe than air attacks by Stuka dive-bombers, he and his men were relieved by No. 6 Commando. 'In some ways,' noted the official history, 'it was an example of a perfectly planned airborne operation, in that mobility was exploited to forestall the enemy.'[8]

Next into action was Hill's 1st Parachute Battalion. Hill had been told on the voyage to North Africa that his first task was to capture Tunis airport at El Alouina in northern Tunisia, but this was cancelled when intelligence was received that 7,000 to 10,000 German air-landing troops had beaten them to it. Instead, on arriving at Maison Blanche, he was ordered by Lieutenant General Anderson – a 'crusty old boy who didn't know anything about parachute troops and didn't like what he had heard about them' – to seize the airfield at Souk-el-Arba in northern Tunisia, and then move 30 miles to the north-east where Vichy French troops were holding key road junctions around the town of Beja. Having done a deal with the French, he was to 'patrol east to harass the enemy, resorting to guerrilla warfare if necessary'. At the same time, the 2/503rd US Parachute Battalion was ordered to seize and hold airfields at Tebessa and Youks-les-Bains to the south.[9]

With the scheduled drop on 15 November postponed because of bad weather, Hill and his men tried again the following day. 'Off we went in Dakota aircraft commanded by a splendid colonel,' he recalled. 'He and his men had never dropped para-chutists before. They also had no intercom between their aeroplanes and no intercom within the aircraft itself. The only map I could get hold of was a one-quarter-inch-to-the-mile French motoring map, which included Beja.'

During the three-hour flight, they were bounced by two Messerschmitt ME-109 fighters. Both were shot down by their escort of Spitfires, 'great little planes' that the chain-smoking Reg Curtis remembered well from Dunkirk. Sweating in the humid heat, the men sang songs and cracked jokes to hide their nerves. At last came the time to jump. 'The order "Go" rang in my ears,' wrote Curtis. 'Before long I was a changed man: I felt much cooler being whisked about in the air. All round me seemed hundreds of parachutes, just like a training exercise, then I realised I had dropped into action. I landed OK.'

One man – Private Webster, a friend of Curtis's from the Guards – was killed when he hit a power line. Otherwise the drop was 'unopposed except for some rather excitable Arabs' who galloped towards the parachutists 'on frisky-looking Arab horses'. Having fired a few shots in the air, 'more in jubilation than trying to be hostile', they rode off.[10]

Once on the ground and formed up, the bulk of the battalion moved off in requisitioned vehicles, mostly buses, for Beja.* Alastair Pearson, the second-in-command, remained behind with HQ Company to collect the parachutes. He also arranged Webster's funeral on the 16th, which was 'an endurance test as the whole population of Souk-el-Arba attended' and they had a walk of about three miles in blazing heat carrying all their equipment to the graveyard outside the town. After shaking hands with about 500 mourners, Pearson 'climbed into the hearse and rode back in state'. He then requisitioned a railway engine and two trucks, loaded all the stores and caught up with the battalion at Beja Station. Battalion HQ was situated in an abattoir.[11]

A day earlier, leaving the battalion on a hill overlooking Beja, Hill had walked into the town with a French liaison officer to speak to Général de Division George Barré, commanding French troops in Tunisia. Barré was, strictly speaking, still answerable to the pro-German Vichy regime of Marshal Pétain; but he also knew the Germans had recently occupied all of metropolitan France, and he was about to switch sides. He told Hill that his

---

* According to Reg Curtis, the 1st Parachute Brigade's famous battle cry originated at Beja when a 'gigantic Arab complete with flowing robe and headgear' emerged from a tent, cupped his hands to his mouth and bellowed: 'Who-oooh-Ma-hamed!' (Curtis, *Churchill's Volunteer*, p. 103)

main concern, if he threw in his lot with the Allies, was how to combat German armour. After Hill had reassured him 'in the most glowing terms' that Allied armoured divisions were rushing to their aid, Barré agreed to let the paratroopers take over key road junctions. He had 2,500 men under his command; Hill only 525. At dusk the next day, Hill marched his battalion through the town twice to make his force look bigger. 'We wanted desperately to bring the French in on our side,' wrote Hill, 'and demonstrate to the local population that the Germans were not infallible.'[12]

They got their opportunity the following day, 18 November, when Major Peter Cleasby-Thompson's mobile column – two platoons of S Company, two sections of sappers and a detachment of 3-inch mortars – ambushed a column of German armoured cars on the highway between Sidi Nsir and Mateur, 35 miles north-east of Beja. There were six enemy vehicles – three heavy eight-wheeled armoured cars and three light recce cars – with 40 yards between each of them. The paratroopers held their fire until the first vehicle had detonated one of the mines laid by the sappers. This was the signal for battle to commence as parties of Gammon bombers★ led by Lieutenants Mellor and Kellass 'quickly immobilised two of the armoured cars' and the scout cars were also 'put out of action'. Those Germans not killed or wounded in the first five vehicles soon surrendered. That just left the armoured car at the rear of the column which 'opened fire with machine gun and sub-machine gun'. But it was targeted with accurate 3-inch mortar fire and eventually knocked out.[13]

★ Officially known as the No. 82 Grenade, and designed by Lieutenant R. S. Gammon of the 1st Parachute Battalion, the 'Gammon Bomb' was an improvised hand-thrown bomb used by paratroopers, special forces and the Resistance as an anti-personnel weapon or to destroy parked aircraft or vehicles. Its charge of plastic explosive was wrapped in fabric and sewn onto an impact fuse that would detonate on contact.

Stationed with the 3-inch mortars on a nearby hill, Reg Curtis remembered everyone letting rip with mines, mortars, small-arms fire and Gammon bombs. There was only one British casualty: Sergeant Sammy Steadman, who was hit in the leg. Otherwise the action had gone like clockwork, yielding a 'pretty good' bag of Luger pistols, German maps and documents, some Zeiss field glasses and one undamaged scout car.[14] The car was used to take Steadman and a badly wounded German back to Beja, while the rest of the force withdrew to Sidi Nsir after destroying the enemy vehicles and burying the 3-inch mortar and some explosives. Cleasby-Thompson recalled: 'The local Arabs were bribed and promised to hide the equipment and look after the four enemy wounded who could not walk. These were given food, water, cigarettes and morphia. The heavy stores were left behind because the remaining two vehicles could not be started and it was supposed that the enemy column had wirelessed their HQ at Mateur.'

Only later did a small group of paratroopers return in a French car to the scene of the ambush and collect the wounded, stores and mortar. Meanwhile, the Arabs had looted the disabled armoured cars and stripped the enemy dead.[15]

Overall the ambush had had the desired effect by impressing the French and making them 'better disposed' to the Allied cause. This was confirmed on 19 November when the French commander at Medjez-el-Bab, 30 miles east of Beja, warned the Germans not to cross the River Medjerda. They tried to do so anyway, in the morning of 20 November, and were opposed by the French and the 1st Parachute Battalion's R Company under Major Conron. Both 'fought magnificently' in beating back the Germans, though the French casualties were particularly high. A day later, after R Company had withdrawn to Beja, the Germans took possession of Medjez.

On 22 November, during a visit to the French at Sidi Nsir,

Lieutenant Colonel Hill learned that an Italian force of 300 men and tanks were laagered each night on Gué Hill, nine miles to the north-east. He decided to attack after dark and was delighted to be given a company of Moroccan troops – Goums – to help carry his mortar ammunition. Deploying the whole battalion apart from R Company in a pincer attack, he led his men towards the hill by the light of the moon. They tried to make as little noise as possible, but every farmhouse they came to 'had a bloody dog that barked'. Even so, they got to the foot of the hill undetected. Hill now sent a troop of Royal Engineers to mine the road leading to the back of the feature to prevent any enemy armour from escaping.

He was preparing the main assault when three loud bangs were heard. 'The sappers had been carrying their Hawkins anti-tank mines in sandbags ready to lay them,' noted Hill. 'Somehow, one of them had accidentally exploded and set off the rest. Three officers and 24 men were killed.'[16]

Hearing the explosions, the Germans opened fire with heavy machine guns. Hill's men attacked regardless. 'Moved platoon forward into dead ground and stopped to try to locate positions,' reported Lieutenant Stan Wandless, a married 27-year-old from Gloucester who was commanding 7 Platoon of S Company. 'Large numbers of grenades were then thrown, so I sent No. 7 Section round to the right to create a diversion and moved quickly with the remaining two sections to the SE side of the hill and proceeded to advance up the hill. On this side there was more cover such as boulders. Soon after we again came under MG [machine gun] fire, this time very heavy, and more grenades, but I was able to identify one MG position. Giving this as a target to the nearest Bren gunner, we advanced in short bounds, covered by the Bren, until we were within throwing distance of the nearest MG. Threw some grenades and advanced to the top of hill and immediately gave rapid fire on to the position and then walked forward in line, firing as we went. By this time all the enemy on the hill were killed or wounded.'

Wandless's typically understated report makes light of the heroism and skill he and his men displayed as they stormed the German position, finding two machine guns, five dead and eight wounded. He had only one casualty: a platoon runner hit by grenade fragments.[17]

While the attack was going in, James Hill had noticed three tanks 'firing rather ad lib down the hill'. Thinking this was too good to be true, and that he must do something about it, he grabbed two or three men and moved up the side of the hill where he could see one of the tanks 'blazing away'. It was a small tank, in a 'hull down' position. Hill noted: 'Most armoured vehicles have a little round hole which they can open up to peep through. I put my revolver in the hole and pulled the trigger and of course the bullet went whee-e-e-e! all the way round the inside of the tank. Up went the hatch . . . and out came a chap shouting, "*Italiano! Italiano!*"'

He repeated the trick with the second tank and the result was the same: a hasty capitulation. The third tank was commanded by a 'great big German', a 'much tougher chap' who also came out with his hands up. But he was holding a pistol which, as he jumped down, he aimed at Hill and fired three times, hitting the lieutenant colonel in the chest, neck and arm.

Taken to the foot of the hill, Hill was placed in the sidecar of a captured German motorcycle with his adjutant, Miles Whitelock, who had lost part of his nose, and the pair were driven back to Sidi Nsir 'down a railway track, bumping all the way over the sleepers for five miles or so'. They eventually arrived at Beja where Hill was operated on by Captain Robb and his parachute surgical team, who 'undoubtedly' saved his life.

Hill's gallantry at Gué was rewarded with a DSO and the French *Legion d'Honneur*, the latter medal pinned on his pyjamas in Algiers General Hospital by the imposing figure of the six-foot-three French General Henri Giraud who assumed command of the French forces in North Africa after the assassination of the Vichyiste Admiral François Darlan on 24 December 1942. Pearson and Wandless were both awarded Military Crosses, as was Philip Mellor for his assault on the armoured column near Sidi Nsir a few days earlier.[18]

14

Primus in Carthago
– Tunisia, November–December 1942

THE SKY WAS 'CLEAR and cloudless' as 44 Dakota transport planes flew over the Atlas mountains, heading east towards northern Tunisia, in the early afternoon of 29 November 1942. They were carrying 600 men of the 2nd Parachute Battalion, a troop of sappers from the 1st Parachute Field Squadron, and a section of the 16th Parachute Field Ambulance. Sudden gusts of wind buffeted the planes as they rose and fell in the formation. They were protected by American Lockheed P-38 Lightning fighters, flying directly above, and British Hawker Hurricanes away on the flanks, but no enemy approached. As the mountains gave way to the plains, they lost altitude until they were skimming the dry brown earth.

Finally, after a frustrating wait of two weeks, John Frost and his men were heading into battle – the last of the 1st Parachute Brigade's three battalions to see action in North Africa. The original plan had been for them to drop near the town of Pont du Fahs in northern Tunisia, 'destroy enemy aircraft, stores and petrol there', and then move in two 12-mile jumps north-west and do the same at the airfields at Depienne and Oudna, the latter just 15 miles south of Tunis. They would then try to link up with advance elements of Lieutenant General Anderson's First

Army at St Cyprien. But last-minute intelligence had indicated that there were no Axis planes at either Pont du Fahs or Depienne, so the revised operation was a drop near Depienne, 'an attack on the landing ground at Oudna', and a withdrawal to St Cyprien.

It was, Frost knew, an extremely hazardous mission. They had no transport, unless they captured some, and 'had a long way to go carrying all the ammunition, food, batteries, and other stores we needed for at least five days'. He was, however, reasonably optimistic. There was talk of a combined thrust towards Tunis and he had visions of himself and his men arriving '*Primus in Carthago*',* the heroes of the hour. They had no information about the local inhabitants, but assumed they would be friendly and were taking along a large quantity of francs to ease their passage. More worrying was the lack of intelligence on the size and strength of the opposition. They could only hope, remembered Frost, that the enemy 'would not be able to spare any armour'.

Following the late change of plan, the pilots were hurriedly rebriefed but there was no time for a detailed study of the map to find a suitable dropping zone. Frost would jump, and the others 'take their cue' from him. The first planes took off from Maison Blanche airfield at noon and, after circling for more than an hour to wait for the others to catch up, the convoy headed east.

As they approached their target after a three-hour flight, the country 'appeared to be smooth and level with no obstacles except an odd dried up watercourse and a few clumps of cactus'. As soon as they had passed over Depienne, Frost jumped, the signal for the other sticks to follow.[1]

---

* A reference to the ancient city-state of Carthage, located north of modern Tunis, that was destroyed by the Roman general Scipio Africanus in the 3rd Punic War in 146 BC.

Leading the way for A Company's 1st Platoon was 22-year-old Lieutenant Dennis Rendell, the only son of a director of Schroder's Bank. Born in London and educated at St Albans School, Rendell was commissioned into the Middlesex Regiment in 1941 and volunteered for airborne duty soon after. 'Cheerful and dedicated', he was one of Frost's best subalterns.[2] Once Frost had jumped, he and his platoon followed suit. Rendell landed softly, and 'was at once aware of the silence with no small-arms fire or shell-fire'.

They had landed unopposed and, as it was his first operation, he was heartened at how easy it had been. A company formed up and moved, as planned, to a defensive position north of the dropping zone. The only casualty was a 'Roman candle', caused by a parachute which had failed to open.[3]

Frost, meanwhile, had made for a small mound where he blew on the copper hunting-horn he had brought back from Iraq. Unfortunately, the battalion had been dropped far and wide, with a deep gulley separating some of the sticks from their weapon containers, and it took some time for the men to rally to his call.

Establishing Battalion HQ in some ruins north of Depienne, Frost issued orders to the separate companies by radio: A was to block the road north of the dropping zone, prevent any local inhabitants from leaving, and commandeer any transport; B was to occupy Depienne and also commandeer transport; and C was to take up position south of the drop zone, block the road running east and salvage all chutes and containers. Frost also summoned the company commanders.

As he waited for them to arrive, three armoured cars appeared on the road running north from Depienne. The cars were British, part of the Derbyshire Yeomanry – an encouraging sign as Frost had not expected Allied forces 'in the area so soon'. The troop commander said he was patrolling as far north as Cheylus, part of the way to Oudna, 'where a German road block was suspected'. He returned an hour later with the news that the obstruction was south of Cheylus at a place called Djebel Oust.

When all his company commanders had assembled, Frost took stock. He had lost one man in the drop, and six were injured. The latter were left with the French at Depienne, to be evacuated 'when the opportunity arose'. Frost's other headache was deterring would-be looters who were keen to get their hands on the discarded parachutes. 'Some held their ground until shots were falling right among them,' he recalled, 'and it was maddening to have to waste valuable ammunition in this way.'

Leaving a platoon of C Company to gather stragglers and salvage parachutes, Frost and the rest of the battalion set off for Oudna at midnight, using a country track to bypass the German roadblock. Despite requisitioning mules and carts to transport some of their equipment and supplies, the men struggled under heavy loads. They were led by Lieutenant Ken Morrison of C Company, an outstanding officer in whom everyone had great confidence. Despite the poor maps, Morrison found his way across the difficult terrain.

Fortunately the moon came out, 'and its light was welcome, for gradually the track became steeper and rougher in places and some were having great difficulty getting their mule carts and trollies over the course'. Shortly before dawn, Frost called a halt. They were well into the hills and it would not take them long to get to Oudna once it was light. The soldiers grabbed what rest they could in deep heather beside the track. Frost was too cold to sleep.

Next morning, at 7 a.m., they were overflown by two German aircraft but not observed. With the sun warming their shivering bodies, they set off again and were soon spotted by Arabs who gave away their progress by shouting from village to village, and lighting fires, but there was nothing Frost could do to prevent it.

By 11 a.m. the battalion was deployed in low hills near Prise de l'Eau with a commanding view of Oudna airfield. Apart from one crashed German aircraft, there was no sign of enemy planes. Civilians confirmed that the strip 'was not being used by the Axis and that all the enemy troops were withdrawing to Tunis'. To make certain, Frost ordered A Company to move by the most direct route to Oudna 'with the object of making a complete recce', while the rest of the battalion kept to the high ground.[4]

Advancing on the right of the company front towards Oudna station, its white buildings plainly visible, was Lieutenant Dennis Rendell's 1st Platoon. 'After about 15 minutes,' recalled Rendell, 'the sound of machine-gun fire, very fast and certainly not our Brens, was heard and we all instinctively fell to the ground in the prone position . . . After a few minutes I thought it reasonably safe to continue, so shouted the order to move on, and this we did.'

Despite a 'good deal of noise, chiefly small-arms fire with the occasional crump of a mortar bomb or shell', Rendell and his Platoon HQ got as far as the tiny station which they occupied. They were joined there by men from two of his three sections. Eventually Rendell went to inspect the nearby airstrip and found it empty but for a few abandoned 50-gallon oil drums, 'which suggested some previous aircraft activity'. Back at the station, they could hear 'the sinister sound of engines and there, to the left of the airstrip, were three or four tanks and an armoured car about half a mile away'. As the armoured car approached, Rendell realised their only anti-tank weapon was a Gammon bomb that had to be used at 'very close range'. Luckily it did not come to that. The armoured car – 'huge, with eight wheels and festooned with wireless masts' – drove by at a range of 50 yards and headed 'merrily on towards Tunis'.[5]

The rest of A Company, meanwhile – very skilfully led by 34-year-old Major Dick Ashford, a former NCO in the East Surrey Regiment who was 'socialistically inclined and disliked regular officers on principle' – had ejected the Germans from positions on a low ridge south of Oudna. They were supported by the men of C Company who occupied a farm to their left front. It was now that four German tanks appeared, close to the airfield, and began shelling and machine-gunning C Company's position. 'Ken Morrison was still in the van,' recalled Frost, who had gone forward to halt his leading companies, 'and now he, with a valiant few, wriggled towards [the tanks], intending to grenade them at close quarters. Ken was killed in so doing, and only one survived.'[6]

German Messerschmitt ME-109 fighters then appeared, and made several low strafing runs. But, thanks to their smocks and camouflage nets, the paratroopers were hard to observe from the air and no casualties were inflicted. By 9 p.m., aware that the battalion was very vulnerable to counter-attack, Frost ordered his men back to their original positions near Prise de l'Eau, which most of them reached an hour later. The order did not get through to A Company's forward platoon – Rendell's – which withdrew on its own initiative during the night, and linked up with the rest of the battalion at dawn on 1 December.

Frost – who had spent an uncomfortable night lying back-to-back with his deputy Philip Teichman for warmth – decided that his next move should be towards the First Army. 'We had been told to make for St Cyprien,' he remembered, 'which was well to the north and not many miles from Tunis. However, bearing in mind the armoured thrust which we were expecting, and encouraged by the contact we had with our own armoured cars on the day we landed, I felt that we should stay where we were for the time being, and continue to try and get in touch with First Army by wireless.'

At about 10 a.m., a small column of vehicles, some of them armoured, appeared from the north and began to shell and machine-gun the 2nd Battalion's position from a range of 2,000 yards. The paratroopers responded with 3-inch mortars, landing one bomb 'slap in the middle of a group of vehicles and men' and forcing them to withdraw to a safe distance. A report came from C Company, facing south, that two tanks and an armoured car were approaching, and that they were displaying yellow triangles, the First Army recognition sign. Frost heaved a sigh of relief. 'All our troubles seemed over,' he wrote, 'and we should soon be on our way with more ammunition, our wounded taken care of, and with the tremendous moral support of some of our own armour.'

Then came the crushing news from John Ross, C Company commander, that the tanks were, in fact, German and must have picked up the yellow triangles from the Depienne party. They had, in addition, taken three C Company men prisoner and were demanding the surrender of the rest of the battalion. Soon after that, Frost received a wireless message from the First Army that the armoured thrust on Tunis had been postponed. He felt a mixture of 'sickness, rage, and utter weariness'. He knew that their only hope now was to move to high ground a mile to the north, and then head west across the plain as soon as it got dark. Having destroyed the wireless sets and mortars – which were respectively out of batteries and ammunition – and informed the medic Jock McGavin that he and his ambulance section would have to remain behind with the wounded, they set off for the hills.

The Germans responded by shelling their line of march, and rock splinters caused terrible wounds. Frost passed one man 'whose face had almost been sliced from his head and he held it on with both hands as he was guided along, blind and stumbling'. As the going got tougher, the requisitioned mule transport ran off, taking with them C Company's haversacks and a 'precious set of bagpipes'.

Heat, thirst and exhaustion took their toll as the men climbed on hands and knees. Frost called a halt when they reached the northern slopes of a hill called Sidi Bou Hadjeba where they were fortunate to find a well. Deploying the men on two summits, Frost could see enemy activity on the plain below and knew an attack was imminent.

It began at 3 p.m. with infantry and light tanks assaulting uphill. The paratroopers held their ground, and even managed to disable a couple of tanks with Gammon bombs, but their casualties steadily mounted. They included the dependable Major Frank Cleaver, the 33-year-old commander of B Company from Essex (and, like Ashford, promoted from the ranks), who 'was suddenly struck down while he was talking to some of his HQ.'

With the enemy pressure at its height, and Frost wondering how much longer they could hold on, enemy fighter planes appeared overhead. But instead of attacking the embattled paratroopers, they mistakenly opened fire on their own side in the valley, giving Frost's men just enough breathing space to survive the day.

They set off after dark, heading west in company groups to reduce the risk of detection. One platoon was left behind to collect the wounded. 'It meant,' wrote Frost, 'that they were almost certain to be made prisoner, but the coming cold of the night, and the uncertainty of the behaviour of the local Tunisians, required that our men be collected and protected despite the cost. "C" Company had practically ceased to exist, and among the killed was Henry Cecil, one of our best-loved and most cheerful subalterns.' Since the drop, the battalion had lost a quarter of its men.

Moving with his Battalion HQ group, Frost called a halt at 1 a.m. When they continued the march two hours later, Major

Philip Teichman, his deputy, and Captain Short, the adjutant, were both missing. The HQ group eventually found refuge in a farm north-west of the Djebel El Mengoub, and at 10 a.m. was joined by A Company.[7] The farm 'lay on the southern slopes of a gentle rise, surrounded by thick cactus hedges which as obstacles were as effective as barbed wire'. There was 'plenty of cover, abundant water and fairly solid buildings'. The Arab owner was friendly, and provided the paratroopers with eggs and other fresh food for their first cooked meal since landing. They were also able to wash and dry their clothes. With the addition of A Company, and the fact that he now had every approach to the farm well covered, Frost would have felt reasonably secure but for the acute shortage of ammunition. To rectify the problem, he asked the intrepid Lieutenant Euen Charteris, one of the heroes of Bruneval and now his intelligence officer, to try to contact the nearest First Army troops who, according to the farmer, were a few miles to the west at a place called Furna. They were to return 'as soon as possible and not later than dark'.

In the early afternoon, German troops were observed setting up machine guns and mortars on a ridge a few hundred yards to the north. Facing the ridge was Dennis Rendell's No. 1 Platoon. A little earlier, Rendell had been 'quietly having a shit' beyond the cactus hedge when he noticed a couple of dots moving along the skyline. Someone was looking at him, or more likely the Battalion position. He quickly finished his toilet and rejoined Platoon HQ, only to find Captain Keith Mountford, the company second-in-command, who told him they would be pulling out as soon as it was dark.

Rendell explained what he had seen, and together they studied the ridge through their glasses. By now there were several dots, easily identifiable as helmets. Who were they? 'Maybe they are Yanks?' suggested Mountford.

But a salvo of mortar bombs, followed by machine-gun fire,

answered that question. They were Germans. Despite the appalling turn of events, Mountford made Rendell smile, and helped to lessen the tension and fear, by saying: 'You know, Dennis, you are probably unique – you must be one of the very few British officers to be caught with his trousers down in the face of the enemy!'

The Germans opened fire at 3 p.m., shortly after the Arab farmer had departed with his family, his friendly smiles replaced with reproachful scowls. To conserve ammunition. Frost had told his men to hold their fire until the enemy were within 50 yards. This passivity seemed to confuse the Germans who sent a small party forward at 5 p.m. to reconnoitre the northern perimeter. They were shot down by Rendell's men, though he 'had a job to stop the men firing'. A little later, they 'scuppered a more determined attack in the same way, but this time the effect was more deadly and the control much tighter'. By now, the 'light was beginning to fade, and various farm buildings were on fire; most of them had straw roofs'. The fires 'gave off a ghostly light which, combined with the smoke, made accurate shooting impossible', and this was a concern because they knew the Germans were getting ever closer.

Mountford reappeared to tell Rendell that the signal to move would be Frost sounding 'gone away' on his hunting horn. The plan, explained Mountford, was for the battalion to withdraw through the farm and head south-east for the Djebel El Mengoub where they would rally before continuing their march to the west. As Charteris had not returned from Furna, Frost had decided to head for Medjez-el-Bab, now back in Allied hands, instead. Pausing their chat, they could hear German voices on the far side of the cactus hedge. They responded by throwing grenades which burst with 'satisfying crumps, and this was followed by cries of pain'. They parted soon after: Mountford returning to Company HQ, and Rendell to brief his NCOs on the plan.

Soon after dark, the German machine-gun and mortar fire intensified. Hearing Frost's hunting horn, Rendell and his men began to withdraw. As he crawled from his Platoon HQ, Rendell could hear mortar bombs falling nearby. His last memory, before he lost consciousness, was of a 'ghastly smell of sulphur just like school chemistry experiments'. When he came to, the following morning, someone was pulling at his belt. He looked up to see a German soldier trying to remove his pistol from its holster. He tried to help him, but failed because his hands were too cold and he was shivering. His right leg was slick with blood, and his trousers torn. The German pulled him to his feet, and dumped him gently but firmly into a motorcycle sidecar. He was taken to an aid post, where he was joined by a few men from B Company and some sappers. 'For you the war is over,' they told him.★[8]

The remnants of the battalion, meanwhile, had rallied on the high ground to the south-east of the farm to the sound of Frost's hunting-horn. Of the original 200 men, only 110 had made the rendezvous. They started heading north-west towards the main Tunis–Medjez-el-Bab road, but on reaching a secondary road at Bou Khail, Frost decided to use that to reach Medjez. They stopped once to fill their water bottles at a well, and again at midnight for an hour's rest. Frost called in the officers to discuss their next move. But even as he was speaking, they all fell asleep, only to be 'woken by the cold about half an hour later'.

At 3 a.m. with the going much easier, they noticed another

★ After treatment for his wounds, Rendell was flown to Italy and held in Sulmona prisoner-of-war camp in central Italy. During the confusion that followed Italy's armistice with the Allies in September 1943, Rendell got away with some other officers and helped to run an escape organisation. A famous picture was taken of him shooting an air rifle at a fairground in Sulmona in November 1943, flanked by German servicemen who were unaware of his true identity. He eventually returned to the UK, via Rome, in July 1944. He was awarded a Military Cross for his gallant service in North Africa, and an MBE for escaping.

column on the track ahead of them. It turned out to be Captain Dennis Vernon and his sappers who had missed the rendezvous after the break-out from the farm. Soon after, they found another large farm with many outbuildings and plenty of water, occupied by a very charming French lady and her two daughters who were only too happy to give the paratroopers a refuge. Their invitation to the officers to take breakfast 'was most welcome, particularly as champagne was served'.

The women said they lived in no-man's land and never knew which side was going to turn up next. This was confirmed when an employee rode up with news that a German armoured column was approaching. Frost ordered a hasty departure. Near Ksan Tyr, barely 10 miles from Medjez, they were resting in an olive grove when three German armoured cars approached a nearby road junction. There was no need to issue any orders. 'All ranks froze where they stood or lay,' wrote Frost, 'and absolute silence prevailed. The prowlers made off down the road to Tunis before we restarted our march.'

They had barely covered two miles when they saw armoured half-tracks moving across open ground to their right. The half-tracks approached, their heavy machine guns at the ready. Luckily, they were Americans from the US 1st Armored Division. They seemed to know nothing about the paratroopers, but agreed to take their walking wounded and a small recce party with them back to Medjez and to report their whereabouts. Frost went with them and eventually reached the headquarters of the British 78th (Battleaxe) Division at Oued Zaaga where he reported to Major General Vyvyan Evelegh. Frost was told that the main battle was being fought further north at Tebourba, on a separate axis of advance, which was probably why so little interest had been taken in his 'abortive mission'. Yet Evelegh reassured him that if the paratroopers had achieved nothing else, they had 'at least drawn off a considerable number of enemy mobile and armoured troops from the main battle', and he agreed to make a sortie the next day to try to find the rest of Frost's battalion.

But the recce was never made because of a false alarm that night, 3/4 December, claiming that Medjez was about to be attacked by German paratroopers. Frost and his men were accordingly deployed to the west of the town in support of a battalion of French Colonials. When the attack did not materialise, the paratroopers were taken back to the nearby Arab village of Sloughia to recuperate, where they were joined by a few stragglers, including 21-year-old Captain John Ross, who had been Frost's second-in-command at Bruneval, and a handful of C Company men. Ross was 'still tender of years for his rank and responsibility', noted Frost, 'but a great heart beat beneath a somewhat dour exterior'.

There was hardly anyone left from B Company. Both Major Philip Teichman, Frost's deputy, and the adjutant Jock Short had been killed with that company 'when they were isolated and attacked by an armoured column'. Euen Charteris had also lost his life attempting to get through to Furna. 'He had been,' noted Frost, 'a magnificently enthusiastic Intelligence Officer, whom I had always thought would bear a charmed life, especially after his amazing performance at Bruneval. However I was soon delighted to hear that Douglas Crawley of B [Company], who had been temporarily blinded on the Bou Hadjeba, had been led all the way back to Medjez by Ronald Stark, another officer of great determination.'

Frost's greatest regret was having to abandon his wounded. On the basis of his briefing from Brigadier Ted Flavell, commander of the 1st Parachute Brigade, he had assumed that units of the First Army would be quickly on hand. Instead, he and his men had 'been virtually abandoned among an apparently hostile Arab population to compete against mobile armoured troops who were fully supported and informed by their own air forces'.

While he was proud of what his men had achieved against the odds, he felt bitter that his fine battalion had been 'cut to pieces on such a useless venture'. He could understand the difficulties of finding a worthwhile mission when the situation in Tunisia was so fluid, and intelligence was incomplete. What he could not forgive, however, once the decision had been taken to use his battalion, was the failure of Forward Headquarters to make every effort to support it, 'to verify information, to get and keep contact and, when their own optimistic appreciations had proved to be so false', they should have 'redoubled their efforts to do some of these things'. Instead, they did nothing.

The real mistake, however, was for the task to have been accepted 'on such flimsy information'. Why had the RAF not been asked to fly a reconnaissance mission to confirm the need for a whole battalion to be dropped? Why had local Frenchmen not been contacted for information? 'The fact of the matter,' wrote Frost, 'was that the British Army had no idea how or when the new airborne capability should be used and our own Brigade Headquarters set-up was woefully inadequate to ensure that really dreadful errors should not occur.'[9]

They could not know it at the time, but the 2nd Battalion's drop at Depienne was the last airborne operation of the North African campaign. Thereafter, as the remaining Axis forces were squeezed between the First Army advancing from the west, and the Eighth Army from the south, the men of the 1st Parachute Brigade were used as conventional infantry.

The previous operation – Freshman – had been a one-off raid with an ambitious strategic objective: to cripple Germany's nuclear programme. It did not succeed, but lessons were learned, including the imperative for better training and intelligence, and a closer liaison with the pilots who would deliver them to the target. Worryingly, many of the same failings were then repeated in North Africa.

Among the recommendations made after Torch by Group Captain Norman and Major General Browning were the need for aerial photographs and better maps, and the use of British aircraft and crews – familiar from training – to carry the men into action on both day and night operations. 'In spite of the gallant efforts of the American air crews,' they noted, 'the drops were inaccurate and the men were widely dispersed. Had the troops met enemy opposition immediately on landing, the effects might well have been disastrous.' True, but the needless destruction of Frost's isolated 2nd Parachute Battalion in the skirmishes that followed was bad enough.

Moreover, the lack of an expert in airborne matters at either Allied Force or First Army Headquarters 'had the inevitable result that 1 Parachute Brigade were not used to their full airborne capacity and arrangements before each drop were not as good as they should and could have been'.

Above all, there was a painful sense of missed opportunity. North Africa should have been the perfect theatre of war for airborne operations; the huge distances involved, the broken terrain, and the absence of prepared defensive positions meant there were 'great opportunities'. No other troops could compare in terms of 'strategic mobility' and the sudden arrival of parachutists where they were least expected could have had 'paralysing effects' on the enemy.

At the very least, the 1st Parachute Brigade should have been dropped on Tunis 'before about 23rd November', and not wasted on relatively minor operations. The messianic Major General Browning was convinced that, had the whole of the 1st Airborne Division been used to spearhead the advance from Bône to Tunis, it would have 'forestalled the Germans' and 'ended the campaign at one blow'.[10]

15

Plugging the Gaps
– Tunisia, January–February 1943

THIRTY MILES SOUTH-EAST OF Algiers, at the centre of the Mitidja plain, lies the small town of Boufarik. Founded by French settlers in 1836, it had been built on a rectangular plan with low white-washed buildings arranged in long, straight shaded streets. Its economy was based on intensive farming: vines, cereals and tobacco. But it was best known for its oranges which, in 1933, an Algerian-born French shopkeeper had used to make a sparkling soft drink called Naranjina. Today it is sold all over the world as Orangina.★

On 10 January 1943, after a three-day train journey from Souk el Khemis in Tunisia, the 1st Parachute Brigade – minus Frost's 2nd Battalion, which the 78th Division had refused to release because of a lack of men – arrived in Boufarik to rest, refit and absorb replacements. It had been quite a journey, with the officers travelling in railway carriages and the men in cattle trucks hung with an assortment of cooking tins and pots. There were frequent stops – a good thing, noted the recently promoted Lieutenant Colonel Alastair Pearson of the 1st Battalion, 'as there were no

---

★ In 1951, the shopkeeper's son Jean-Claude relaunched the drink with its new name and a distinctive 8-ounce bottle shaped like an orange.

washing or other conveniences on board'. He added: 'Every time the train stopped the men were out like a flash to answer the call of nature or to get hot water for shaving from the engine driver. Then on we'd go with horses or Arab beggars chasing after us.'[1]

The long, tiring journey away from the front was worth it as they approached Boufarik through acres and acres of 'big, beautiful jaffa-sized oranges just waiting to be picked'. Corporal 'Lofty' Curtis, for one, could not wait to try a few. They were billeted in a long, low white-painted building, 'clean, spacious and, above all, dry'. The paratroopers competed for the best spots, usually 'staked by a kit bag flying through the air to land before anyone else's'.

When they tired of eating oranges and Boufarik's limited opportunities for entertainment, Curtis and his mates were taken by liberty truck to nearby Algiers, with its terraced boulevards, houses with bright red rooftops and shuttered windows, and 'pleasant parks with French and Arab intermingled with American and English servicemen taking a leisurely walk'. Those in need of 'horizontal refreshment' were wise to stick to the properly regulated French brothels in the city centre. 'On entering,' recalled Curtis, 'it was like approaching a smart hotel, with its spotless frontage and glass doors. But inside the aroma of cheap perfume knocked you for six, the soft lights dazzled you, and quite lush young mademoiselles glided by most flimsily dressed, leaving very little for the imagination to ponder.'

Curtis and a pal surveyed the scene from the bar, drinking a 'ghastly' overpriced beer before switching to wine. The young Londoner was intrigued by the sheer variety of soldiers in the brothel, particularly the Americans who were having a field day with their 'fat wallets'. Girls sat with their customers 'beneath dim lights, kissing and cuddling as if they were life-long lovers'.

A nod from the girl and the 'soldier would eagerly grip his partner's arm, then glide her almost impatiently through a curtained opening to a place where he could satisfy his whim'. Almost overpowered by the fug of cigar smoke, perfume and body odour, Curtis and his mate left to find some grub.[2]

While his men enjoyed themselves, Alastair Pearson was beating off not one but two attempts to usurp his command. The first was from Lieutenant Colonel Geoffrey Gofton Salmond, the former commander of the 2nd Battalion who had been replaced by Frost while ill. Healthy again, he arrived at Boufarik and advised Pearson he was taking over the 1st Battalion. 'I told him to get lost,' recalled Pearson. 'I was the CO till somebody senior to me told me otherwise or until I got it in writing. He went off in a huff.'

The second challenge – from James Hill, the former CO – was more serious. Since his grievous wounding in the attack at Gué on 22 November, Hill had been impatient to return to the battalion and, though forbidden to take exercise, had climbed out of his window at night to stroll through the hospital grounds. Seven weeks later, he declared himself fit and discharged himself. But he failed to convince either Brigadier Ted Flavell or Doc Haggie, the 1st Battalion's medic, that he was ready to resume his duties and, instead, was sent back to England on medical grounds where he eventually took command of the recently formed 9th Parachute Battalion, part of the 3rd Parachute Brigade. Pearson, as a result, was confirmed as CO of 1st Battalion.

On 24 January, the 1st Parachute Brigade – still minus the 2nd Battalion – was moved back to the front for infantry duty, this time with the 6th Armoured Division. It travelled by sea from Algiers to Bône, on the 'very comfortable' commando troopship HMS *Princess Beatrix*, and then on by road in the pouring rain to Souk el Arba in Tunisia where an obstreperous military official tried to block the 1st Battalion's advance. Pearson had a blazing row with him and said he was going through his 'bloody town' whether he liked it or not. The town major threatened a court-martial, but eventually backed down and Pearson's men reached Ghardimaou in the early hours of the morning. There was no food to be had, and everyone 'crawled into bed exhausted, wet and hungry'. A day later, they reached their lying-up area in a rain-soaked orange grove at El Aroussa, 20 miles south of Medjez-el-Bab, after a hellish night drive.[3]

Elsewhere, the fortunes of war had changed in favour of the Allies. In the British Solomon Islands in the south Pacific, American marines and army troops had held on to Guadalcanal after a brutal five-month arm-wrestle with the Japanese in the air, at sea and on land. It was a pivotal battle: described by a Japanese general as the 'graveyard' of his army;[4] and by the US Army Chief of Staff General George C. Marshall as the 'turning point in the Pacific' thanks to 'the resolute defence of these Marines and the desperate gallantry of our naval task forces'.[5]

On 23 January, the second-last day of the top-level Anglo-American conference at Casablanca in Morocco, where Churchill, Roosevelt and their respective staffs had met to plan the next phase of Allied strategy *after* Axis forces had been cleared from North Africa, news arrived that General Montgomery's Eighth Army had captured the Libyan port of Tripoli without a fight. At Stalingrad, the encircled German Sixth Army was about to surrender to the Russians, a catastrophic defeat that would mark a turning-point on the Eastern Front.

Yet, despite the optimism at Casablanca, the fighting in Tunisia was far from over. Since the turn of the year, the front line had run south from Cap Serrat on the coast to Bou Arada, via Medjez, and then along the edge of the Eastern Dorsale mountain range to Sened, leaving the Axis in control of the long stretch of coastal plain that runs from Tunis to the Libyan border. On 18 January, General der Panzertruppe Hans-Jürgen von

General Sir John Dill, Chief of the Imperial General Staff (CIGS), inspecting parachute troops at the Central Landing Establishment at RAF Ringway near Manchester, December 1940.

Parachute troops on parade in front of a Whitley bomber at Ringway, January 1941.

The Tragino Aqueduct.

X Troop (No. 11 Special Air Service Battalion) who participated in Operation Colossus – February 1941.

A 'stick' of parachute troops entering a Whitley at Ringway, April 1941.

Parachute troops jump
from a Whitley during
a demonstration for
the king near Windsor,
25 May 1941.

Parachute troops, bare-
headed and wearing
'jump jackets', in
Norwich during exercises
in Eastern Command,
23 June 1941.

Low-level oblique of the 'Würzburg' radar near Bruneval, France, taken by Sqn Ldr A.E. Hill on 5 December 1941. Photos like this enabled a raiding force to locate, and make off with, the radar's vital components in February 1942 for analysis in Britain.

Wing Commander Charles Pickard, CO of No. 51 Squadron, inspects a captured German helmet with troops from 2nd Parachute Battalion after the Bruneval raid, 28 February 1942.

Major General F.A.M. 'Boy' Browning observes paratroop training at Netheravon.

Paratroopers inside the fuselage of a Whitley, August 1942.

Vermork heavy water plant in Norway, target of Operation Freshman.

Officers from the 2nd Battalion, Parachute Regiment resting near Beja after returning from a drop on Depienne. From left to right: Captain Stark, Lieutenant Brayley and Major Ashford.

A jeep being loaded in a Waco glider, prior to Operation Ladbroke in Sicily, July 1943.

British airborne troops wait to board an American Waco CG-4A glider, July 1943.

The Primosole Bridge after its recapture, July 1943.

Primosole Bridge, 1943: the Royal Engineers are shown repairing damage to the bridge over the Simeto after its recapture.

British airborne troops approaching Taranto in a landing craft, during the invasion of Italy, 14 September 1943.

Major General Richard Gale, commanding the 6th Airborne Division, addresses his men (4–5 June 1944)

Arnim, the Axis commander in northern Tunisia, had launched a series of attacks against French units holding the passes of the Eastern Dorsale, with a diversionary attack by the 10th Panzer Division in the north at Bou Arada where the British gunners of the 17th Field Regiment were supporting the French. The latter attack was beaten off; but further south, Axis forces (including the dreaded Mark VI 'Tiger' tank) advanced into the Ousseltia Valley and captured 3,500 French troops.[6]

Among the British and American troops who were sent to plug the gaps were the men of the 1st Parachute Brigade. On 1 February, Pearson's 1st Battalion was ordered to capture two German-held features astride the Bou Arada–Pont-du-Fahs road: the vital 2,000-foot high massif of Djebel Mansour and its neighbouring feature El Alliliga. They would be supported by a company of the French Foreign Legion and a battery of the 17th Field Regiment, while a second company of the Foreign Legion created a diversion at the southern end of El Alliliga.[7]

On the morning of 2 February, a 'warm clear day', the battalion struck camp and marched to the jumping-off point that Pearson and a fighting patrol led by Captain Coxon had selected the night before (capturing three Germans from the Mountain Division, but losing Lieutenant Norton, who was shot in the thigh, in the process). It was an arduous march, as Lieutenant Alan Clements, commander of T Company's 9 Platoon, recalled, 'but this was not regretted, since the hills we climbed covered us all the time from the view of the enemy'. Finally they arrived at the back of a height known as Djebel Kentlar, where they were fed and told to rest under the trees until evening. Clements and the officers, meanwhile, moved to a vantage point held by the Foreign Legion to observe the objective. It lay 'long and green, rising from what seemed to be a perfectly level plain of a mile's width'. Its 'even mass' seemed to be broken by just a single gully, towards its right-hand end, and, even with binoculars, they could see no sign of the enemy. The gully was in fact the dividing point between Mansour and the neighbouring El Alliliga (a 'long whale back'), to the south.

The mood among the officers was 'elated' and 'carefree'. One was Lieutenant Philip Mellor, the London-born son of a High Court judge and Cambridge University blue, who entertained the others by adopting an 'inimitable American drawl'. Meanwhile, the Foreign Legionnaires – proper soldiers, with their bushy beards – waxed lyrical about their newly issued Garand M1 semi-automatic rifles, courtesy of the US Army. Once they had all had a good look at the mountain through a periscope, the company commanders briefed their subalterns on the plan of battle. The battalion would advance up the more gentle northerly slope on a two-company front: R on the left and T on the right. Battalion Headquarters would follow T Company, with S Company in reserve. When Djebel Mansour had been taken, they would move on to El Alliliga.

Returning to their lying-up position at dusk, the officers ate a hot meal and then tried to get some rest. Lieutenant Alan Clements – whose mother had spent so many months scrutinising a photograph of paratroopers in the *Evening News*, in case she could spot him – lay on his back awake, looking at the stars and contemplating the battle. He felt 'quite composed', and was 'more interested in, than concerned, for the prospects of the coming action'. As he did every evening, he recited the Lord's Prayer, finding comfort in the beauty of the words.

Roused at 12.30 a.m. on 3 February, the battalion set off half an hour later in a long column of route with R Company in the lead, followed by T Company, Battalion HQ and S Company. Moving in single file by the light of the moon, they followed the same tortuous route – twisting and turning, ascending steeply and then descending just as abruptly – that the officers had taken the night before. Eventually they reached the mouth of the gorge where white tapes had been put out to mark the route. Far from being the flat stretch of country they had imagined, the plain was 'cut by numerous gullies which proved arduous in the crossing'. Generally, the men marched 'very well under their heavy loads' and kept their night discipline by not talking. But the game was given away, nonetheless, when someone in the leading company fired a careless shot.

Clements later absolved the miscreant by suggesting that the enemy were already expecting an attack. They certainly were now. As the paratroopers neared the end of their march, noted Clements, 'the country opened out and we traversed a level plan with Djebel Mansour broad on the starboard bow'. The mountain seemed 'grey and forbidding', a huge mass rising from the flats 'like a great whale'. Skirting a farm, whose dogs raised a terrific din, they reached the base of the mountain at 4 a.m. and lay down to wait for zero hour.

At 5 a.m. they crossed the starting line and began to climb through thick undergrowth. 'We had only advanced a few paces,' wrote Clements, 'when the firing started, sporadic at first but swelling in volume. It was machine-gun fire and all tracer. The crash of a mortar bomb occasionally varied the high staccato of this fusillade. These bursts of fire [send] coloured parabolas across the darkness.'

Noticing that most of this fire was un-aimed – either wild or on a fixed line – Clements was not overly concerned. Yet he found it increasingly difficult to keep in contact with Sergeant Osborne and the rest of his platoon, and soon drew well ahead, stopping only for the 30 seconds that it took for the enemy's flickering white Very lights to burn out. He saw no enemy, but fired two pistol shots at the flash from a nearby machine gun that he later suspected was British. Either way, it kept firing.

Finally reaching the summit with other members of T Company, he gave orders for two Italian prisoners – 'wretched, shivering little boys' who had been found in a slit trench just under the crest – to be taken to the rear. Delighted to hear the voice of Major Bull, his company commander, rising above the noise and firing, he ran over and learned that two of his fellow officers had been wounded. The plan now, said Bull, was to advance south along the crest to the gulley that led to the neighbouring height of El Alliliga, clearing enemy trenches as they went. Clements's No. 9 Platoon would keep to the right.

They moved off and soon realised it was not flat table land, but rather an undulating piece of ground, varying in width, and clothed in thick undergrowth. Progress in the dark was slow, with Major Bull well to the fore and Clements slightly to his right. They discovered that the summit was crisscrossed with small trenches, some occupied, others abandoned. Approaching one, with grenades going off all around him, Clements felt a sharp pain in the left shoulder and fell to his knees. 'I'm hit!' he shouted, half in shock.

Corporal Meadows ran over, took a primed grenade from Clements's hand and threw it down the hill where it exploded harmlessly. 'You all right?' asked Major Bull.

Clements nodded. Adrenaline had numbed the pain. He got back to his feet and set off with Sergeant Thornton at his side. A short way ahead, they were challenged in German, probably by a defender who had mistaken them for his retreating comrades. Thornton responded with a quick burst from his Sten gun.[8]

Also advancing along the top of the mountain was Private A. A. Brown, a Bren gunner in R Company. 'I came to a German officer lying face downward,' he remembered, 'coughing his life away, a horrible sound, and as I stood there in a flash Sergeant Guest had run up to him, relieved him of his wristwatch and Luger, and scuttled away again. A group of about 20 Germans had surrendered and two or three riflemen had them covered and were shepherding them along the rear.' At that moment, the

No. 2 on his Bren appeared and, drawing his Colt .45 semi-automatic, started to shoot at the prisoners. Fortunately, he was a poor marksman and no one was hit before shouts from Brown and the escort brought him to his senses.

Brown and his No. 2 should have continued on to the gully that led to El Alliliga. Instead they set up the Bren at a point overlooking the main road, on the far side of the mountain from where they had launched the attack. They were collecting rocks to build a defensive sangar when Brown received a sledgehammer blow in the left hip. He had been shot. Rolling over, he undid his trousers to inspect the wound. It was a jagged bleeding hole that extended from hip to groin, and poking out of his abdomen was the sharp point of a bullet. Pulling it out, he applied a dressing to the injury and did up his trousers to create a pressure point. He then checked the two fused grenades in the lower pocket of his jumping smock, and found that one had absorbed the shock of the bullet which had hit his abdomen. He threw the grenade down the mountain.[9]

Lieutenant Clements, meanwhile, was evading the fixed line of machine-gun fire which periodically swept the summit by keeping below the lip on its extreme right. Eventually, he and his remaining men reached 'a truly immense fissure cutting into the mountain side'. They plunged down the steep hill, negotiating the 'most appalling scrub', and on the gully floor found Majors Bull and Conron with the remnants of T and R Companies: a total of only four officers and 40 men out of an initial 200. Conron was very irritable and out of sorts, telling Clements that he was in the wrong place. 'The width of the mountain had caused R and T companies to contract together,' recalled Clements, 'and this brought me next to him, still on the right, which is where I should have been. He seemed to imagine that I was wrong or lost or something. He apologised later.'

Despite being down to just a handful of men, Bull and Conron had already decided to continue with the original plan to capture El Alliliga which, from their position in the gully, rose up before them like the bulwark of a ship. As they climbed, there was more shouting and firing, and hand-to-hand fighting. Four German prisoners were captured in one dugout. It was here that Clements dumped his webbing because the shoulder straps had been cut through by shrapnel. With dawn breaking, they burst through some trees into a clearing where a party of Germans immediately threw up their hands. Before they could disarm them, the Germans had darted into the undergrowth, followed by a hail of bullets.

Soon after, Clements and a Bren gunner called Bowmer were moving forward when they heard a burst of firing and saw Private Hughes, a tall man armed with a rifle and bayonet, go down screaming. He had been shot and killed by Germans manning a trench. 'Bowmer let them have a whole magazine firing from the hip,' wrote Clements, 'and I contributed with my pistol. Then we charged and found three Germans cowering in a veritable spasm of terror at the bottom of the trench and a fourth already passing out.'

Other parachutists now appeared and, having witnessed Hughes' death, were demanding an eye for an eye. Clements refused to bow to mob justice, and instead ordered the captives to be taken to the rear. He doubted his instructions were carried out. 'I rather think,' he later confessed, 'the Germans were shot. I have never before seen such abject terror on men's faces.'

Having picked up a German Mauser semi-automatic pistol to replace his own pistol, Clements was approaching El Alliliga's bare summit when he met two officers: Major Bull and Second Lieutenant 'Ginger' Rickey. The major seemed calm, but was clearly unhappy at the way the battle was unfolding; Rickey had blood on his face and looked shaken.

Bursts of machine-gun fire forced Clements to the ground. He took cover with Sergeant Osborne behind a rotten tree stump, but the bullets simply tore through the wood, fanning Clements' face and body, and hitting Osborne in the helmet and head. 'Oh, sir! Oh, sir!' he moaned.

It was 9 a.m. and, with barely 30 men left, Major Bull thought it was best to withdraw. 'That summit,' remembered Clements, 'was perfectly bare and could be swept by fire. Mortars might have neutralised it for a time, but where were our mortars? So it was decided to retreat: Conron agreed with Major Bull and accepted his orders.'

Clements was given the thankless task of covering the retreat with Bowmer and his Bren gun. They chose a good position, 100 yards below the summit, and waited side by side. Suddenly a large party of Germans – some wearing Afrika Korps sun helmets, firing their weapons and shouting – retook the position they had just vacated. They both opened fire and saw the Germans 'going down like nine-pins'. Eventually they rejoined the remnants of the two companies manning a defensive position in the gully between the two heights of El Alliliga and Djebel Mansour.[10]

16

'We lost a lot of grand fellows'
– Djebel Mansour, 3–5 February 1943

THE 1ST PARACHUTE BATTALION's successful night attack on Djebel Mansour was a considerable achievement. Yet by narrowly failing also to capture the neighbouring feature of El Alliliga, which lay a short way to the south, the battalion had left itself in a precarious position, facing an enemy on two fronts. To shorten his defensive lines, therefore, Lieutenant Colonel Alastair Pearson ordered Major Bull to pull back the remnants of R and T Companies to the summit of Djebel Mansour.[1] 'After an exhausting climb,' remembered Lieutenant Alan Clements, 'I arrived at that part of the summit which T Company was to occupy for the next 36 hours. Just below the crest were numerous dug-outs.'

The battalion was deployed on Mansour with T Company on the right, R Company in the centre and S Company on the left, the latter occupying a northern extension of the height known as Hill 648. After a unit of the Foreign Legion had arrived to take over Hill 648 in the afternoon, S Company joined the others on the thin spine that formed the summit of Djebel Mansour. Battalion Headquarters was in a large dugout behind the junction of R and S Companies.

Setting up his platoon headquarters in a two-man dugout with a branch roof, with Bull's HQ a little further down the slope, Clements was shocked to see the original 16 survivors of T Company gradually swell to 60. 'Most of these new arrivals,' he noted, 'were fresh as paint, all with the proper amount of equipment and ammunition – 110 rounds and two grenades. They all had stories of being on some other job, such as shepherding prisoners or looking after a wounded man, or getting involved with other companies. I gave some of these gentlemen very black looks. There was no excuse at all for their dereliction. They were given a good lead by their officers. They only had to follow.' One of the offenders, Clements was horrified to admit, was the company sergeant major, who should have known better.

After a medical orderly had applied a dressing to his shoulder wound, Clements received a visit from Alastair Pearson, who himself had been wounded in the foot. Pearson told the young officer what had happened to the rest of the battalion. 'S Company,' recorded Clements, 'was the most badly cut up. They had arrived late at the foot of the mountain and do not seem to have been coolly controlled. They were pinned down for some time on the northern slopes of the mountain by machine-gun posts that we had left behind in our advance – probably only one, but these things are always magnified. They were now reorganising at the far end of the mountain.'

Soon some of the more serious casualties were brought on stretchers to T Company's position. Placed in unoccupied dugouts and trenches, and covered with captured blankets and greatcoats, they all looked grey and cold.[2] Much of the day was spent digging in and evacuating the 105 wounded and 35 prisoners. Corporal Reg Curtis carried a mate called Taffy, who had been shot five times ('all clean flesh wounds'), and was 'saturated in blood but cheerful', back to the aid station in the valley below. It took Curtis three hours to complete the exhausting six-mile trek through 'wooded country, ravines and open waste'. Harassed by shells and sniper fire, and at times crawling with Taffy on his back, Curtis eventually reached the aid post. 'I saw him put into a Jeep with other wounded,' he recorded. 'That was the last I saw or heard of him.'[3]

Meanwhile, Pearson had requested urgent support from a nearby battalion of the Grenadier Guards. The response – conveyed by Major Peter Cleasby-Thompson when he arrived with a mule train loaded with ammunition and rations in the afternoon – was that the Guards would attack the southern end of El Alliliga that afternoon. The attack failed, prompting the commander of the 1st Guards Brigade to agree to make a fresh attempt on the El Alliliga feature by the whole of the 3rd Grenadier Guards the following day.[4]

That night, 3/4 February, Lieutenant Alan Clements was ordered to man a listening post well beyond the defensive perimeter in case the enemy attacked from El Alliliga. Taking five men with him, he set up the post behind some small trees, 100 yards down the hill. Though desperately tired, he found it impossible to sleep when it was not his turn to keep watch because it was so bitterly cold. On duty, he remained motionless as he stared at the floor of the gully and the slopes of El Alliliga beyond, watching for any sign of movement. It was a spooky thought that the enemy might be forming up in the darkness. The only sound was the occasional shell fired by British 25-pounders 'which swished overhead and landed with a thump on Alliliga'. He withdrew the patrol just as dawn was breaking, and had never been happier to reach British lines. It felt, he wrote, 'like returning home'.

After a breakfast of two squares of the 'sickly emergency ration', some chocolate, biscuits, tinned pears and half a pint of tea, Clements went for a walk around the 1st Battalion's defensive perimeter. At the far end he shared a flask of wine with 23-year-old Lieutenant Bob Wharrier from Wickford, Essex, in a dugout overlooking Hill 648. Wharrier broke the news that Philip Mellor, the popular lieutenant who had amused them with an American drawl, had died, 'which hurt me very much', wrote Clements. 'His leg had been severed by a mortar bomb in S Company's assault and as he lay a bullet had penetrated his head. He spent his last few moments with [S Company's commander, Major] Martin, imploring him not to worry about him, but to move on with the company.'

Clements also visited the Foreign Legion detachment on Hill 648, and picked up some German postcards and rifle ammunition from the abandoned German dugouts, then returned to T Company in time to witness the 3rd Grenadier Guards' assault on El Alliliga. It began, just before 3 p.m., with a heavy barrage on the crest of the hill, which then lifted to the neighbouring heights. They could see 'small steel-helmeted figures slowly ascending the hill in an open formation'. Soon they were 'winding in and out of the trees and were lost to sight in the thicker foliage'. The firing and shelling continued for two hours, then died down. The result of the attack was uncertain, but there was no sign of a success signal being fired from the summit.[5]

In fact, the 3rd Grenadiers had only been able to advance two-thirds of the way up the slope of El Alliliga, failing to stop the German troops on the summit from shooting at Pearson's men on Mansour. The situation worsened when the Legionnaires on Hill 648 were overrun by a German counter-attack during the morning of 5 February, leaving the paratroopers trapped between two hostile forces. 'By now,' noted Lieutenant Colonel Pearson, 'we were in big trouble; we needed reinforcements PDQ [pretty damn quick] as we'd suffered a lot of casualties and our mortars had run out of ammunition. But I decided to hang on as long as possible.'

At 10.10 a.m., under heavy shell and mortar fire, Pearson radioed for permission to withdraw. It was denied. Instead,

Brigadier Ted Flavell, commander of the 1st Parachute Brigade, wanted Pearson's 1st Battalion to join the 3rd Grenadiers on El Alliliga and form a 'tight perimeter'. Pearson felt this was 'impossible as the intervening ground was under fire and that it would entail coming down the hill and then going up again to obtain a covered approach'.

At 10.30 the German mortars ceased fire, which meant an assault was imminent. Fifteen minutes later, by which time the enemy had closed to within 40 yards of S and R Companies' trenches, Pearson repeated his request. 'I was told,' he remembered, 'to hang on for another five minutes and I'd get an answer. I told them that if I hung on for two minutes more there would be no one here to take their bloody answer. I got permission and told the companies to withdraw, leaving the seriously wounded behind.'[6]

Reluctant to expose the Grenadier Guards, Brigadier Flavell had only allowed Pearson to withdraw after the commander of the 1st Guards Brigade said the 3rd Grenadiers would do the same. The move was covered by the guns of the 17th Field Regiment of the Royal Artillery and the tanks of the 26th Armoured Brigade which laid a smoke screen in the plain between Mansour and British positions to the rear.[7]

Told to fall back by Major Bull, Lieutenant Clements toured the company position shouting for members of his platoon. No one answered. The survivors had already left and the trenches were empty. He made his way down the steep slope to the plain. On the way he met Pearson, 'standing by a tree in an exposed position', who told him to move back to the gully. To get there he would have to cross the plain which had little cover. Rounding up some of his platoon at the bottom of the hill, they moved out into the open in an extended line. Some of the men began to run, but he ordered them not to. He wanted the retreat 'to be orderly and in any case increasing one's speed from three to five miles an hour does not serve to dodge a bullet moving at several thousand feet per second'.

The enemy were firing from the vacated position on Mansour. Fortunately, their shooting was inaccurate and not many paratroopers were hit, particularly after they reached the relative safety of the gully winding its serpentine way across the plain. It was, remembered Clements, a 'scene of indescribable confusion' with men 'coalescing into an ill-armed, ill-equipped mob without any leadership'. Only the retreating Guardsmen seemed to have retained their discipline.

Finally reaching the remnants of the battalion in its old lying-up area, Clements spoke briefly to Major Peter Cleasby-Thompson who told him: 'We lost a lot of grand fellows.' Asked if he had any tobacco, Cleasby-Thompson generously gave Clements his pouch – a wedding present – and in return got the lieutenant's sniper's rifle. Clements wanted to remain with the battalion, but was ordered into an ambulance and jolted off to the rear.[8]

Clements's parents were hugely relieved to receive a telegram from their son on 19 February, informing them that, though wounded, he had survived the battle. 'It dissipated at once,' replied his father Reginald, 'the horrible uncertainty in which we had been living for the past fortnight, and we were delighted that you were able to write so cheerfully . . . [We] are most anxious to know every detail of the action itself that you are able to tell us in a letter. I fear from a daily perusal of the Times that the regiment has suffered dreadfully heavily. We were intensely sorry to hear about poor [Philip] Mellor; I know the high esteem in which you held him both as a soldier and a man.'

In a later letter, Clements mentioned the death at his side of Platoon Sergeant Reginald Thornton, a 26-year-old Dubliner, who had been with him since the early days, and the tendency for the 'better man' to die while the 'wastrel' survived. His father responded: 'It puzzled the writer of the Book of Job; his answer was unsatisfactory, but so far as I know it is the only one there is. And those Germans who bolted after surrendering. Don't they see, besides knaves, what fools they are? Innocent blood will pay for their treachery another day.'

Clements's father also mentioned they had had a telephone call from a Guards officer called Willis who had occupied the bed next to Clements at the field hospital. 'He said that in the hospital he was operated on before you were, and came round sooner. While you were still unconscious your C.O. and Adjutant came in, and they asked him to tell you how well you had done. Evidently they gave the same message to the doctor. "Magnificently" was the word Willis used . . . When I say that I feel proud of you, I give you a very faint idea of my feelings. Mummy I think did not sleep that night; she said it was useless to expect her to.'[9]

Clements had indeed done well, yet only received a mention in despatches. Alastair Pearson, meanwhile, was awarded the Distinguished Service Order for his leadership on Djebel Mansour. It was scant consolation for what was, in effect, the destruction of his command. Of the 1st Battalion, 35 were killed, 132 wounded and 16 missing – almost 50 per cent of its strength for no discernible gain. Among the injured was Private A. A. Brown, the Bren gunner, who lay immobile for more than 24 hours until he was found by a Foreign Legion officer and taken down the mountain on a Guards Bren gun carrier.

Less fortunate were Major Conron, commanding R Company, Captain Stanley Wandless MC ('a great little guy with fair bushy eyebrows, quietly spoken, yet another pipe smoker!'), and the popular Lieutenant Philip Mellor. 'The cream of our men,' as Corporal Reg Curtis put it, 'were disappearing fast in the foot-hills of Tunisia.'

An exasperated Pearson wrote later: 'To this day I have never been able to discover the importance of Djebel Mansour or El Alliliga. For the overall battle all we did was to occupy about a regiment of a crack German division for four days which may have helped the general situation, but I always ask myself: was it worth the cost?'[10]

17

'They have proved their mastery over the enemy' – Tunisia, February–May 1943

O N 4 FEBRUARY, AS its sister unit fought for its life on Djebel Mansour, Lieutenant Colonel John Frost's 2nd Battalion was moved south from its position near Medjez-el-Bab to defend a vital crossroads in the Ousseltia valley. 'If you are attacked,' the local infantry brigade commander told Frost, 'you must be prepared to accept heavy casualties. It is vital that you impose as much delay as possible.'

'Yes, I see,' responded Frost.

'There are reports of 10 infantry battalions with about 100 tanks up the road in front of where you will be, but I don't suppose they will use all that lot.'

'Those seem to be rather heavy odds. Can you let me have some anti-tank guns?'

'No, I am afraid all mine are fully deployed and dug-in, but I will send you six tanks.'

'Thank you very much, sir. I am sure they will make all the difference.'

'Not much I'm afraid,' admitted the brigadier. 'You see, they are no use against German tanks.'

'Oh.'

The brigadier had more bad news: the tracks to the position

were mined, so the battalion would have to move across country, as quickly as it could.

Before dawn on 4 February, Frost sent one company forward in the dark, assisted by a guide, while he and his command group followed at daybreak in carriers, by which time the tracks were supposed to have been cleared of mines. They approached the crossroads 'very gingerly and got out of the carriers just short of it'. The whole area was 'sprinkled with trip-wires connected to mines', which fortunately they noticed before any harm was done. It was eerily silent and 'stank of death'.

Having issued his orders, Frost moved everyone back to the carriers and started off to the assembly area, where the battalion would be waiting. He was in the lead carrier, with two others following, and this time they moved at speed. Suddenly Frost noticed that the surface of the road in front had recently been disturbed. There was no way to stop, but as soon as his carrier was clear, he turned to shout a warning to the following vehicles.

It was too late. Frost watched in horror as the third vehicle 'bucked savagely on to its side as a sheet of flame appeared beneath it, immediately followed by a tremendous explosion'. The convoy stopped and Frost and others ran to assist those people who had been thrown clear of the stricken carrier. Two of his key men were beyond help – Major Dick Ashford and Captain 'Dinty' Moore, commanding A and HQ Companies respectively – and several seriously injured. Though 'not a cosy subordinate', Ashford had been with the battalion since its formation and 'his keenness was a byword'; Moore was a larger-than-life character with an appropriate comment for any occasion and a 'great man for summing-up'.

What made their deaths even harder to bear was the fact that the anticipated German attack never came. On 7 February, having suffered a few more casualties from sporadic shelling, Frost's battalion was moved back from that 'dreadful crossroads' to spend an uncomfortable night in the hills behind. With no blankets or groundsheets to ward off the cold, the men slept huddled together – all except Frost who, conscious of his role as commanding officer, chose to sleep alone. He awoke almost frozen to the ground, and was relieved to hear the battalion would be returned to the command of the 1st Parachute Brigade for the first time in a month.[1]

Stationed just to the south of Bou Arada, the brigade spent much of February on the defensive, defeating several minor enemy attacks and taking a number of prisoners during aggressive night patrols. The most serious assault they had to face was part of a three-pronged attack by von Arnim's panzer army – *Unternehmen Oschenkopf* (Operation Ox-Head), designed to push the British back in northern Tunisia – on 26 February. The southern prong (or 'horn', hence the naming of the attack after the Zulu tactic of encirclment known as the 'horns of the Buffalo') was aimed at Medjez and Bou Arada, guarded by the 17th Field Regiment and the 1st Parachute Brigade.[2] The heaviest blow fell on Pine-Coffin's 3rd Battalion, with Frost's men in action soon after. 'We all knew,' wrote Frost, 'we were as fully prepared as possible, plenty of ammunition had been stocked, the defensive fire-plan had been carefully worked out and neatly fitted in, the positions had been properly dug, revetted and concealed. Moreover the men were fit, fresh and should know exactly what to do.'[3]

In the event, the 2nd and 3rd Battalions held all their positions, inflicted 400 casualties and took 200 prisoners, at a cost of 18 killed and 54 wounded. It was a magnificent defence – but all in vain as the infantry brigade on their left were penetrated by enemy armour and by nightfall had been all but overrun.[4]

The 1st Parachute Brigade's next major challenge came in early March when it was moved north to defend positions astride the Tamera–Sedjenane road, close to the Mediterranean coast. On 8 March, a strong enemy force attacked the front held by the 1st and 2nd Battalions. Frost's men were on a steep-sided feature, covered in cork oak woods, known as Sidi Mohammed el Kassin. By 10 a.m., A Company was completely surrounded. 'Do not worry,' radioed Major John Lane, the company commander, 'I can assure you we shall be perfectly all right.'

As the day wore on, the enemy infiltrated small parties between the forward companies and Battalion HQ. The adjutant Willoughby Radcliffe, a successful solicitor before the war, volunteered to lead a mule train with ammunition for the beleaguered A Company, but was shot and killed en route. Another fatality was Geoff Rotheray, the new commander of HQ Company, who perished during a machine-gun duel with Germans on the hill above.

Frost was cheered, however, by the capture of a whole German platoon. 'We were told that the English soldiers on this hill would offer little resistance,' admitted its leader. 'Now we find your parachutists here. There is no end to damn propaganda.'

By the end of the day, assisted by a company of the 3rd Battalion, Frost's men had driven back the German infiltrators and taken 60 prisoners. The final riposte was by Lieutenant John Timothy, the Bruneval veteran, who single-handedly attacked a small party of German machine-gunners who were digging in near his platoon. 'Having killed six of them,' wrote Frost, 'he returned with two brand new MG 34s.'★ As liaison officer to the US 503rd Parachute Infantry Regiment, Timothy had become the first British parachutist to be awarded American jump wings. For his gallantry on 8 March, he was awarded the Military Cross.[5]

★ A German recoil-operated air-cooled medium machine gun that could fire up to 900 rounds a minute.

After more enemy attacks had forced it to concede some ground, the 1st Parachute Brigade was ordered to prepare for a general offensive on the night of 27 March with two neighbouring infantry brigades. The intention was to capture the Tamera position within 48 hours, but with two intermediate objectives. As Pine-Coffin's 3rd Battalion had been holding the line, the attack would be made by Pearson's 1st Battalion and Frost's 2nd Battalion. The night before, Frost's men attended a church service in a big machine shed. 'The men sat on shelves,' remembered Frost, 'in tiers round the sides of the building, and Padre Watkins officiated from a table in the middle. Everyone who could, went, and everybody sang, led by a small harmonium. Now that the hour of fresh battle approached, there were many amongst us who wondered what really happened if our number came up.'

When the service was over, Frost said a few words of encouragement and concluded: 'I don't know what you think of us, but I know I speak for all my officers when I say we have nothing but the highest possible regard for every single one of you.'

Advancing behind a creeping barrage, the forward companies of both battalions were able to capture much of the high ground that marked their initial objective, and a number of German and Italian prisoners, before dawn. But a fierce counter-attack by German paratroopers was only narrowly stopped by the 2nd Battalion's C Company, an action that cost the life of Lieutenant Dickie Spender, a renowned poet, who fell riddled with bullets, having killed four of the enemy.

By the evening of 28 March, the 1st Battalion – attacking on the left – had taken its second objective and six enemy guns. At one point during the assault, Pearson's men were advancing so fast they were hit by their own artillery. Corporal Reg Curtis saw Pearson crouched by a rock, bellowing into a radio handset: 'What do you think you're doing? You're killing all my bwoody men!'

Meanwhile the 2nd Battalion, facing stiffer opposition, was down to the strength of a single company. Reinforced by two companies from the 3rd Battalion, Frost agreed to continue the attack after dark. When his men moved forward at 3 a.m., there was little opposition as the bulk of the enemy had withdrawn. 'By the time we reached our old positions in Cork Wood,' wrote Frost, 'we had collected no less than 50 [prisoners], together with a great deal of booty.'

The Battle of Tamera ended with the 1st Parachute Brigade in possession of all its objectives. One man not surprised by the paratroopers' success was Lieutenant General Charles Allfrey, commander of the British V Corps, who noted in his diary that the parachute brigade 'as usual have done a magnificent job, and throughout the day pressed on, and at 1630 hrs beat off a counter-attack personally led by [Major Rudolf] Witzig' and his crack battalion of German parachute engineers. They had, added Allfrey, in conjunction with French colonial troops on their left, captured 'about 800 Italians, 150 Germans and 5 guns . . . Sent Para Bde a "Hurrah" notice in the evening which they richly deserved.'[6]

The brigade had been in action since 7 March, and in that time had 'withstood every attack until, through the failure of others, it had been called to withdraw to prepare and execute a counter-stroke, which was, in effect, the start of the whole successful offensive to clear North Africa'.[7]

In truth, the Axis troops – particularly the Germans – were still fighting tenaciously and some of the First Army's relatively inexperienced British infantry had a tendency to withdraw under pressure. By contrast the men of the 1st Parachute Brigade – all hand-picked volunteers, superbly fit and effectively led – rarely took a backwards step and were as formidable in defence as attack. Even when not used in their specialist airborne role, they were a formidable proposition.

Towards the end of April, the brigade returned by train to Boufarik where it bade farewell to its boss, Ted Flavell, who returned to the UK to become the commander of Airborne Establishments. Awarded the DSO in recognition of the brigade's outstanding service in North Africa, Flavell was replaced by 36-year-old Brigadier Gerald Lathbury, the original boss of the 3rd Battalion, who had been commanding the 3rd Parachute Brigade since December 1942. Lathbury was succeeded, in turn, by Brigadier James Hill.[8]

Before leaving the 1st Parachute Brigade, Flavell was delighted to receive a letter of congratulation from General Sir Harold Alexander, the theatre commander. It read:

> Now that it has been possible to relieve the Parachute Brigade who have for so long a time played a most valuable role in the north, I should like to express my thanks to, and admiration for, every Officer, NCO and man for the conspicuously successful part they have taken in the recent fighting. They have proved their mastery over the enemy who have a whole-hearted respect for this famous Brigade which is best described in their own words for them – 'THE RED DEVILS'.

He received a separate message from his immediate boss, Major General 'Boy' Browning, explaining in a little more detail the origin of the brigade's famous nickname. 'General Alexander directs that 1st Parachute Brigade be informed,' wrote Browning, 'that reliable information from German forces in Tunisia stated that [the brigade] have been given the title by the Germans of "Red Devils". General Alexander congratulates the Brigade on achieving this high distinction. Such distinctions given by the enemy are rarely won in battle except by the finest fighting troops.'[9]

Historians have tended to take at face value the claims by

Alexander and Browning that the 'Red Devils' name originated with the enemy. Yet the fact remains that no German source has ever been produced to confirm their version of events. Could it have been, instead, a clever bit of PR by the British generals to boost recruitment and instil fear in the enemy? It is certainly possible.

The derivation of the name is also a mystery. It has generally been assumed that 'devils' was a grudging acknowledgement of the paratroopers' pugnacity. As for 'red', it may have been inspired by the colour of their berets (though they were seldom worn in battle), or their appearance after fighting in the African mud, with which they were regularly coated, coupled with the tail-like fasteners on their parachute smocks that gave them a Lucifer-like appearance. We can only speculate. What is not in doubt is that they were inordinately proud of a nickname that is still used today to refer to members of the Parachute Regiment.[10]

However it came about, the title was not undeserved. During the course of the campaign – which officially ended on 13 May 1943 when the Italian General Messe surrendered the last of 250,000 Axis troops to the Allies – the brigade carried out three parachute operations and fought for five months as ground infantry with the First Army in Tunisia, capturing 3,500 prisoners and inflicting an additional 5,000 casualties (killed and wounded) on the enemy. It, in turn, lost 1,700 men. 'They had more battles than any other formation,' wrote the official historian of airborne forces, 'and in the Tamara valley, in the period 6th March to 14th April, did most of the fighting for 46 Division. In fact, it may be safely said that the brigade bore the brunt of the original operations of First Army.'[11]

A year later, in his account of the Tunisian campaign *Birth of an Army*, the war correspondent A. B. Austin described the men of the 1st Parachute Brigade as the 'flower of our infantry'. He added: 'Handicapped as they were, and not able to do the kind of work for which they had been specially trained, they held difficult gaps in the line and fought off the enemy while the later arrivals of the First Army were being trained in Tunisian fighting.'[12]

The official history of Britain's paratroopers in the Second World War was even more effusive, noting that in just 90 days the brigade had earned a 'reputation for gallantry, discipline and initiative unsurpassed by that of any other troops in Africa'.[13]

Frost was happy to admit that the compliments showered on the brigade by senior generals made its veterans feel 'quite prima-donna-ish'. Yet the tribute he appreciated most was given by German veterans as the battalion came close to one of the biggest prisoner-of-war camps in North Africa. 'The word that our train was passing,' wrote Frost, 'very soon got round the camp, and as it drew slowly by, scores of Germans came tumbling out of their tents. They ran towards us, throwing their hats in the air, and cheered us to the echo.'[14]

The Tunisian campaign made Britain's airborne forces legendary, but it was also an agonising missed opportunity. 'Boy' Browning had hoped to see the 1st Parachute Brigade deployed in a mass parachute jump – the role for which it had been trained.[15] Instead it was restricted to three battalion combat jumps at the start of the campaign that were executed with inadequate planning and varying degrees of success. Thereafter the brigade was used as emergency infantry, to plug holes in the line, and was frittered away as a result.

But Browning was undeterred and, just a few months later, he would get the opportunity to see if airborne forces really could make a difference when both the 1st Airlanding Brigade and the 1st Parachute Brigade dropped into action in Sicily.

18

Operation Ladbroke
– Sicily, 9–10 July 1943

A T 6.25 P.M. ON 9 July 1943, the first of 144 planes – Halifax and Albemarle bombers, and C-47 Dakota transports – took off from six airfields near Sousse on the Tunisian coast and headed due east towards Malta, the first leg of a 340-mile flight to the south-east coast of Sicily. They were towing eight Horsa and 136 American-built Waco CG-4A gliders, containing a total of almost 1,740 members of the 1st Airlanding Brigade whose task – codenamed Operation Ladbroke – was to capture and hold the Ponte Grande road bridge and port of Syracuse, a mile to the north, until they were relieved by men from the British 5th Division, who were due to land on beaches nearby in the morning of 10 July.

The invasion of Sicily – Operation Husky – was the largest amphibious operation of the war. It involved more than 3,000 warships, supply vessels and landing craft converging on a 100-mile stretch of the southern coast with 160,000 troops, 14,000 vehicles, 600 tanks and 1,800 guns.[1] But no task was more vital than the one given to the glider force, the 1st Airlanding Brigade, which, until then, had been untested in war, was only partially trained and equipped with just a handful of Horsa gliders.

Since its formation in October 1941, the development of the 1st Airlanding Brigade had been painfully slow. This was chiefly the result of RAF Bomber Command's unwillingness to supply the necessary tug aircraft. The dearth had continued despite the creation of the RAF's No. 38 Wing to train and operate with the 1st Airborne Division in April 1942. In a paper submitted to the War Office in January 1943, Major General 'Boy' Browning complained that there were only 48 aircraft available for dropping paratroopers or towing gliders, none of which 'was capable of towing a fully loaded Horsa Glider on operations'. Bomber Command, he said, had displayed 'no interest and carry out no training in parachuting or towing'. He added:

> The writing on the wall had been painfully obvious in N. Africa where months of hard fighting and grievous losses lie ahead; this for no other reason than that aircraft were not available at the right place and time to accomplish the capture of Tunis which, in the circumstances, was a practical certainty by Airborne troops up to 23 November, 1942 – how many thousands of valuable British lives will be lost during the next year due to the practical non-existence of suitable aircraft?

Browning went on to point out that, because of a lack of resources, glider pilots were only able to gain 15 hours of flying time a year which made them 'quite unfitted' to perform the vitally important task of transporting men and weapons.[2]

The upshot was that the Air Ministry agreed to the War Office's request to replace No. 38 Wing's obsolete Whitleys with 90 modern aircraft: 80 Albemarle and 10 Halifax bombers. But not all of them would be delivered until September 1943, while a further 66 Albemarles were assigned to the various glider and parachute training units.[3] This was too little, too late, as far as the Glider Pilot Regiment (GPR) was concerned. After arriving at Oran in Algeria in late April, two squadrons of the GPR were then moved 60 miles to Tizi on the Macara Plain where they were joined by the various elements of the 1st Airborne Division – including the 1st Parachute Brigade – and the 51st Wing of the American Troop Carrier Command.

The 1st Airborne Division had undergone a number of changes that would have far-reaching consequences. The first was the detachment of the 3rd Parachute Brigade to form the core of a second airborne division, the 6th – the number was chosen for security reasons – commanded by Major General Richard 'Windy' Gale, which would be based in the UK.* The 2nd Ox and Bucks Light Infantry and the 1st Royal Ulster Rifles – two of the four original battalions in the 1st Airlanding Brigade – were also left behind in Britain as the spine of the new 6th Airlanding Brigade. They would be joined later that year by a new 5th Parachute Brigade and supporting units.[4]

But the most significant alteration to the 1st Airborne Division was the replacement of its commander Major General 'Boy' Browning, who had been appointed Airborne Advisor to General Sir Harold Alexander's 15th Army Group in North Africa, with 47-year-old Major General George 'Hoppy' Hopkinson, the former commander of the 1st Airlanding Brigade.

Born in Retford, Nottinghamshire, Hopkinson had been apprenticed to an engineering firm when the Great War broke out. Commissioned into the North Staffordshire Regiment, he won a Military Cross during the retreat of the British Army in the spring of 1918. 'His example of fine personal courage and coolness under fire,' read the citation, '[are] worthy of the highest praise.' After the war he completed a degree in civil engineering at Cambridge University and, having travelled widely in Europe

---

* A third airborne division, later known as the 44th, was also envisaged for India.

and Russia, returned to the army where he excelled at cross-country running and other sports. Short and light on his feet, he was immensely fit and fiercely competitive.

At Dunkirk, he commanded the GHQ Reconnaissance Unit with distinction, then volunteered for the fledgling parachute force, injuring his back during his first jump and later flying as a passenger in RAF bombing raids over Germany to 'relieve the tedium of training'. Hopkinson took part in one of the earliest military glider flights and, having become the 1st Airlanding Brigade's first commander, was a vigorous and enthusiastic cheer-leader for glider operations.[5]

Having nominated Hopkinson as his successor, Browning might have imagined that he could control his wilder impulses. He was wrong. With the invasion of Sicily imminent, Hopkinson was determined that the 1st Airborne Division would take part, and in its proper role. He was particularly keen to test the capability of his glider troops and, aware that Browning had reservations about their training and equipment, went over his superior's head and appealed directly to General Sir Bernard Montgomery who was to command the British Eighth Army on Sicily.

With no experience of airborne operations, Montgomery allowed himself to be persuaded by Hopkinson that glider troops should be assigned the vital task of seizing the Ponte Grande road bridge over the Anopo Canal, a mile south of Syracuse, and hold it until relieved by seaborne forces of the 5th Infantry Division who would, if all went to plan, arrive seven hours later.[6]

Hopkinson only had eight Horsa gliders, all towed from the UK to North Africa by Halifax bombers. They were to be used to land the *coup-de-main* (direct assault) party of two companies of the 2nd South Staffords in fields either side of the canal spanned by the Ponte Grande. This was Phase One of the oper-ation. Phase Two was the main landing by the rest of the 1st Airlanding Brigade – 1st Border and 2nd South Staffords, with supporting units – on two landing zones a little further to the south, followed by an advance to the bridge. Phase Three was for the 2nd South Staffords to hold the area of the bridge, while the 1st Border passed through and captured Syracuse.[7]

The main body of the 1st Airlanding Brigade would be transported in 136 American Waco CG-4A gliders, dubbed the 'Hadrian' by the British, that Hopkinson had acquired from the US 51st Troop Carrier Wing. The tugs were 27 Albemarle bombers and 109 C-47 Dakotas flown by American pilots. To avoid anti-aircraft fire, the plan was to release the gliders 3,000 yards out at sea so they could arrive silently and unannounced. The heavier Horsa gliders would be released at an altitude of 4,000 feet; the Wacos at just 1,800 feet.[8]

Described by one pilot as 'a dark green blunt-nosed dragonfly', the Waco was of steel, wood and fabric construction, 49 feet long and with a wingspan of 84 feet. It could carry 13 men, a Jeep and its crew or cargo.[9] The problem was that the Wacos were wholly unfamiliar to the men from the Glider Pilot Regiment who were to fly them into Sicily; nor had these pilots done much night flying, despite the plan being to land in darkness, and in a terrain crisscrossed with rocks and stone walls.

The man tasked with overcoming these obstacles was 30-year-old Lieutenant Colonel George Chatterton, who had succeeded as commander of the 1st Glider Pilot Regiment after the pioneering John Rock had been killed in a night flying accident in October 1942. Originally destined for the Merchant Navy, Chatterton had switched to the RAF after leaving Pangbourne Nautical College and had become an accomplished aerobatic pilot. But he was confined to ground duties after a mid-air collision in 1935 and, with war looming, transferred to the army and fought with the 3rd Grenadier Guards during the Dunkirk campaign. In late 1941 he leapt at the chance to return to the skies by volunteering for the new glider unit.

Even before he succeeded Rock, Chatterton was convinced that the GPR needed men who could fight as well as fly, and to that end he employed drill sergeants from the Brigade of Guards to oversee a brutal training regime. 'We will forge this regiment as a weapon of attack,' he told his men in 1942. 'Only the best will be tolerated. If you do not like it, you can go back whence you came.'[10]

Chatterton could drill his men all he liked on the ground, but he could do nothing about the scarcity of tugs and gliders. He was well aware that his men lacked the night flying experience to cope with an operation as challenging as Ladbroke, and in unfamiliar gliders to boot. He voiced these concerns in Algiers on 1 April 1943 at a meeting with Hopkinson. 'Hoppy', remembered Chatterton, 'was an amusing little man. Very short, with black wavy hair, he was very ambitious, and delighted at having been made up to a General.' On this occasion he 'was in splendid form and had obviously pulled off something that pleased him'.

Hopkinson began: 'Well, George, it's nice to see you. I have a very interesting operation for you to study. I've been to see General Montgomery and he has agreed to use the 1st Airborne Division on a night assault on Sicily.'

This sounded ominous to Chatterton. He held his breath as the general motioned to a map of the island on the wall. 'I have agreed,' continued Hopkinson, 'to land the Airlanding Brigade on the night of July 9th/10th on the beaches in the neighbourhood of Syracusa. Another force of parachutists will be dropped at Catania, and a further force, supported by a glider squadron, at Augusta.'

Chatterton did a quick mental calculation and realised there were barely three months to find the necessary airstrips, tugs and gliders. It was not enough time, and his fears only increased when Hopkinson showed him aerial photos of the prospective landing zones that were strewn with obstacles. 'Well,' said the general, 'what do you think?'

After a brief pause, Chatterton replied: 'You know, sir, that the pilots have had no flying experience for at least three months, and little or no experience of night flying at all.'

'Oh,' said Hopkinson, as if it were nothing, 'we will soon put that right. The US Air Force are going to supply tugs and gliders.'

'American gliders?' asked Chatterton incredulously.

'Yes, what difference will that make.'

'Difference, sir? Why, they hardly know our own gliders, let alone American!'

'Well, you'll have to put up with it, won't you,' said Hopkinson, none too pleased by his glider chief's lack of enthusiasm.

'Yes, sir, I will try to do so,' responded Chatterton. 'But this looks a pretty stiff landing place, don't you think, sir?'

Hopkinson frowned. 'Now look here, Colonel Chatterton,' he said, sternly. 'I'm going to leave you for half an hour, and in that time you can study the photographs. If at the end of that time you still think that this is too difficult, you can consider yourself relieved of your command.'

The general stalked out, leaving Chatterton with an awful dilemma. His pilots lacked the training to undertake such a 'mad' operation; but if he refused to lead them, they would be sent anyway – and with someone less experienced. He would have to go. When Hopkinson was given the good news by Chatterton, he behaved like a spoilt child who had got his way.[11]

Chatterton was right to be concerned. For various reasons, seven tugs with Waco gliders failed to leave mainland Tunisia on 9 July. Approaching Sicily in the darkness from around 10.15 p.m., the remaining 137 planes – towing 8 Horsas and 129 Wacos – climbed to their cast-off heights as the moon came out. But strong winds were causing dust storms on the ground, 'and

the landmarks, so prominent in aerial photographs seen before
take-off, were obscured in rolling clouds of dust, making it more
difficult for the tug pilots to fix their positions or even to see
the shore'.

The air was soon crowded with tugs and gliders heading in
all directions, blown off course. Most of the intercom sets were
ineffective, and the complete lack of battle experience was felt
as searchlights and enemy flak prompted the majority of tugs to
release their Waco gliders more than the stipulated distance of
3,000 yards out to sea, 'putting a landfall out of the question'.
Of the 73 Wacos that were released too soon, only 9 reached
the Sicilian coast; whereas 46 of the 50 who were let go within
3,000 yards made it ashore, but were widely scattered along a
25-mile stretch of the Sicilian coast. A further two diverted to
Malta and Tunisia, and 10 returned to base.[12]

One of the many gliders that ditched in the sea was Chalk
54A, carrying 13 men of the 2nd South Staffs. One recalled:
'Bumpy flight. Glider released 2230hrs at unknown height. Pilot
said, just after releasing, "We are at 600 feet", next moment
glider landed in sea about 8 miles from the coast. All men got
out of glider, but both pilots and seven [men] missing.' Only
seven of the 15 occupants survived, after waiting eight and a half
hours in a life raft to be rescued by a naval launch.[13]

Among the survivors was Lance Corporal Jack Baskeyfield,
the 20-year-old son of a sliphouse worker from the pottery town
of Burslem, near Stoke-on-Trent. A hardworking, ambitious
young man, he had worked his way up from errand boy to
manager of the local Co-op butchers at the age of just 18. A
few months later, in February 1942, he was called up for military
service and joined the South Staffordshire Regiment, later transferring to the regular 2nd Battalion in the 1st Airlanding Brigade.
His airborne instruction included fitness, insertion techniques,
familiarity with weapons and tactics. To be issued with the

famous maroon beret was, for him, to be confirmed as the member of a corps d'élite. But nothing could have prepared Baskeyfield for his first glider flight into action. A fellow airlanding soldier recalled: 'Who would like being cooped up in a confined space for hours wearing full kit with vomit sloshing around their feet, providing a nice slow target for ground fire, awaiting the crash landing – and then having to fight a battle?'[14]

It never came to that for Baskeyfield, but he was lucky to survive the ditching. Many others in the 1st Airlanding Brigade and the Glider Pilot Regiment 'paid a high price for Hopkinson's childish enthusiasm and personal ambition'. The brigade suffered 313 fatalities, including 225 drowned in ditched gliders; a further 101 of the 272 pilots were killed, wounded or missing, a horrific casualty ratio of over one in three.[15]

Incredibly, despite the fact that only two of the eight Horsas carrying the *coup-de-main* party reached their designated landing zone – two small fields covering two acres of ground – the operation to capture the Ponte Grande was a success. It helped that one of those two Horsas, Chalk No. 133 with No. 15 Platoon of the 2nd South Staffs on board, was released within five miles of the target and at an altitude of 5,000 feet to counteract the high winds. Despite being hit by flak, the tug pilot Flight Lieutenant Tommy Grant managed to deliver the Horsa to the 'right spot and at the right height before turning to fly back to his base, 400 miles away'. Having cast off, the Horsa pilot Staff Sergeant Dennis Galpin flew on the predetermined course for several minutes until he saw Syracuse beneath him. Realising he was too far north, he turned to where he thought the objective lay.

Eventually he recognised the landing zone, 'just as depicted on the night map'. They were flying at about 2,000 feet when a searchlight caught them in its beam and flak opened up. Taking evasive action, Gilpin headed back out to sea and returned at low level. But he failed to shake the searchlight which followed the glider down to the ground 'and conveniently illuminated its approach on to the field, highlighting the bridge at the same time'.

The glider touched down 'fairly smoothly, but after it had run a few yards the nose wheel went into a ditch and broke, and the under part of the nose was damaged'. Luckily 'the only casualty was the platoon commander, who sprained his ankle'. His injury notwithstanding, Lieutenant Lennard Withers and 29 men deployed from the glider and, supported by Gilpin and his co-pilot, advanced on the bridge.[16] To execute a pincer attack, Withers and five men swam the canal and assaulted a pillbox on the north bank to draw fire, while the rest of the platoon attacked from the south. The attack was successful, detonators were removed from demolition charges and telephone lines cut.[17]

The second glider to reach the landing zone, piloted by Captain John Denholm (formerly of the 1st Cameronians) was not so fortunate. It hit the canal bank, causing a Bangalore torpedo★ to explode and kill everyone on board.[18]

At 4.30 a.m., by which time it had been joined by a tiny reinforcement of Lieutenant William Welch and seven men from the Brigade Defence Platoon, No. 15 Platoon fought off a determined attack by three enemy armoured cars, killing the commander of one and forcing the other two to retire. Half an hour later, Major Beazley and 15 men of the 9th Field Company, Royal Engineers, fought their way through to the bridge and completed the dismantling of the demolition charges. They were soon joined by Lieutenant Colonel A. Gordon Walch and another

---

★ Invented by Captain R. L. McClintock of the Royal Engineers while attached to a unit of the Indian Army at Bangalore in 1912, the torpedo was an explosive charge placed within one or several connected tubes and used by combat engineers to clear obstacles like barbed wire.

15 stragglers from various units, including the 1st Borders; and then, at 6.30 a.m., by two more officers and 23 men. By now there were seven officers and 80 men guarding the bridge, armed with one 3-inch mortar, two 2-inch mortars, four Bren guns and one Sticky Bomb.

From 8 a.m. onwards, the bridge and forward positions came under 'heavy and accurate mortar fire', forcing Walch to withdraw everyone into defensive positions by the canal, with Lieutenant Welch and two sections on the east side of the bridge, and the remainder on the west side. Soon after, Major Beazley was killed by mortar shrapnel and, owing to a shortage of ammunition, the defenders were 'only able to return the enemy's fire intermittently'. This now included a field gun on the ridge west of Syracuse, a gun 300 yards north-west of the bridge, and a couple of 3-inch mortars.

At midday, the fire from Italian mortars and machine guns was incessant, and the counter-attacking force around the bridge was thought to be at least a battalion. With casualties mounting, Walch withdrew the remnants of his force into a position astride the canal to the east of the bridge. As long as the canal and bridge could be held, and enfilade fire from a bend in the canal prevented, this was a sound decision. Walch felt he could hold it for several hours.

But at 2 p.m. an Italian machine gun was established at the north end of the bridge that could enfilade the canal; and half an hour later Italian troops had moved to within 300 yards of the defensive position from the north, west and south-west. By 3.15 p.m., all the outlying posts had been wiped out and there remained only 15 to 20 unwounded officers and men, 'cornered at the point where the canal joins the sea, where there was no cover whatsoever'.

A quarter of an hour later, almost out of ammunition, Lieutenant Colonel Walch and the last defenders were overrun.

Only Lieutenant Welch and seven men managed to escape by crawling down a ditch and hiding under a stone bridge. They eventually linked up with the forward elements of the 2nd Royal Scots Fusiliers, travelling up from the south in trucks, who quickly recaptured the bridge, allowing the casualties to be evacuated.

Incredibly, Lieutenant Colonel Walch and the main body of prisoners were being marched due west when their Italian guards bumped into and were overpowered by men from the Northamptonshire Regiment. Reporting to the commander of 17 Infantry Brigade, Walch received permission to take the party back to the bridge and resume command.[19]

One of the Waco gliders that did manage to reach terra firma – carrying men from the 2nd South Staffs, four handcarts of ammunition and a Bangalore torpedo – was piloted by Staff Sergeants Ivan Garrett and Tommy Moore. Cast off at 2,300 feet, a mile and a half from the coast, it came down well north of its intended landing zone on a rocky slope about 100 yards from the beach, and barely 20 yards from an Italian pillbox. The glider came to a shuddering halt when a large rock smashed through its nose, breaking Moore's ankle and pinning his legs under the seat. Garrett was unhurt, and able to kick his way through the side of the cockpit. But within seconds of landing the fabric roof of the glider was set on fire by fragments of Italian grenades, which in turn ignited the boxes of phosphorus grenades and mortar bombs that the glider was carrying. Six of the 12 soldiers on board managed to escape, but the others all perished.

As Garrett was rescuing one injured man, he was hit in the left arm by a piece of shrapnel which tore away most of the elbow joint. Undeterred, he went back for Moore who could feel the cushion on his seat beginning to burn. Reaching the nose of the glider, Garrett used his right arm to lift it a little.

Knowing this was his only chance, Moore threw himself forward and wrenched his leg free. As he did so he felt the bone break.

Once free, Moore tried to help Garrett pull an unconscious and badly burnt soldier to safety. Unable to do so, they moved to the cover of rocks, 30 yards away, and stayed there while the ammunition continued to explode. Moore used a puttee as a tourniquet to stem the bleeding from Garrett's mangled arm, but both were suffering from the intense cold. In the morning, their hopes rose when they saw landing craft approaching beaches to the south.

Moore knew they were unlikely to survive another night in the open, so he left Garrett and set off south towards Avola, using a captured Italian carbine as a crutch. On reaching the beach, he managed to 'tickle' a large fish and ate it raw. Then he started to swim towards the shipping offshore, having first swallowed two Benzedrine tablets, but thought better of it and later joined a wounded corporal in a deserted farmhouse down the coast.

They were found there by British troops who went to collect Garrett. He was conscious, recalled Moore, 'but suffering from gangrene, loss of blood and exposure'. All three survived, though Garrett lost his arm and the corporal was unable to bend his knees. Garrett's bravery and self-sacrifice had undoubtedly saved Moore's life.[20]

George Chatterton, meanwhile, had endured an eventful first 24 hours in Sicily. Flying a Waco glider (Chalk No. 2) with the 1st Airlanding Brigade commander 'Pip' Hicks and some of his staff on board, he had been at the controls for more than four hours when they finally picked out the coast of Sicily, recognising its shape from the map and charts they had studied. Too far north, they changed course and flew down the coast at 1,900 feet, avoiding heavy flak as they passed Syracuse.

'Can you see the release point, Peter?' Chatterton asked his co-pilot.

'Another five minutes or so,' replied Harding, looking at his watch. Soon after, he shouted: 'There it is!'

'I can't see a damn thing,' said Chatterton, reaching for the release lever. As he did so, the tug started to turn and dive.

'My God,' yelled Chatterton, 'he's pushing off!' He pulled the release lever and turned the glider – now 'light and easy to handle' – back towards Sicily. But a dust storm meant he was unable to see the coastline until, descending to a height of just 200 feet, he spotted a cliff face directly ahead. Climbing desperately to avoid it, he flew into a bust of flak that hit his port wing and forced him to ditch in the sea. Fortunately, they were just 100 yards from land and, having survived a scary moment when they were picked out in the water by a searchlight and targeted by a machine gun, they all got safely ashore. Moments later, a Royal Navy pinnace appeared and dropped off men from the Special Raiding Squadron (formerly the 1st SAS Regiment) who had been tasked with spiking a battery of guns on the Murro di Porco peninsula. Joined by Chatterton and the others, the SRS men spent the rest of the night attacking and silencing a number of enemy positions, and taking 150 Italian prisoners.

'Later the next day,' recalled Chatterton, 'we came to the bridge, Ponte Grande, where we found the aftermath of the battle. Galpin's glider was still in the field, a memorial to an epic piece of glider piloting, and the pattern of much that was to come.'

On the far side of the canal was the grim sight of Captain Denholm's glider. It had hit the bank and the effects of the explosion inside the glider 'could clearly be seen'. Chatterton wrote: 'The crew and passengers had been blown forward as if down a funnel, but of the pilot there was no sign. As I stood looking at this macabre and tragic pile of bodies I thought back to the gay Denholm. I remembered that as I was briefing the pilots, he had appeared at the door. His beret was at a jaunty angle and his long fair hair showed beneath. He had just arrived, after having been towed 1,500 miles across the sea and desert in one of the Horsa gliders. As he leaned on the door, he said, in his typical drawl: "I say, I've come to see a man about an operation.'"

Chatterton walked back to the bridge 'deeply affected, and somewhat overwhelmed'.

Galpin was rewarded with the Distinguished Flying Medal. Of the other gallant bridge defenders, Lieutenant Colonel Walch got the OBE, and Lieutenants Withers and Welch the Military Cross. Lieutenant Colonel Chatterton received the DSO for landing his glider 'under the most trying and exhausting circumstances without damage to the crew', and for his outstanding leadership thereafter.[21]

The divisional commander 'Hoppy' Hopkinson, who accompanied the 1st Airlanding Brigade in a glider, came down in the sea so far from the coast he had to be picked up by a Royal Navy destroyer – whose skipper turned out to be an old friend and fellow oarsman from Cambridge. As Hopkinson later put it: 'I was late for the battle having landed in the sea, but they got on without me for the first few hours.'[22]

Airborne historian William F. Buckingham described the landing on the night of 9/10 July 1943 as a 'fiasco, partly due to light winds, alert anti-aircraft defences and a light mist over the landing area', but mainly 'directly attributable to Hopkinson's insistence on committing men to battle with insufficient training and practice'.[23]

Yet, once on the ground, the 1st Airlanding Brigade had performed miracles, a point emphasised by General Montgomery in a congratulatory message to Hopkinson that was passed on to the men. Hopkinson wrote:

General Montgomery asked me to let the Airlanding Brigade know that their contribution to the success of the landing operations had been invaluable. He regretted that the airborne operation had, through no fault of the Brigade, proved more difficult than anticipated, but he wished to emphasise the important and gallant part played by all ranks. In spite of all difficulties and setbacks, the main objective had been captured and held. For those responsible for this particular operation he was filled with admiration. Others, who, by their own initiative, fought isolated actions in various parts of the battlefield, had played no small part in this most successful landing action. Had it not been for the skill and gallantry of the Airlanding Brigade, the port of Syracuse would not have fallen until much later, because the enemy would inevitably have formed a strong defensive line on the canal to the south of the town.[24]

These were baby steps, of course, and the subsequent use of the 1st Parachute Brigade in Sicily was far from an unqualified success. But here, undoubtedly, was confirmation of 'Boy' Browning's vision: that airborne forces could be used in a strategic role that really could alter the course of a battle, a campaign, and ultimately a war.

19

'I floated down like a fairy queen'
– Sicily, 13–14 July 1943

S TATIONED BY THE DOOR of one of the first Dakotas to take off from four sandy airstrips near the holy city of Kairouan in north-east Tunisia at just after 7 p.m. on 13 July 1943, a few nights after the capture of Ponte Grande, was Platoon Sergeant Johnny Johnstone of the 2nd Parachute Battalion. As the senior rank in the aircraft, he was the last to embark, and would be the first to exit, after he had pushed out a hamper of spades and picks.

Determined to make himself as comfortable as possible for the three-hour flight to Sicily, he had put his gear on the hard metal seat and was sprawled on a pile of canvas next to it. For much of the trip he read a slim Penguin volume, looking out from time to time through the open door to 'watch the blue of the Mediterranean gradually darkening to indigo as darkness fell'.

Born and raised in Aberdeen, Scotland, Johnstone had volunteered to join the 2nd Parachute Battalion in the autumn of 1941 because, like many others, he was 'bored with uninspired training and coast defence'.[1] He had taken part in the disastrous Oudna drop in North Africa with A Company's No. 1 Platoon, under the gallant Lieutenant Dennis Rendell, and was later wounded in the jaw by mortar shrapnel at the Battle of Tamera.

By the time he returned to the battalion a couple of weeks later, A Company had been reduced to the strength of a platoon.

Once the fighting was over, A Company was addressed by General Dwight D. 'Ike' Eisenhower, the Supreme Commander of Allied Forces in the Mediterranean, near Boufarik. With the men drawn up in a hollow square, a Jeep pulled alongside and Ike jumped out. Beckoning with both hands, he drawled: 'Bring 'em in. Bring 'em in.'

When the men had crowded to within a few feet, Eisenhower grinned and said: 'We Anglo-Saxons don't go in for this kissin' stuff so I'll just say . . .' – leaving a slight pause – 'You're so gooood!'[2]

To prepare for its next operation, the 2nd Battalion was moved in early July to a camp near Kairouan, a few miles west of the Tunisian port of Sousse. There the men of No. 1 Platoon were given the details of their mission by Lieutenant Tony Frank who explained that it was a 1st Parachute Brigade 'affair': the 1st Battalion would capture a bridge in Sicily, while 2nd and 3rd Battalions secured bridgeheads south and north of the river respectively.[3]

The original airborne plan had been for the capture of three bridges to speed the northward advance of General Montgomery's Eighth Army from its landing beaches in the south-east of Sicily to the port of Messina, opposite the toe of Italy. They were (from south to north): the Ponte Grande, near Syracuse (1st Airlanding Brigade); a bridge to the south-west of Augusta (2nd Parachute Brigade); and the Primosole Bridge over the River Simeto, just south of the Catania plain. In the event, the operation planned for the 2nd Parachute Brigade never took place because the advance of the ground troops was faster than expected. That just left the final operation – codenamed Fustian – by Brigadier Lathbury's 1st Parachute Brigade. Originally planned for the night of 12 July, it was delayed 24 hours because of bad weather.

During the hard training that preceded the operation – including two practice drops at night – the parachutists had developed a new system of dropping with their personal weapons attached to their bodies, rather than in separate containers, and a method of rallying at the drop zone by a series of sound signals.[4]

Shortly before the invasion of Sicily, General Montgomery arrived at the parachutists' camp near Kairouan to give his customary pep talk. 'His Jeep drew up in our olive grove,' remembered Sergeant Johnny Johnstone, 'and we clustered round while the fierce little man stood up in the Jeep, and in his now well-known and somewhat easily satirised clipped, nasal tones, told us we were "going on a party" . . . He closed by giving us the password "Desert Rats", no doubt an encouraging reference to recent successes, with the counter sign, [the] suitably belligerent "Kill Italians".'[5]

Assigned to capture three high features to the south of the Primosole Bridge – codenamed Johnny I, II and III – the men of the 2nd Battalion were scheduled to land in cornfields a little to the west, between the hills and the canal that flowed into the Simeto river. The route from the drop zone to the features was fairly straightforward, even by moonlight: first a bund (or high bank) south of the river, and thence the main road to the 'Johnny' heights. Italian troops were known to be holding the heights, and just in case they panicked when they saw the planes, Frost had detailed Johnstone's No. 1 Platoon, commanded by Lieutenant Tony Frank, to make straight for Johnny II, the nearest feature to the drop zone and one from which a determined enemy could easily disrupt the battalion's assembly and subsequent movement.

Johnny I was the central and most important of the three features, and possession gave absolute control of the main road leading to the bridge. This was the key location on which Frost intended to put most of the battalion. Johnny III was away to the east and the least important of the three.[6]

Though he had not known him long, Johnstone was impressed by the quiet efficiency of his 25-year-old platoon commander Tony Frank, a noted sportsman who had attended the Jesuit boarding school of Stonyhurst before reading Classics at St Catharine's College, Cambridge. Johnstone also had confidence in the section commanders and the handful of other veterans who had survived the North African campaign. He was, however, uneasy about the raw youngsters who made up the bulk of the platoon.

After they had distributed ammunition, hand grenades, 2-inch mortar bombs, Hawkins anti-vehicle mines and American K-rations, Frank said a few words of quiet encouragement. Johnstone followed this with a 'rather nattering injunction to the youngsters to just do what they were told'. It occurred to him later that 'nattering does not inspire confidence and that in any case most of them would be pathetically dependent on the commanding word once they experienced what [Ernest] Hemingway called "the ultimate loneliness of contact [with the enemy]"'.

It did not help when word spread that the 1st Airlanding Brigade's attack near Syracuse 'if not a failure, had been pretty much of a mess, since many of the gliders had gone astray, some into the sea, and of course the Yank tug pilots were blamed'. Johnstone, ironically, was glad when Operation Fustian was delayed for 24 hours. He had been in a very depressed mood on 12 July, but this had lifted by the time the planes took off on the 13th. He mused later: 'Military writers talk easily of "seasoned troops" and "battle-hardened veterans", but I doubt if many men who have experienced it go easily and willingly into battle. The only advantage the veteran has is that he may know a few tricks of survival. Just as the first impact of the reality of battle can flatten the excited enthusiasm of the tyro, so the steel of a man's resolution is in the end made brittle, not tempered, by too frequent contact with the fire of war.'

On 13 July, as his Dakota neared the east coast of Sicily at around 10 p.m., Johnstone wandered up the plane to speak to the pilot. They were on schedule and on course, came the reply, and were about 10 minutes out from the drop zone. Having warned his men, Johnstone decked himself in his gear 'like the proverbial Christmas tree'. Apart from his parachute, he had a side pack loaded with a mess tin and 48 hours of rations, while his pockets and pouches were stuffed with Sten gun magazines, grenades, a Hawkins mine, map case, compass and binoculars. The Sten gun itself was attached to the webbing on his chest. He also carried the platoon 38 radio, and in his right hand the slim canvas case containing the radio antenna.

Before hooking up, he checked on his men, and then stood by the door. The pilot made a 90-degree turn, and he caught 'a glimpse of beach, white under the moonlight and the outline of the estuary, before the mysterious shadowy shapes of the land were sliding beneath'. Suddenly 'the shadows were enlivened by a regular firework display of flares and tracer streaming up'. When the green light came on, he shoved the hamper out, shouted 'good luck' to his men, and jumped. He 'floated down like a fairy queen', with a radio aerial clutched in one hand until it was time to pay it out beneath him on a length of parachute cord attached to his belt.

As the 'flat shadows' rushed up to meet him, he clamped his feet together and landed with a 'breath-taking wallop'. Lying still for a moment, he eased himself up and banged the quick-release box to unfasten the harness. Getting to his feet, he felt physically fine. He had, in fact, landed heavily on his left shoulder and it would be some weeks before he could raise his arm above shoulder height.

He looked around and could see no one near. He would learn later that, just after his jump, the pilot took evasive action to avoid flak and the rest of the stick landed much further up the drop zone. Away to the east he could see the 'looming bulk' of high ground that was the battalion objective. Much farther off, and equally prominent in the moonlight, was the great mass of Mount Etna dominating the northern skyline.

Johnstone eventually met up with one of his section commanders and five men, and together they headed towards the battalion rendezvous. They had not gone far when a burst of fire caused them to dive to the ground. Johnstone levelled his Sten and pulled the trigger. The only sound was a disappointing clunk. It was a new weapon, issued the day before, and had never been used. He cocked it and tried again, but it refused to fire.

As they moved forward, a haystack to their left rear burst into flames and they could hear German voices ahead. They took cover in a large shell hole, armed with Stens and rifles, but no Bren guns. Eventually they spotted some 'shadowy figures moving in column eastwards along the drop zone', at a distance of barely 50 yards. Johnstone was about to shout the password, but something odd about the way they were moving made him pause. They were marching in a long straggling column and seemed to be dragging something behind them. Only later did he realise that they were German *Fallschirmjägers* who had been dropped at the same time.

Once the column had passed, Johnstone continued with his small group along the drop zone. He was puzzled by the silence as, by now, it was well past midnight and the whole brigade should have been in action. After narrowly avoiding a hostile armoured vehicle that roared across their line of march, they finally reached the road where they were challenged by the brigade major who informed them that Lieutenant Colonel Frost and some of the 2nd Battalion had gone off up the road towards the high ground which was the objective. Johnstone and the men followed, keeping just off the road, and were soon joined by a couple of NCOs.

With dawn about to break, Johnstone ordered the men to take cover in a small vineyard. He felt 'very tired and empty of initiative', and later blamed the after-effects of the Benzedrine tablets they had all taken on the plane, just before jumping. He lay down next to the section commander and, pillowing his head on the small pack, 'gazed up through the leaves and clusters of small green grapes at the now rapidly lightening sky'.[7]

The Dakota carrying Lieutenant Colonel Frost and some of his HQ staff also had an uneventful flight until the approach to the drop zone when it was fired on by streams of tracer. Below, the dark landscape was speckled with flames. Frost landed awkwardly in a shallow, empty ditch, his left leg taking most of his weight. He heard a 'pop' in his left knee, but the pain came later.

Having gathered his stick, he headed for the pre-arranged rendezvous nearby. But long after the time had passed when the whole battalion should have assembled, only a handful of his HQ Company, the majority of Major Dickie Lonsdale's A Company, and a few other stragglers were present. 'There could be no doubt,' he wrote later, 'that few of the other squadrons had flown in as staunchly as ours.'[8]

This was not a problem confined to the 2nd Battalion. Of the 116 Dakotas and 19 tugs and gliders that had taken off from Tunisia – carrying the 1,900 men of the 1st Parachute Brigade – three planes and three glider combinations returned to base soon after. The rest headed for Sicily, and more than 70 per cent of the pilots remembered being fired at by Allied naval ships en route. Some were shot down; others forced off course. Those that reached the coast were then targeted by enemy flak and searchlights, prompting many to take evasive action. This made it harder to locate drop zones and some parachutists – like Johnstone's stick – were thrown to the floor and unable to jump at the correct time.[9]

As a result, only 39 aircraft dropped their troops on or within half a mile of their drop zones, 48 did so farther afield, and 17 returned to base with their paratroopers still on board. A further 12 were unable to reach or find their dropping zones at all. Of the gliders, only four landed successfully in the right place. This meant that a paltry 20 per cent of the 1st Parachute Brigade – 12 officers and 283 men – 'were available for the battle for which they were intended'.[10]

Frost had managed to gather 112 officers and men at the 2nd Battalion's rendezvous by 1 a.m.[11] There was, however, no sign of Victor 'Dicky' Dover, the adjutant, or Johnnie Lane, the second-in-command, the two officers with whom Frost had discussed the detail of the operation. But as Dickie Lonsdale – a boisterous 29-year-old who had been a founding member of 151st Parachute Battalion in India, before transferring to 2nd Battalion – was confident he could hold Johnny I with his company alone, Frost decided to make for the objective with the force that he had. With his injured knee beginning to stiffen, he was forced to use a rifle as a crutch.

On the road he met up with the 1st Parachute Brigade's commander, Brigadier Gerald Lathbury, who, having failed to find his signallers, had little idea of what was happening elsewhere. But he could hear signs of firing from the direction of the Primosole Bridge, a mile and a half to the north-east, and, confident that the 1st Battalion would soon be in possession, Lathbury ordered him to continue towards his objective.

Frost and his group passed a 3rd Battalion officer and a few men, busy destroying all the telephone lines they could find, and lots of Italians moving about in the dark. Some were keen to surrender; others wanted to fight on. At the bottom of the hill they met Lieutenant Tony Frank, commanding A Company's No. 1 Platoon, whose job it had been to secure Johnny II.[12] Frank explained that he and a small force of men had fought their way through 'superior German forces, inflicting many casualties on them', before meeting up with other stragglers from A and B Companies, a total force of three officers and 25 men. Together they decided to assault Johnny I from three directions: one section moving round the north of the feature; another round the eastern edge; while the third, with Frank in overall command, moved up the north-eastern slope. Facing light opposition, they silenced a number of machine guns and captured 130 Italian soldiers, many of whom were hiding in caves.[13]

Frost sent Lonsdale and the rest of A Company to secure Johnny I, and remained with a small party at the base of the hill to direct the battle. He now had 140 men on Johnny I, covering all approaches, but with no supporting weapons or communications.[14]

At around 6.30 a.m. on 14 July, Frost's positions on Johnny I were counter-attacked by German paratroopers from the west, supported by machine guns and mortars. From his hiding place in the vineyard, Sergeant Johnny Johnstone could hear the sounds of a firefight nearby. First the 'solid thunk of a Bren in reply to the Spandau cobra hiss', and then 'the swish and crump of mortars coming from the German side on to what we now know was a handful of A Company on Johnny I'.

Soon after, there was the sound of movement in the vines nearby, and a barked command: 'Hände hoch!'

Crouched on his knees, Sten at the ready, Johnstone could see the back and left side of a stocky little figure whose Schmeisser sub-machine gun was levelled at the burly form of Sergeant 'Biff' Whitehead, an international rugby player before the war. He was about to open fire when Sergeant Fisher hissed from beside him, 'Not now, Johnno!'

Johnstone lowered his weapon, and seconds later he and Fisher were surrounded by German paratroopers. 'What a splendid target for grenades and Schmeisser fire we would have been,' wrote Johnstone, 'in our little green hollow on the hillside. Oh, we might have added a word or two to the Red Devil legend, but I am pleased to think that most of the group are probably alive today [because we did not open fire].'[15]

On Johnny I the mortar fire was, noted Frost, 'all the more deadly on the rocky ground and the number of our casualties began to grow'. They were also being targeted by machine-gun fire from Johnny II, a few hundred yards to the west, and a fighting patrol was despatched to knock this out. Unfortunately, the patrol encountered German armoured cars that forced it back with many casualties. Meanwhile, the long grass to the south of A Company's positions had caught fire, and the smoke became an effective screen behind which the Germans were able to advance.

With A Company pushed back into an ever-tighter perimeter, it looked as if the position on Johnny I was about to be overrun. It was saved by the timely arrival of naval gunfire from a cruiser offshore that had been contacted by Captain Vere Hodge, the Forward Observation Officer. 'Almost immediately,' wrote Frost, 'the high-velocity medicine began to arrive with a suddenness and efficiency that completely turned the scales. The principles of surprise, economy of effort, concentration of force and flexibility were amply demonstrated by one young officer, a signaller and a wireless set. What seemed like imminent defeat was staved off and from then on the danger receded.'

This gave Captain Stanley 'Bombs' Panter and his 3-inch mortar crews the chance to locate and bring into action an abandoned but fully operational Italian Howitzer in the valley between Johnny I and II. 'No sights could be found that day,' noted the battalion war diary, 'but 15 shells were eventually fired onto enemy positions.'[16]

During the course of the morning, Frost was visited in his Battalion CP by Brigadier Lathbury who, despite suffering from painful shrapnel wounds sustained during the night, had walked from his command post near the bridge. He confirmed what Frost had long suspected: that less than a third of the brigade had arrived and nearly all the heavy weapons were missing. Even so, the bridge and the bridgehead on both sides had been firmly secured and, thus far, the enemy had made no attempt to retake them.[17]

This inactivity would not last.

20

'I've no hesitation in shooting him'
– Sicily, 13–17 July 1943

LIEUTENANT COLONEL ALASTAIR PEARSON, commanding the 1st Parachute Battalion, realised all was not going to plan when one of his signallers told him the plane was over Mount Etna, a good 25 miles north of Primosole Bridge. He made his way to the cockpit. 'The drop zone's down there,' he said to the American pilot, pointing to the south, 'what are we doing?'

The co-pilot had his hands over his face and was crying. The pilot was only marginally more composed. 'We can't,' he replied, 'we can't.'

'Can't do what?' Pearson demanded.

'We can't go in there.'

Pearson could see 'blobs of fire', and realised the pilot thought they were burning Dakotas. He said to the pilot: 'There's nothing for it boy, we've got to do it. If your co-pilot's no good, I've no hesitation in shooting him.'

As if to emphasise the point, he drew his revolver. When the pilot continued to protest, Pearson offered to shoot him as well.

'You can't do that,' the pilot replied, 'who'd fly the aeroplane?'

'Don't worry about that. I've got a bloke in the back who can fly this.' It was true: one of his men was a former RAF officer.

'Yeah,' said the pilot, 'but he won't know how to land it.'

Pearson laughed. 'You don't think he's going to hang out to land it, do you? He'll be stepping out very sharp.'

Very reluctantly, the pilot agreed to make for the drop zone and Pearson returned to his seat. Minutes later the bell rang and they all stood up. The plane seemed to be going too fast and dropping in altitude, instead of levelling off. They jumped anyway, Pearson going at number 10 and his batman following. They were so low, Pearson could not remember his parachute opening before he hit the ground hard. His knees hurt, but otherwise he was all right, as was his batman. 'The remainder of the stick,' he said, 'all suffered serious injuries or were killed. I was very angry. We all got to our RV and soon discovered the burning Dakotas were no more than haystacks alight.'[1]

Arriving a little before Pearson on the drop zone to the south-west of the bridge was Second Lieutenant Dick Bingley, commanding S Company's No. 5 Platoon. A former Territorial with the Middlesex Regiment, Bingley had joined No. 2 (Parachute) Commando as a sergeant in October 1940. Sent on an officers' training course in late 1942, he missed the North African campaign, but rejoined the 1st Parachute Battalion in time for Operation Fustian. Like Pearson, he had had to 'persuade' the terrified pilot of his Dakota to drop his stick – platoon HQ, one section and two medical orderlies – in the correct place. He found out later that the other half of his platoon – the platoon sergeant, two sections and two signallers – had been dropped in Malta by error.

Once on the ground, Bingley set off with his small force. On the way he met and joined forces with Regimental Sergeant Major John Lord of the 3rd Battalion, a 35-year-old former Grenadier Guardsman who should have been dropped north of the bridge. Closer to the bridge, they were augmented by a section from the 1st Battalion's HQ Company and Lieutenant

Colonel E. C. Yeldham,★ the 3rd Battalion's commanding officer, who had also gone astray.[2] The task of Yeldham's battalion was to capture and hold the northern approaches to the bridge. Yet only the equivalent of two platoons were dropped anywhere near the bridge, and they all joined the 1st Battalion as it was 'quite impossible for them to attempt their task to the north'.[3]

Guarding the southern end of the 400-yard-long steel Primosole Bridge were two pillboxes. As Bingley's group approached, they encountered a patrol of four Italians and killed two of them. They then assaulted the pillboxes with Gammon bombs and, after a brief struggle, 18 Italians surrendered. In the fracas, Bingley was shot through the hand by a bullet from a Beretta *Modello* 38 sub machine gun. 'A medical orderly expertly smothered the wound with penicillin powder,' remembered Bingley, 'and the bandaging sufficed for the next 24 hours, for which I was most grateful. We took possession of the pillboxes, and with a small guard escorted the prisoners to the bridge.'[4]

A group of about 50 parachutists, under Captain Rann, soon arrived from the northern drop zone. They included the fit-again Lieutenant Alan Clements, commanding No. 9 Platoon, who later wrote a graphic account of the parachute drop and the battle that followed in a letter to his parents:

Dramatic indeed was my first sight of the island. Immense red fires were burning all over the plain; streams of varied coloured tracer bullets were pouring up into the air and forming curves and cascades – very pretty were they not lethal and aimed at us . . . We had struck the land at an angle and now the pilot made

---

★ Yeldham had replaced Geoffrey Pine-Coffin when the latter returned to the UK to take command of the 7th Battalion, The Parachute Regiment (Light Infantry), in June 1943. For commanding the 3rd Battalion with 'skill and gallantry' during the North African campaign, Pine-Coffin had been awarded the Military Cross.

a great circle to effect a proper landfall – the mouth of the river Simeto. The land receded, we banked steeply, almost skimming the water. Then suddenly the land re-appeared, fires and all and we turned in. The engines roared at full throttle and we climbed. I caught a glimpse of a long, straight road, then a serpentine river. The red light went on, followed simultaneously by the green and out we went. A few twists and jerks and I hit the ground – a comfortable point of impact – a corn stook!

Soon after meeting up with Dick Bingley at the northern end of the bridge, Clements saw a convoy of five German trucks appear from the direction of Catania. The parachutists immediately took cover in drainage ditches on each side of the road and waited for the trucks to hit the line of mines that had been laid in the road. The first one triggered a mine and swerved off the road, causing the others to brake violently. One was blown up by a Gammon bomb while the others were targeted by small-arms fire.[5]

Before long, the first three lorries were ablaze, exploding their cargoes of petrol and ammunition. Bingley was shocked to see men 'engulfed in burning petrol' and found their screams 'sickening'.[6] The occupants of the last two lorries got out firing their machine pistols and headed for the cover of the drainage ditches where they were shot by the concealed British parachutists.[7]

An hour later, at around 3 a.m., Brigadier Gerald Lathbury was approaching the southern end of the bridge with some of his staff when he was wounded by a grenade thrown by a stray Italian.[8] Lathbury had his trousers round his ankles and was bent over having field dressings applied to his backside when Lieutenant Peter Stainforth of the 1st Parachute Squadron, Royal Engineers, walked up. Rising above the indignity of his pose, Lathbury told Stainforth to remove the demolition charges from the bridge as quickly as possible. Stainforth and his men did just that by climbing up the girders at both ends and chopping at the tangle of cables – detonating wire mixed with telephone lines – with machetes. Everything went in the river: cables and explosives. Then they examined the piers and found that, like a lot of continental bridges at the time, they had been built with chambers to hold sacks of powder explosives. These, too, were dumped in the river. Within half an hour the job was complete.[9]

By 4 a.m., the bridge was being held by about 120 men of the 1st Battalion, commanded by Alastair Pearson, and two platoons from Yelham's 3rd Battalion. Their supporting arms were two 3-inch mortars, one Vickers medium machine gun and three hand-held anti-tank weapons known as PIATs.* They would be supplemented, over the next couple of hours, by three 6-pounder anti-tank guns that had been flown in by glider, but communications were still very sketchy. They had a No. 22 wireless radio set, sited on the south bank of the river, but it did not have the range to contact either the seaborne forces or Advanced Divisional HQ. At 9.30 a.m., the brigade major was able to get through to a British armoured unit – later identified as the 4th Armoured Brigade – and report the capture of the bridge. After the unit had responded that they could not yet get through to relieve the 1st Parachute Brigade, wireless contact was lost and never regained.

At around 10 a.m., two German Messerschmitt ME-110 fighter-bombers strafed the bridge area. This was followed, at midday, by a prolonged artillery bombardment from Axis positions to the north.[10] Corporal Reg Curtis, dug in with other

---

* First used in combat in 1942, the PIAT – Projector, Infantry, Anti Tank – could fire a 2.5 lb projectile up to 115 yards in a direct fire anti-tank role, and 350 yards in an indirect fire role. Spring-loaded, the hollow-charged grenade would travel at 300 feet per second and explode on impact. The PIAT had no back-blast to reveal the position of the user but was often inaccurate, except at very close range, and difficult to cock.

members of the Mortar Platoon in a slit trench at the southern end of the bridge, remembered 'ugly black balls of smoke' and the whirring of shrapnel. One lump of metal hit the bridge above him and, ricocheting dangerously near his head, embedded itself in the back of the trench. Another piece penetrated his webbing, airborne smock, trousers and shirt, and came to rest in his flank. It 'stung sharply for a few seconds', and was still warm as he gently extracted it.[11]

The expected counter-attack from the north was put in at 1.10 p.m. 'with enemy infantry advancing down both sides of the road under cover of smoke, and with close support from enemy fighters'. At first the two 3rd Battalion platoons, with their strength reduced to five officers and 35 men, reported the situation to be under control. But as the enemy attack – supported by self-propelled guns, artillery and anti-aircraft guns – became more intense, the defenders were forced to contract their perimeter and eventually evacuate the northern bank.[12]

Though ordered to conserve ammunition, and fire only when they were 'absolutely certain of a kill', the British paratroopers on the south bank were still able to prevent the enemy from reaching the bridge. They made good use, according to Clements, of a captured Italian Breda machine gun which was sited in a two-storey pillbox. They were forced to abandon the position when it was targeted by heavy artillery.

Unable to infiltrate on foot, the Germans poured heavy machine-gun and artillery fire on all the British positions south of the river, and brought up anti-tank guns to engage the pill-boxes. They also sent infantry across the river, 400 yards to the east of the bridge.

By 6.45 p.m., German machine guns and small arms were firing into the bridge from the high ground to the south-east. The situation was now desperate: the 1st and 3rd Battalions had been forced into a small perimeter on the south side of the bridge which was under bullet and shell fire from three directions; casualties were mounting and ammunition running out; nothing was known of the situation of Frost's 2nd Battalion which had been tasked with securing the night ground – the 'Johnny' features – to the south; and there was no sign of a relief force. Taking all of these factors into account, Brigadier Lathbury reluctantly gave the order for the bridge force to withdraw south in small parties.[13]

The decision was not to Alastair Pearson's liking. In his view, they were in no danger of being overrun, and could surely hold out until dark. 'But in the end,' he recalled, 'I had to do as I was told and withdrew my battalion to the hills.' Before doing so, he and his provost sergeant 'Panzer' Manser and batman Jock Clements made a recce of the river bank because he had a 'gut feeling' he would soon be coming back. About 400 yards to the west of the bridge he found a ford across the river, and made a mental note before retracing his steps.[14]

Most of the bridge force headed west in small groups of three to six men, skirting their original drop zone before moving south along a dried-up wadi. Reg Curtis and two mates were shot at from a hill-top to the west, but not hit. Next they encountered, and disarmed, a group of Italian soldiers, mostly youngsters and those 'beyond the age for soldiering'. Telling the Italians to wait for Allied troops, they pressed on and reached a deserted farmhouse as it got dark. They chose not to stop and, after covering another five miles, dozed for an hour in an orchard until awakened by the sound of marching feet on the road nearby. It was a 10-strong German patrol, 'heavily armed with Schmeissers and rifles'. Curtis shrank back into the shadows and the patrol plodded by, unaware of their presence. A short while later, the sound of automatic gunfire suggested that the patrol must have met other British paratroopers. Curtis and his mates eventually reached Augusta, via Lentini, more than 15 miles from the bridge, and were relieved to find the town crawling with British armour and infantry.[15]

Lieutenant Alan Clements was in a group of six that spent the night in the bakery of a large farmhouse, expecting capture at any minute. 'You can have no idea,' he told his parents, 'of the relief with which we heard the rumble of the first heavy tanks of the 8th Army, and the next day our own 25s [25-pounders] opened fire on the enemy defences at the bridge, a sight which it was only human to relish after our own experiences of the day before. Moving back we passed long columns of prisoners, passing to the rear – a forlorn sight! – and Montgomery standing up in his car greeting the passing soldiers with cheerful bonhomie.'[16]

Dick Bingley had earlier escorted a group of wounded back to Lentini where they were met by the battalion quartermaster who gave them a hot meal, relieved them of their weapons and despatched them in ambulances to a hospital in Syracuse. From there they were shipped back to Tripoli to recuperate.[17]

The withdrawal of the bridge force in dribs and drabs had been witnessed by Lieutenant Colonel Frost and his men from their position on top of Johnny I, just over a mile to the south. Frost had had no contact with brigade HQ since Lathbury's visit that morning, and was now down to 60 effectives, having lost two officers and 40 men killed, with the same number wounded. They had done all they could 'to collect as many of these small parties as possible by waving and shouting and sending out patrols'. It was not easy to persuade some of the fugitives that they were 'still firmly established', yet by the time it got dark they had been 'considerably reinforced and were in a much stronger position than before'. It got so crowded on Johnny I, in fact, that there was no longer room for the 500 or so Italian prisoners within the perimeter who were 'ordered to fall out for the night, but to make quite sure they reported again at first light in the morning'.

At 7.45 p.m., much to Frost's amazement, a troop of Sherman tanks from the 4th Armoured Brigade, the leading element of Montgomery's Eighth Army, rumbled down the road. They reported that infantry were moving up fast behind them to relieve the 1st Parachute Brigade. At midnight, more tanks and the infantry arrived, with a company of the 9th Durham Light Infantry joining Frost's men on Johnny I. They explained that they had covered 20 miles in the heat of the day and were in no fit state for immediate offensive operations. An attempt to recover the bridge would, however, take place the following morning.

If Brigadier Lathbury had only held on at the bridge for a few hours longer, this new assault would not have been necessary. His failure to inform Frost of his intention to withdraw was also a mystery. One man who did reach Frost's position before midnight was Pearson, commanding the 1st Battalion, with a few of his men.

Early on 15 July, Frost and Pearson watched the preparations for a full-scale tank and infantry assault on the bridge by the 44th Royal Tank Regiment and the 9th Durham Light Infantry. After a huge artillery bombardment, smoke was used to cover the advance of the tanks and infantry over 'the last and most dangerous stretch'. But the Germans held their fire until the infantry, plodding relentlessly on with bayonets fixed for the final assault, were within some 50 yards of their positions. Then they opened up, mowing down the leading platoons. They also 'fired burst after burst of machine gun fire at the tanks, which had the effect of forcing them to remain closed down and therefore unable to identify targets'. Without protection, the infantry attack 'faded away and both Durhams and tanks came back'.[18]

Four of the 44th Royal Tank Regiment's Shermans were lost and 18 men captured in the assault, while the commanding officer and medical officer were also killed.

While all this was happening, Brigadier Lathbury – who had spent the night below Johnny I – came up the hill and met the commander of the 4th Armoured Brigade, John Currie, who was watching the battle from Frost's HQ. Brigadier Currie told him that another daylight battalion assault, using exactly the same axis and method, would take place in the afternoon. Overhearing this, Pearson said in a voice loud enough to hear: 'If you want to lose another battalion, you're going the right way about it.'

The two brigadiers glared at Pearson. But Lathbury then persuaded Currie to listen to what Pearson had to say. The commander of the 1st Parachute Battalion advised cancelling the frontal attack, and instead taking the 8th Durham Light Infantry across the river to the north bank by the ford he had scouted. They would then be in a position to assault and recapture the Primosole Bridge from a direction the German defenders were not expecting.

'All right, Pearson,' said Currie, 'what else do you need?'

'Just 2,000 yards of white tape.'

'What's that for?'

'To mark the route. If we're going to get lost, we'll all get lost together.'

'All right. You can have it.'

Pearson added that it was to be a silent attack by two companies of the Durham Light Infantry, and that he wanted the rest of the battalion with its armoured support 'to be in position on the road, ready to move as soon as they saw the success signal, a green Very light'.

At midnight, Pearson asked Major Lidwill, the boss of 8th DLI, and the two company commanders to walk with him to the ford. Betraying his nerves, Lidwill asked: 'What's out in front?'

'My bloody batman, I hope!' replied Pearson.

'Panzer' Manser was leading with the white tape, followed by Pearson, the officers, and the two companies of 8th DLI. As they were approaching the river, a Durham accidentally shot and killed the man in front of him. 'The noise was unreal – a single shot at night,' remembered Pearson. 'I really thought we'd passed a line of no return. But the Germans made no response.'

At the ford they found Pearson's batman Jock Clements. 'Away across the river, Jock,' said Pearson.

'What me, sir?'

'Aye, you, yes. Here's my torch. If you see anything, give it a wee wave.'

Clements frowned. 'If there's anyone on the other side you'll soon know about it.'

Lidwill looked surprised that a batman would talk to a lieutenant colonel like that, but Pearson was used to it. He told Clements to mark the approach to the bridge with the tape, and they would follow him across.

They did so at 2.10 a.m., using two fords 50 yards apart, and moved through thickly planted vineyards to the bridge where they found little opposition. Assuming the Germans would counterattack at first light, Pearson told Lidwill to place his two companies at the edge of the vineyards, on either side of the Catania road, because if the enemy got in there he would be in trouble. But Lidwill refused.

By this time, it was getting light and Pearson had done his job. So he and his two men withdrew back up the road. He expected to meet the Durhams going into action – 'streams of Jeeps and tanks' – but the only person he met was a War Office observer on his bike, who pedalled back with Pearson's report. Even so, it was dawn before the Durhams crossed the bridge.[19]

The delay was partly because the mortar flares had got separated from the mortars, and the wireless sets were not working.

Eventually the rest of the battalion came forward and established a hard-won bridgehead at the north end of Primosole which, despite being forced to concede ground on a number of occasions, the 8th DLI did not relinquish. Reinforced the following night – 15/16 July – by the other two battalions in the 151st Infantry Brigade, the 6th and 9th, the Durhams finally broke the savage resistance of the German paratroopers on 17 July when Allied tanks crossed the bridge. The 151st Brigade had lost more than 500 men in the fight for the Primosole Bridge.

Of the 12 officers and 280 men of the 1st Parachute Brigade who had taken part in the battle, 27 were killed, 78 wounded and 10 missing.[20] Yet despite the fact that less than 20 per cent of the brigade 'dropped at the right place and at the right time' – resulting in an effective force that was 'very depleted and disorganised' – the original plan was 'carried out as far as possible'.[21]

In Sicily, airborne warfare had come of age. The Sicily campaign was what 'Boy' Browning, now airborne advisor to the 15th Army Group, had long sought for airborne troops: to land behind enemy lines and capture and hold vital bits of infrastructure – in this case bridges – until relieved by rapidly advancing ground forces. It was the 'first time in history a force of 4,000 fully armed British soldiers, with anti-tank artillery, was launched into battle by air for an attack on enemy positions'.

Unfortunately, the two operations, Ladbroke and Fustian, were poorly planned and had to make do with unfamiliar equipment and inadequately trained personnel, particularly pilots. These problems were exacerbated by high winds and alert anti-aircraft defences. resulting in exceptionally high casualties and a failure to land more than a fraction of the original force at the right time and the right place. Once on the ground, however, these small numbers performed heroically, underlining the tantalising potential of Britain's airborne force if only it could be used more effectively.

As ever, there were chastening lessons for the staff of the 1st Airborne Division to absorb. The post-mortem raised the need for 'full scale rehearsals, so far as possible under similar conditions of landfall, terrain and moon'; close liaison between glider pilots and the pilots of their tug aircraft; all ranks to train in the use of enemy weapons, and after landing to 'move as rapidly as possible to the main objective, without allowing themselves to become involved in incidents en route'; good liaison with ground forces, 'certainly on the Brigade level and whenever possible on the Battalion level'; better air support, particularly with regard to the neutralisation of enemy anti-aircraft fire and searchlights; regardless of the severity of enemy fire, pilots were to 'fly a steady course' once the red jump light had been switched on to give parachutists the best chance of hitting their drop zone.[22]

Unless accuracy improved dramatically, the writing was on the wall. Similar operations in the future – came the stern message – could only be justified if the air force could reliably drop at least a substantial portion of the parachute force where it was meant to be. Liaison between the army and air forces could therefore never be too close.[23]

Lieutenant Colonel John Frost, shipped back to Sousse in North Africa with the remnants of the 1st Parachute Brigade on 17 July, struggled at first to see any silver lining. He felt hugely frustrated by what he regarded as 'another humiliating disaster for airborne forces and almost enough to destroy even the most ardent believer's faith'. Then, as temporary brigade commander, while Lathbury recovered from his wounds in hospital, Frost had to look in detail at what had gone wrong. 'Almost every day,' he recalled, 'stragglers from Italy got back and they all told us how they had been bundled out of their aircraft all over the place, some even being dropped on the slopes of Mount Etna 20 or 30 miles away from the correct [drop zone].'

Gradually he and his staff built up an accurate picture of what had happened, which tended to contradict the debriefing reports put in by the returning pilots. They discovered that a 'considerable number of aircraft had returned to base without dropping their sticks at all, the pilots claiming they couldn't find the way'. One or two, as in the case of Pearson's air crew, had been forced to fly in at pistol point. But it was hard to believe that any pilot could have failed to see the fireworks round the Primosole Bridge, as they claimed.

While Major General Hopkinson was averse to a distasteful and awkward post-mortem, Frost felt that the American pilots' shortcomings 'would jeopardise all future operations at night, and that it was essential that they be invited to make good their navigational deficiencies'. He asked them to a presentation at Brigade HQ with copious supplies of Scotch whisky to lighten the atmosphere. After the Brigade Intelligence Officer had unfolded the tale, Frost invited the Americans to join them in the mess. Their commander responded that they would be happy to do so, but only after he had spoken to his pilots with the aid of the map. What followed must have been a savage dressing-down. 'It was at least three-quarters of an hour,' wrote Frost, 'before the Americans joined us and by then they were in no mood for a party. It was obvious that their Commander had had no idea of the extent of the fiasco. We all knew that they would do their best to ensure that it would never happen again.'[24]

Nearly a month after the operation, Frost was delighted to welcome his adjutant Dicky Dover back to the battalion. His stick had been dropped on the slopes of Mount Etna and, over the next few days, most of them were captured. Dover, however, had remained at large for 23 days with Corporal T. Wilson, a brigade signaller, living off apples and scraps. They successfully dealt with the odd German sentry, and made a considerable nuisance of themselves by attacking enemy transport and sabotaging communications and water supplies. Finally, on 5 August, they came across a patrol of the DLI, and only narrowly avoided being mistaken for the enemy and shot. 'Are you paras?' asked the DLI scout.

'No, you stupid bastards,' replied Wilson, 'we're the babes in the wood.'[25]

Deservedly awarded the MC and MM respectively, Dover and Wilson had shown the sort of tenacity, courage and aggression that Frost expected of all parachutists. The same could not be said of another of Frost's officers, despite his having 'previously been decorated for gallantry' and having been dropped, unlike Dover, quite close to the correct drop zone. When the officer in question eventually reported to Frost with half a dozen men, after the battle was over, he appeared to be fresh, clean and unconcerned.

'Hullo,' said Frost, 'and where have you been?'

The officer pointed to an area just beyond the drop zone and said: 'Things seemed to be rather boisterous between where we were and where you were so I decided to wait till things quietened down.'

Such pusillanimity was not expected of a parachute officer and Frost arranged for his removal from the battalion soon after. The officer was never named by Frost, to spare him embarrassment, but he was almost certainly 25-year-old Lieutenant Desmond 'Slapsie' Brayley, commanding A Company's No. 2 Platoon. A grammar school boy from Pontypridd in Wales, Brayley had been awarded a Military Cross for 'gallant and distinguished services' during the withdrawal from Oudna. Barring injury or capture, his career should have prospered. Yet he left the 2nd Battalion soon after the Sicily campaign and ended the war with the modest rank of captain.*[26]

---

* Frost hinted at the officer's identity when he wrote: 'The officer left the

Other officers and men of the 2nd Battalion who performed well during their brief time in Sicily included Major Dickie Lonsdale, awarded the DSO, Captain Stanley Panter and Lieutenant Tony Frank, both given the Military Cross, and 30-year-old Corporal Neville Ashley of Frank's No. 1 Platoon who won the Military Medal for helping to beat off an enemy attack on Johnny I on 14 July. 'With complete disregard for personal safety,' noted Ashley's citation, 'he moved his [Bren] gun well forward and destroyed [an enemy machine gun] crew. Later, having shot a German soldier at short range, he went out and brought him into the R.A.P. as he was in danger of being burned alive.'[27]

A similar act of heroism was performed during the same German attack on 14 July by another member of Frank's platoon, 26-year-old Sergeant John Bardwell from Consett, County Durham, who showed 'great skill, initiative and coolness' in withdrawing his section as it was 'in danger of being cut off'. Then, having taken up a new position on Johnny I, Bardwell 'went back under heavy fire and brought back two of his men who had been wounded and were in danger of being burnt alive as the dry grass was on fire'.[28]

Oddly enough, Frost received nothing for his bold leadership in Sicily, even though Alastair Pearson of the 1st Battalion got a well-deserved second Bar to his DSO. Pearson was fast asleep in the front of a truck, heading for Syracuse with the remnants of the 1st Parachute Brigade on 17 July, when he was woken by his batman Clements and told that General Sir Bernard

---

battalion, prospered very greatly and became a byword in more ways than one (Frost, *A Drop Too Many*, p. 187). That was Brayley to a tee. After the war, he became a successful businessman and, following generous donations to the Labour Party, was knighted and then made a life peer. He served a very short stint as Under-secretary of State for Defence in Harold Wilson's second administration (1974–1976), but resigned after allegations of financial irregularities.

Montgomery was on the road behind. 'Just at that moment,' remembered Pearson, 'the familiar khaki Humber passed with its pennant flying and signalled for us to stop. I thought a rocket was impending for being asleep but not so. He greeted me by name like a long-lost friend and congratulated us on our efforts and then said he'd like talk to the men.'

As the pair took a stroll down the road, Monty told Pearson that, despite the high casualties, the operation had been a success. When they got to the trucks, Monty was greeted by cheering men, all smoking his cigarettes and saying, 'How's Alamein, sir?' It was, Pearson thought, 'very, very clever how he knew where I was and a great morale raiser'.★[29]

★ Back in Sousse, Pearson was stricken with a 'bad dose' of malaria – probably caught in Sicily – and, after a spell in hospital, was sent back to England in November 1943 to join the staff of the 6th Airborne Division. He had lunch with 'Windy' Gale, the divisional commander, who told him: 'You'll make a bloody bad staff officer.'

'I'm inclined to agree with you,' said Pearson. 'What are you offering?'

'I have just sacked the commanding officer of the 8th Battalion which is in the 3rd Parachute Brigade commanded by James Hill. Would you like that job?'

'Yes, that will suit me fine.' (Pearson, quoted in Arthur, *Men of the Red Beret*, pp. 122, 209–10)

21

'Get over the side!'
– Apulia, Italy, September–November 1943

S HORTLY BEFORE MIDNIGHT ON 9 September 1943, the 2,700-ton fast minelayer HMS *Abdiel* was about to dock to offload stores and troops in Taranto harbour, on the inner heel of Italy, when it struck two mines. Gus Platts, a member of the 6th Parachute Battalion's mortar platoon, heard 'an unholy bang', immediately followed by what he thought 'were tracer bullets, but which were actually sparks shooting out of the funnel'.

Within seconds, the crippled ship broke into two and started to sink by the stern. Platts was catapulted into the bottom of the lifeboat under which he was sheltering. As he got to his feet, a naval officer shouted: 'Get over the side!'

By now the ship was listing so badly to port that he had to climb up the deck to get to the starboard rail, and was able to sit on the ship's side as she turned over. He paused for a moment to help a friend blow up his inflatable life-jacket, then leapt into the water, swimming away from the vessel as fast as he could. He had swum about 100 yards in water thick with fuel oil when he turned to see the *Abdiel*'s bows, with men still hanging on, sink beneath the surface.

Eventually rescued by a rowing boat, he and some of the other survivors spent the night in a cinema near the docks. They were the lucky ones. Forty-eight crew and 58 men from the 6th Battalion went down with the ship, including the commanding officer Lieutenant Colonel J. A. Goodwin, and Regimental Sergeant Major F. T. Langford. A further 150 men were wounded. It is ironic that it was the sinking of a ship that accounted for the most serious casualties suffered by British airborne forces as they took part in the second phase of the invasion of southern Italy.[1]

The final decision to extend the Sicily campaign to mainland Europe was taken only after Benito Mussolini, the Italian dictator, had been toppled by a coup d'état on 25 July and the new head of government, Marshal Badoglio, initiated secret peace negotiations with the Allies. On 3 September, a couple of weeks after the last Axis troops evacuated Sicily, the armistice was signed at the headquarters of General Sir Harold Alexander, commander of the Allied 15th Army Group. That same day, the first phase of the invasion of the Italian mainland began with Operation Baytown, the crossing of the Straits of Messina and the bloodless occupation of Reggio by General Sir Bernard Montgomery's Eighth Army.

Five days later, the Italian armistice was announced by the BBC, prompting German forces to occupy Rome, and Marshal Badoglio and the Italian royal family to flee to Brindisi, where they set up an anti-fascist Italian government. The announcement was timed to coincide with the second phase of the invasion on 9 September: Operation Avalanche, the landing of General Mark Clark's US Fifth Army at Salerno, 35 miles south of Naples; and Operation Slapstick, the arrival of George Hopkinson's 1st Airborne Division at the Italian naval base of Taranto, after the departure of the Italian fleet to Malta.

Hopkinson had hoped his men would be deployed by air. He was desperate for another opportunity to prove the worth of his airlanding troops after the Sicily fiasco, and even tried to persuade

John Frost, when he was deputising for Lathbury, to mix glider-borne and parachute units in the 1st Parachute Brigade. But while Frost accepted that the glider 'was probably the best means of introducing the supporting and heavier weapons', the parachute was, in his view, the optimal way to bring in men.[2]

Neither method would be used by the 1st Airborne Division in Italy because of a lack of aircraft and suitable airfields in Sicily. Instead, they would be sent in by sea to seize Taranto and exploit the lightly defended area to the north, on the eastern flank of the main advance. To defend the whole of the province of Apulia, the Germans had only one formation, the 1. Fallschirmjäger-Division (1st Parachute Division), which, weakened by losses in Sicily, was believed to number around 8,000 men. The divisional headquarters was at Altamura, 50 miles northwest of Taranto, and elements were scattered as far north as Foggia.

In the same area there were more than 100,000 armed Italians, including the 152ª Divisione di fanteria 'Piceno' (152nd Infantry Division), under the command of XI Corps at Bari, but an agreement had been made with Badoglio's government that these troops would cooperate with the Allies against the Germans once the armistice was announced. Hopkinson's plan, therefore, was to 'advance inland, contacting Italian military leaders and spreading Allied influence as far afield as possible, particularly in the towns of Brindisi and Bari, [and] at the same time thwarting any attempt by the Germans to impose their authority in this region'.[3]

Transported from the Tunisian port of Bizerta in Royal Navy cruisers, the 4th Parachute Brigade – formed in North Africa and the Middle East in late 1942 and assigned to the 1st Airborne Division prior to the Sicily campaign – landed first on 9 September and secured the port. It was during the follow-up operation to land the 2nd Parachute Brigade that *Abdiel* was sunk by a mine.

At this early stage of the campaign, the airborne troops had very few supporting arms and practically no transport. They relied instead on local resources and any captured enemy equipment.[4] Their opponents, as they had been at times in North Africa and also Sicily, were German parachutists. 'Sometimes,' noted Captain Tony Hibbert of Brigade HQ, 'there were battalion or full company attacks, but mostly it was just really vigorous patrolling on both sides, with the occasional bump. There was a great deal of hanging around which made people impatient, especially the unit commanders. When this happens they tend to go out in front themselves instead of sending patrols.'[5]

Some of the stiffest opposition was encountered at the town of Castellaneta, 25 miles north-west of Taranto, where the Germans had established a strong defensive position on either side of the main road. On 11 September, as he watched the 10th Parachute Battalion assault the road-block, Major General Hopkinson was hit by machine-gun fire and mortally wounded. He died the following day – the only British airborne general to be killed in action during the war – and was replaced by Eric Down.

'"Hoppy" was very much a front-line general,' noted one of his senior officers, 'and any brigade or battalion in trouble would very soon find him in its midst.' His courage was not in doubt; what seems to have been in shorter supply was judgement and common sense. A 'restless, endearing character', he died because his impatience got the better of him.[6]

Imprudence was also displayed by Lieutenant Colonel Tony Deane, commanding the 4th Parachute Battalion. Determined not to be caught in an ambush, he had armed his personal Jeep with two light machine guns facing forward, and two Stens guarding the rear. All could be fired by the driver pulling on a piece of string. But none of these weapons were any use when Deane dismounted from the Jeep to inspect a bridge and was captured by German paratroopers hiding nearby.[7]

The day after Hopkinson's death, 1st Airlanding Brigade came ashore and joined the 2nd and 4th Parachute Brigades in harassing patrols against the enemy. For several days there were minor engagements as the Germans disputed the advance towards Altamura. The last brigade to land at Taranto was Lathbury's 1st. It was, according to John Frost, 'given very little to do, for the 8th Army was moving slowly in those days and while the 5th Army fought desperately for its beach-head at Salerno, the 8th was maintaining its balance. We spent four days digging in at Taranto in case the Germans produced a sudden riposte which might force us back to the sea.'

On the night of 20/21 September, Lathbury's brigade took over the advance to Altamura from the 2nd Parachute Brigade, entering the town unopposed on 22 September. That same day – in an ironic mirroring of the airborne force's first ever mission, Operation Colossus – the retreating Germans blew up the Apulian aqueduct at Atella, 'cutting off the water supplies not only of the province of Apulia, but of the whole Foggian plain'. By now, the 1st Airborne was under the command of the British V Corps which had disembarked at Taranto with the 78th Infantry and 8th Indian Divisions, and the 4th Armoured Brigade.

After the 1st Airlanding Brigade captured Foggia on 28 September – the Germans having abandoned the city a day earlier – the division was charged with rescuing the many former Allied prisoners of war who, as a consequence of the Italian surrender, were roaming the Italian countryside behind enemy lines. Codenamed Operation Simcol, the plan was to drop five 10-man sticks of parachutists in the centre of Italy to find the former POWs and arrange for their rescue by sea. One of the sticks was American, another from the 2nd SAS, and the remainder were drawn from the three battalions of the 1st Parachute Brigade. Captain 'Tim' Timothy, who had missed the Sicily campaign with in-growing toenails (since cured by an operation), led the 2nd Battalion's contingent, composed of himself, an Italian-speaking American soldier, and eight volunteers.

In total, Operation Simcol helped around 500 POWs to return to Allied lines. For his part in the mission, Timothy was awarded a Bar to his Military Cross. In his report, he gave due credit to Italian civilians for looking after the escaped prisoners and giving them clothes. 'There are,' he wrote, 'numerous instances of Italians buying medicine for those of our men who are sick. The POWs are generally being treated as honoured guests.'[8]

Although Timothy got back safely, most of his men were captured. This was counter-balanced by the return of some 2nd Battalion men who had been taken prisoner in North Africa, including 'a party who had spent three weeks on active service with the 2nd German Parachute Battalion'. They had managed to escape, wrote John Frost, 'during an excellent evening's carousal'.[9]

Meanwhile, the 1st Parachute Brigade had been sent to Barletta on the Adriatic coast on 25 October to 'deceive the enemy into thinking that a landing on the East coast was imminent, and compel him to dispose his forces to meet this threat'. They did this by conducting brigade exercises in which men and vehicles were loaded and put to sea as if a genuine seaborne assault was intended.

In late November 1943, with little prospect of future airborne operations in Italy, the bulk of the 1st Airborne Division was returned to the UK by sea to prepare for D-Day. Left behind was the 2nd Parachute Brigade which, henceforth, would serve as an independent formation in Italy, the south of France and Greece.

'The short days and cold nights of November,' noted Frost, 'gave us a foretaste of what an Italian winter could be like. The

Germans were fighting hard for every inch and the rain was no friend to offensive mobile operations. We knew that we were probably being saved for the coming operations in north-west Europe so when we were finally ordered back to Taranto on the first stage of our journey to the UK there were no regrets.'[10]

22

Sheldon's Corner and Sangshak
– Assam, north-east India, 19–24 March 1944

AT 9:00 A.M. ON 19 March 1944, Major John Fuller received word from scouts that 900 Japanese soldiers were approaching his position at Point 7378, a hill feature that guarded the winding rollercoaster track that led north to Kohima and south to Imphal. Both towns were keystones of the Indian IV Corps' defences in the Manipur district of Assam in north-east India, and the targets of a major offensive – Operation U-Go – that had been launched across the Chindwin river from Burma by Major General Renya Mutaguchi's Japanese Fifteenth Army, with the rail and road hub of Dimapur as its ultimate objective.[1]

Fuller was commanding C Company of the 152nd Indian Parachute Battalion, part of the 50th Indian Parachute Brigade★ which, after the cancellation of a full-scale drop into the Arakan peninsula, had been sent in early 1944 to a camp near Kohima

---

★ Raised in Delhi in October 1941, the 50th Indian Parachute Brigade was made up of the 151st (British), 152nd (Indian) and 153rd (Gurkha) Parachute Battalions, together with sappers, signals and medical units. In November 1942, the 151st was re-designated the 156th and sent to the Middle East where it joined the 1st Airborne Division's 4th Parachute Brigade and later served with it in Italy and Holland. It was replaced in the 50th Brigade by the 154th (Gurkha) Parachute Battalion which, by the spring of 1944, was still in training.

for jungle warfare training. Briefed a few weeks later by Major General Ouvry Roberts, commanding the 23rd Indian Infantry Division, the brigade commander had been assured that 'the expected main Japanese threat against India could only develop from well south of Imphal', as 'several thickly jungle-clad mountain ridges, rising up to 3,000 or 4,000 feet', would discourage an approach from the east. The brigade's orders, therefore, were 'to keep the area clear of Japanese patrols and infiltration agents'.

On 10 March, following intelligence reports that the Japanese were about to cross the Chindwin further south, the 50th Brigade was ordered to move with all speed to Imphal. As transport was scarce, the move would be done in stages and take several days. The first unit to move was the 152nd Parachute Battalion – uniquely recruited from across the Indian Army on a no-class, no-caste basis – under Lieutenant Colonel Paul 'Hoppy' Hopkinson, the 37-year-old son of a professor of archaeology turned Anglican priest (and no relation to the late commander of the 1st Airborne Division). Having left school at 16, Hopkinson joined the Indian Army and saw service in Waziristan and up the Khyber Pass. He and a fellow officer, Captain B. E. Abbott, were attending a staff course in England in 1940 when they were sent to Ringway to earn their 'wings' and glean what information they could, before returning to the sub-continent to help set up a parachute force for the Indian Army. After a stint as the 50th's first brigade major, he was promoted to lieutenant colonel and given command of the 152nd Battalion. Small and slightly built – looking more like a scholar than a military man – Hopkinson was 'winsome and diffident, with a quiet sense of humour'. Yet his character 'inspired immediate trust from all who served with him'.

Arriving in Imphal on the evening of 10 March 1944, Hopkinson was ordered to set up a patrol base at a track junction called Sheldon's Corner, 10 miles east of Sangshak, a 'small Naga village on a piece of high ground, tactically very well sited'. It was, noted a brigade staff officer, 'breathtaking country but progress anywhere was slow because of the narrow muletracks and footpaths (vertical in places) which had to be followed much of the time. One false move by man or mule could result in a 1,000-foot plunge down the "khudside".'[2]

At Sheldon's Corner the battalion was to 'take over, complete and be prepared to occupy certain fixed defence works' that Lieutenant Colonel Trim's 4/5th Mahratta Light Infantry were in the process of constructing. The position comprised two outposts monitoring the tracks that led from Sheldon's Corner down to the Chindwin: Point 7378, occupied by C Company; and another hill feature known as 'Gammon', defended by B Company. 'They were not mutually supporting,' noted Hopkinson, 'being some two to three miles apart. Before these positions could be effectively occupied much work was necessary; besides which they required stocking with ammunition, rations etc and arrangements made for the storage of water. The remainder of the [battalion] was located in a "hide out" in the jungle about 2 miles [to the] rear on the northern slope of a hill known as "Badger". No defence works had been started here and the only water points were further down the slope.'

The plan was for the two forward company positions to act as 'pivots of manoeuvre' for a mobile striking force from the battalion operating from the hideout. It was adequate to deal with small parties of the enemy, but against a large force there was a danger that one or both of the forward companies would be isolated and overrun. A further problem was that a parachute battalion had only three rifle companies, which was insufficient to garrison both the outposts and also leave enough men to provide a relief force and defend the hideout. There was, more-over, 'a shortage of tools, barbed wire, other defence stores and above all the water problem'. The 152nd Parachute Battalion would just have to make the best of it.

Hopkinson's 700 men took over the positions at Sheldon's Corner and its outposts from the Mahrattas on 15 March. Like the rest of the brigade, the men of the 152nd had removed their distinctive red berets and embroidered 'wings', and were wearing standard jungle green uniforms with a 'patch pocket' on the front right leg. On their heads they sported slouch hats, woollen caps or, in the case of the Gurkhas of the 153rd Battalion, broad-brimmed felt hats. Only the mortarmen wore steel helmets. Each 10-man rifle section was led by a naik (corporal) armed with a 9mm Sten gun. The rest of the section had .303 Lee-Enfield rifles, a single Bren gun, grenades, bayonets and the Gurkhas' famous curved fighting knife, the kukri.

Both forward companies of the 152nd were supported by a section of 3-inch mortars and a pair of medium machine guns. When Major Fuller joined C Company at Point 7374 on 17 March, having just arrived from Kohima with mortar ammunition, the garrison numbered 170 men, including seven British officers. His orders were to hold the hill until relieved, to keep an eye out for enemy patrols that might cross the Chindwin, and to continue to improve the unfinished defences.

On 18 March, Hopkinson drove to advanced Brigade HQ, which had been sited at Sangshak a day earlier, for a conference with acting Brigadier M. R. J. 'Tim' Hope Thomson, a 32-year-old regular officer who had won a Military Cross in Palestine with the Royal Scots Fusiliers before volunteering for airborne duty. 'Tall, fair and athletic in build, impassive and reserved in manner', noted one officer, Hope Thomson was unable to speak either Urdu or Gurkhali, and had no experience of commanding Indian troops. He did, however, have 'one indisputable asset: his up-to-the-minute knowledge of airborne techniques in Britain, supplemented by a visit to the 1st Parachute Brigade in action in North Africa, where he had seen and assimilated the lessons learned in fighting there. In 1943 he was the only officer in India Command with any real knowledge of airborne matters.'

Hope Thomson's chief contribution to the brigade's training, however, was to order all sub-units to conduct regular sessions of PE and unarmed combat, field firing, battle drills and night movement. The mastering of these skills would prove invaluable in the fighting to come. Hope Thomson told Hopkinson to start operating long range patrols from 21 March. There was no suggestion that an attack was imminent.

That night, Fuller reported to Hopkinson by radio that he had credible intelligence from an officer from V-force, a 'stay behind' reconnaissance outfit set up by the British in 1942, that the Japanese 'were across the Chindwin in considerable strength' and had occupied the village of Pushin, a couple of miles east of Point 7378. It was Hopkinson's first indication that a major Japanese advance in their sector had begun. 'We all felt thankful,' he wrote, 'for the very hard work put in on improving the defences, occupying them and in having moved all the ammunition, supplies etc from the Basha camps into the positions. We had largely got over the water problem in the forward localities by digging tanks and lining them with tarpaulins.'[3]

By 9.30 a.m. the following day, 19 March, Fuller – who had been informed by his scouts that a large Japanese force was approaching – knew an attack was imminent. It began at 2 p.m. after the 900 men of the Japanese 3/58th Regiment, under Major Shimanoe, had encircled his position. The first assault was beaten off, as were two night attacks, though at a heavy cost in men and ammunition. At first light on 20 March, Hopkinson received word from Point 7378 that Fuller, three other officers and 40 men had been killed, and many more were wounded, including the second-in-command, Roseby. Just as desperate was the shortage of ammunition.

The only source for what happened next is the Japanese 58th Regiment's war diary:

By mid-morning the enemy's fire slackened considerably. Suddenly, from the top of the hill, a small group of about 20 men charged down towards us, firing and shouting in a counter-attack. However, between us was a wide ravine which they had been unable to see, and of those who were still alive some fell into it in their rush onwards while the rest had no choice but to surrender.* A few escaped. At the very top of the position an officer appeared in sight, put a pistol to his head and shot himself in full view of everyone below. Our men fell silent, deeply impressed by such a brave act.

At Point 7378 the 3rd Battalion suffered 160 casualties in the action, with one company and two platoon commanders killed and another four officers wounded . . . The enemy had resisted with courage and skill.

That an Indian Army officer preferred suicide to capture – a mirroring of Japanese practice – is harrowing to learn. He may have been shamed by the defeat, or aware that the brutal conditions in Japanese prisoner-of-war camps were tantamount to a slow death. Whatever the explanation, he has never been identified.

Hopkinson, meanwhile, had attempted to relieve the pressure on Fuller's men by despatching A Company, under Richard Gillett, on a flanking route that would bring them round to Point 7378 from the east. But they were slowed by the steep terrain and the difficulty of navigating through the jungle at night. When they did reach a point half a mile to the east of 7378, the battle was all but over.[4]

---

* A month later, taking advantage of the post-battle confusion, 24 C Company men escaped from captivity and made their way to safety.

By 19 March, the 50th Indian Parachute Brigade was all that lay between two Japanese divisions and Imphal, and the Indian plains beyond. The security of British India was hanging in the balance. Hope Thomson had been ordered by IV Corps to form a 'strong box', a self-contained post, at Sangshak, 10 miles from Sheldon's Corner. He 'somehow managed to contrive order out of chaos' by gathering in all his units, which included Hopkinson and the remnants of the 152nd Battalion who began the withdrawal to Sangshak on 20 March. Hopkinson's men carried as much as 70 or 80 pounds of equipment through the mountainous terrain. Yet none of this would have been possible 'without the valour and self-sacrifice of the doomed company at Point 7378' who had held up the Japanese for just long enough to make a retreat possible.

The only prepared defences at Sangshak were a two-company position on the eastern edge of the plateau that had been dug by the local Kalibahadur Regiment. This was incorporated into the brigade 'box', thus saving vital time. Little else about the position, however, was in the brigade's favour. It was, noted Hopkinson, a 'barren hill-top, some half a mile long by a quarter wide'. The jungle came up to the outer edge of the perimeter and a track, leading from Imphal to Sheldon's Corner, and on down to the Chindwin river, ran along the southern face of the position. The village of Sangshak was just outside the south-west corner, and slightly below it. Overlooking the position, at the north-west corner of the perimeter, was a small wooden church belonging to an American Baptist Mission. Near the church were large stacks of brush wood.

There were, moreover, no water points within the perimeter 'and the springs from which the the Kalibahadurs drew water were outside and very small'. Sangshak was, in Hopkinson's opinion, 'far too isolated for prolonged defence even if supply by air could have been guaranteed'. It had been selected as a patrol base – rather than a position to be properly fortified and supplied – because senior commanders 'had been deluded into thinking that the country was far too difficult for the Japanese to be able to move large forces across the mountain ranges and through the very dense jungle'.

The race to reach Sangshak first was only just won by the 50th Brigade. On 22 March, as the last units were occupying the position, the Japanese were converging in a pincer attack from both the north and west. As Hopkinson put it: 'It was mayhem: 15th Battery of the 9th Mountain Regiment Indian Army was in action shelling enemy columns coming down the track from Ukhral, 4/5th Marathas were covering the concentration of the brigade from a ridge about 500 yards west of the perimeter (West Hill). The Medium Machine-Gun Company were digging in as fast as possible. 153 Battalion had arrived the night before and were occupying part of the western perimeter. We (152) had been allotted the northern and part of the western face including the vital Church area, but there was too little daylight left when we arrived on the 22nd to do more than occupy the Kalibahadur slit trenches and weapon pits.'⁵

The garrison had about 2,000 men in position when the Japanese attacked as night was falling on 22 March. They came sweeping in from the west against the trenches occupied by the 153rd Battalion, recruited exclusively from the tough Nepal hillmen who had served in European-officered Gurkha battalions since the early 19th century. The Gurkhas waited until the leading Japanese soldiers had set foot on level ground before opening fire, bringing down the enemy in heaps. As they fell, noted Harry Seaman, a young officer of the 153rd, 'still more enemy soldiers were coming into view over the brow of the hill, silhouetted against the evening sky, to be cut down by rifle fire'.

Soon, the medium machine guns 'began to spray West Hill with spectacular bursts of tracer, and the mortars started lobbing their three-inch bombs onto the enemy still out of sight behind the hill'. The first assault was stopped in its tracks, costing the Japanese 2/58th Regiment's 8th Company 90 of its 120 men in just 15 minutes of combat.[6]

But with darkness came a second assault from the south, which continued, on and off, for much of the night. It was a terrifying experience for the Gurkhas and their officers, many of whom were in combat for the first time. Renegade Indian troops – members of the Indian National Army who had been recruited from former POWs to fight alongside the Japanese – tried to deceive the defenders by shouting 'Cease fire!' in English, Urdu and Gurkhali. British officers hurled insults in response. The night was lit up by Very lights, tracer and exploding Japanese two-inch mortar bombs, 'which seemed to burn with a phosphorous glow'. Before long, the village just outside the perimeter caught fire, and it was touch and go whether the company would have to retire; but at the critical moment the wind changed. From the regimental aid post half way down the forward slope, the 53rd's medical officer Captain F. G. Neild had 'a magnificent view across the dip at the bottom to the burning village on the opposite slope'.

All night long, the wounded came to Neild's aid post, but there was little he could do, except staunch the bleeding and administer morphia, before evacuating the worst cases to the field ambulance that had been set up in a little dip, about 200 yards from the centre of the perimeter. There the senior medical officer and surgical team carried out multiple operations.[7]

Dawn revealed the ground outside the perimeter to be littered with the bodies of 3 Japanese officers and 86 men. Aware that officers and senior ranks might be carrying important documents, Hope Thomson gave orders for their recovery, no easy task as the ground was swept by enemy machine-gun fire. The closest corpses were just below the church, on the enemy side, and Captain 'Dicky' Richards hoped to pull them in with an improvised grappling hook he had made out of a 'decapitated wireless aerial and some line'.

While he was scanning the dead through binoculars, a Japanese machine gun opened up and began traversing. Bullet holes 'started to appear in a line from the far end of the whitewashed mud and wattle wall, about 18 inches from ground level'. Richards froze, until Major John Bull shrieked 'Down!'

This broke the spell, and he flung himself to the ground. The fire passed over him 'with only an inch or two to spare, going to and fro for some minutes'. Bull called for mortar support which caused the Japanese to keep their heads down long enough for Richards 'to pull in a few bodies and get clear'.

Incredibly, one of the Japanese officers did have 'some very interesting maps showing the plan and intended routes for the attacks by the Japanese 15th and 31st Divisions on Imphal and Kohima', which were taken back to IV Corps Headquarters at Imphal by Captain Lester Allen, the brigade intelligence officer, and an NCO 'who bravely penetrated through the Japanese attackers unscathed'.

A study of the maps also made it quite obvious to Hope Thomson and his staff that their position at Sangshak would have to be eliminated if the Japanese were to carry out their plan. This was confirmed by a message back from the corps commander at Imphal that Sangshak needed to be held at all costs. He was, he added, making plans to reinforce the brigade, but they would not be completed any time soon. Despite the lack of immediate support, the garrison was cheered by this news.[8]

Daylight, however, laid bare the weakness of their position. Guarding the north-west corner of the perimeter, the men of

Hopkinson's 152nd Battalion were manning slit trenches that were far too shallow, unprotected by barbed wire and with no communication or crawl trenches back to the rear. Hemmed in by the jungle, their forward posts had restricted fields of fire, and all ranks were at constant risk of being shot by snipers or machine gunners if they made the slightest movement in the open. Hopkinson soon lost quite a few officers and NCOs to this harassing fire as they attempted to visit platoon and section posts. But the unit worst affected was the 50th's Medium Machine-gun Company, dug in near Brigade HQ at the left centre of the perimeter, because the upright firing position of its gunners was so exposed. Major Bull, the company commander, and his deputy Captain Graydon were both shot in the head and killed as they tried to keep the guns firing after their original Number Ones had been hit.

During the morning of 24 March, Hope Thomson's patrols reported large enemy columns of motor transport and elephants moving in from the east. They brought forward Japanese artillery which began to shell the position from midday, followed by more probing infantry attacks. It took fierce hand-to-hand fighting to push them back. Hope Thomson called for air support and a number of Allied fighters did come over and engage the enemy but as the jungle targets were very difficult to locate, some of their own positions were accidentally shot up as well. Hopkinson was watching the fighters from Battalion HQ when one headed straight for him. He had just enough time to take cover 'before the post was riddled with machine-gun fire'.

Fatigue and hunger were now showing in every face, and water-collecting parties were sniped at as they bravely ventured out to the three nearby springs. The heat and discomfort of the packed trenches only compounded the strain.

They were, however, urged to hold on by the local divisional commander, Major General Ouvry Roberts, who signalled to

Hope Thomson: 'Well done indeed. You are meeting the main Jap northern thrust. Of greatest importance you hold your position. Will give you maximum air support. Convey to all ranks my greatest appreciation of what you have already achieved.'[9]

23

'Fight your way out'
– Assam, north-east India, 24–31 March 1944

A T DAWN ON 25 MARCH, the Japanese attempted to over-whelm Sangshak's Anglo-Indian defenders by launching a combined assault with a company of Major Nagoya's 2/58th Regiment and two from Major Shimanoe's 3/58th Regiment which, briefly rested after its costly action at Point 7378, had arrived a day earlier. The attack was directed against the church and the north-west corner of the perimeter, an area defended by Hopkinson's battered 152nd Battalion. The Japanese regiment's war diary charted the progress of the attack:

> Some of the men broke into the position after savage hand-to-hand fighting, but then came under fire from the enemy's position on the left and right. Those who had entered the enemy's position were annihilated and the remainder withdrew with heavy losses in killed and wounded, including Lieutenant Nakamura, killed. So this attack ended in failure again.[1]

For the hard-pressed defenders, meanwhile, a supply airdrop on 25 March was hugely welcome. But only a small fraction of the parachute loads was collected by the garrison; the rest fell into enemy hands. Essential supplies were dwindling fast, particularly artillery shells and mortar bombs. Hopkinson's battalion was out of grenades completely, rations were at a bare minimum, and 'what little water there was had to go to the Field Ambulance for the wounded'. There was only enough water for one small mug of tea per man each day. No praise was enough, wrote Hopkinson, for the manner in which his Indian soldiers 'stuck it out although exhausted by lack of sleep, food, water and ammunition'.

By now down to just two heavily depleted companies, Hopkinson asked Hope Thomson for permission to contract the perimeter a little by withdrawing his men to a natural position behind the church, while leaving a small garrison in the building itself. Hope Thomson agreed, and the withdrawal took place late on 25 March. Unfortunately, it was observed by the Japanese who then prepared to attack the church in the early hours of the next day. It was a savage assault, preceded by heavy mortar and artillery fire, and eventually gained its objective after the garrison had all been killed or wounded and Hopkinson's men were unable to retake it. By now, all Hopkinson's company commanders had been killed or badly wounded, and most of his junior officers and many of the VCOs* and NCOs were also casualties. In Battalion HQ, both the Signal and Intelligence officers had been killed. The weapons pits 'were a shambles of dead and dying', both their own and Japanese.[2]

At 7.30 a.m. on 26 March, with the Japanese just 100 yards from Brigade Headquarters, Hope Thomson ordered his defence platoon, led by the young and intrepid Lieutenant Robin de la Haye (nicknamed the 'Red Shadow', because of his habit of

---

* A Viceroy's Commissioned Officer (VCO) was a senior Indian soldier who held a commission issued by the Viceroy. Also known as an Indian or Native Officer, he was superior in rank to warrant officers in the British Army, but only had authority over Indian troops.

doing the rounds at night wearing a pair of red silk pyjamas under his webbing), to restore the situation. De la Haye and his men made a 'spirited attack but were cut to pieces by enemy fire from West Hill'.[3]

In desperation, Hopkinson collected every man he could find at Battalion Headquarters – including runners, signallers and orderlies – and himself led a counter-attack which recovered some of the lost positions. Badly wounded in the leg by a grenade, Hopkinson was taken to the field ambulance for treatment, while the rest of his men were outflanked and forced to retire.[4]

The line was eventually stabilised after a gallant charge by Gurkhas of the 153rd Battalion's A Company. A Japanese warrant officer remembered: 'The Gurkha soldiers, famous for their courage, rushed on and on though many had fallen, screaming as they advanced despite their wounds. Hand-to-hand fighting was everywhere and hand grenades flew everywhere . . . Thus the top of the hill turned to a hell on earth.'

It had been a day of almost non-stop fighting – from before dawn to three in the afternoon ('11 and a half hours of continuous mayhem') – the 'climactic fury' of which had been almost 'impossible to chronicle in detail'. Most of the participants would remember only fragments of that grim day when losses for both sides would exceed the butcher's bill for the whole of the previous week. Only by mid-afternoon did an 'exhausted lull and a semblance of order' return to Sangshak.

Just before six that evening, a message from Major General Ouvry Roberts: 'Fight your way out. Go south then west. Air and transport on the lookout for you. Good luck, our thoughts are with you.'

Sent uncoded and on a frequency that had been unchanged for five days, the message was thought to be an enemy hoax. But when it was confirmed by Imphal, the 'initial euphoria at this last-minute chance of survival was soon dampened by the enormous problems of evacuating the seriously injured, who would have to be carried'. Colonel Bobby Davis, the senior medical officer, offered to stay behind with the worst cases, but he was overruled by Hope Thomson who knew from harsh experience of the Japanese that neither 'the gallant doctor, nor his patients, would have any chance of survival'. After 'much argument and heart-searching', therefore, it was decided that 'those who were unfit to be moved should be made as comfortable as possible and given heavy sedation'; while those capable of walking would be helped by comrades to withdraw with the rest.[5]

With no time to prepare a tactical retreat, Hope Thomson ordered a mass break-out at 10.30 p.m. in a south-easterly direction to avoid Japanese positions to the south at Koushou. As the start time approached, the tension mounted. Japanese fire that evening had been limited to a few short bursts, but everyone knew that a full-scale attack on the weakened garrison was bound to succeed. Fortunately, it never came. Documents captured later confirmed that an attack was scheduled for 3 a.m. the next day, which may explain the lack of enemy activity that evening.

After a final bombardment of West Hill and the village beyond – intended to deceive the Japanese and fire off any remaining ammunition – the guns were disabled and the withdrawal began. In pitch darkness, with the silence 'broken only by a cough or muffled curse as men tripped or fell into empty trenches', the garrison headed down the few hundred yards of steep, dense woodland that surrounded the position.

Moving at different speeds, depending on the type of casualty, the brigade soon fragmented into smaller parties that varied in size from three men to 30. The most depleted unit, by far, was the 152nd Battalion, commanded since Hopkinson's shrapnel injury by Major Reggie Steward. He was one of two unwounded officers out of the original 25 who had gone jungle-training at

Ukhrul a fortnight earlier; of the officer casualties, a scarcely credible 18 had been killed. A further 500 NCOs and men were out of action. Many of the dead officers had been with the unit since it was raised in late 1941, including Tom Roseby, 'another long-haired boy whose career at Oxford had been interrupted by the war', and Archie Buckle, who with his 'fair hair, freckled face and irresistible humour was like a ray of sunshine on a dismal day'.

By 6.30 a.m. the escapees had reached the valley floor and were faced with the task of turning west and climbing the same elevation – 2,000 feet – that they had just descended. Progress was very slow, on account of the jungle terrain and the many wounded. Fortunately, although the Japanese had known of their departure since midnight – and, thereafter, took relatively good care of the badly wounded paratroopers left behind – they were too exhausted to pursue.[6]

In all, the escapees had to climb three mountain ranges – some extending 4,000 feet above the valley floors – to reach Imphal. One halt was so long that Major Harry Butchard of the 153rd Battalion 'moved up the column to find out why, only to discover that the men waiting to cross the ditch had fallen into a deep sleep'. They were so exhausted that he had to kick them into action. That evening he came upon Colonel Abbott, the brigade deputy commander, a large, heavily built officer with a ruddy complexion who, the day before, while the battle was raging in Sangshak, had said to him: 'Harry, I am determined I am going to die of an excess of port in my old age.'

Abbott was half-carrying Hopkinson who, with his arms around the colonel's neck, was hopping up the hill. They joined Butchard's party which, shortly after, settled down for the night in a wood. After a meagre meal of a biscuit or two, and a cigarette or a puff from a pipe, they retired hungry and exhausted to sleep.

At dawn they continued the trek, uphill this time, and eventually met up with and were joined by Brigadier Hope Thomson, concussed by a bad fall and with his head swathed in a blood-stained bandage, and his Pathan orderly. Two days later – having narrowly avoided 'walking into an armed Japanese supply column' by 'rolling into the thick elephant grass and lying "doggo" as the enemy passed within feet of them' – they stumbled across a party of British officers and men brewing up tea in a mess tin. The officers were unsure of the situation to their rear, and had no idea whether they were in front of or behind Japanese lines.

Finally reaching the outskirts of Imphal on 31 March, Butchard was relieved to see the familiar khaki of an Indian sentry. The group closed up and marched in like soldiers, though they resembled a band of scarecrows. Of the many casualties loaded onto ambulances, most would live to fight another day.[7]

The heroic defence of Point 7378 and Sangshak had all but destroyed the 50th Indian Parachute Brigade, the only airborne formation east of Suez. The 152nd Battalion, for example, lost almost 90 per cent of its original strength of 700, most of them killed. Only 2 officers and 90 men had reached Imphal unscathed. The units next hardest hit were the Medium Machine-Gun Company and the Brigade Defence Platoon, both with 75 per cent casualties. Meanwhile, the 153rd Battalion had lost a third of its men, and both supporting gunner units a quarter. Yet the brigade group had exacted a fearsome toll on the enemy, killing and wounding an estimated 2,000 Japanese.

Given the scale of their sacrifice, many in the brigade were mystified when the corps commander Lieutenant General Geoffry Scoones congratulated the 4/5th Mahrattas and the two gunner formations for their part in the battle, but said nothing to Brigadier Hope Thomson and his surviving paratroopers. They were even more disconcerted when rumours began to fly around

Imphal and further afield that the Gurkha and Indian battalions of the 50th had 'faltered' and 'run away'. The exact source of the rumours is hard to trace. They were probably fanned by a message from high command for all units around Imphal to look out for 'stragglers' from Sangshak. It is also likely that Lieutenant Colonel Trim of the 4/5th Mahrattas exaggerated the contribution made by his own men to the defence of Sangshak, while at the same time diminishing the role played by the paratroopers. Yet it may not be a coincidence that Scoones – soon to be knighted and promoted to full general for stopping the Japanese at Kohima and Imphal – later wrote in his report of the battle that the 50th Brigade was at full strength (in reality it had only two battalions, not three) at Sangshak, and that Hope Thomson had both misjudged the direction of the Japanese advance, and mismanaged his response.

This was unfair. Hope Thomson had only become aware of Japanese movements after he was alerted by the 152nd's C Company at Point 7378. But Scoones may have felt the need to deflect attention from his own failings in the days preceding the battle and Hope Thomson was the perfect fall guy because, having returned to Imphal, he was immediately flown back to Madras for hospital treatment. There Hope Thomson was visited by a senior staff officer from Delhi and told he was being posted back to the UK, where he found himself reduced in rank to major and effectively 'busted'. He did not even have a chance to say goodbye to the men he had commanded since 1942, and who had fought so hard for him at Sangshak.

Instead, they were simply told that their brigade commander had been 'invalided home as a result of injuries'. It was only later that some began to suspect that the reason Hope Thomson was removed from the scene was because he was the only man 'who was in a position to ask – and answer – awkward questions about the events that nearly destroyed IV Corps'. It was, noted one young officer of the 153rd (who penned an account of the battle), 'impossible to avoid the conclusion that the 50th Indian Parachute Brigade and its commander had been made the scapegoats for the errors and omissions of those above them'.[8]

The unjust criticism of Hope Thomson was repeated many years later by historian Louis Allen, who wrote in his 1985 book *Burma: The Longest War* that the brigade commander was at various points during the Battle of Sangshak 'on the verge of madness', squatting 'on the floor of his trench clutching his water-bottle', and 'in no fit state at that time to command a retreat and [Lieutenant Colonel Trim] took over'. Hope Thomson rejected all of these claims, and demanded a retraction. 'It is indeed a matter of historical record,' he wrote to Allen's publisher,

> that when I reached Imphal, after many vicissitudes, I was evacuated as a case of severe physical and nervous exhaustion . . . I have [never] sought to deny or conceal the fact that for a very brief period during the last two days of the continuous eight-day battle I did suffer a short collapse from exhaustion, which collapse was only witnessed by, and at the time known to, one other officer. On quickly recovering I resumed my duties and continued them until the evacuation of Sangshak, not cowering in my trench . . . During the eight-day battle, with the brief exception of the above incident, I was at duty either at my HQ or, for the last six days, frequently out and about on the perimeter at Sangshak, doing the best I could do to sustain and coordinate our resistance in desperate circumstances.[9]

A fairer assessment of the battle was provided by the divisional commander, Major General Ouvry Roberts, who, a few days after the survivors reached Imphal, told Captain 'Dicky' Richards, who had served under him in the Middle East, 'that the brigade, with its attached units, fighting under what must have developed into most appalling conditions, had undoubtedly saved Imphal and Kohima from the danger of being immediately overrun by the Japanese spearhead troops'.[10]

This was certainly the opinion of Lieutenant Colonel Paul Hopkinson, commanding the 152nd Battalion, who described the brigade's last stand at Sangshak as 'magnificent'. He added: 'By seriously disrupting Japanese forces when speed was vital to them, we gained the time necessary for defences to be built up in Kohima and non-combatant units to be evacuated. We also inflicted very heavy casualties on the Japanese which they could not afford so early in their campaign and were not able to replace.' He estimated that the total enemy casualties were 450 to 500 at Sheldon's Corner and 2,000 at Sangshak.

On the debit side, 'the only Parachute Brigade in India had suffered severe casualties fighting in an infantry role', and to replenish these losses would take a long time. The situation was exacerbated by the fact that, as the move to Imphal had been 'for training purposes, nearly every available man who had completed his parachute training had gone with the brigade'.[11]

General Sir William Slim, commanding the Fourteenth Army, would later commend Lieutenant General Scoones for his calm response to the sudden invasion of Assam. 'The fog of war had descended,' wrote Slim. 'He was deluged with reports and rumours of Japanese columns which seemed to flit in and out of the jungle, now here, now there; little was definite and certain . . . Rightly he decided to hold to our plan for the battle and to follow the course which would, if successful, more quickly concentrate his corps in the Imphal Plain.'[12]

In reality, as noted by Frank McLynn in *The Burma Campaign*, Scoones of IV Corps reacted far too slowly to the Japanese offensive, particularly the threat to his 17th Division south of Imphal, and only ordered it to withdraw north when it was almost too late. Fortunately, the divisional commander, Major

General David 'Punch' Cowan, acted unilaterally – and technically against Scoones' specific orders to stand firm – by giving
the order to retreat. 'Slim,' wrote McLynn, 'charateristically, took
the blame for this slow reaction, thus covering up for his favourite
[Scoones] . . .. Even so it was touch and go for a while.'[13]

Slim himself was partly responsible for leaving the eastern
approach to Kohima uncovered and undefended. He might have
tried to shift the blame on to Scoones. Instead he used his 1956
memoir, *Defeat Into Victory*, to commend the 50th Indian
Parachute Brigade and the 4/5th Mahrattas (part of the 23rd
Division) for slowing the advance of the Japanese 15th and 31st
Divisions long enough for Kohima and Imphal to strengthen
their defences. 'After dark on 26 March,' he wrote, 'what was
left of the brigade was ordered to break out and make for Imphal.
The 10 days' delay and the heavy casualties this small force and
the RAF who supported them had inflicted on the enemy were
of inestimable value at this critical stage of the battle.'[14]

After the war, former members of the Japanese units that had
fought at Sheldon's Corner and Sangshak went further by insisting
that 'the heavy casualties they suffered and the seven-day delay,
completely disrupted their plans and worse still threw out their
timetable'. If the 50th Parachute Brigade 'had cracked or been
over-run in the first fierce onrush of the attack, as they fully
expected it would be', the whole of the Japanese 15th Division
would have 'poured straight down the last 36 miles of excellent
road into the Imphal Plain (which at the time was denuded of
our troops who had all gone South), annihilated IV Corps HQ
[and] seized the air fields'.[15]

Hope Thomson's men had performed heroics in the hills of
Assam. Yet the near destruction of the only two fully trained
parachute battalions in India was to have a severe impact on
India's airborne capability. The original plan – thrashed out
between Mountbatten, the newly appointed Supreme Allied

Commander in South-East Asia, Browning and others – was for four airborne divisions to be available in the theatre 'for the season 1944/45, two American and two British'. Of the two British divisions, one would come from the UK and the other – to be called 44th – would be formed in India from the existing 50th Indian Parachute Brigade, the British 2nd Parachute Brigade (sent from the Middle East), and a new airlanding brigade and support troops to be raised in India in January 1944. While the Chiefs of Staff in London gave the scheme broad approval, they could not guarantee the arrival of the 2nd Parachute Brigade, and warned that it might be difficult to employ the 44th Airborne 'because of the lack of tug aircraft, gliders, trained glider pilots and suitable airfields'.

Plans had been drawn up to deploy all or part of the putative 44th Division in airborne operations against the Japanese in Burma in late 1944 and early 1945. But they were badly disrupted by the losses suffered by 50th Brigade in Assam and, in the event, the formation of the division was postponed until January 1945.[16]

Despite his mean-spirited demotion in rank, 'Tim' Hope Thomson later served with distinction in north-west Europe as second-in-command of the 5th Dorsets and commanding officer of 1st Worcesters, winning a DSO with the latter for personally leading an assault on the Goch escarpment on the German-Dutch border in February 1945. He also fought in Malaya with his old battalion, the 1st Royal Scots Fusiliers, and retired with the substantive rank of brigadier in 1967.[17] Asked after the war by an officer of the 50th Brigade what the fighting in Europe was like, he replied: 'Well I can tell you this. I would go through the whole campaign in Europe again rather than those seven days in Sangshak. The tempo and fierceness of the fighting did not compare.'[18]

PART III

Triumph, June 1944

24

'The spearhead of the invasion'
– Dorset and Normandy, 5 June 1944

MONDAY, 5 JUNE 1944, was another filthy day with high winds and rain, and Major John Howard felt only sympathy for the many thousands of men being thrown around on ships in the English Channel. In the afternoon, he was handed a message with the codeword 'Cromwell' and was told 'that the meteorological boys had confidently predicted a spell of clearer weather overnight'.

Howard had received the same message a day earlier, only for heavy rain and gales to postpone Operation Tonga, the British airborne component of Operation Overlord, the long-awaited Allied plan to use 5,300 ships and 12,000 aircraft to land or drop 150,000 men and 1,500 tanks on or behind five beaches in Normandy, northern France. Tonga required the insertion of 8,500 glider-borne infantry and paratroopers from the 6th Airborne Division on the eastern flank of the D-Day beachhead. At the same time, 13,000 men of the US 82nd and 101st Airborne Divisions would secure the western flank. But leading them all into action – the point of the spear – would be the 180 men of Howard's D Company, 2nd Ox and Bucks Light Infantry, part of the 6th Airlanding Brigade. Their task: to land in six Horsa gliders at around midnight and capture, by *coup-de-main*, the vital road bridges over the River Orne and the nearby Caen Canal. Possession of the bridges was vital, not only to defend the eastern flank of the D-Day beachhead from a German counter-attack, but also to allow an Allied breakout once the landings were secure.

Under canvas in a sealed transit camp near Tarrant Rushton in Dorset, Howard and his men – D Company, two platoons from B Company and a small force of sappers – spent the next few hours in a state of excitement and apprehension that gradually rose to fever pitch. The men tried to get their heads down for an afternoon nap, but 'with so many thoughts and fears running through their heads it was impossible to sleep'. Instead they 'listened to their shared wireless sets for more news and tried to pass the time'.

In the evening, after a fatless meal to reduce the chance of airsickness, Howard and his men got dressed and checked their weapons, ammunition and equipment. Howard noticed that 'some of the chaps were visibly sagging at the knees under their heavy loads'. This was because many of them had taken on extra ammunition, including grenades and bandoliers of .303 ammunition, making a mockery of the order not to exceed 231 pounds per man.

After the men had blacked their faces, necks and hands with multi-coloured grease paint, they were ordered to parade by the senior NCO, Platoon Sergeant Peter Barwick, 'a tall, good-looking young Londoner with a happy-go-lucky attitude'. Howard then addressed the men and, his voice faltering with emotion, wished them luck and thanked them 'for all their hard work and untiring cooperation during training'. He could tell from their eyes that all of them were confident and excited, and he was convinced that every man would do his best.

Ordered onto waiting army trucks for the short ride to Tarrant Rushton airfield, some of the overloaded men lost their balance and fell into the arms of their comrades; others had to be shoved up from behind. As the trucks passed the airfield's administrative buildings, they were met by waving WAAFs and airmen who knew something big was in the air. They stopped next to six Horsa gliders, tucked unobtrusively away in a corner of the airfield and chalk-marked Nos 1 to 6: the first three would take half the force, under Howard, to the Caen Canal bridge; the remaining three the other half, commanded by Howard's deputy Captain Brian Priday, to the Orne river bridge. A short way off, standing in herringbone formation beside the runway, were the six battle-scarred Halifax bombers that would tow the gliders over the Channel. Both gliders and tugs had three white stripes freshly painted on their wings to alert Allied aircraft and ships that they were friendly.[1]

Climbing out of the trucks, Howard and his men were met by the 12 glider pilots who would attempt to land them close to the bridges. He shook hands with the pair who would pilot No. 1 Glider: Staff Sergeants Jim Wallwork and John Ainsworth. A self-confident 24-year-old Mancunian, Wallwork was 'a witty fellow, with a smiling, open face and slicked back hair' who had left the infantry to volunteer for the Glider Pilot Regiment in 1942. Howard had liked him instinctively at their first meeting and was glad to know he would pilot Chalk 91 – also known as No. 1 Glider – with Ainsworth. Wallwork's defining attribute was his unflappability. When told by Howard, just days before the operation, that intelligence photos indicated the presence near the canal bridge of anti-air landing poles known as 'Rommel's Asparagus', Wallwork had responded: 'That's just what we want, sir! You see one of our main worries has been running into this embankment on landing if we over-ran the LZ. We knew that if we had a bad landing and even just a grenade went off, sympathetic detonation could cause the whole bloody lot to go up – just like what happened in Sicily! What will happen now when we come into the LZ is that the poles will take a bit off one wing, and a bit off the other. That'll pull us up nicely!'

With the loading of the last of their kit complete, the men stood on the edge of the runway drinking tea, chain-smoking and telling corny jokes to relieve the tension. Howard made a last check that the men had enough blacking on their hands and face, and told a couple they needed to reapply it. With no grease paint to hand, they used soot from the exhaust pipes of lorries and motorbikes.

Joined for a last smoke and a chat by the pilots of the tugs, Howard was told by one of them: 'I've got to hand it to you boys. We've flown on some sticky jobs in our time but what you lot are going to do – well that takes some guts!'

The words were kindly meant, but Howard did not need reminding of the risks. He distracted himself by calling on everyone to synchronise their watches to 10.40 p.m. Before giving the order to 'emplane', he walked up to each glider in turn and shook the hands of the officers and called out words of encouragement to the men. Several responded by shouting 'Ham and Jam!', the codewords for the successful capture of both bridges intact. He felt a sizeable lump in his throat.

As Howard climbed aboard No. 1 Glider, Lieutenant Colonel Mike Roberts, commanding the 2nd Ox and Bucks, who had travelled 60 miles from his base at Harwell to see them off, called out: 'See you on the bridge tomorrow, John.'

The tone was so calm and matter-of-fact that Howard felt a surge of confidence and certainty. He took his place opposite the front exit door, with Lieutenant Den Brotheridge to his right and Platoon Sergeant Ollis on the left, and fastened his seat harness. To let the 'Top Brass' know that they had made the right choice in selecting them for such an important mission, his men were singing at the top of their voices.

At 10.56 p.m., recalled 19-year-old Private Denis Edwards of 25 Platoon, travelling on No. 1 Glider, 'the steady hum of the bomber engines suddenly increased to a deafening roar. A cold shiver ran up my spine, I went hot and cold, and sang all the louder to stop my teeth from chattering. Suddenly there was a violent jerk and a loud "twang" as our tug plane took up the slack on the 125-foot towrope. The glider rolled slowly forward and my muscles tightened as the flying plywood box gathered speed, momentarily left the ground, then set down again with a heavy thump, and, finally, a jerk as with a loud roaring of the bomber's engines we became airborne.'

As Edwards had climbed aboard, he had felt 'tense, strange and extremely frightened', much as he imagined a condemned man must feel on the morning of his execution. The idea of carrying out a night-time airborne landing with such a small force seemed to him a sure way of getting killed, yet at the moment the glider parted company with the ground he experienced 'an inexplicable change'. The 'feeling of terror vanished and was replaced by exhilaration'.

The other five tug–glider combinations followed at one-minute intervals. Once in the air, the tugs climbed to 6,000 feet before levelling off. It was a moonlit night with ragged patches of cloud and a stiff wind, causing Howard to curse their bad luck. In fact the unsettled weather played to the airborne soldiers' advantage because it had convinced the chief German meteorological officer in Berlin to declare that there would be no invasion on 4 or 5 June.

With the glider flying level, Howard unclipped his harness and went forward to speak to the pilots. He was surprised to find they were all alone in the sky and could see no other planes. As the cover plan was for the Halifax tugs to continue on to bomb Caen, as part of a larger raid, he had fully expected to see more aircraft. They were nowhere visible.

After 40 minutes in the air – and Howard now back in his seat – Wallwork spotted the white line of surf breaking on the Normandy beaches and told Ainsworth: 'Two minutes from cast–off!'

From the tug he received the windspeed, height and heading, and a final wish of 'Good luck!'

Wallwork called back to Howard: 'Prepare for cast–off.'

Howard ordered the men to stop singing as complete silence was necessary for the approach to the target. Moments later they felt a jerk as Wallwork cast off from the tug, and put the glider into a steep dive. He was desperate to get below the cloud layer so he could see the ground and get his bearing.

To speed up their exit from the glider, Den Brotheridge and Wally Parr at the rear got up from their seats, unfastened the doors and heaved them upwards, while Howard and others clung to their wrists and equipment for safety.

'Suddenly,' remembered Howard, 'we were all aware of the sweet, damp night air over the Normandy countryside as it filled the glider and we all breathed in, for the first time, the smell of France. The glider was now down to 1,000 feet and, looking down through the open door, I could see the dark and un-believably peaceful fields of Normandy with cattle grazing in them. The patchwork of fields was so similar to the countryside of England, it was hard not to believe that we weren't on just another exercise. The silence was uncanny and all we could hear was the air swishing past the sides of the glider; it was a sound that none of us would ever forget.'[2]

As the hardest of taskmasters, Major John Howard was feared and respected by his men in equal measure. He was 'proud of having come up from the ranks to achieve his position', noted Private Denis Edwards, 'having once been an Oxford City Police sergeant, and he took his responsibilities very seriously indeed'.

This meant that his company 'had to be the best at everything, be it sport, marches, field exercises or physical and endurance training' – and it was.[3]

Private Wally Parr of No. 25 Platoon, a garrulous Cockney who had volunteered for airborne duty after three years with the Gloucestershire Regiment, felt that Howard was strict and firm but fair, and 'never asked anybody to do anything he wasn't prepared to do himself'. The training was so tough that there were times Parr almost gave up. 'When your feet were blistered and raw and bloody,' he recalled, 'and your back's aching, and you're spending night after night on Salisbury Plain, just laying down there on the freezing solid ground in the fog, with no cover, obviously you get a little pissed off with it. But the camaraderie, the spirit, within that company was so great that I wouldn't have missed it for all the world. It was a great company, led by a great company commander.'[4]

Howard's drive was not unrelated to his tough upbringing. Born in a tiny two-up, two-down house in Camden, north London, in December 1912, the eldest of nine children, he had left school at 14 to become a broker's clerk in the City. When his firm went under in 1931, he joined the King's Shropshire Light Infantry and left after seven years as a corporal to join the Oxford City Police. Called back to his regiment at the start of the war, he was rapidly promoted to regimental sergeant major before being offered a commission in the Oxfordshire and Buckinghamshire Light Infantry, a unit descended from the 52nd Light Infantry that had performed with such distinction for the Duke of Wellington during the Napoleonic Wars. At first, Howard found it hard to gain acceptance by his fellow officers who looked down on his Cockney origins and 'cut' him in the mess. He would never forget or forgive those humiliations. It made him determined to show 'those bastards' that he 'would be a better officer than they could ever be in their wildest dreams'. While they were off at shooting parties and playing golf, he was planning his training routines and drilling the men.

Howard's work ethic paid off in early 1942 when, having accepted a demotion to join his new regiment's 2nd Battalion – recently converted to an airborne function as part of the 1st Airlanding Brigade – he was instructed to take over command of C Company from Digby Tatham-Warter, 'a likeable enough fellow but a typical "top drawer" officer, with a Sandhurst back-ground'. Assuming Tatham-Warter was just another arrogant 'blue blood', Howard changed his mind when he got to know him better. He was, in fact, 'an easy-going chap with an attrac-tive manner' and to his surprise, Howard found himself warming to him.

He spent barely a month knocking C Company into shape before he was given a new job: command of D Company, the unit with which his name is forever associated. Among its young officers were Captain Brian Priday, his second-in-command, a dependable and trustworthy man with whom he forged a special bond that was to carry them through to D-Day, and Lieutenant Henry 'Tod' Sweeney, commanding No. 23 Platoon, a sensitive and deeply spiritual man who had almost entered the priesthood before plumping for a secular calling instead.

Aware that he would need more officers like Priday and Sweeney, in whom he could trust, Howard picked Second Lieutenant Herbert Denham 'Den' Brotheridge, a superb sportsman from Smethwick, near Birmingham, to command his No. 25 Platoon. Also promoted from the ranks, the 26-year-old Brotheridge 'was to become an immensely popular platoon leader, able to talk easily to the men under his command and earn their undying allegiance'. The last two members of Howard's junior leadership team – commanding No. 22 and 24 Platoons respec-tively – were Tony Hooper and David Wood, the latter 'a fresh-faced, sandy-haired lad with a very agreeable disposition, even-tempered and ready for a bit of fun', who joined the company as a 19-year-old freshly minted second lieutenant. At first, Howard was unconvinced that Wood would make the grade. 'Isn't of much use to me,' the company commander noted in his diary after their first meeting, 'but may shape up in time.' He did. Within a year, Howard had revised his opinion. Wood was, he wrote, 'a rattling good Officer!!' and he 'wouldn't lose him for the world'.

Recently married (and soon to have his first child), Howard missed his young wife Joy dreadfully and struggled to cope with the tragic news that his younger brother Percy had been killed in action against the Japanese. He dealt with the emotional turmoil by throwing himself even more wholeheartedly into his work as a company commander, a dedication not unnoticed by his CO.

In early 1943, there were rumours that the battalion would soon be sent overseas to join the rest of the 1st Airborne Division in North Africa. But these were scotched in April when it was decided to keep back two of the 1st Airlanding Brigade's four battalions – the 2nd Ox and Bucks and the 1st Royal Ulster Rifles – to form the core of the new 6th Airborne Division's 6th Airlanding Brigade at Bulford Camp. Though deeply depressed by the news, Howard kept training hard and would later realise how fortunate they were not to have been part of the disastrous first use of glider-borne troops in Sicily. The lessons learnt from those mistakes would make them much better prepared for their own baptism of fire in Normandy. A fellow company commander who was not so patient was Digby Tatham-Warter who left the battalion in late 1943 to transfer to the paratroopers, telling Howard: 'I want a chance to see some action!'

Howard was genuinely surprised by Digby's decision because he could imagine few worse situations than jumping out of an aircraft, praying his parachute would open and unsure where he would land. It was, in his view, infinitely preferable to arrive by glider with a pilot in charge. The 'para-boys', as they were known, felt just as strongly that they didn't want to 'prang into action'. It was, as a result, very unusual for people like Tatham-Warter to cross over, though parachutists received more risk money than glider lads: two shillings a day extra money, compared to a single shilling, the cause of much ill feeling among the glider troops. The irony of Tatham-Warter's decision is that, bar a largely bloodless campaign in Italy, he would not see proper combat with Frost's 2nd Battalion until the Arnhem campaign a year later.

In early 1944, all the talk was of the opening of the Second Front at a location in northern France yet to be announced. The first concrete hints that the 2nd Ox and Bucks Light Infantry would be involved were given by Lieutenant General 'Boy' Browning, the commander of Airborne Forces, in a lecture to the officers and senior NCOs on the 'Invasion set-up' on 26 February. Afterwards, recalled Howard, the general feeling was that the invasion plans were at an advanced stage and that, before too long, the command at battalion level would be briefed on what was going to take place. He was convinced that the 6th Airborne Division would play a pivotal role.

Just how important his own part would be in the invasion was made clear on 23 March when he was briefed on a full-scale divisional exercise – codenamed Bizz – that involved his D Company landing in gliders near to, and capturing intact, three small bridges near Lechlade in Gloucestershire.* Howard was

---

* Howard and D Company had been nominated for this vital and extremely dangerous role in the D-Day plan by Brigadier Hugh Kindersley, commanding the 6th Airlanding Brigade. When asked by 'Windy' Gale who was the best company commander in the brigade, Kindersley replied: 'I think that all my men are jolly good leaders, but I think Johnny Howard might do this one rather well.' (Ambrose, *Pegasus Bridge*, p. 53)

elated to hear that it was considered a 'VC job': highly dangerous, and possibly worthy of Britain's highest gallantry award. The three-day exercise went well, though Howard's men only narrowly fought off a counter-attack by 'enemy' troops before they were relieved by the rest of the battalion.

At the debriefing for the exercise on 15 April, the divisional commander 'Windy' Gale praised D Company's spirited and efficient capture of the bridges. 'What you gain by stealth and guts,' he added, 'you must hold with skill and determination.' These words would remain with Howard as he prepared for D-Day. His exact role was confirmed later that day by his commanding officer, Mike Roberts, who told him that D Company, plus two platoons of B Company and thirty airborne sappers, would have the vital task of capturing and holding two unnamed bridges, a quarter of a mile apart. 'You realise, John,' said Roberts, 'that your company will be the spearhead of the invasion. It is a great honour for the Regiment to be selected to find troops for this highly important job. But I feel absolutely confident that you will be able to pull it off.'

Howard returned to his billet in a state of nervous exhilaration. He longed to be able to confide in his second-in-command, Brian Priday, but he had been told to keep the information under his hat until after the final dress-rehearsal for the operation – codenamed Exercise Mush – in late April.

Howard selected two platoons from B Company, commanded by Lieutenants Dennis Fox and 'Sandy' Smith. Both were experienced and would, Howard felt, work well with the D Company officers. Fox and Smith were not so sure. Both were former Cambridge students and keen athletes who enjoyed chasing women and having a good time; they regarded Howard and his officers as fanatical workaholics and wanted to stay as far away from them as possible. At the same time, the chance to take part in a top-secret mission was a big lure, and as they got to know the D Company officers they were surprised at how well they got along.

After the exercise, Howard was told he was now officially on the 'X' list – officers cleared to receive documents with the Top Secret security classification 'Bigot' – and would be given the outline of the whole invasion plan, Operation Overlord, as well as the details of the 6th Airborne's plan (Tonga), and the specifics of his role. His written orders began: 'Your task is to seize intact the bridges over the Canal at Bénouville and the River Orne at Ranville and hold them until relieved by the 7th Parachute Battalion. If the bridges are blown, you will establish personnel ferries over both water obstacles as soon as possible.' The capture of the bridges, he was instructed, would be a '*coup-de-main* operation depending largely on surprise, speed and dash for success'. As long as the bulk of his forces landed safely, he should have 'little difficulty in overcoming the known opposition on the bridges'. His difficulties would arise 'on holding off an enemy counterattack on the bridges' until he was relieved.[5]

Over the next month, Howard made regular visits to the divisional planning house – codenamed 'Broadmoor' – at Brigmerston Farm House, near Durrington, to fine-tune his role in the invasion. Overall the 6th Airborne Division had four main tasks: to secure intact and hold the two bridges; to neutralise an enemy artillery battery at Merville near the coast; to secure a bridgehead between the Rivers Orne and Dives; and to prevent enemy reinforcements (including panzer units) moving towards the British left flank from the east and south-east.[6]

The first of Howard's targets was the steel-girder road bridge that crossed the Caen Canal at the village of Bénouville, roughly half way between Caen and the small coastal port of Ouistreham. Hydraulically operated by a huge water tank at its eastern end, the bridge could be raised almost to the perpendicular to allow ships to pass beneath. The canal was 190 feet wide and 27 feet deep, but as 50-foot abutments projected into the water from either bank, the lifting span of the bridge was only 90 feet. The asphalt and steel road that crossed the bridge was 12 feet wide.

A quarter of a mile up the road towards Ranville was the second target, a two-span cantilever bridge over the River Orne, which ran parallel to the canal from Caen to the sea. This road bridge was 350 feet long and 27 feet wide, including walkways, and spanned a river with steep, muddy banks.

According to intelligence reports – gleaned from aerial photos and local members of the French Resistance (one of whom, Georges Gondrée, ran the café on the west bank of the canal crossing) – both bridges were defended by a small garrison of just 50 men, armed with up to six light machine guns, four light 20mm anti-aircraft guns and possibly two anti-tank guns of less than 50mm calibre. The strongest defences were on the east bank of the canal bridge. They included, just south of the road and close to the canal, a large circular concrete emplacement that was believed to contain an anti-tank gun; and, 30 yards farther south, an anti-aircraft machine-gun post, mounted on an eight-feet-high tower. Sixty yards north of the road, and also near to the canal, were three machine-gun nests, 12 yards apart, in a line facing north-east. A short way beyond these emplacements was a concrete pillbox. There were more machine-gun nests on the west bank of the canal, on either side of the bridge approach.

The river bridge, meanwhile, had only a camouflaged pillbox (possibly housing an anti-tank gun) and two machine-gun nests on the east bank, and a small anti-aircraft machine-gun emplacement on the west bank. None of these defences was wired.[7]

The defenders were members of a motorised battalion of the German 736th Grenadier Regiment, part of the 716th Infantry Division, a low category formation that consisted of troops who were mostly under 20 or between 35 and 40 years old. Only half were thought to be ethnic Germans; the rest were Poles and Russians. The 'fighting value of this division', Howard was told, 'has been assessed at 40% static and 15% in a counter-attack role. Equipment consists of an unknown proportion of French, British, and Polish weapons.' The main counter-attacking threat would come from the rest of the motorised battalion, based at Bieville, seven miles east of Bénouville, with up to 12 tanks under its command, while the veteran 21st Panzer Division was laagered just east and south-east of Caen.[8]

As both bridges had been prepared for demolition, it was felt that only glider-borne troops were capable of landing at night, surprising the defenders and capturing the bridges before they could be blown. 'The idea,' remembered Lieutenant Tod Sweeney, 'was to land three gliders as close to each bridge as possible. We would all land within two waterways, so that if the Germans did blow the bridges, then we wouldn't be cut off from one another.'[9]

The six Horsa gliders would each contain 2 pilots, 5 sappers and twenty-three officers and men of the 2nd Ox and Bucks Light Infantry. The three under Howard's command were due to land south of the road that linked the two bridges, and the other three, under Brian Priday, to the north. To avoid the danger of collision, they would approach the targets from opposite directions.

To assist his planning, Howard was given aerial photographs, maps, intelligence reports and a large model of the two bridges and the ground in between, 12 feet by 12 feet, that had been 'lovingly recreated' with 'every building, tree, bush, ditch, trench and fence', and was constantly updated as new information came in. It was, Howard felt, the nearest he could get to a personal reconnaissance of the area.

The last-minute training for Howard's force included the 'capture' of two bridges near Exminster. They were a little smaller than the targets in Normandy, and the distance between them only 150 rather than 500 yards, but they were similar in that one was over a canal and the other over a river. The drills included cooperation with the men of the 7th Parachute Battalion, commanded by Lieutenant Colonel Geoffrey Pine-Coffin (formerly of the 3rd Battalion), whose task once they had landed east of the River Orne was to make straight for the bridges and relieve Howard's force.

True to form, Howard worked his men until they ached, insisting that every platoon practised each of the jobs, 'so that no matter who landed where and in what order, they would all automatically know what to do'. The training was so repetitive that Cockney Wally Parr, one of Howard's 'scallywags' whose constant infractions resulted in regular demotions in rank (from corporal and lance corporal back to private), told a pal as they washed in cold water outside Exminster's village hall one morning: 'I flippin' 'ave bin doin' it all in me ruddy sleep, 'aven't I? – dreamin' it all bloody night!'

Howard's plan was for the first platoon on the ground to pierce the enemy defences, race across the bridge and take out any opposition on the far side. Meanwhile the second platoon into action would mop up the inner defences, while the third, if it arrived safely, would help whichever platoon was most in need. The sappers were to go straight for the chambers on the bridge holding the explosive, 'cut wires, de-prime and remove it'. Since the opposition was expected to be weakest on the road bridge, Priday was expected to send his third platoon to reinforce Howard at the canal bridge as soon as he was in control. 'Speed and dash,' were Howard's watchwords.[10]

To Denis Edwards, however, it seemed little more than a suicide mission in which a tiny force of around 180 men would 'crash-land in gliders without heavy weapons or armoured vehicles, to capture a couple of bridges from the Nazis, with no guarantee of being relieved or supported for some hours at the very least'.

Even if they succeeded in taking the bridges – which was possible as they had surprise on their side – the task of holding them until reinforcements arrived by air or fought their way through from the beaches seemed, to him, 'like a pipedream'.[11]

25

'Ham and Jam!'
– Normandy, D-Day, 6 June 1944

A S NO. 1 GLIDER began its final descent to the target, all that could be heard was air rushing down the fuselage and the co-pilot John Ainsworth counting down the seconds on his stopwatch, lit by a small hand-held lamp, before instructing Jim Wallwork to 'Turn' 90 degrees to starboard. The second of these turns brought the glider on to a northerly heading and directly ahead, clearly visible by moonlight, was the outline of the canal bridge the pilots knew so well from the detailed model.

The 28 passengers behind them were silent, each man thinking of what was to come and those he had left behind. Major John Howard had visions of Joy and his two children sleeping peacefully in their beds in Oxford, and could feel the small lump in his tunic's breast pocket where he had placed one of his son's first pairs of red leather shoes. Out of the open door he could see the instantly recognisable River Orne and knew they were on course.

With the glider losing height rapidly, and rocking from side to side, Ainsworth yelled, 'Hold tight!'

It was the signal for the men to adopt their landing positions by linking arms in a butcher's grip and lifting their legs off the floor to minimise the possibility of fractures. Gripping their weapons tightly, the men tensed their bodies for impact. 'I gritted my teeth,' recalled Howard, 'and tried to pray but all I could think was "Please God, please God" as we came in to land with a terrific crash, a splintering noise and sparks flying past outside the doorway.'

Skidding and bouncing twice on the uneven ground, the glider lost its wheels and landed on its metal skids at 80 miles per hour. Howard thought they were under fire, but in fact the flashes were just caused by the skids striking the stony ground. With a final thunderous roar, the glider came to a juddering halt with its nose through the bridge's barbed wire defences, just as Howard had requested.

It was 12.16 a.m. on Tuesday, 6 June 1944, and the D-Day landings had begun.

Briefly knocked unconscious by the impact, Howard opened his eyes – and realised he could not see. Terrified he was blind, he quickly worked out that his 'battle-bowler' helmet had been forced down over his eyes and, pushing it up, he was confronted with 'the smashed doorway, the air full of dust, the holes torn in the side of the glider and the sound of the pilots groaning in the smashed cockpit'.

The good news was an absence of gunfire and the glorious realisation that they had achieved their first objective of complete surprise.

Wrenching off his safety harness and grabbing his Sten gun, Howard rolled head-first out of the broken doorway. Directly ahead, barely 50 feet away, stood the large water tower on the east side of the canal bridge. The pilots had clearly done a marvellous job. He was soon joined by Lieutenant Den Brotheridge who, like many others, had used his weapon to smash his way out of the other side of the glider and was limping. 'You alright, Den?' asked Howard.

'Yes, I'm okay.'

'Good, get cracking with your first section.'[1]

Once the men were assembled, Brotheridge shouted, 'Come on lads!' in his rich Brummie accent, and started running towards the bridge with his platoon in close pursuit. They were spotted by a lone German sentry on the bridge who fired a white Very light which made him the target of multiple Sten guns fired from the hip.[2]

One section, under Corporal Bailey, peeled off to deal with the pillbox across the road. It was led by best pals Wally Parr and Charlie Gardner who spotted two entrances. Parr dashed to the first one, put down his rifle, and got out a type 36 grenade. With Gardner covering him with a Bren gun, Parr hauled open the door and chucked in the grenade. There was a deafening explosion. Gardner then stood in the doorway and sprayed the room with his Bren. They repeated the operation at the second door. As Parr picked up his rifle, he could hear a voice groaning and moaning inside. The door was open, so he took out a phosphorus grenade, took off the tab, and threw it in. It 'went off a treat'.[3]

Meanwhile, Den Brotheridge had led the charge across the bridge. He 'limped as he ran but was oblivious to the pain in his leg and was firing from the hip as he went'. Following close behind Brotheridge were 19-year-old privates Bill Gray, a good friend of Parr and Gardner, and Denis Edwards, who remembered a Spandau machine gun opening up on them from the far side. They returned fire and kept going. 'As we neared the far side of the bridge,' wrote Edwards, 'still shouting, firing our weapons and lobbing hand grenades, the Germans jumped to their feet and ran for their lives, scattering in all directions. Relief, exhilaration, incredulity – I experienced all these feelings upon realising that we had taken the bridge.'[4]

Gray, Lance Corporal Tom Packwood and others assaulted a group of outhouses with machine guns and grenades. Another section 'cleaned out the slit trenches on either side of the bridge and between them they all took a number of prisoners'. As Gray came back towards the bridge he saw to his dismay the body of his officer lying beneath the window of the Gondrée café, just south of the road. 'Brotheridge had been shot in the throat,' recalled Gray, 'and also appeared to have been hit by a phosphorous smoke grenade. He was unconscious but still alive; his airborne smock was still burning.'[5]

John Howard heard the burst of fire that mortally wounded Den Brotheridge as he was making his way towards the bridge with his wireless operator, Lance Corporal Ted Tappenden. At the same time, he heard the shout 'Charlie, Charlie, Charlie', the codeword for Lieutenant David Wood's platoon which had landed in No. 2 Glider a minute or two after Howard, having narrowly avoided a collision with No. 3 Glider, carrying Sandy Smith and his men. Wood's glider had made a reasonable landing, stopping 30 yards or so behind No. 1, and its occupants were quickly into action. But No. 3 glider was not so lucky. Landing hard between the other two, and at an angle, it ended up partly submerged in a pond, into which both pilots were thrown. The crash caused a number of casualties in Smith's platoon – codename 'Easy' – including a Lance Corporal Fred Greenhalgh who was knocked unconscious and drowned in the shallow water, the first fatality of the D-Day landings.*

Moments after hearing 'Charlie, Charlie, Charlie', Howard was approached by a panting David Wood. Aware that Wood and his platoon were ready for action, Howard ordered them to clear the inner trenches on the east side of the canal. They 'immediately went in, firing from the hip' and the 'air was rent

---

* In a grisly quirk of fate, a Lance Corporal Darren Jones of the Royal Engineers drowned trying to swim the Caen Canal, near Pegasus Bridge, during the celebrations to mark the 75th anniversary of D-Day in 2019.

with gunfire and explosions'. Much later, they discovered the corpse of a German soldier who had been 'in the act of laying ready-primed mines in the trenches'. Howard 'was profoundly grateful that he had been prevented from accomplishing his task'.

Sandy Smith was the next platoon officer to appear. In the bad landing, he had broken his wrist, but he had tucked it into his battledress and he was keen to carry on. Howard ordered him to take his platoon over the bridge and deploy to the right of the road, while Brotheridge's men took up positions on the left. Howard had been told to expect the first counter-attack from a motorised battalion of the Wehrmacht's 736th Grenadier Regiment, stationed west of the canal bridge. He had been briefed that its battle group would probably comprise 'one company of infantry in lorries, up to 8 tanks and one or two guns mounted on lorries', most likely coming down roads, but a 'cross-country route' was also possible.[6]

It was only then that Howard received the news that Brotheridge had been hit in the neck and badly wounded by machine-gun fire. His first instinct was to cross the bridge and check on his friend's condition, but he knew that, as CO, he should never leave his command post without a deputy in charge. That deputy, Brian Priday, had still not landed at the river bridge. Tappenden confirmed, however, that he had received no radio message from Priday either. Howard soon had other concerns when a runner arrived with the news that both David Wood and his platoon sergeant were 'out of action, having run into machine-gun fire from the trenches'. Within a few minutes of landing, Howard had 'only one infantry officer left and that was Sandy Smith who only had the use of one arm'.[7]

The other three gliders – Nos 4 to 6, carrying the force under Captain Brian Priday – should have landed near the bridge over the River Orne only a few minutes after Howard touched down.

But a navigational error by the crew of the Halifax tug caused No. 4 Glider, with Priday and Lieutenant Tony Hooper on board, to cast off near Varraville, eight miles to the east, and they eventually came down near a bridge over the River Dives, which they captured before realising their mistake. They bravely decided to work their way back through enemy-held territory to rejoin D Company, but would not do so until the early hours of 7 June.[8]

That left just two gliders to capture the second bridge. They had both released at the correct point, near Franceville-Plage on the coast, and immediately made a slight turn to the right, flying three more compass bearings for 90 seconds each time until they were pointing due south. As No. 5 Glider came down, Lieutenant Tod Sweeney pulled open the door as his batman held on to his belt. Through the open doorway, Sweeney could see cows grazing in the fields of Normandy. He strapped himself in and they landed, only for the glider pilot to confess: 'I'm sorry but I've dropped you short.'

They were more than a quarter of a mile from the target, partly the result of hitting an air pocket, and it would take them 10 minutes to make their way across two dark fields, laced with ponds and water-filled culverts, to the bridge.[9]

No. 6 Glider, meanwhile, after its own cast-off, had been almost impossible to control because it was overloaded. It was descending at too steep an angle – 'going down at 90 mph like a streamlined brick!' – causing its pilot Staff Sergeant Roy Howard to shout to Lieutenant Dennis Fox, whose platoon he was carrying, 'Two men to the back – on the double!'

This helped raise the glider's nose, but Howard had been too successful in losing height and the landing zone was a little further away than he expected. He 'ripped the flaps off very quickly and stretched the glide, flattened the glide path and brought her down'. She came to a rest just six yards from her allotted spot and 100 yards from the bridge. After a brief moment of stunned silence, Howard turned and said, 'Mr Fox, you are in the right place, sir. Off you go!'

It was 12.19 a.m. Surprised to find they were the only glider in sight – the other two should have been even closer to the target – Fox led his men towards the bridge which they captured after destroying a machine-gun post with a mortar round.[10]

When Tod Sweeney and his men arrived a few minutes later, shouting their call sign 'Baker', the place was ominously quiet. They began to trot across the bridge, expecting at any moment that it would be blown up beneath them. Reaching the far side they heard the call sign 'Fox', and realised that the occupants of No. 6 Glider had got there before them. Puffing from exertion, Sweeney greeted Lieutenant Fox, his fellow platoon commander. 'Hallo, Dennis, how are things?'

'All right, Tod,' responded Fox, 'but I haven't seen any bloody umpires yet.'

Soon after, Sweeney's radio operator got through to Tappenden to report that they had captured the bridge but there was still no sign of No. 4 Glider containing Brian Priday and Hooper's platoon. The enemy, meanwhile, had 'run off, leaving their guns in weapon-pits, still warm from the sentries' occupancy'.[11]

Howard was elated. Already the sappers with him had 'searched the bridges, cut all the wires and found the chambers ready to receive their charges of explosive, but in fact no charges had been laid'. They were found later in a magazine near the canal bridge.

The time was 12.26 a.m. Barely 10 minutes had elapsed since No. 1 Glider touched down, and both bridges were in British hands. Howard instructed Tappenden to send out the success signal, 'Ham and Jam'.

He was hoping it would be picked up by Brigadier Nigel Poett, commanding the 3rd Parachute Brigade, who had been dropped with a team of Pathfinders ahead of the main force. The message was prefaced by Poett's call sign: 'Hello, Four-Dog, Hello Four-Dog, Ham and Jam, Ham and Jam.'

Tappenden repeated this so many times, without response, that Howard eventually heard him say 'Ham and Bloody Jam!' Brigadier Poett, they would later discover, had been separated from his radio operator and never received the message.

Meanwhile, Sandy Smith had run back over the bridge to report that the situation on the west bank was quiet, though he suspected some German soldiers were holed up in houses on the edge of Bénouville village. 'You are to coordinate the defence of both your and Den [Brotheridge]'s platoons,' Howard told him. 'I'll send someone else over to deal with the Germans. Have you seen anything of Doc Vaughan?'

'Not recently, sir,' said Smith. 'I think he might have been injured on landing.'

This was troubling news. Vaughan's job was to set up the casualty command post (CCP) in a small tree-lined lane between the two bridges. If the medic was hors de combat, who would treat the badly wounded?

'All right, Sandy,' said Howard, 'off you go.'

Howard then yelled across to Corporal Godbold, who had taken command of Wood's platoon after both Wood and his sergeant had been wounded, and told him to go over the bridge and clear the houses on the edge of Bénouville. Howard also sent orders by radio for Sweeney to remain on the river bridge while Fox and his platoon reported to the canal bridge to lend a hand as he feared that 'counter-attacks from the enemy could not be long in coming'. This was in rough conformity with his original plan – once both bridges were secure – to leave one platoon at the river bridge and defend the more vulnerable canal bridge with the other five: two platoons forward, covering Bénouville and a small hamlet, Le Port, to the north; two defending the west bank of the canal bridge; and one, in all-round positions, on the east bank. With only five platoons now available, thanks to the errant glider, this plan would have to be adapted.

Howard had been told to expect the first elements of the 7th Parachute Battalion to reach the bridges about an hour after he did, so he sent the 7th Battalion's liaison officer, Lieutenant MacDonald, who had landed on one of the gliders, to make contact with his commanding officer, Lieutenant Colonel Geoffrey Pine-Coffin.

As MacDonald stole into the night, Howard was approached by two stretcher-bearers carrying Lieutenant Brotheridge. Told the officer was unconscious, Howard bent over, felt for his pulse and tried speaking to him, in vain. His friend was still alive, but barely. 'I watched them carry him away with a lump in my throat,' remembered Howard. 'Brotheridge had been incredibly brave and had been the first man wounded in action in the invasion, and his platoon had then made short work of the gun crew that fired the Spandau.'

Howard then went to help a man with a bloodied face who was carrying supplies from the gliders to the command post near the bridge. It was the unflappable pilot of No. 1 Glider, Jim Wallwork. Dumping a box of ammunition at Howard's feet, he said: 'What next, sir?'

Another glider pilot was taking messages for Howard to the forward platoons on the west bank of the canal. He was impressed. As a group, the pilots 'refused to keep clear of the battle and did stalwart work to aid the troops'.

When Dennis Fox arrived with his platoon soon after, Howard sent him over the canal bridge 'to form a fighting patrol out beyond the perimeter defences facing west, in order to detect any reconnaissance parties, or to stop any enemy forming up to counter-attack'. Howard followed him over the bridge soon after, and found that Sandy Smith had done his job well and was in control. But at Brotheridge's platoon HQ, south of the road, Sergeant Ollis was in 'great pain, having been injured in the back and ribs on landing', so Howard sent him back to the CCP for treatment, and put his senior corporal, Caine, in charge. This meant that out of the three original platoons, one was commanded by a lieutenant with his arm in a sling, and the other two by corporals.

Returning to his command post, Howard found his missing medic, Doc Vaughan, wandering about in a dazed state, and covered from head to foot in slime and mud. He had been thrown into a pond on landing, and was obviously concussed. 'Have you seen any of the casualties?' asked Howard.

'No, John,' replied Vaughan. 'Where are they?'

Howard gave Vaughan a slug of whisky from a hip flask and sent him off with a runner to make sure he found the CCP. Leaning back against one of the metal panels of the bridge, Howard heaved a sigh of relief that, thus far, the plan had worked. But he was short of officers, down a whole platoon and would be hard-pressed to hold off a determined German counter-attack if reinforcements did not arrive soon.

26

'Blimey, we've 'ad it now!'
– Normandy, 6 June 1944

A T 12.50 A.M., THE drone of engines caused John Howard to look up. Countless low-flying planes were approaching from the coast. Then ground flares appeared on the other side of the River Orne, where the 3rd and 5th Parachute Brigades were due to land. Finally parachutes filled the moonlit sky, a spine-tingling sight that Howard and his men would never forget. Even as tracer fire rose from German positions to meet the parachutists, Howard blew the 'Victory-V' signal on his pea-whistle – three dots and a dash, 'carrying as clear as a bell on the night air' – to guide those blown off course to the bridge.

Soon after, the tall figure of Brigadier Nigel Poett arrived at Howard's HQ from the direction of the river bridge. Howard was a little put out that Lieutenant Tod Sweeney, who was manning the bridge with the men from No. 5 Glider, had not given him advance warning of the brigadier's approach. But he quickly forgave his platoon commander when Poett congratulated Howard on his brilliant success in capturing both bridges. The brigadier went on to explain that he had been unable to respond to the 'Ham and Jam' signal because he had become separated from most of his staff – including his wireless operator – during the jump. Satisfied that Howard had the situation well in hand, he then stole off into the night to join the rest of his brigade on the far side of the Orne.[1]

The precariousness of Howard's position, however, was now underlined by noise from two different directions. First, from Bénouville, came the ominous sound of powerful engines and the 'clanking and rattling' of tank tracks. Then shots were fired near the river bridge. An outpost of Sweeney's platoon had spotted four men approaching up the riverbank from the south. When challenged, one of the men shouted 'Englanders!' and opened fire, wounding one of Sweeney's men. The paratroopers responded with Bren gun fire and 'annihilated the lot'. They only discovered later that one of the 'Germans' was British, a Pathfinder from the 22nd Independent Parachute Company who had been taken prisoner and was killed in the crossfire. 'Such tragedies,' noted Howard, 'were bound to happen in battle.'

Minutes later, a car and a motorbike approached the river bridge at speed from the direction of Ranville. The car, an open-topped Mercedes, contained Major Hans Schmidt, the commander of the under-strength company of the 736th Grenadier Regiment that was defending both bridges. He had been carousing in Ranville with his French girlfriend when he learned that the bridges were under attack. He leapt in his car and ordered the driver to return to his HQ in Bénouville as quickly as possible,

The car and escort were 'moving so fast that they flashed through Sweeney's outer defences and were immediately engaged with light machine-gun and rifle fire, which brought the motorcycle crashing to the road'. The Mercedes continued on over the bridge where it was engaged by Sweeney and others, their bullets shooting out the tyres and forcing it to skid to a stop. Three men jumped out and tried to escape. Two were shot and killed, the other one – Schmidt – badly wounded in both legs. 'He declared, in excellent English,' noted Howard, 'that he had lost his honour and demanded to be shot. Sweeney's men took him along to the CCP where he lay propped up against a tree, haranguing Doc Vaughan about the futility of the Allies believing for one moment that they could win the war against the master race.'

Vaughan administered a hefty shot of morphine, at which point Schmidt became more docile and thanked the doctor profusely for treating his wounds. A search of Schmidt's car, meanwhile, yielded 'wine, glasses, plates that had evidently been used for a recent meal, and also ladies' lingerie and cosmetics'. It was easy to conclude that the glider landings had interrupted Schmidt in a 'most intimate soirée with an obliging local lady in Ranville'.[2]

Private Denis Edwards was helping his seven-man section dig in along the single-track railway that ran along the west bank of the canal, just south of the Gondrée café, when he heard the sound of armoured vehicles approaching the crossroads that led to the canal bridge. It was a terrifying moment and they stopped digging. 'Our main concern,' wrote Edwards, 'was their size, as we had nothing to stop larger tanks. No doubt the guards who had fled from the bridge had been able to warn a nearby unit and the tanks were sent to investigate. By now they were less than 50 yards to my rear, and moving towards the bridge.'[3]

A short while earlier, Wally Parr had been sent from his position near the Gondrée café to collect a PIAT anti-tank gun – its 2½-pound projectile capable of penetrating 4 inches of armour – from No. 1 Glider. He found a gun and two crates of bombs, and took them back across the bridge, reaching his position just as two armoured vehicles approached the T-junction. He was about to load the weapon when he realised it had been damaged in the crash and was unusable. 'For Christ's sake,' he said to Charlie Gardner, 'the PIAT's smashed!'[4]

From the far side of the canal bridge, Howard could see an armoured vehicle – almost certainly a half-track with a 37mm gun – turn right at the T-junction and begin 'slowly and menacingly to grind and clank its way down the road towards us'. It was the lead vehicle of two platoons of the 1st Company, Panzerjäger Battalion 716, that had been sent up from Biéville with the mission of 'cleaning up the situation' at the canal bridge.

Howard knew that Fox's forward platoon had a PIAT assembled and ready to use. But as it was dark, and the weapon was only really effective at a distance of 50 yards, the operator would have a very nervous wait until the half-track was within range. Even then he would only have time for one shot, and unless it was a direct hit the missile would bounce harmlessly away. Howard held his breath, fully aware that the success of D-Day – the greatest invasion in history – might hinge on his ability to defend the two bridges. Why, he wondered, was the PIAT gunner not firing? Should he order his men to attack the tank with grenades?[5]

One of those men, young Bill Gray, was lying with Lance Corporal Tom Packwood in the garden behind the café. 'Blimey,' he told Packwood, 'we've 'ad it now.'

Their last hope was Fox's platoon sergeant, Charles 'Wagga' Thornton, who was lying beside the road ahead, aiming a PIAT.[6] A pre-war regular, Thornton was quiet and unobtrusive in barracks, but 'absolutely first class' in action. 'He virtually commanded the platoon,' admitted Fox. 'I was the figurehead and did more or less what he told me to do.' After landing near the river bridge, Thornton had used a mortar to knock out a German machine-gun post before arranging the defensive positions. Now only Thornton and his PIAT were in a position to stop the German armour from recapturing both bridges. He was, he admitted later, 'shaking like a leaf'.

Part of the reason was his lack of faith in the PIAT which he regarded as a 'load of rubbish'. Its effective range was no more than 50 yards and it was fatal to miss with the first shot. 'If you do,' wrote Thornton, 'you've had it, because by the time you reload the thing and cock it, which is a bloody chore on its own, everything's gone, you're done. It's indoctrinated into your brain that you mustn't miss.'

Thornton lined up the sights on the large black shape approaching and, when it was just 30 yards away, squeezed the trigger.[7]

The German half-track* exploded 'with a mighty bang'. Howard later surmised that it 'must have been carrying a full load of ammunition, for it continued to explode for a long time, creating an amazing firework display accompanied by deafening cracks and thuds, that could be seen and heard over a large area'.

It was fortunate for Howard and his men that the commander of 1st Company, Panzerjäger Battalion 716, was riding in the armoured half-track and had been killed. His subordinates obviously thought better of taking on the defenders of the bridge – who they assumed were armed with 6-pounder anti-tank guns – and, amidst much 'revving of engines and general commotion they withdrew in disorder'. Howard knew that the PIAT operator had brought the defenders of the bridge 'precious time', and was very proud of the way his well-trained men were dealing with the enemy. But his satisfaction quickly turned to sorrow

---

* To this day there is uncertainty as to the type of armoured vehicle destroyed. Some of the sources mention a 'tank', with Thornton convinced it was a Panzer Mark IV with a 75mm gun. Denis Edwards, on the other hand, thought it was a 'light machine', while Brigadier Lord Lovat, arriving from the beaches later that day, referred to a 'German half-track, upturned in a ditch'. (Lovat, *March Past*, p. 321) An 'armoured half track' with a 37mm gun, hit near the crossroads by a PIAT, was also mentioned by Private John Butler of the 7th Battalion. (Ambrose, *Pegasus Bridge*, p. 129; Edwards, *The Devil's Own Luck*, p. 45; www.pegasusarchive.org/normandy/john.butler.htm)

when Doc Vaughan sent word that Den Brotheridge had died without regaining consciousness. With Brian Priday missing, and Brotheridge gone, he was without his two closest friends. On the plus side, Vaughan had clearly recovered from his earlier concussion and would carry out his duties magnificently, saving many lives and easing the suffering of others (Germans included).

Howard's chief fear, now, was that the Germans would quickly regroup and launch a more serious attack on the bridge, with infantry and armour, that would easily overwhelm his thin screen of men. He desperately needed support from Pine-Coffin's 7th Battalion, and he needed it soon.[8]

The hold-up was caused, as ever, by the fact that many 7th Battalion men had been blown off course or dropped in the wrong place. Pine-Coffin remembered the pilots of his Stirling bomber having considerable trouble pinpointing the drop zone because the moon was obscured by clouds. He then twisted his ankle on landing, and spent the next hour or so collecting stragglers who were looking for the RV, as was he. 'It was,' he remembered, 'a most desperate feeling to know that one was so close to it, but not knowing in which direction it lay. Time was slipping by and the coup-de-main party might well be in difficulties. Everything could so easily be lost if the Battalion did not arrive in time.'

He was unable to identify a landmark until a chance flare, dropped by one of the aircraft, illuminated the church at Ranville, with its distinctive double tower. This enabled Pine-Coffin to reach the RV at 1.45 a.m. where he found about a quarter of the battalion's strength. Faced with the urgent need to get to the bridges as soon as possible, he decided to leave as soon as half the battalion had assembled. He ordered his second-in-command, Major Steele-Baume, to stay behind and round up the stragglers.[9]

Racing ahead of Pine-Coffin was C Company, commanded by Major R. J. N. Bartlett who had orders to 'go at best speed and link up with John Howard'.[10] Bartlett missed the correct drop zone by at least three miles, landing in an apple orchard instead of cornfields, so a vanguard of about 40 men was led towards the bridges by Major Nigel Taylor of A Company. He, in turn, ordered 19-year-old Private John Butler of C Company's No. 9 Platoon to scout 50 yards ahead of the column because he was armed with a Sten gun. Shortly after landing, Butler had watched a fellow soldier 'jerk and then hang limp and lifeless' below his parachute after he was hit by German tracers. He himself had been shot at before he got to the RV. Now, despite his exposed position at the head of the column, he remembered an uneventful walk as the one or two places where they expected trouble were deserted. When they got to the bridges, they were relieved to find the situation well in hand and both intact. This meant they could jettison the dinghies which they had brought with them in kit bags in case the bridges had been blown.[11]

Howard recorded the time when Taylor's party reached the canal bridge as 2.50 a.m, with Pine-Coffin arriving with the main body about 10 minutes later.* They were over an hour and a half behind schedule, but better late than never. Pine-Coffin now assumed command of the bridges, and ordered Howard to withdraw his men over the canal bridge and act as a battalion reserve with responsibility for the river bridge and the area between the two crossings. He sent his reduced A and B Companies to occupy Bénouville and Le Port, while C Company was used more flexibly in support of the other companies and in reserve. Pine-Coffin's men, reported Howard, 'soon

---

* Pine-Coffin insisted that he reached the canal bridge no later than 1.40 a.m. But this is highly unlikely, given the delays, and Howard's timings are more reliable.

made up for lost time and despite their depleted numbers pushed out the bridgehead towards the west'.[12]

Arriving at the canal bridge at the same time as Pine-Coffin was the assistant adjutant of the 7th Battalion and future film star, Lieutenant Richard Todd. Born in Dublin in 1919, the son of a British Army medic, Todd was an unknown actor with the Dundee Repertory Theatre when war broke out. In 1941 he joined the King's Own Yorkshire Light Infantry as a junior officer, and two years later – desperate to see action – volunteered for parachute training. He was posted to the 7th Battalion which had been raised in late 1942 by the conversion of the 10th Somerset Light Infantry to parachute duties. Initially part of the 3rd Parachute Brigade, the 7th Battalion was soon switched to the 5th Brigade alongside the 12th and 13th Parachute Battalions.

Todd wrote a memorable account of the pre-battle drumhead service that the battalion padre, Captain the Reverend George 'Pissy Percy' Parry, 'a wiry little Welshman with a nature as fiery as his red hair, and a heart and courage to match', held in a meadow near Fairford Airfield as the shadows lengthened on 5 June. They were drawn up in a semi-circle, 610 men facing 'inwards towards the padre who stood on an ammunition box'. A 'more unlikely or piratical congregation could not be imagined, every man abristle with weapons, his face and hands besmirched with black cream, his helmet on the ground before him, his rifle or Sten gun laid across it'. They sang hymns: '*Onward Christian Soldiers* went well. *Abide with Me* was rather more ragged.' It 'was not easy to sing that in such a setting and at such a moment'.

His description of the jump from the Stirling bomber is just as graphic. 'The moment I felt my canopy snap open,' he wrote, 'I pulled the rip-cord to release the leg-bag, holding on to its rope with the other hand. [. . .] I let it slip through my hand and felt it skin my palm and fingers. "Bugger!" I shouted. With the kit-bag dangling 20 feet below me, I reached up to my lift-webs and had a few seconds look around. The sky seemed full of other paratroopers, their canopies silhouetted against the moonlight and the flashes of shells and anti-aircraft gunfire.'

Trotting over the river bridge, Todd got his first sight of a D-Day casualty: a legless German lying by the roadside. Normally the sight of blood turned his stomach, yet he felt only mild curiosity. As he doubled along the causeway towards the canal bridge, he could see heavy explosions, flashes and tracer bullets light up the night sky like a spectacular firework display. He thought: 'Christ! This is it. Here we go!'

In fact, the explosions died down as quickly as they had begun. 'An old tank probing the bridge had been hit by a PIAT bomb,' he wrote, 'and this was its ammunition exploding.'

Reaching the Gondrée Café at the west end of the bridge, Todd was ordered by Pine-Coffin to set up Battalion HQ '300 yards away below the hamlet of Le Port, whose church could be seen on the crest'. Here, in the darkness, the remnants of the HQ party began to dig in, with Todd's own efforts hampered by his skinned right hand. They eventually resorted to using explosives to create their foxholes.[13]

27

'About bloody time!'
– Normandy, 6 June 1944

MAJOR HANS VON LUCK, commanding Panzergrenadier-
Regiment 125 of the 21st Panzer Division, was working
on training schedules in a sparsely furnished house on the edge
of the village of Bellengreville, 12 miles south-east of Caen,
when he heard the growl of low-flying aircraft shortly after
midnight on 6 June. Soon after, his adjutant called from the
command post in the village. 'Major,' said Leutnant Liebeskind,
'paratroops are dropping. Gliders are landing in our section.'

A 32-year-old veteran of the fighting in Poland, Belgium,
Russia (where his reconnaissance battalion had reached the
outskirts of Moscow in December 1941) and North Africa, the
holder of the Knights Cross and a favourite of Field Marshal
Erwin Rommel, von Luck immediately ordered the bulk of his
regiment – armed with self-propelled guns and armoured vehicles – to be put on alert and divisional HQ informed. He also
instructed his 2nd Battalion, which was stationed to the north
and closest to the coast, to 'go into action wherever necessary'
and all prisoners to be brought to him.

Von Luck then received word that the commander of his 2nd
Battalion had already started a counter-attack towards Troarn, 4
miles north of Bellengreville, where his 5th Company was

concentrated. He telephoned the company commander Oberleutnant Brandenburger, in a cellar, and told him to hold on until the battalion reached him. 'Okay,' replied Brandenburger, 'I have the first prisoner here, a British medical officer of the 6th Airborne Division.'

'Send him along,' replied von Luck, 'as soon as the position is clear.'

Meanwhile, Liebeskind had telephoned divisional HQ at St Pierre-sur-Dives, eight miles south-east of Bellengreville, and was told that the commander Generalmajor Feuchtinger and his senior staff officer were both on private business in Paris. Having given a brief situation report, Liebeskind asked Feuchtinger's adjutant to obtain clearance for the regiment to make 'a concentrated night attack the moment the divisional commander had returned'.

As they waited for permission to mobilise, von Luck learned from the first captured parachutists that the task of the 6th Airborne Division was to 'take the bridges over the Orne at Ranville intact and form a bridgehead east of the Orne for the landing by sea planned for the morning of 6 June'.

Von Luck was fully aware that only an immediate night attack could take advantage of the initial confusion among their opponents, and that every minute counted. He also knew that Liebeskind's report would have been quickly passed on 'via division to the corps and to Army Group B (Rommel)'.[1] Why, then, was there no order to attack?

The answer lay in a confused command structure, a disagreement among senior commanders on how best to respond to an invasion, and, crucially, the absence of key decision makers on the night of 5/6 June. Generalfeldmarschall Erwin Rommel, the man responsible for the defence of Germany's Channel coast, had long argued that panzer divisions needed to be placed as close to the sea as possible to prevent any invasion force from gaining a foothold in the first place. General der Panzertruppe Geyr von Schweppenburg, commanding all armoured forces in France, disagreed. He preferred the 10 available panzer divisions to be kept well away from the coast – as a strong operational reserve in the forests near Paris – so that they could react to any crisis. Hitler eventually brokered a compromise: three panzer divisions, including the 21st, would come under Rommel's tactical control, and be stationed near the coast; three more would come under Generaloberst Johannes Blaskowitz, commanding a new army group – G – with responsibility for defending the Atlantic coast; and the remaining four panzer divisions, collectively known as the I SS Panzer Korps, would be kept in the centre of France as the German high command's operational reserve.

In the weeks before the invasion, Rommel had stressed to his subordinate commanders the vital importance of reaction time. 'Every leader,' he told them, 'from the commander in chief down to a squad leader must, in every situation and upon receipt of every order, consider with lightning speed what he must do "as an immediate response", and before anything else.'

On 30 April, he specifically ordered the 21st Panzer Division, stationed closest to the coast in the Caen sector, to 'consider its assembly area as a strongpoint, in which the division is to be ready, with its weapons dug in, to totally destroy even tenfold superior enemy forces, day or night'. It was to be ready to tackle airborne forces, engage in the battle at the coast within the first hours of an enemy landing, and deploy rapidly within the whole Army Group B sector. Such an attack order, however, would be issued by Rommel alone.

By this point, the division had two panzer grenadier regiments stationed on either side of the River Orne: Regiment 192 to the west; and von Luck's Regiment 125 to the east. Its chief armoured component – the Panzer Regiment 22, equipped with 110 tanks, most of them Panzer Mark IVs – was just to the south of Caen.

It was, therefore, inevitable that the panzer grenadier regiments would be first into action. They had been given, moreover, discretion to act thanks to a general instruction from Hitler that 'in the event of an airborne landing, all formations under attack were to immediately counterattack from their existing positions in order to destroy the enemy'. This general order, however, had not been passed on to von Luck by his divisional headquarters.

The confusion of those first vital hours of the airborne invasion was further complicated by the absence from their command posts of not only Rommel, who had returned to Germany on 4 June to celebrate his wife's 50th birthday, but also Generaloberst Dollmann, commander of the Seventh Army which was responsible for protecting the French coastline from St Nazaire to the mouth of the Dives river in Normandy. Dollmann was in Rennes for a map exercise, and Feuchtinger and his chief of staff were in Paris 'to attend to personal affairs'.[2]

As the hours passed and no orders were received, von Luck's anger mounted. They had set up a defensive front yet were 'condemned to inactivity'. The rest of the division, including the panzer regiment and Panzer-Grenadier Regiment 192, was 'equally immobilized, though in the highest state of alert'. Von Luck's adjutant got back in touch with divisional HQ and spoke to the intelligence officer. He said he was 'unable to alter the established orders' and that Army Group B had insisted 'that it was a matter of a diversionary manoeuvre: the British had thrown out straw dummies on parachutes'.*

---

* The dummy parachutists were part of an Allied deceptive operation (code-named Titanic): 200 were dropped south of Carentan at the base of the Cotentin peninsula, 50 more east of the River Dives and 50 to the south-west of Caen. They were equipped with a device to make them explode and catch fire on landing. Reports of these 'exploding puppets' made most commanders think they were part of an elaborate diversion from the main landing, probably in the Pas de Calais. (Beevor, D-Day, p. 54)

As the disaster unfolded, von Luck paced up and down, clenching his fists at the 'indecision of the Supreme Command in the face of the obvious facts'. After he got more information about the parachute landings and the gliders, he felt 'that a night attack would be the right way to counterattack, starting at three o'clock or four o'clock in the morning, before the British could organise their defences, before their air force people could come, before the British Navy could hit us'. They were quite familiar with the ground and he was convinced they 'could have been able to get through to the bridges'.

As well as isolating the two British parachute brigades to the east, such a manoeuvre would have enabled von Luck to stay in touch with the other half of the 21st Panzer Division. But he was not able to act on his own initiative and, as vital minutes ticked by, the bulk of his regiment sat immobile.[3]

However, on the far side of the Caen Canal, the 2nd Battalion of von Luck's sister regiment, Panzer-Grenadier 192 – reinforced with a battery of artillery and the remnants of the 1st Company of the Panzerjäger Battalion 716 – was ordered to move out with a Kampfgruppe and recapture the bridges at Bénouville before pushing on to Ranville. Spearheading the attack was the 2nd Battalion's 8th Company, commanded by Oberleutnant Braatz. At 3.10 a.m., Braatz led his company of panzer grenadiers – equipped with self-propelled guns, light anti-aircraft guns and some grenade launchers – north from its base at Cairon.[4]

The sudden arrival of Braatz's men at the southern end of Bénouville at 4 a.m. caught Major Taylor's depleted A Company by surprise, and drove it out of part of the village. This exposed the two aid posts which had been set up in houses on the lower road: No. 32, manned by the padre George 'Pissy Percy' Parry and some medics, for the walking wounded; and No. 34, run by Captain Wagstaff of the 225th Parachute Field Ambulance, for more severe cases.

Panzer grenadiers entered No. 34 first, but failed to find the seriously wounded who had been moved to the upper floor. They continued up the road to No. 32 where they discovered Parry and the other casualties. According to eyewitnesses, the Germans began a frenzied attack on the wounded, shooting and bayoneting them. When Parry tried to intervene, he was stabbed and killed with bayonets or knives and fell beside the men he tried to save. Only later, when the 7th Battalion retook that part of the village, was this war crime exposed.[5]

'Our position had developed into a classic airborne situation,' recalled Richard Todd, near the hamlet of Le Port. 'There was no front line as such and the battalion had evolved into four pockets of resistance: the three rifle companies and the Battalion Headquarters group, largely out of touch with each other, but each in positions of their own choosing.'

Minutes before first light, the defenders were cheered by the sound of hundreds of Allied aircraft, British and American, raining bombs on the 'strip of gun-positions, trenches and pill-boxes' that menaced the landing of the seaborne invasion force. The bombardment was supplemented by naval guns and rocket-launchers that pulverised the beach defences. 'From our grand-stand position at Le Port,' wrote Todd, 'I felt sorry for the poor sods cowering in those German bunkers. How could they possibly emerge and fight back? But they did, and with impres-sive vigour.'[6]

Meanwhile the fighting around the canal bridge, noted Pine-Coffin in his report, was 'very confused and fierce and almost continuous', particularly in A Company's area which was out of wireless contact and could not be reached by runners.[7] By dawn, A Company's strength was down to fewer than 20 men, with all the officers either wounded or killed. Todd remembered: 'From time to time, we could hear its Officer Commanding, Nigel Taylor, shouting encouragement. We knew that he was lying by the window of a house, one leg shattered, when his second in command, Jim Webber – himself shot through the chest – got through to us to report. Things might have been worse for A Company but for the action of one man, 19-year-old Private McGee.'[8]

Born in 1924 in County Monaghan, Ireland, Michael McGee reacted first when a Panther tank threatened to overrun the position held by himself and some of his comrades. Leaping from his foxhole, he engaged the Panther at point blank range by firing his Bren gun from the hip. This caused the tank to stop and allow McGee's comrades to destroy it with a Gammon bomb. McGee's 'complete disregard for his personal safety was largely responsible for the successful and gallant action fought by his Company'. Unfortunately, he was wounded by machine-gun fire from the Panther and died from his wounds later that day. He was awarded a posthumous DCM.[9]

Thanks to its stubborn resistance, A Company was able to prevent Braatz's panzer grenadiers from reaching the canal bridge. The Germans dug in and fought with their mortars and self-propelled guns from parkland to the south of the village, patiently awaiting the arrival of German armour 'with whose cooperation they hoped to break through to the bridges'. Meanwhile their comrades in Panzer Regiment 22 'stood inactively by their tanks in villages north and east of Falaise, waiting for an operations order that did not arrive until 8 a.m. on 6 June,* by which time

---

* The initial order to the 21st Panzer Division, issued by the German 7th Army HQ, was to attack airborne forces east of the Orne; this was later switched, by the commander of the LXXXIV Corps, to an attack 'on the enemy landing from the sea on the coast north of Caen'. Hampered by this change of direction, and attacks by Allied aircraft, elements of the division eventually reached the

the opportunity to advance under cover of darkness had long gone'.[10]

Pine-Coffin's intention was to hold the enemy 'on the line of the road running north–south from Le Port to Bénouville'. His plan was for Major Roger Neale's B Company 'to infest the southern half of Le Port and the wood on the north side of the road junction and to prevent any break-through to the bridge from the north'. He would keep his counter-attack force – a platoon of C Company, and some men from the mortar and medium machine-gun platoons, armed only with pistols – near his HQ so that it could cover the small wood. The gallant fight being put up by A Company would, he hoped, prevent any large-scale attack developing from the south. In case it did develop, he placed a platoon of B Company just south of the bridge and was confident it could hold any attack until he was able to support it.

In an emergency, he would have brought some of Howard's men back to the west side of the bridge, as the 7th Battalion was now 'pitifully weak in numbers'. He wrote: 'The actual number available, in all ranks, did not quite touch 200, excluding Howard's party which could produce 70 more. This plan worked well and during the course of the day's fighting the enemy launched eight separate attacks in addition to nagging constantly with small parties and occasionally armoured cars.'

Each attack, launched by at least a company of German troops from Grenadier-Regiment 736, was driven off with heavy losses. There was, however, a constant threat to the 7th Battalion defenders and French refugees trying to cross the canal bridge from German snipers firing from the church tower at Le Port

---

coast near Lion-sur-Mer at 7 p.m. before the counter-attack ran out of steam. (Kortenhaus, *The Combat History of the 21st Panzer Division*, pp. 94–109)

and the upper floors of the Chateau de Bénouville, south of the village. The former were periodically dealt with by B Company's No. 5 Platoon using Bren gun fire and, at one point, a PIAT bomb fired by Corporal Killeen; the latter by rounds from a German 40mm gun on the west bank of the canal bridge that two B Company men had managed to fix and operate.

At around midday, the defenders heard the welcome sound of bagpipes to the north, signalling the arrival of the vanguard of Brigadier the Lord Lovat's 1st Special Service (Commando) Brigade which had landed earlier at Sword Beach. It was, recalled Private Denis Edwards (whose section had moved closer to Le Port to support the 7th Battalion's B Company), a noise that made the hairs stand up on the back of his neck – 'a sound like the wild wailing of banshees'.

One of his comrades shouted: 'It's them – it's the Commando!'

They all cheered as the noise grew louder and they recognised it 'as the high-pitched and uneven wailing of *bagpipes*'. For 'excessively tired young soldiers, out of ammunition and in an impossible position, the sense of relief and exhilaration can only be guessed at'. Abandoning all caution, they leapt to their feet, yelling things like, 'Now you Jerry bastards, you've got a real fight on your hands!'[11]

But as the Commandos had to march through the hamlet of Le Port, and part of it was still in German hands, Pine-Coffin told his bugler not to respond to the sound of the bagpipes. The Commandos, as a result, made a slower and more cautious entry into Le Port than they might have done.[12]

Lord Lovat, the handsome 25th Chief of the Clan Fraser, was a veteran of two Commando raids: the first, in March 1941, had successfully destroyed factories producing fish oil and glycerine in the Lofoten Islands off Norway; the second was the disastrous assault on Dieppe in August 1942, although his 4th Commando was the only unit to achieve all its objectives. On D-Day, he had been tasked with marching the six and a half miles from the beaches to the canal bridge in just three hours. In the event, having landed at 8.40 a.m., it took his spearhead No. 6 Commando, under Lieutenant Colonel Derek Mills-Roberts, a little longer because of German opposition and difficult terrain.

From the village of Saint-Aubin-d'Arquenay, Lovat could hear the crack of small-arms fire as Mills-Roberts's men advanced. Despite the lack of cover, he and his staff 'pushed up the road – at best pace, with scouts ahead and thrown wide on the flanks through crops red with flowering poppies'. Below them, in a slight hollow, was the road junction at Bénouville. The main road continued inland, sloping imperceptibly up to Caen. Down to the left, close to the houses, Lovat could see the bridge across the Caen Canal.

'Burning transport smoked ahead,' he wrote. 'A German half-track, upturned in a ditch, provided some protection for wounded men. Dead of both sides sprawled about the hollow, where airborne troops dug deeper into slit trenches. Others brewed up tea: the scene reminiscent of some Indian swoop on the wagon train in a western movie.'[13]

There was 'great jubilation' as Lovat was welcomed by Pine-Coffin, and 'red and green berets mingled on the road'. The two officers agreed that the crossing of the canal bridge was to be something of a ceremony, and it finally took place at 2 p.m. with Piper Bill Millin leading the way, skirling away on his bagpipes, followed by Lord Lovat and some of his Commandos. As they ran across, Lovat recalled, there was a 'fair amount of mortaring, a machine gun up the water pinged bullets off the steel struts, but no one noticed and the brave fellows from the gliders were cheering from their fox-holes at the other end'.[14]

At the far end of the bridge, Lovat shook hands with Johnny Howard, who told him: 'About bloody time!'

Howard then apologised for the mortaring that was coming from Chateau de Bénouville. 'The bastards have got the range,' he told Lovat, 'but it happens to be a maternity hospital and I have strict orders not to disturb the inmates.'

He advised the brigadier to keep moving as it was dangerous to hang around. Lovat headed off towards the other bridge, and was followed by Nos 6 and 3 Commandos, and then No. 45 (Royal Marine) Commando who had their CO picked off by a sniper. Beyond the river bridge, Lovat was met by Brigadier Poett and Major General Gale's chief of staff who told him that the situation was serious: the Germans were attacking from the south; most of the 3rd Parachute Brigade had been blown miles off course by strong winds; and Commando assistance was urgently needed to protect the airborne bridgehead.

Not long after the Commandos had crossed the canal bridge, a gunboat loaded with enemy troops was seen approaching from the direction of Caen. It was fired on by Wally Parr who, with two mates Bill Gray and Charlie Gardner, were manning the 50mm anti-tank gun on the east side of the bridge. The first shell fell 30 yards short, but stopped the gunboat which tried to turn back. The second hit the gunboat's stern, causing it to billow black smoke as it headed back to Caen as fast as its engines would allow. Parr and his mates 'whooped and yelled in glee'.[15]

By mid-afternoon, according to Johnny Howard, the enemy attacks on the bridges were waning and an uneasy quiet seemed to have settled over them. At around 9 p.m., as dusk fell on a glorious evening, they saw many gliders coming in to land around Bénouville and Ranville. It was the 6th Airlanding Brigade, with elements from the 2nd Ox and Bucks who were bringing in the heavy equipment: Jeeps, lorries and anti-tank guns, as well as stores. After some time they began coming across the bridges in the army vehicles, and the soldiers who had been there for almost a day shouted to their comrades: 'You're a bit late on parade, mate!'[16]

Pine-Coffin's 7th Battalion was relieved by the 2nd Warwicks arriving from the beaches at 9.15 p.m., although it would take another couple of hours to extricate the survivors of A Company from their positions in Bénouville. As the exhausted paratroopers marched back over the canal bridge – heading for an area north of Ranville to join brigade reserve – they were thanked by the Gondrée family: Georges, Thérèse, and their two young daughters. Georges had earlier celebrated his family's liberation by digging up bottles of champagne he had buried in the garden and sharing the contents with Howard and his men.[17]

'The Gondrée family was there, smiling and waving as the men passed by,' noted Richard Todd, who had not closed his eyes or eaten for more than 24 hours. 'All day they had helped to tend the wounded and many of us owed a great debt of gratitude to those brave, kindly people. Already fastened to the canal bridge was a crudely painted sign: "Pegasus Bridge", a name derived from the badge worn by British Airborne Forces, the winged horse of mythology. Since our landing 24 hours earlier, approximately half the battalion had been killed, wounded or were missing.* But as we headed through the darkness, the pace was that of light infantrymen – brisk and buoyant – laden and weary though the men were. It had been a day to remember.'[18]

The last two men over the bridge, after a final check to ensure no one was left behind, were Pine-Coffin and his intelligence officer, Lieutenant Mills. It was 1 a.m. on 7 June.

---

* Todd's casualty figures seem slightly inflated because so many 7th Battalion men were dispersed during the drop, but later turned up safe and sound. They had, in fact, lost 3 officers and 16 men killed during the defence of the bridge, and another 3 officers and 38 men wounded. (TNA, WO 106/4315, 6 Airborne Division: Immediate Report No. 2, 11 June 1944)

Pine-Coffin wrote later: 'It had been a particularly full day and had cost much blood and sweat. But the objective had been achieved, and it was a comforting thought to reflect that, during the whole 23 hours of the operation, not a single German other than prisoners had set foot on the bridge.'[19]

Howard and his depleted force had left a little earlier to rejoin their battalion at Ranville. As he moved away from the canal bridge, he glanced back at its distinctive bulk that had come to mean so much to him. 'We all felt a kind of sadness at leaving this place where we had achieved so much,' he wrote, 'only to hand it over to the men of the Warwicks. Bill Bailey described it rather well in the years that followed when he said, "You see, we rather felt that it was ours."'

In capturing the bridges, Howard had lost five officers – one killed, two wounded and another two missing – and 15 men (only one killed). He was also missing a platoon – Hooper's – and his second-in-command Brian Priday. Of his original four platoon commanders, only Sweeney was left. The injured included two platoon sergeants, meaning that two platoons were commanded by corporals.

After taking a couple of wrong turnings – and almost bumping into German armour in the village of Hérouvillette – Howard and his men finally reported to Major Mark Darrell-Brown* at Battalion HQ in Ranville in the early hours of 7 June. Soon after, Howard's spirits were given a tremendous boost when in walked Brian Priday and Tony Hooper. They explained that they had been released in entirely the wrong place, coming down close to a bridge over the River Dives. Fired at by German

---

* Darrell-Brown, formerly the second-in-command, had taken over the 2nd Ox and Bucks Light Infantry from Lieutenant Colonel Mike Roberts who had badly injured his leg when his glider crash-landed. This was not good news for Howard who did not have the same confidence in Darrell-Brown. (Howard, The Pegasus Diaries, p. 141)

sentries, they assaulted and captured the bridge before heading across country to Ranville. Hooper was taken prisoner as he scouted ahead – then Priday killed his captor, and released him. Slowed by the flooded terrain, they found refuge on a French farm and continued their march the following morning. It was dark by the time they reached Ranville, and were joyfully reunited with the rest of D Company.

Early on 7 June, Darrell-Brown received orders to occupy and hold the village of Escoville, two miles south-east of Ranville. Unfortunately, elements of the 21st Panzer Division were already there – concealed and waiting – and the battalion took heavy casualties as it entered Escoville. Howard went forward to visit his advanced platoon, pinned down by enemy snipers, and was shot through the helmet, the bullet grazing his head. Blood loss and a probable concussion meant he could no longer command D Company, which he handed over to Priday. They eventually withdrew to Hérouvillette, taking as many of the wounded as they could carry.

Totting up the casualties was the saddest reckoning of Howard's life. D Company had lost 58 men – nearly half its strength – who were killed, wounded or missing. Howard, holed up in Hérouvillette for the next four days, nursed his head wound and fell into a 'deep trough of near-despair over what had befallen D Company since our glorious success of capturing the two bridges'. It had all happened so quickly that he was engulfed by feelings of guilt and bewilderment. 'I never again entered that village without experiencing a feeling of loss and grief,' he admitted. 'It even overshadowed the triumph of "Pegasus Bridge" for me.'[20]

In its initial report, the 6th Airborne Division staff put the success of the *coup-de-main* operation down to the 'skill and daring of the glider pilots', the 'speed and surprise' achieved by Howard's men, the quality of the intelligence, and the failure of the Germans to place demolition charges and react quickly enough to retake the bridge. They might have added a sentence praising Pine-Coffin's 7th Battalion for defending the canal bridge from multiple counter-attacks.[21]

Both Howard and Pine-Coffin were rewarded for their fine work on D-Day with DSOs, the former decorated by Field Marshal Montgomery himself in a field in Normandy on 16 July 1944. Lieutenants Smith and Sweeney of the 2nd Ox and Bucks received the Military Cross, as did Lieutenant Pool of the 7th Parachute Battalion, who held the western bridgehead of the Caen Canal for 21 hours. Sergeant Thornton, who took out the German armoured carrier with the PIAT, was given the Military Medal. Eight of the glider pilots – including Wallwork and Ainsworth – were awarded Distinguished Flying Medals for what Air Chief Marshal Sir Trafford Leigh-Mallory described as 'one of the most outstanding flying achievements of the war'.[22]

If Operation Tonga had failed, and the Germans *had* been able to retake the bridges, there might have been two immediate consequences: the isolation and destruction of the bulk of the 6th Airborne Division east of the River Orne; and a cohesive armoured counter-attack by the whole of the 21st Panzer Division against the eastern flank of the five D-Day landing beaches that would have caused untold casualties and threatened the very success of the invasion itself.

By 'exploiting the initial confusion among the enemy after their descent', wrote Major von Luck, 'we would have succeeded in pushing through to the coast and probably also in regaining possession of the two bridges over the Orne at Bénouville. Parallel operations would then have been started also by Regiment 192 and the panzer regiment.' This might not have been enough to defeat the invasion as a whole, 'but there would probably have been a delay in the seaborne landing, with great losses for the British'.[23]

The failure of senior German commanders to order the 21st Panzer Division to counter-attack until it was too late had been pivotal; but so too were the courage and tenacity of the untested British 6th Airborne Division.

28

'Grade A stinker of a job!'
– Dorset and Normandy, April to June 1944

MAJOR TERENCE OTWAY, DEPUTY commander of the 9th
Parachute Battalion, was enjoying a spell of leave in
London with his wife Stella when the phone rang. It was Bill
Collingwood, brigade major of the 3rd Parachute Brigade, asking
him to return at once to Bulford Camp for an urgent meeting
with Brigadier James Hill. Catching the next available train from
Waterloo, Otway was met at Andover station by a staff car that
ferried him to Bulford. Hill was waiting for him in his small,
spartan office.

Once Otway was seated comfortably with lit pipe and a cup
of tea, Hill said: 'You can put up another pip because you're
taking over the 9th Battalion. The "Big Show" – the invasion
of Europe – is definitely on and the 9th has been allocated a
very special job, namely the neutralisation of a heavily defended
German battery. It will be, I'm afraid, a Grade A stinker of a
job!'

Unable to say more, Hill told Otway that all would be revealed
at 'Broadmoor', the divisional planning house at Brigmerston in
Wiltshire. Otway was ecstatic: at the age of 29, he had achieved
his ambition to command a parachute battalion; and, moreover,
one picked for a very special, if highly dangerous, job.

Accompanied by Collingwood, Otway was driven to Brigmerston farmhouse and led up to a room on the first floor. The walls were lined with aerial photos, maps and diagrams. Dominating the centre of the room was a detailed model of a gun battery, complete with barbed wire, minefields, trenches and four heavy concrete gun casements, all pointing along the coast (from east to west). 'You see that?' said Collingwood. 'That's a battery.'

'Yes, I can see that,' replied Otway.

'You have got to take it.'

Collingwood explained that the guns were suspected of being 150mm calibre, and were sited to protect the beaches that had been chosen for the D-Day landings.* Unless they were knocked out, the guns would cause havoc among the landing craft and the bigger ships offshore. But they would be a particularly tough nut to crack. Each gun was protected by a six-foot-thick concrete emplacement, covered by another 12 feet of earth, and resembling a huge burial mound. The largest – No. 1 – was made from 1,400 cubic metres of concrete; the other three had used just 500 cubic metres each. All were accessed by steel doors. Clearly, special equipment and explosives would be needed to destroy the emplacements.

The garrison protecting the guns was believed to number from 180 to 200 men, chiefly located in an underground control room, in the emplacements themselves and in a number of concrete pillboxes. There was a 20mm dual-purpose gun and up to a dozen machine guns. The whole position was circular, about 400 yards in diameter, and surrounded by a double-apron of

---

* In reality, the guns were Czech-built 100mm howitzers, manned by German artillerymen, and their main task was to guard the locks and estuary of the Orne Canal in case Allied assault troops attempted to capture Caen by moving up the canal in boats. Their secondary task was to guard the flat ground east of the Orne estuary, in the event of an enemy landing; and their third to hit enemy ships in the Channel. (Jefferson, *Assault on the Guns of Merville*, p. 74)

barbed wire and a minefield that was, in places, 100 yards deep. The closest village, just a few hundred yards from the guns, might contain more troops.

The vital factor, explained Collingwood, was time. The battery had to be destroyed by 4.50 a.m. on 6 June. Yet, owing to naval and air commitments, the earliest anyone could be dropped by parachute or landed by glider was 12.20 a.m. The nearest suitable drop zone was 2,400 yards south-east of the battery.

Otway's immediate task was to formulate a plan of attack. For reasons of security, he was unable to take anything from the room. But he could return whenever he liked.

A few days later, he was told the location of the battery: close to the Normandy village of Merville, a mile inland from the seaside resort of Franceville-Plage and double that distance from the town of Ouistreham where the Caen Canal and River Orne flowed into the Channel. Its guns commanded 'Sword' beach and would jeopardise the planned landing of the British 3rd Division, and the entirety of Operation Overlord itself.

Otway studied the model (which was constantly being updated) and all the available intelligence, and soon came up with his plan. There were, he realised, only two sides from which they could attack. From the north was a double-apron barbed wire fence, outside which was a minefield about 30 yards deep. Beyond this was an anti-tank ditch 14 feet wide and 16 feet deep, which they 'assumed would be full of horrors'. On the south side 'there was the same double-apron fence and the same 30-yard minefield, but instead of the ditch there was another barbed wire fence some 12 to 15 feet thick and 5 to 6 feet high'. The whole battery was 'surrounded by a minefield 100 yards deep which was protected by a barbed-wire cattle fence, possibly electrified'. Such was the 'nut to be cracked'. Since they were to land to the south-east of the battery, he decided to attack from that direction.

The first 7th Battalion men – 12 members of the Rendezvous (RV) and Battery Reconnaissance (BR) parties – would land with the Pathfinders at 12.20 a.m. One officer and five men would establish the battalion RV on the drop zone. The BR party, meanwhile, would split into two: one officer and two men to head for the Merville Battery to conduct a study of the defences; and another officer and two men to proceed to the site of a separate battery to establish if, as Allied intelligence believed, it was a fake. Before the first RV party got to its destination, 100 RAF bombers – Lancasters and Halifaxes – would plaster the battery with 400-pound bombs at 12.30 a.m. in the hope of destroying it or its defences.

At 12.35 a.m, five Horsa gliders would land as close to the RV as possible with the heavy equipment which included two 6-pounder anti-tank guns and three Jeeps containing scaling ladders, lengths of explosive Bangalore torpedoes and aluminium foot bridges. Once the rest of the battalion had landed at 12.50 a.m., and assembled at the RV point, it would make its way to the battery, preceded by a taping party of one officer and eight men whose job was to lay tapes as directed by the Reconnaissance Party to the most suitable points for breaching the inner wire defences. They would be equipped with mine detectors.

Once a firm base had been established 300 yards from the perimeter, the taping party would clear four-foot-wide lanes through the minefield to each intended gap. Shortly before the assault proper began at 4.30 a.m., a diversion party – armed with five PIATs and two Bren guns – would attack the main gate, while two sniping groups used Brens, anti-tank rifles and Lee-Enfields to target bunkers and machine-gun positions. While this was going on, the Breaching Company – B – would lay Bangalore torpedoes to clear the wire, with one platoon assigned to each gap.

At exactly 4.30 a.m., having been released from their tugs six minutes earlier, the first of three Horsa gliders would land – daringly – inside the battery positions. They would be carrying the Glider Assault Detachment of 4 officers and 54 men – mostly A Company and a detachment of Parachute sappers – with Stens, grenades and explosive charges to blow up the two centre gun positions.

Justifying this highly dangerous glider manoeuvre, Otway explained: 'It seemed to me daft to go over what was then known as the Atlantic Wall, the heavily defended French coast, fly over that and drop outside another fortress, i.e. the Merville Battery. So I decided to see if I couldn't . . . put troops directly inside.'

As soon as the first glider had touched down, a bugle would signal the nearby mortar crew to cease firing star shells. The Breaching Company would then blow the Bangalore torpedoes and the Assault Company – C – would charge through the gaps in the wire and rush the four concrete gun emplacements, followed by a troop of sappers who would destroy the guns.

If all went to plan, the accompanying naval party would inform the light cruiser HMS *Arethusa* that the mission had been successful. If the ship's company did not get this message by 5.30 a.m., it would assume the attack had failed and open fire on the battery with its 6-inch guns.[1]

Terence Otway, the man responsible for this vital mission, was a tough character who did not suffer fools. One sergeant noted: 'You're daren't make a mistake with the Colonel.'

His command style bore more than a passing resemblance to John Howard's. 'I wanted to be respected,' wrote Otway, 'and I wanted to be considered a fair person, but I wouldn't go out of my way to get popularity. I wanted an efficient, well run, happy Battalion, and I reckon I had it.'[2]

Born in Egypt on 15 June 1914, the son of an Irish civil

engineer, Otway was educated at Dover College and the Royal Military Academy, Sandhurst, where he passed out 18th of 200 in 1933. He was commissioned into the Royal Ulster Rifles and served in Hong Kong, Shanghai – a baptism of fire, repelling daily Japanese raids – then India, on the equally lively North-West Frontier, before returning to the 1st RUR which, by then, had been converted to glider troops as part of the 6th Airlanding Brigade. Told by the commanding officer that there were too many majors, and he would have to drop to captain, Otway walked out, but thanks to the intervention of Major General Gale, he was reassigned as second-in-command of the 9th Battalion.[3]

Otway's new unit had been known as the 10th Battalion, The Essex Regiment, before it was converted to airborne duties and renamed the 9th (Eastern and Home Counties) Parachute Battalion in late 1942. Around 200 of the 10th's originals were awarded their wings and formed the spine of the new battalion, which was assigned to the 3rd Parachute Brigade with the 7th and 8th Battalions (the latter commanded by the legendary Lieutenant Colonel Alastair 'Jock' Pearson). In August 1943, a couple of months after James Hill had become the 3rd's brigadier, the 7th Battalion was moved to the newly formed 5th Parachute Brigade and replaced by the 1st Canadian Parachute Battalion.

While sad to lose Pine-Coffin's 7th Battalion, Hill was impressed by the Canadians. He found them similar to the 1st Parachute Battalion 'inasmuch as they were formed from soldiers who wanted to fight and the sooner the better, soldiers of fortune really'. As a lone parachute battalion was 'no good to anybody', they were assigned to the 3rd Parachute Brigade.

To prepare for the brigade's role in Normandy, Hill insisted that both officers and men were extremely fit and capable of doing multiple jobs. Every battalion and company had an A and B Headquarters, 'so that if one was knocked out, the other could take over'. Each man was 'trained to use other people's weapons and to drive Bren carriers – anything that kept the battle going'. Hill's four rules of battle were: speed, control, simplicity (of thought and action), and effective firepower.

Hill's brigade had three tasks on D-Day: to capture and put out of action the Merville Battery; to destroy five bridges over the River Dives (spread over seven miles of waterlogged terrain) and hold a vital wooded ridge which overlooked the whole of the Orne valley from Bréville in the north to Troarn in the south; and to harry the enemy by sending out strong fighting patrols to the south of Troarn.[4]

But the job given to the 9th Battalion – neutralising the Merville Battery – was the most important, and, aware of this, its keen new commander left no stone unturned as he prepared his men for the big day. Spotting a suitable location near Newbury from the air, Otway got permission to construct a replica of the Merville Battery and the surrounding countryside so that his men could practise both the march from the RV and the assault. Assisted by sappers, he supervised the construction in just seven days of the anti-tank ditch, the four huge gun emplacements, made from tubular steel and hessian, the barbed wire defences and the dummy minefields (complete with skull-and-crossbones signs that read '*Achtung Minen*'). After incessant training, his battalion carried out a full dress rehearsal that went remarkably well, albeit lacking in parachutes, gliders or actual opposition,

Paranoid about 'loose talk' giving the game away, Otway recruited 12 attractive young women from the Women's Auxiliary Air Force (WAAF) and told them to go to Newbury as spies to flirt with his troops 'and see if you can get any hint of what we're going to do'. When the honeytrap reported back, Otway was proud to find that 'not one single man had broken security. It was that vital. Lives, all our lives, depended on it.'[5]

★

The 24-hour postponement of D-Day on 4 June, due to bad weather, was a nerve-racking time for many of the airborne troops, but for Otway, it was a godsend. He 'had been working so hard for months that he was exhausted, and the postponement allowed him some much-needed rest'.[6]

At 11.10 p.m. on 5 June, Otway's advance parties took off in two Albemarle bombers from RAF Harwell, southern Oxfordshire. The three-man BR (or 'Trowbridge') Party, which had the vital job of scouting out the battery's defences, was made up of Major George Smith and two experienced NCOs, Company Sergeant Majors Bill Harold and George 'Dusty' Miller. A phlegmatic Geordie, orphaned as a boy, Miller had joined the Green Howards in 1933 before switching to the Army Physical Training Corps and later the Parachute Regiment. Like Smith and Harold, he was an expert map and compass reader who had practised the march to the battery so many times he could probably have done it blindfolded. Teak-tough and imperturbable, he was chosen to jump first.

An hour into the flight, with the pilot dodging increasingly heavy flak, Miller's only concern was that they were dropped on target. At 70 minutes, the team were all standing, their static lines hooked up, when the green light went on. Miller opened the hatch – which he likened to a 'big hole in a coffin' – and jumped. The moon was obscured by cloud and the darkness lit up by flashes from anti-aircraft fire. It took just a few seconds to descend from 500 feet to the exact field at which the pilot had been aiming. Harold and Smith landed soon after, both within hailing distance of Miller. Hearing the sound of approaching bombers, they took cover in a ditch to await the completion of the huge aerial bombardment of Merville Battery that was scheduled for 12.30 a.m. The bombs fell on time, but not in the right place. Most exploded to the south-east, some just 200 yards from where Miller and his comrades were cursing the inaccuracy of the RAF and the irony of nearly being killed by their own side.

Narrowly avoiding a German patrol, they made their way past the burning village of Gonneville-sur-Merville to the outer perimeter of the Merville Battery where they could hear the German sentries chatting. Having cut through two layers of barbed wire, they hid in a bomb crater to await the arrival of the taping party.[7]

The six-man RV party, meanwhile – led by Major Allen Parry (younger brother of the 7th Battalion's ill-fated Padre George 'Pissy Percy' Parry) – had not found things quite so easy. Jumping with a large kit bag lowered from his right leg, containing his personal equipment, a signalling lamp and batteries, Parry landed on time – at just after 12.20 a.m. – but in a location he did not recognise. There was no sign of the large, bushy tree on the bank of a wide ditch that he was expecting to see, and no other members of the RV party in sight. He pulled out his 'Ducks, bakelite' recognition whistle★ – which made a sound like a quacking duck – and blew it. Nobody responded. Panicking slightly, he set out on a westerly compass bearing that he hoped would lead to the RV, hauling his heavy kit bag behind him.

The drone of RAF bombers filled him with fear that he might have landed in their target area. 'I had just reached a ditch,' he remembered, 'when the bombs descended all around me. I felt certain I couldn't be missed . . . When they ceased to fall I breathed a sigh of relief.' The next sound he heard was a rustling in the hedge. He raised his Sten and prepared to fire.

'Punch,' whispered a voice nearby.

'Judy,' responded Parry.

★ To signal to their men in the dark, British airborne officers carried little bakelite 'ducks' that made a quacking sound. Their soldiers responded with small bird-call whistles. American airborne troops, on the other hand, recognised each other by clicking little metal crickets, of the type used by children on Halloween.

Two Canadian paratroopers appeared, as lost as he was and without weapons. 'Do you know where our RV is, sir?' asked one.

'No,' said Parry, 'but you can come along with me. You'd better have this.' He handed one his Sten, as he also had a pistol.

At 1 p.m., having collected a dozen more strays, Parry spotted a red light and made his way over to it. It was held by Lieutenant Joe Worth, the Intelligence Officer, and with him were Major Eddie Charlton and Captain 'Hal' Hudson, the adjutant, 'but precious few others'. Soon after, he spotted the bushy-topped tree and found Private George Adsett, his 21-year-old batman, standing beneath it. 'Good evening, sir,' said Adsett. 'What kept you then?'

'Oh nothing much. I had one or two little jobs to do on the drop zone and here I am.'

Parry extricated the Aldis lamp from his kit bag and said to Adsett: 'Now you go up that tree and I will hand you the lamp. When I give you the word you can start flashing.'

'Oh no,' replied his batman, 'you're in charge. You go up the tree and I will hand *you* the lamp.'

Parry scrambled up the tree and began signalling.[8]

The CO, Terence Otway, meanwhile, had taken off from Harwell in the first of 34 C-47 Dakotas carrying the rest of the 9th Battalion at 11.30 p.m. As is the way with paratroopers, he and his men were overloaded with kit, weapons and ammunition. They were all wearing battledress jacket and trousers, topped with the camouflage Denison smock★ that was worn over webbing equipment to prevent snagging before and during the

---

★ Designed by a Major Denison of the camouflage unit, and first introduced in 1942, the Denison smock was a coverall jacket issued to all airborne troops and the GPR, as well as SOE agents and Commandos, and scout and sniper platoons in infantry battalions. Most paratroopers wore it over their webbing equipment for the jump, but then under after they had landed.

jump. Their heads were protected by the brimless Para helmet – which Otway insisted they wear at all times on operations – though they also carried their red berets.

Otway slept for the first half of the 70-minute flight to France, waking only as they left the British coast behind. To celebrate, he pulled out a hip flask of whisky and passed it to the other passengers, who included his batman Corporal Joe Wilson, the taping party – comprised of eight men led by Captain the Honourable Paul Greenway – plus duplicate RV and BR parties in case the originals had 'gone astray'.

As they reached the French coast the flak began, with one explosion narrowly missing the tail of the aircraft. Minutes later, as Otway stood behind Wilson in the door of the aircraft, another shell exploded to the side of the Dakota, its shock-wave shooting Wilson out of the door 'like a bullet, but he wasn't hurt'. Of the descent, Otway remembered 'incendiary bullets coming up at me, and actually going through my chute, which was disturbing, in fact I was bloody angry about it'.[9]

A combination of wind, poor navigation and enemy opposition meant that the battalion was scattered over 'an enormous area, one stick being dropped 30 miles east of the battery position'.[10] As a result, every component of the attacking force was under-strength. Of the original eight members of the taping party, for example, only Captain Greenway and two of his men were able to link up with the BR party at the battery. They arrived without any tape, mine detectors or other equipment – all of which had been lost in the drop, much of it submerged in the marshland. This did not deter Paul Greenway and 'Dusty' Miller of the BR party from crawling into the minefield, removing mines and cutting trip wires as they went, and marking out two separate paths by 'digging heel marks in the dust'. It was, noted a report, 'an amazing fact that these two parties accomplished what they did without mine detectors, and without a single casualty'.[11]

Meanwhile, Otway and his batman Wilson had come down on a farmhouse that the Germans were using as a command post. Wilson crashed through the roof of its greenhouse, and Otway bounced off a wall. The noise caused the Germans to open fire, but both got away in the dark. Wading through marshland with water that at times was chest-high, Otway saw a lot of drowned men, but there was nothing he could do. He and Wilson finally reached the RV at 2.30 a.m., where there was 'desultory firing' and the 'moans of a sapper with a broken leg'. Otway was met by his second-in-command, Major Eddie Charlton, who told him that only 110 of the original 600 or so members of the battalion had appeared, with 10 lengths of Bangalore torpedo and no scaling ladders. There was also no sign of the five gliders carrying stores and vehicles.★ Otway decided to wait another 15 minutes, by which time an extra 40 men with an additional 10 lengths of Bangalore torpedo had arrived.

He did a quick inventory: each company was now about 30 men strong; they had, in addition, a single machine gun, four members of the diversionary party minus most of their weapons, half of one sniping party, six medical orderlies and enough signallers to get by. There were, on the other hand, no sappers or members of the field ambulance, and no working radios, 3-inch mortars, 6-pounder guns, mine detectors, and Jeeps or trailers with the glider stores. The task seemed hopeless. 'What the hell am I going to do, Wilson?' he asked.

A former professional boxer with a flat nose and big cauliflower ears, Wilson might have looked as if he 'hadn't got a brain in his head', wrote Otway. In fact, he was 'extremely intelligent and knew me backwards'.

★ The gliders had run into a squall in mid-Channel, causing their tow-ropes to part. They came down in the sea and were never seen again.

The batman replied: 'Only one thing you can do, Sir, no need to ask me.'

Otway knew he was right. How could he face his friends and colleagues if he gave in now? He had to give it a go. 'I went on and put all thoughts of failure out of my head,' he remembered. 'It was a question of move off or give up. In the Parachute Regiment giving up is not an option.'[12]

En route to the battery, they had to be careful to avoid the huge bomb craters – some eight to nine feet deep – that littered the countryside. They were useful to hide in, however, when a patrol of 20 German soldiers crossed the front of their march; and also when they were shelled by German artillery and mortars. Eventually the head of the column reached the outskirts of Gonneville-sur-Merville, about 300 yards from the battery perimeter, where Major Smith had set up the 'Firm Base' and was waiting to brief Otway. Despite the lack of men and specialised equipment, Smith explained, they had cut through the outer wire and marked two gaps through the minefield. That made up Otway's mind: his reduced breaching party of 30 men would blow two gaps through the inner wire with Bangalore torpedoes, not four as planned, and then lie in the gaps and against the jagged edges like a human mattress; this would allow the assault party – subdivided into four assault groups, each of a dozen or so men – to race through both gaps and attack the casemates.

As Major Ian Dyer of C Company was missing, Otway gave overall command of the assault party – now a composite force of A and C Companies – to Major Allen Parry who had successfully set up the RV and navigated the column to the battery. There was always the possibility that they would be joined in the assault by the last three gliders. But given the mishaps thus far, and the lack of mortar star shells to guide them in, Otway knew better than to rely on their turning up. They were, he decided, on their own.

Despite the immense responsibility heaped on his shoulders, Otway remained remarkably cool and collected. He gave his orders 'concisely and clearly', wrote Major Smith, and it was 'incredible that everything was arranged and organised on the spot, amidst what seemed the most awful chaos'. Otway's 'calm set a fine example which was followed by all ranks'. His thoroughness in training had paid a dividend as 'the troops were on their toes and ready for the job'.[13]

What had always been an extremely tough ask was now, thanks to their reduced numbers, mission impossible. Yet they would give it a go nonetheless.

29

'Get in! Get in!'
– Normandy, 6 June 1944

A s Otway's men were forming up for the assault, they were spotted and fired on by six enemy machine guns: two outside the battery's defences, one on each flank, and another four from inside the wire. Seeing his closely packed paratroopers felled like corn, Otway yelled: 'Get those bloody machine guns!'

The single Vickers medium machine gun that had survived the drop – manned by Sergeant Patrick McGeevor and Corporal James 'Marra' McGuiness – took on and eventually silenced the firing from the left flank. Sergeant Sid Knight, commanding the remaining four men of the diversionary party, was told to do the same on the right flank as he made his way to the main gate. One of the 10th Essex originals, he identified three German machine guns, 'one outside and two inside the perimeter'. After silencing the outside machine gun, he led his men into the battery, where he spotted one of the gunners by a broken piece of concrete. 'His tracer gave him away,' wrote Knight, 'so I got right round behind him and put my gun on him which quietened him down. I had a go at the third one, whether I got him or not I don't know but it all went quiet.'[1]

It was now just before 4.30 a.m. and, although there were no star shells to guide them in, Otway decided to wait and see if any of the assault gliders made an appearance. Suddenly one came into view. It was circling overhead, searching for the battery, when it was hit near the tail by flak and forced to crash land in an orchard a hundred yards to the south-east.

With no more gliders in sight, Otway decided to wait no longer. He gave the order to attack and Major Parry blew his whistle. This was the signal for the Bangalore torpedoes to be detonated and the assault groups to move through the gaps in the wire, while the breaching party provided covering fire. Otway encouraged the assault by shouting: 'Get in! Get in!'

The attack began with a cacophony of noise as the defenders shot at the gaps in the wire, booby traps and mines went off 'all over the place', and the sound of a second battle came from the south-east where the survivors of the glider clash were engaging a platoon of German troops. Otway sent two assault parties through each gap, one after the other.[2]

Heading for the No. 1 gun, on the extreme right of the battery, was Lieutenant Alan Jefferson and his assault party of nine men, all from his No. 12 Platoon; he had left two men behind because they had lost their weapons. As they ran, 'shouting blue murder', Jefferson felt something nick him between the shoulder-blades and saw one of his men falling, just behind him. Then he felt a sharp blow in his left thigh, and tumbled to the ground. There was no pain, but he couldn't get up. He dragged himself over to a stack of wooden poles to watch his remaining men charging straight for the rear of the biggest of the four flat-topped concrete gun emplacements. Amidst 'yells, agonised cries and clouds of smoke', they charged through the open steel doors. Jefferson could not have been prouder.[3]

Following up, Major Parry was also shot in the leg as he entered the battery, and lay for some minutes dazed and winded by his fall.★ He then applied a tourniquet to his leg and limped towards No. 1 emplacement, where he discovered a scene of carnage. The ground was littered with the dead and wounded of both sides, and other Germans were being herded out of the emplacement with their hands up. Parry went inside, past more wounded, and eventually found the gun. It was not the 150mm monster they had been told to expect, but an old-fashioned field piece, mounted on a carriage with steel-rimmed wooden wheels. Sick with disappointment, and faint from the loss of blood, he told a sergeant with his party to use two sticks of plastic explosive to try to destroy the gun's breech block. This was done and, having inspected the damage, Parry was 'reasonably satisfied that sufficient damage had been inflicted upon it to prevent it playing a part in the seaborne assault'.

He then visited No. 3 emplacement 'after the party responsible for its destruction had withdrawn', and heard the news that the gun in No. 4 emplacement had 'been successfully neutralized'.[4]

Already inside the battery, Company Sergeant Major Sid Knight and his diversionary party moved towards the main gate where they found some Germans trying to surrender. 'Shoot them!' shouted Knight's men.

'You can't shoot them,' the CSM responded. 'They've got the white flag up.'

They were taken prisoner.[5]

While all this was going on, Otway had moved forward to the right-hand gap in the wire to direct operations. Up ahead, he could hear a storm of German machine-gun and mortar fire tearing holes in the attacking ranks. Eventually, Lieutenant Mike Dowling reappeared and said, 'Battery taken as ordered, Sir.'

'What about the guns,' said Otway, 'have they been destroyed?'

★ Parry's batman, George Adsett, ran on into the battery and was killed.

'I think so.'

'Bloody well get back up there,' ordered Otway, 'and make sure those guns are out of action.'[6]

To snuff out the remaining German resistance, Otway led the rest of his force into the battery. Machine guns opened up on both sides, but they kept going, ignoring the wounded. 'Once the Germans saw that we were parachutists,' wrote Otway, 'they put their hands up. They shouted, I could hear them, "para-trooper", and we killed or wounded the whole garrison except for 23 [who] we took prisoners.'

Incredibly, the fearsome reputation of British airborne troops had helped to persuade the German defenders to throw in the towel, thus saving lives on both sides. As the fighting died down, Otway saw what he thought was a dog tied up outside a pillbox and moved towards it to investigate. 'Don't touch that, you bloody fool,' said an officer lying nearby who had failed to recognise his CO. 'It's a booby trap.'

The officer was Alan Jefferson, lying with one of his legs shattered. Eager to evacuate the casualties, Otway instructed the German prisoners to show them the paths through the minefields. When they refused, Otway had his men fire bullets into the ground behind them, which changed their minds. He was about to make a thorough inspection of the guns, to make sure they could not be fired, when German troops shelled and mortared the battery from their positions in nearby Franceville Plage 'with complete disregard of their own troops'. Otway took cover in the nearest emplacement, and finished his inspection very carefully. All the guns were out of action. Despite being laughably understrength – down 550 men, thanks to the botched drop – Otway had achieved the unthinkable, and taken the battery.

It was time to fire the success signal. This was done by the signals officer, Jimmy Loring, who used a Very-light pistol to fire a cartridge that emitted yellow smoke. At the same time, he released a carrier pigeon, which he had been keeping in a special container inside his Denison smock, to carry the same message back to London.

As day broke, Otway ordered the remnants of his force to withdraw to the RV point at Calvary Cross, half a mile to the south. His orders were to occupy high ground close to the village of Le Plein, capturing a small naval radar station en route. But given that he had only 80 men still on their feet – having lost 5 officers and 65 men at the battery – he decided to make straight for Le Plein, using back country lanes. Encountering stiff German resistance as he tried to enter Le Plein, Otway took his men to the nearby Chateau d'Amfreville where they were finally relieved by elements of No. 3 Commando on 7 June.[7]

By then, some of the more serious casualties from the assault – including Major Parry, Captain Hudson, Lieutenant Jefferson and Private Mower – had been saved from German captivity thanks to the courage and ingenuity of the 28-year-old battalion padre, John Gwinnett. Dropped seven miles too far to the east, Gwinnett had 'wandered about the swamps all night' before linking up with 10 paratroopers at dawn. They finally reached the 3rd Brigade HQ at a crossroads near the village of Le Mesnil at 6 p.m. on 6 June, where Gwinnett discovered that 22 wounded men of the 9th Battalion had been left in a farm close to the Merville Battery where they were being looked after by German medical orderlies.

Gwinnett at once commandeered a truck – originally a British model, captured at Dunkirk – and drove to the farm with a 9th Battalion medic, Private Anderson. Only able to liberate four casualties at a time, they made multiple trips ferrying the wounded to the parachute field ambulance at Le Mesnil. Major Parry, who was in the last batch, remembered narrowly avoiding an ambush en route, and sheltering for half an hour at a chateau housing refugees. A woman at the chateau made them a Red Cross flag which was waved by a German orderly on the bonnet of the truck, which seemed to do the trick.[8]

The 'silencing' of the Merville Battery by Otway's 9th Battalion has acquired legendary status. 'We successfully attacked and destroyed a very important enemy battery of guns,' wrote Otway to his wife on 14 June, 'which threatened the beaches over which our troops were landing from boats the next day.'[9]

The 6th Airborne Division's official report noted: 'It was a disappointment to the battalion to find that the guns were of 75mm [calibre] only, and these were destroyed by Gammon bombs. It does not detract however from a magnificent feat of arms, and a display of absolute determination to overcome all handicaps.'[10]

It was, indeed, an extraordinary achievement to capture the battery with so few men. But one burning question remains: were *all* the guns put out of action, as Otway claimed in his letter? He was evacuated from France on 19 July 1944 with 'severe concussion' – having narrowly survived the explosion of a stray shell – and never returned to active service.

John Golley's 1982 history of the raid, *The Big Drop*, insists that Otway's injuries were as much psychological as physical, and that he took the news of his recall extremely badly. 'Introverted and suffering from battle fatigue,' writes Golley, 'his mind could only dwell on his own inadequacies and the loss of so many of his men . . . He could find nothing good in anything except his Battalion, which he had lost.' Even the award of the DSO★ – for 'conspicuous bravery and outstanding leadership'

★ Other 9th Battalion gallantry awards for the assault on Merville Battery include: the Military Cross for Major Allen Parry (awarded jointly for 6 June 1944 and 24 March 1945); and the Military Medal for Company Sergeant George 'Dusty' Miller, Sergeant Sid Knight, Sergeant Patrick McGeevor and Corporal James 'Marra' McGuiness.

during the assault on the battery and the defence of le Plein – and his status as a war hero meant little to him at first.[11]

Interestingly, in one of his last staff jobs before leaving the army in 1948, Otway wrote the official history of Britain's Airborne Forces in the Second World War. Of the 9th Battalion's action at Merville, he wrote: 'the battalion . . . penetrated and finally assaulted and overran the position, destroying two out of four guns completely and rendering two useless for at least 48 hours.'[12]

Even this modified claim about how many guns were destroyed was contradicted by Leutnant Rudolf Steiner, the 24-year-old Austrian-born acting battery commander, who was in his bunker OP on the beach at Franceville-Plage when the assault began in the early hours of 6 June. He headed towards the battery, but was forced back by heavy fire as the 9th Battalion assault was underway. After Otway's men withdrew, the German battery sergeant major and his surviving men emerged from their bunkers to reoccupy the battery and, according to Steiner, discovered that three of the four guns were still able to fire. At least two were used during the afternoon of D-Day, but only to fire 'on Ouistreham, on the Orne estuary and along the canal'.[13]

The 6th Airborne Division had been given four tasks on D-Day: to secure intact and hold two bridges over the Caen Canal and Orne river; to neutralise an enemy artillery battery at Merville near the coast; to secure a bridgehead between the Rivers Orne and Dives; and to prevent enemy reinforcements (including panzer units) moving towards the British left flank from the east and south-east. Despite the inaccuracy of the drops – thanks to damaged Eureka sets, not enough Pathfinder teams, poorly trained aircraft crews and adverse weather – the division still achieved all of its objectives, and, over the next 10 weeks, was able to consolidate the bridgehead east of the Orne and beat off repeated enemy attacks.

On 18 August 1944, the division crossed the Dives Canal – as part of the Allied breakout from the Normandy bridgehead – and by the 27th had captured Pont Audemer on the River Risle, just 10 miles from the Seine, an advance of 45 miles in nine days, 'carried out largely on foot against heavy enemy opposition and through difficult country'. Lieutenant General Harry Crerar, commanding the First Canadian Army, congratulated 'Windy' Gale on the 'immense contribution' his division had made during the recent fighting, particularly the impressive 'determination and speed with which his troops have pressed on in spite of all enemy efforts to the contrary'.

By the time it re-embarked for England in early September, to prepare for its next big airborne operation, the division had lost 4,457 men: 821 killed, 2,709 wounded and 927 missing.

But it is for its valiant and costly efforts on D-Day, and not the Normandy campaign as a whole, that the previously unblooded 6th Airborne will forever be remembered. 'It is doubtful,' noted a British newspaper report of 22 June, 'whether there has ever been a body of troops have been brought to a higher pitch of physical fitness, self-reliance and fighting skill. The gallant deeds of that magnificent division made history . . . As General Montgomery said yesterday: "the men of that division who died did not die in vain."'[14]

Indeed, they did not. The brigade-strength drops in Sicily had underlined the huge potential of an airborne force, but that potential was only realised a year later by the men of the untested 6th Division who, brilliantly led by Richard 'Windy' Gale and his subordinate commanders – notably James Hill, Nigel Poett, Terence Otway and John Howard – overcame formidable setbacks to achieve all their D-Day objectives, including the capture of the bridges over the Caen Canal and River Orne, the silencing of the Merville Battery, and the protection of the Normandy bridgehead's eastern flank.

Confidence in the airborne project had been restored. The possibilities now seemed endless and, as the Allied forces drove into Europe, the question on the mind of every Para Boy and Glider Lad was: where next?

PART IV

Disaster, September 1944

30

'It will be some blood bath'
– Lincolnshire, UK, September 1944

I N EARLY SEPTEMBER 1944, Lieutenant Colonel John Frost briefed the officers of the 2nd Parachute Battalion in the library of Stoke Rochford Hall, a neo-Jacobean mansion near Grantham in Lincolnshire that had served as Battalion Headquarters since the turn of the year.

'We have a new divisional show,' he told them. 'It's called Operation Comet, and involves the 1st Airborne Division and the Polish 1st Parachute Brigade seizing a series of river crossings in Holland and holding them until relieved by the ground troops of XXX Corps. The three main crossings that need to be captured are the road bridges over the rivers Maas, Waal and Lower Rhine at Grave, Nijmegen and Arnhem respectively, a total distance of 64 miles. The 1st Parachute Brigade has been given the job of taking the furthest bridge at Arnhem. It is, I know, a long way from XXX Corps' starting point on the Dutch border. But if the other bridges are captured intact, it is possible that the leading elements can reach Arnhem within 24 hours.'

His officers listened with little enthusiasm. The 1st Airborne Division had planned no fewer than 15 airborne operations since D-Day – including drops near Caen, St Malo, Falaise, Rambouillet,

Boulogne and, most recently, Tournai in Belgium – and all had been cancelled. Why would this one be any different?

Commanding A Company's No. 1 Platoon was 20-year-old Lieutenant Robin Vlasto who had joined the battalion after its return from Italy. He, too, assumed this grandiose operation was another false alarm. 'All hope of the 1st Airborne Division being given a chance before the Armistice was signed had been given up long ago,' he wrote. 'The Second Front had gone much too well from our point of view. The men were so jealous of the newly formed 6th Division that they daren't go home and tell their people that the 1st Brigade – the Cream of the Elite – were still at Grantham and would probably be having the brigade Swimming Sports soon.'[1]

The frustrating idleness of the airborne troops was, as Vlasto conceded, partly the result of Allied success: ground troops had swept forward so fast that intended airborne targets had already been taken. Since winning the battle for Normandy in late August, for example, the million-strong Allied armies had crossed the Seine and raced for the German and Belgian borders. Spearheaded by the armour of Lieutenant General Brian Horrocks's XXX Corps, the British Second Army had captured Arras on 1 September, Brussels on the 3rd, and the vital port of Antwerp a day later, a lightning dash of 250 miles from the Seine in less than a week. But instead of pressing on immediately towards the Rhine, Horrocks's two leading armoured divisions – the Guards and the 11th – paused on 4 September to allow supplies to catch up. This was an error. 'I believe that if we had taken the chance and carried straight on with our advance instead of halting at Brussels,' admitted the hatchet-faced Horrocks, 'the whole course of the war in Europe might have changed.'[2]

Moreover, if the 11th Armoured Division had advanced just 18 miles further north from Antwerp to the narrow neck of the

South Beveland peninsula, it would have intercepted the German Fifteenth Army, 150,000-strong, in its flight from the north Belgian coast. As it was, the majority of General der Infanterie Gustav-Adolf von Zangen's army was allowed to escape – including two weak SS panzer divisions, the 9th and 10th, which by a freak of fate were sent to regroup in the Arnhem area – and turn the nearby Albert Canal into a strong defensive position.

Undeterred, Field Marshal Sir Bernard Montgomery pushed hard for a reallocation of resources so that his northern army group could make the decisive breakthrough. 'I consider,' he cabled Eisenhower on 4 September, 'we have now reached a stage where only one really powerful and full-blooded thrust towards Berlin is likely to get there and thus end the German war.'[3]

Eisenhower disagreed. Replying on the 5th, he told Montgomery that his aim was to cross the Rhine 'on a wide front' and place a stranglehold on Germany by seizing the main industrial heartlands of the Saar and the Ruhr. In any case, he said, it was necessary to open the ports of Le Havre and Antwerp, vital for resupplying the Allied armies, before any 'powerful thrust' into Germany could be launched.[4]

Montgomery had other ideas. On 3 September, he had ordered his chief of staff to begin work on a plan to seize the bridges 'between Wesel and Arnhem' and launch his 21st Army Group across the Lower Rhine, north of the Ruhr. He was determined to establish the bridgehead over the Rhine, and felt that Eisenhower would then reward him with the lion's share of military supplies and reinforcements out of General Omar Bradley's US 12th Army Group. Thus was born, from Montgomery's arrogant determination to lead the charge into Germany, the first plan to capture the bridges, Operation Comet.[5]

As Frost continued his briefing of Comet at Stoke Rochford Hall, Vlasto's earlier doubts gave way to optimism as it became clear that his A Company, commanded by Major Digby

Tatham-Warter, would take the starring role. 'The plan,' said Frost, 'is for A Company of the South Staffordshire Regiment to land their gliders close to the southern end of the bridge at Arnhem and capture it before the Huns have even thought about their acorn coffee. Then our own A Company, and another from the 3rd Battalion, will do a forced march from the drop zone, seven miles from the bridge, on the north bank of the Rhine, and hurry through the town of Arnhem to relieve the glider party. The rest of us will join A Company as quickly as we can. The brigadier has assured me that the 2nd Battalion will, without any doubt, be involved in the bloodiest part of any battle we may have, and believe me it will be some blood bath.'

Vlasto was delighted: the 1st Parachute Brigade had been given the plum role of taking the bridge at Arnhem, and its 2nd Battalion had 'the choicest task of all with A Company right ahead'. He recalled: 'We were pretty pleased with this job, although it did seem a rather complicated method of committing suicide.'[6]

Comet was scheduled for 10 September. But at 2 a.m. that day, just four hours before the leading elements of the 1st Airborne Division were due to take off from airfields in southern England, it was cancelled because of stiffened German resistance along the Albert Canal, and the fear that the ground forces of XXX Corps would not be able to link up with the airborne forces quickly enough.[7]

Vlasto and his fellow officers drowned their sorrows in a two-day drinking spree. 'Believe me,' he wrote, 'when I say there was quite a party in Nottingham . . . On our return late Friday night, after two extremely thick days, we were informed that the same Flap was on again so we went to bed.'[8]

★

Frustrated by the cancellation of Comet, Montgomery instructed General Miles Dempsey, commanding the Second British Army, to prepare a replacement operation that would use not one but three airborne divisions – the British 1st and American 82nd and 101st – to capture the same number of river crossings. The operation was doubly attractive because the Germans had just begun their V-2 rocket attacks on London from launch sites in western Holland, and the British government had asked Montgomery how long it would take his army group to seal off the area.

Later that day, 10 September, Montgomery met Eisenhower aboard a plane at Brussels aerodrome, and poured out his frustrations at his superior's flawed strategy. Despite suffering from a painful knee injury, Eisenhower kept his cool. Leaning forward and putting his hand on the field marshal's knee, he said: 'Monty, you can't speak to me like that. I'm your boss.'

This brought Montgomery to his senses and he mumbled an apology. But while Eisenhower would not agree to Montgomery's requests to transfer to his army group two American corps from Hodges' American First Army, and to rule out a simultaneous advance by Patton's American Third Army in the Saar, he was prepared to give Montgomery priority in supplies and broad authorisation for the new airborne operation. 'I'll give you whatever you ask to get you over the Rhine because I want a bridgehead,' Eisenhower told him. 'But let's get over the Rhine first before we discuss anything else.'

Meanwhile, Dempsey had summoned Lieutenant General 'Boy' Browning – who was now commander of the British I Airborne Corps and deputy commander of the First Allied Airborne Army – to his Brussels headquarters where they formulated the new plan, Operation Market Garden. Market was the airborne component, in which the US 101st and 82nd Airborne Divisions would seize river and canal crossings from Eindhoven to Nijmegen, including the huge bridges over the Rivers Maas and Waal. The British 1st Airborne Division and the Polish 1st Independent Parachute Brigade, meanwhile, would drop near Arnhem to capture the road bridge over the Lower Rhine. They would, said Browning, lay out an airborne 'carpet' for the ground troops to advance over.*

Garden would consist of the tanks and infantry of Horrocks' XXX Corps advancing up a single road, with polderland flood plain on either side, dotted in places with woods and plantations. Having crossed the Arnhem bridge – hopefully within 24 to 48 hours of the start of the operation – they would occupy the nearby airfield at Deelen to allow the 52nd (Airlanding) Division to be flown in, and from there XXX Corps would continue to the shore of the Ijsselmeer, a total distance of more than 90 miles from the start line.

That afternoon, having flown back from Belgium, Browning briefed his boss Lieutenant General Lewis H. Brereton and other senior officers on the plan at the First Allied Airborne Army's HQ at Sunninghill Park,† a Georgian mansion near Ascot, Berkshire. A pivotal decision was whether they should launch the operation by day or night. There were pros and cons. German night fighters would be more effective than their daylight counterparts, but flak would be more accurate by day. As there would be no moon during the week beginning 17 September (the

---

* In Cornelius Ryan's classic account of the operation, *A Bridge Too Far*, Montgomery briefed Browning after his meeting with Eisenhower. On being told that the armour would reach Arnhem in two days, Browning is said to have replied: 'We can hold it for four. But, sir, I think we may be going a bridge too far.' (Ryan, p. 79) This conversation is almost certainly apocryphal as Montgomery does not appear to have met Browning on 10 September.

† Demolished after a fire in 1947, the house was rebuilt in red brick by HRH Queen Elizabeth II for her son Prince Andrew, Duke of York. He lived there with his family from 1990 to 2004.

earliest the operation could be launched), Brereton decided to go in daylight, in the belief that flak positions could be knocked out in advance, or suppressed during the mission itself.

The other fateful contribution made during the meeting was by Major General Paul Williams, commanding the USAAF's IX Troop Carrying Command whose planes would transport the 30,000 paratroopers and gliders to Holland. Browning had calculated that, using two lifts per day, all the troops and their kit could be delivered over 48 hours. But Williams insisted that the 'lift would have to be modified, due to the distance involved, which precluded the use of double tow lift'. This meant that, with each plane towing only one glider, instead of two, as Browning had calculated, double the number of lifts would be required. Moreover, as mid-September days were shorter and the mornings misty, Williams ruled out two lifts a day.

These changes meant it would take at least three days to transport the airborne divisions to Holland, and longer if the weather was poor. Operation Market, as a result, would not be landing any more assault troops on the crucial first day than had been planned for the much smaller Operation Comet, because half the force would have to guard landing and drop zones. So much for the airborne carpet.[9]

That evening, Browning briefed his senior commanders at the headquarters of his British I Airborne Corps – which would oversee the operation – in the beautiful Neo-Palladian mansion of Moor Park in Hertfordshire. They included Major General R. E. 'Roy' Urquhart, a 42-year-old English-educated Scot who had taken command of the 1st Airborne Division when Eric Down was sent to India to raise a new division in January 1944. A tall, heavyset man with a thick black moustache who had impressed Montgomery with his command of the 231st Independent Brigade Group during the Sicily campaign, Urquhart was delighted to leave his staff job with XII Corps for airborne duty. The appointment had been cooked up by Montgomery, who wanted Down's replacement to come from outside the close-knit airborne world, and Browning, whose chief requirement was that the candidate came 'hot from the battle'.[10]

Inevitably, the replacement of the respected Down with an outsider like Urquhart was resented by many within the division, particularly those who felt the experienced Brigadier Gerald Lathbury deserved the promotion. There was also the question of how long it would take him to understand airborne warfare. For John Frost, the 'snag of bringing in a complete newcomer, was that however good they may be, they were inclined to think that airborne was just another way of going into battle, whereas in fact the physical, mental and indeed spiritual problems were, when the battle might have to be fought without support from the normal army resources, very different'.[11]

Frost's fear that Urquhart did not 'get' airborne warfare was justified. 'The basic rules,' wrote Urquhart, 'were the same. An airborne division was a force of highly trained infantry, with the usual gunner and sapper support, and once it had descended from the sky it resorted to normal ground fighting. Infantry rules operated, if under rather different conditions.'[12]

His feeling was that the division 'contained a great collection of individuals' and 'wonderful material', but that they lacked training as formations. Many had done well in North Africa and Sicily, and believed they were the finished article. Urquhart did not agree, and the next few months of drilling were 'very busy'.[13] There was also the disappointment of 'getting his Division to battle-pitch time and again, only to have operations called off because the Allied land forces in Europe had overrun the proposed objectives'.

No wonder, then, that Urquhart took the Market Garden briefing with a pinch of salt. 'Had it been the first operation for which we had been briefed,' he noted, 'we would have taken it more seriously, but we took it in our stride because we were very practised planners at this stage.'[14]

On 12 September, Urquhart briefed his divisional 'O' Group on the plan, shortly before receiving confirmation that the operation would take place on the 17th. Two days later, he visited his three brigade commanders, and also Stanisław Sosabowski, commanding the Polish 1st Independent Parachute Brigade. He explained that the divisional objectives were to capture at least one, but preferably all, of the three bridges over the Lower Rhine at Arnhem: the great road bridge; a pontoon bridge; and a railway bridge. They were then to establish a 'sufficient bridgehead to enable the follow-up formations of 30 Corps' to deploy north of the Lower Rhine. Lastly, their task was 'to destroy enemy anti-aircraft defences in the area of the dropping zones and landing zones, and in the area of Arnhem, to ensure the passage of the subsequent lifts of the division'.

There was scanty information about the enemy, though it was known that 'the whole of the operational area was being prepared for defence as quickly as possible' and the Germans were expected to fight hard on the line of the Rhine. The Arnhem vicinity, moreover, was known to be an important training area for armoured and motorised troops. Yet the general picture painted by divisional intelligence was that 'major enemy resistance would be of a strength of not more than a brigade group, supported by some tanks'.

The major problem facing Urquhart was where to locate his glider landing zones (LZs) and paratroop drop zones (DZs). Ideally, they would be on both sides of the river, but the south bank was thought to be unfavourable as it was low-lying polder land 'with numerous deep ditches and few roads, very exposed, and considered unsuitable for mass glider landings'. Even so, Urquhart had wanted to drop part of the first lift here, but he was overruled by the RAF because their planes would have had to fly through German flak positions close to the Arnhem bridge.

After much debate, most of the zones were eventually sited on the north bank on a slight plateau, fringed by woodland, where 'extensive, open, firm areas' were perfect for dropping parachute troops and landing gliders. They included the four zones to be used for the first lift – DZ-X, LZ-S, LZ-Z and DZ-X – which were between six and eight miles west of Arnhem; and the drop zone for the second lift – DZ-Y – which was ten miles from the town. The zones for the third lift – LZ-L and DZ-K – were five miles west of Arnhem and a mile south of the bridge respectively. The RAF had agreed to drop the Poles on the south bank because they assumed that, by D+2 (the third day), the 1st Airborne Division would have knocked out most of the German flak batteries.

Comet had allowed for *coup-de-main* parties to be landed at all the major bridges, including Arnhem, but this option was removed from Market Garden because the air plan was complicated enough already, and the gliders would be subjected to heavy anti-aircraft fire if they got too close to the targets. Now, on the first day, all the gliders and paratroopers would land well away from the bridges. This would give the Germans time to organise their defence. When the experienced Major General 'Windy' Gale was told, he warned Browning that the omission of the *coup-de-main* parties was likely to end in disaster and he would resign before accepting such a plan. Browning disagreed, and asked Gale not to mention it to anyone for fear of harming morale. Urquhart's solution was to use the 1st Airlanding Reconnaissance Squadron, mounted in Jeeps armed with Vickers machine guns, to race ahead of the parachutists and capture the bridge.

As well as divisional HQ, two brigades would land on the first day: the 1st Parachute Brigade, whose task was to secure the bridges; and the 1st Airlanding Brigade, to protect the dropping and landing zones until the arrival of the 4th Parachute Brigade in the second lift on the afternoon of D + 1 (18 September), when the brigade would form a perimeter defence line on the western outskirts of Arnhem. The 4th Parachute Brigade, meanwhile, would form the perimeter line on high ground to the north of the town. In the third and final lift on D + 2, the Polish 1st Independent Parachute Brigade would land its heavy equipment in gliders north of the river and drop paratroopers on the south bank, opposite the town, who would immediately cross the river and form the eastern perimeter.[15]

In his post-war account of the operation, Roy Urquhart made no mention of feeling any serious reservations at the time. Yet, according to Browning's aide Captain Eddie Newbury, Urquhart arrived at Browning's office at Moor Park on 15 September and said: 'Sir, you've ordered me to plan this operation and I have done it, and now I wish to inform you that I think it is a suicide operation.'

Urquhart then turned on his heel and walked out.[16]

Another key figure 'quite frankly horrified' by the plan was 25-year-old Major Brian Urquhart (no relation to Roy), the British I Airborne Corps' chief of intelligence. A fiercely bright young man – the son of the Scottish artist Murray Urquhart who had abandoned the family when Brian was just six – he won a scholarship to Westminster School and studied at Christ Church, Oxford, before joining the Dorsetshire Regiment at the start of the war. Transferring to the 1st Airborne Division as an intelligence officer in 1942, he had been badly injured in a parachute accident, but recovered to serve in North Africa and the Mediterranean. His new job, with regard to Operation Market Garden, was 'to try to evaluate what the enemy reactions were going to be and how our troops ought to deal with them'.[17]

He was not optimistic. On hearing Browning say the intention was to lay a carpet of airborne troops, along which the Allied armies would advance, he asked: 'Is it to be a carpet of live troops, or dead ones?'

He did not believe the northern route was the 'best way to get into Germany', and struggled to see how the ground troops were going to get to Arnhem 'in time to relieve' the 1st Airborne Division. Far more alarming, however, was information from Dutch intelligence sources that there were 'two strong SS Panzer Divisions – possibly the 9th and 10th – being refitted near Arnhem'. They had been 'very badly mauled' in Normandy, but were still composed of the 'best fighting troops in the German army and they had heavy weapons'. But when Brian Urquhart first mentioned the potential presence of these troops to Browning and his chief of staff, Colonel Gordon Walsh, on 12 September, his concerns were brushed aside. 'I made a horrible nuisance of myself,' remembered Urquhart, 'because I felt this was an awfully dicey operation. There seemed to be a desperate desire on everybody's part to get the airborne into action.'

Part of the problem was overconfidence. Browning and his senior officers 'were all extremely gung-ho and were talking about Christmas in Berlin'. Someone even told Brian Urquhart that they were going to take their golf clubs 'because it was going to be a pushover'. With time running out, they were desperate to outdo the hard-charging American commander George S. Patton whose US Third Army had reached the River Moselle in the Saar. 'They felt,' noted Brian Urquhart, 'they had been left in a stodgy, static role and they were all wrapped up in dash and a stupid notion of competition. I think they were also influenced by a false idea of a complete collapse of the German Army. Browning, I know, was thinking of 1918 and another "great breakthrough".'

Brian Urquhart, on the other hand, was convinced the Germans would fight as tenaciously as ever, particularly the SS troops. The final proof was the arrival on 15 September of five low-level aerial photos taken by a British reconnaissance aircraft that clearly showed the presence of German armour in the Arnhem area. He showed them to Browning who replied: 'I wouldn't trouble myself about these if I were you. The tanks are probably not serviceable at any rate.'

This was the last straw for Urquhart who became, in his own words, 'rather hysterical about the whole thing'. He had tried to get his point of view across – arguing that the troops needed to be dropped in a different place 'so that they could immediately capture the bridge', that he doubted the relieving troops could arrive in time, and that the German opposition would be much more formidable than they imagined – but he had been ignored. When he continued to protest, he was 'removed, against my will, from the scene. I was sent away – exhausted, they said. I had become such a pain in the ass that the medical officer told me to go home and have a rest.'[18]

31

'Blizzard of silk'
– Lincolnshire, UK, 15–17 September 1944

O N THE DAY THAT Major Brian Urquhart's warnings fell on deaf ears, Brigadier Gerald Lathbury briefed his senior officers at Belton House, the magnificent 17th-century mansion that was serving as the 1st Parachute Brigade Headquarters, near Grantham, Lincolnshire. 'You are about to take part,' he told them, 'in a great offensive which has the ultimate aim of surrounding the Ruhr and making it impossible for the Germans to continue the war. Operation Market is similar to Comet. But now the whole 1st Airborne Division will concentrate on holding the bridges at Arnhem, while the American 101st and 82nd Airborne Divisions take care of the other bridges. Our brigade's role is to seize three bridges at Arnhem – the main road bridge, the neighbouring pontoon bridge, and the railway bridge – and hold them until the arrival of the rest of the division during the afternoon or evening of D + 1. The brigade will continue to hold the inner perimeter of the bridges until it is relieved by XXX Corps at any time after 24 hours. In the event of the main bridge being blown, we will seize the railway bridge instead.'[1]

Lathbury then explained that the 1st Airlanding Reconnaissance Squadron, commanded by Freddie Gough, a 'cheerful, red-faced, silver-haired major', with a platoon of sappers attached, would land first in gliders and use Jeeps to enter the town from the north-west, capture the bridges by *coup-de-main*, remove any demolition charges and hold them until relieved. It would be followed to the bridges by John Frost's 2nd Parachute Battalion, a troop of 6-pounder anti-tank guns and some sappers, who would take the southern, minor road along the north bank of the Rhine, codenamed 'Lion'. Once in possession of the bridges, the 2nd Battalion would form close bridgehead garrisons at both ends, and hold the western half of the town. Meanwhile the 3rd Parachute Battalion, having moved down the main Heelsum–Arnhem road (codenamed 'Tiger'), would take and hold the eastern half of the town. The 1st Parachute Battalion, part of the brigade commander's reserve, would move last by the northern route ('Leopard') to occupy high ground to the north of the town from where it could prevent the enemy from observing the inner defensive perimeter, and cover the approaches from that direction. Lathbury and his staff would follow the 2nd Battalion to a position close to the north end of the road bridge and set up their headquarters.[2]

Though Frost was 'delighted to be given a really worthwhile task at last', he could see several glaring snags in the plan. First, as the drop zones 'were several miles from the objectives and on the north side of the great main river obstacle only', it meant a long approach march on foot, 'through enclosed country and built-up areas'. If there was 'anything in the way of opposition, surprise would be lost and the enemy would have plenty of time and opportunity to destroy the bridges'. Furthermore, the capture of bridges in general was 'extremely difficult and hazardous' if you were on one bank only because the defender could concentrate his fire on all the approaches to the bridge from the comparative safety of the other side.

The reasons given for not dropping troops on both sides of

the bridges were, to him, unconvincing. The flak near the town could have been 'destroyed or neutralized' by Allied fighters and fighter bombers, which had 'complete ascendancy over the Luftwaffe'; and, far from being unsuitable for paratroopers, the farmland south of the river was where the Polish Brigade was due to be dropped on D + 2.

The unsatisfactory selection of drop zones might not have mattered so much if the air forces had been willing to fly two sorties on the first day of the operation, 17 September.[3] But instead, to avoid early morning fog, the departure time had been set for 9.45 a.m., with an arrival time over Arnhem of 1.15 p.m. Thus, had two lifts been attempted on the first day, the second would not have arrived until after nightfall, 'resulting in an inaccurate and possibly scattered drop as in Normandy'.[4]

Given that he was largely on his own for the first 24 hours, Lathbury might have chosen to concentrate his brigade for the advance on the bridges. Instead he split it into three battalion columns, relying on speed, surprise and the weak opposition that he had been told to expect. If those intelligence reports were unduly optimistic, however – as Brian Urquhart had suggested to Browning – there was a real danger that one or more of his battalions would be held up before they reached the bridges.

Shortly before Frost briefed his own officers on Operation Market at Stoke Rochford Hall on the morning of Saturday, 16 September, he was informed that 'the pontoon bridge which had been functioning west of, and close to, the main bridge had now been dismantled'. This left him two objectives: the main road bridge and the railway bridge, two miles west of the town. But the former was his 'real task and the raison d'être of the divisional operation'. He had 'every confidence in being able to take it and hold the north end', but was well aware that they would be on the wrong side of the river for capturing the southern end.

Major General Richard Nelson Gale OBE MC, the commander of 6th Airborne Division, talking to troops of 5th Parachute Brigade before they emplane at Royal Air Force Harwell on the evening of 5 June.

Halifax glider-tugs along with Horsa and Hamilcar gliders waiting at RAF Tarrant Rushton to take off for Normandy.

Discarded parachutes and Airspeed Horsa gliders lie scattered over 6th Airborne Division's landing zone near Ranville in Normandy, 6 June 1944.

Transport moving across the Caen Canal bridge at Bénouville on 9 June 1944. The crossing was renamed Pegasus Bridge, after the mythical winged horse on the shoulder flash of British airborne forces.

An aerial view of the Merville Gun Battery, after an air bombardment on 3 June 1944.

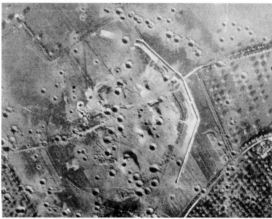

General Sir Bernard Montgomery (right) talking to Maj Gen Windy Gale and Brigadier Nigel Poett of the 6th Airborne Division after both men had been decorated by the commander of the United States 1st Army, General Omar Bradley, on behalf of President Roosevelt at General Montgomery's headquarters in Normandy. July 1944.

Douglas Dakotas dropping paratroops of 1st Airborne Brigade on to Dropping Zone (DZ) 'X', at Heelsum, west of Arnhem, 17 September 1944.

Generalmajor Friedrich Kussin, Arnhem garrison commander, lies dead in his car after being ambushed by No. 5 Platoon, B Company, 3rd Parachute Battalion, 1st Airborne Division, on 17 September 1944.

German SS troops search equipment left behind during the fighting on 17 September.

Men of the 2nd Battalion, South Staffordshire Regiment entering Oosterbeek along the Utrechtsweg on their way towards Arnhem, 18 September 1944.

Aerial view of the bridge over the Neder Rijn, Arnhem; British troops and destroyed German armoured vehicles are visible at the north end of the bridge, 19 September.

Lieutenant John Hollington Grayburn (1918–44), VC.

Maj Gen Urquhart outside his HQ at Hartenstein, 19 September.

Survivors of the 2nd Parachute Battalion's Support Company (including Private Albert Adams, left, with Bren gun) defending the Oosterbeek perimeter, *c.* 21 September 1944.

A German StuG III assault gun at Arnhem.

Allied tanks of British XXX Corps cross the road bridge at Nijmegen during its capture, 20 September.

Sergeants J. Whawell and J. Turl of the Glider Pilot Regiment search for snipers in the ULO (Uitgebreid Lager Onderwijs) school in Kneppelhoutweg, Oosterbeek, 21 September 1944.

British paratroops being marched away by their German captors. Some 6,500 of the 10,000 British paratroops who landed at Arnhem were taken prisoner, a further 1,485 had been killed.

A German photo of Arnhem bridge immediately after the battle.

Indian paratroops jumping from Douglas C47 Dakota transport aircraft as they run up to the dropping zone south of Rangoon, 1945.

Brigadier Poett talking with Field Marshal Montgomery during the Battle of the Bulge in January 1945. Left to right: Major-General Eric Bols (CO 6th Airborne Division), Field Marshal Bernard Montgomery, Brigadiers Edwin Flavell (6th Airlanding Brigade), James Hill (3rd Parachute Brigade) and Nigel Poett, and Lieutenant Colonel Napier Crookenden (CO 9th Parachute Battalion).

Glider troops after landing near Wesel, as part of Operation Varsity, 24 March 1945.

British airborne troops study a sign outside Hamminkeln during operations east of the Rhine, 25 March 1945.

British airborne troops with a 6-pdr anti-tank gun in Hamminkeln, 25 March 1945.

The plan he explained to his officers – many, like Robin Vlasto, nursing hangovers from their two-day drinking spree – was for A Company under Major Digby Tatham-Warter to move off from the drop zone first and make straight for the road bridge (codenamed 'Waterloo'). Having consolidated the northern end, Tatham-Warter was to send one platoon over the bridge to the south side. Frost and his headquarters, meanwhile, would follow close behind him with Dicky Dover's C Company, 'which was to capture the railway bridge near Oosterbeek, and then pass across so as to reach the south end of the main bridge'. This action would be supported by the battalion's mortars and machine guns. B Company, under Douglas Crawley, would bring up the rear and act as 'reserve for any eventuality'.[5]

Tatham-Warter, who had joined the 2nd Battalion from the Ox and Bucks Light Infantry, was chosen to lead the advance to the road bridge because he was a thruster; or, as Frost put it, 'a Prince Rupert of a man; he would have been a great cavalry commander on the King's side in the war with the Roundheads'. Dover remembered him as 'cool, calm, and collected', a tall man, 'a little aloof but full of confidence'. Unwilling to trust the reliability of the American hand-held SCR536 'walkie-talkie', which had a range of a mile and was used to communicate between Company HQ and the platoons, Tatham-Warter had trained his men to understand bugle calls that dated from the Napoleonic Wars. He was also fond of twirling an umbrella, and would carry one into his first battle.[6]

Dicky Dover's C Company were tasked with capturing the railway bridge. Dover was told that if it was blown before his men could cross it, he was to enter the town of Arnhem by Utrecht Street and capture the main enemy headquarters. The rest of the battalion, meanwhile, would approach the road bridge by way of the towpath north of the river bank.[7]

The success of their mission, said Frost, would come down

to three things: surprise, speed and grim determination. It would
also depend upon the arrival of XXX Corps within the allotted
time of two days, or three at the outside. There was, added
Frost, who had clearly not been made privy to the intelligence
that Brian Urquhart had desperately tried to circulate, 'no armour
in the vicinity at all'.[8]

Woken at 6 a.m. on Sunday, 17 September 1944 – and with
almost four hours to kill before their take-off from nearby Saltby
airfield – the 2nd Parachute Battalion officers enjoyed a leisurely
breakfast in the mess at Stoke Rochford. Frost ate eggs and
bacon, and read the newspapers. Others – including Robin
Vlasto and fellow A Company platoon commander Jack Grayburn
– tucked into 'two poached eggs on haddock, masses of toast
and marmalade, washed down with coffee'.

Everyone, remembered Frost, was 'in the best of spirits and no
worries anywhere', quite a contrast to some of his previous operations. Digby Tatham-Warter had a perpetual smile on his face, as
if to say 'This is too good to be true'. Eventually, having donned
their kit, weapons and ammunition, they staggered downstairs and
got the platoons on parade. They were a 'remarkable sight', recalled
Vlasto, with everyone festooned 'with packs, guns, bits of rope etc'.[9]

Parading with the Mortar Platoon, part of 'Bombs' Panter's
Support Company, was 19-year-old Private James Sims from
Brighton who had transferred from the Royal Artillery in
February 1944. One of only 60 men of his contingent of 165
to qualify as a parachutist, he remembered being awarded his
'wings' and red beret as one of the proudest moments of his life.
He had hoped to be assigned to one of the Independent Parachute
Companies, 'Pathfinders' who went ahead of the main body to
mark and defend the drop zones. Instead he was sent to Frost's
2nd Battalion which already had a 'splendid war record'.

Drilled relentlessly in the use of the 3-inch mortar – a simple but devastatingly effective weapon that could drop a 10-pound high-explosive bomb onto a target a mile and a half away – sent on morning runs, and served food in huge tents that was 'good and plentiful', Sims quickly became an enthusiastic member of the airborne fraternity who held as their ideals a 'willingness to fight anyone at any time, a determination not to let down our officers and comrades, and a resolve to uphold the formidable reputation of the Parachute Regiment'.

They were shown propaganda films and given lectures to inspire them with a sense of what they were fighting for, but the impact was minimal. Getting British soldiers worked up enough to defend democracy was, Sims felt, an 'uphill task'. Most soldiers had three basic interests: football, beer and crumpet. For parachutists, 'the order was reversed'. Few of Sims' comrades 'seemed to take anything seriously, but their weapon expertise was obvious'. They regarded their German enemies with a mixture of admiration and contempt.

Commanding the Mortar Platoon was Lieutenant Bryan Woods, a 25-year-old Ulsterman who had been studying at Cambridge when war broke out in 1939. Like Tatham-Warter, he initially joined an airlanding battalion – in his case the 1st Royal Ulster Rifles – before switching in the spring of 1943 to the Parachute Regiment. A tall, slim man, he was 'rather quiet, but very efficient and cool under fire according to the veterans of the platoon who had seen action with him in Sicily'.* He was also extremely solicitous of his men, 'refusing to sit down or even have a mouthful of tea' after a long arduous march until everyone had a hot meal inside them and were bedded down for the night. Naturally, wrote Sims, 'the men responded to such positive treatment, but for all this discipline was strict'.

---

* During the Sicily campaign, Woods had commanded A Company's No. 3 Platoon.

Just before the operation, Sims was told that he and two other 19-year-olds were too young to be parachuted into Arnhem and would accompany the baggage train by road and sea instead. But when three veterans failed to return from the fleshpots of Nottingham – probably assuming that this was just another abortive operation – the three youngsters were roped into the mission after all. Designated as bomb carriers, they were given a harness with six 10-pound mortar bombs to cart into action. They were also issued with 'Dutch occupation money, maps, escape saws, forty pounds of .303 rifle ammo, two 36 grenades, an anti-tank grenade, a phosphorus bomb, and a pick and shovel'.

Transported in lorries to Saltby airfield, the 509 officers and men of the 2nd Battalion found rows of Douglas C-47 Dakotas parked along the runway 'like horses in the paddock waiting to move to the start-line'. The place was a hive of activity with groups of men checking containers by each aircraft, and officers in Jeeps driving in all directions.[10]

Having drawn their parachutes, the men were given mugs of tea and bacon sandwiches. When a camera crew arrived on a truck to film them, they jumped about and waved their mugs in the air. 'The excitement was beginning to build up,' wrote Sims, 'everyone was laughing and shouting; the atmosphere had suddenly become like a school outing or picnic. All our doubts seemed to be swept away in a sudden surge of confidence. At last we were going and we somehow knew that this time there would be no stand-down.'[11]

Assigned with his staff to Chalk 16, Frost found the American pilot 'a reassuring type of man who exuded confidence', and his crew – co-pilot, navigator and radio operator – in good spirits. Once Colonel Styles, the American group commander, had wished him good luck, he went down the column of planes to do the same to his men.[12]

On the order 'Emplane!', they clambered aboard the Dakotas

– 16 per plane – and settled into the metal bucket seats on either side of the fuselage interior. Soon after, the planes' two powerful Pratt and Whitney 1,200hp engines roared into life and the first strings of the flight began to move out of their parking areas and on to the runway.[13]

One by one the planes took off, climbed and circled the runway while others joined the formation. They were part of a huge armada of 1,534 aircraft and 491 gliders that were carrying the first lift of more than 20,000 Allied troops, members of the American 82nd and 101st, and the British 1st Airborne Divisions. The first to leave were carrying each division's Pathfinders who would parachute onto the drop and landing zones, fight off any Germans, set up Eureka homing beacons to guide in the waves of troop carriers, and set off colour smoke grenades on their approach. Frost and his men were preceded by 12 RAF Stirling bombers carrying the Pathfinders of the 21st Independent Parachute Company, at least 20 of whom were German and Austrian Jews who had transferred from the Pioneer Corps. All carried dog-tags and identity papers with fake Christian names in case they were captured.

Next to go, spaced at 20-minute intervals, were the tug planes and gliders carrying the 1st Airlanding Brigade and then Browning's I Airborne Corps HQ, divisional HQ and the field ambulances. The Horsas were filled with Jeeps, trailers, motorcycles and 6-pounder anti-tank guns, as well as troops, supplies and ammunition; while the larger Hamilcars contained Bren gun carriers and 17-pounders. The glider carrying 'Boy' Browning, his batman, doctor, cook, tent and Jeep – due to land with the 82nd near Nijmegen, from where the corps commander could direct the battle from a central position – was flown by Colonel George Chatterton himself. He remembered Browning 'immaculately dressed in a barathea battle-dress with a highly-polished Sam Browne belt, knife-edge creased trousers, leather revolver holster, all gleaming like glass, a swagger cane in one hand and wearing kid gloves'. Browning was in 'tremendous form because he realised that he had reached one of the climaxes of his career'.

Last to leave, half an hour after Browning, were the C-47 Dakotas carrying six American parachute regiments and the British 1st Parachute Brigade.[14]

The planes and gliders flew down two five-mile-wide air corridors to the English coast and beyond. The Northern Route was assigned to aircraft carrying the American 82nd Airborne and British 1st Airborne. It crossed the English coast at Aldeburgh in Suffolk, and proceeded south-east across the North Sea to the Dutch island of Schouwen, where it dog-legged east to Eindhoven. There the route split, with the 82nd heading north-east to Nijmegen, and the 1st directly north to Arnhem.

The Southern Route, reserved exclusively for the 101st Airborne, crossed the coast near Colchester in Essex, and headed across the Channel to its landing zones near Eindhoven, via Antwerp in Belgium. The transport aircraft were preceded by a force of bombers and fighter-bombers from the RAF and USAAF whose main task was to attack flak sites along the Market route. More than a thousand Allied fighters – mostly RAF Hawkers, Tempests and Typhoons – were airborne to protect the transport planes.[15]

Having crossed the Dutch coast – and with just 10 minutes to H-Hour (the time at which the attack was due to begin) – Lieutenant Colonel John Frost stood in the Dakota's open doorway and tried to compare the country with his memory of the map. He spotted the distinctive Maas river and, as they crossed it, the pilot warned them to get ready. The atmosphere was one of tense excitement. Forced smiles, and furious last-minute puffing on cigarettes, reminded Frost that the business of 'jumping far behind the enemy lines was no small test for anyone's nervous system'.[16]

Young James Sims, due to jump second last in his stick, had passed the flight reading an article in *Reader's Digest* about a plane crash. Crossing the North Sea, his Dakota was targeted by machine-gun fire from a German naval vessel, the tracer bullets 'whipping past the open doorway like hornets'. The only 'casualties' were paratroopers being sick into brown paper bags as the pilot took evasive action. Flying inland at an altitude of around 2,000 feet, Sims could see that the RAF had marked the route to Arnhem 'with one blazing flak tower after another'.

Warned by an American crewman that they were dropping to 700 feet for the run in, Sims and his colleagues put on their close-fitting helmets and adjusted the rubber chin-guards. Then they hooked on to the static line and heaved their kit bags containing six mortar bombs, pick, shovel, rifle and small pack on to their legs, securing them with special web straps, an extra weight per man of at least 100 pounds. Finally they stood up and, in single file, closed up behind one another, right hand holding the kit-bag grip and left on the shoulder of the man in front.

Lieutenant Woods, due to jump first, was framed in the doorway, the 'slipstream plucking impatiently at the scrim netting on his helmet'. The 'red light glowed steadily and then the green light winked on. Go!'

When Sims jumped, the slipstream caught him and whirled him around. He found himself in the middle of a colourful 'blizzard of silk . . . conscious of taking part in one of the greatest airborne descents in the history of warfare'.[17]

For Major Dicky Dover, dropping with a stick of C Company, the descent was uneventful as he oscillated in his parachute harness. Below him he could see tiny figures scurrying about the drop zone in all directions, and the comforting sight of a huge cross of white tape that confirmed they were in the right place.[18]

32

'You made it this time, Dicky'
– Holland, 17 September 1944

GIVING A LAST SUDDEN jerk on his parachute's lifters to slow his descent, Lieutenant Colonel John Frost hit the ground hard but unharmed. It was 1.50 p.m. on 17 September 1944, and he had found the drop zone, seven miles west of Arnhem, with perfect accuracy and just 10 minutes behind schedule. There was no sound of enemy action, 'just the steady continual drone of aircraft approaching, leaving rows and clusters of parachutes in the air, followed by the fiercer note of their engines as they wheeled for home at increased speed'.

He quickly made his way to the battalion RV on the edge of some woods, marked by yellow smoke, where he found Digby Tatham-Warter and a number of his officers and men, including Robin Vlasto and Jack Grayburn, who had not been fooled by a separate yellow signal at the wrong end of the drop zone. 'Gradually,' noted Frost, 'the sections, platoons and companies began to take form. It was now about half-past two in the afternoon and quite hot. The sweat was pouring off the cheerful faces of the men as they filed past me into the wood.'[1]

When Major Dicky Dover reached C Company's area, he discovered that two of his men had been injured in the drop, the spare Bren gun was missing, all the lightweight motorcycles were damaged and only one folding bicycle was in working order. On the bright side, most of his men were there and the Company wireless set was in communication with Battalion HQ. Dover caught sight of the tall, hawk-like figure of Brigadier Gerald Lathbury who waved and said: 'You made it this time, Dicky.'[2]

Avenging the memory of their last, disastrous drop in Sicily, the battalion had arrived as a body, with only a handful of injuries, and was ready to move. But just as Frost was congratulating himself on a great start, the sound of firing came from the woods nearby. He fought off the temptation to investigate, knowing it was vital not to delay the battalion's departure or use up its valuable supply of ammunition. He discovered later that his men had engaged a small party of Germans who suddenly appeared in two open-topped lorries and an armoured car. The car soon fled, leaving the shot-up lorries and several prisoners. They were members of the reconnaissance troop of the SS Panzergrenadier Depot and Replacement Battalion 16, commanded by SS-Sturmbannführer Sepp Krafft, who, informed by radio of the landings, had placed the bulk of his 435 men to cover the two central routes that led into Arnhem: the railway line near Wolfheze and the main Utrecht highway to the south – 'Tiger' to the British – that was about to be used by the 3rd Battalion. According to the Krafft battalion's war diary, the reconnaissance troop was 'wiped out'.

Soon after 3 p.m. – by which time he had been joined by five Jeeps, a Bren gun carrier and some anti-tank guns – Frost received a message from Brigade Headquarters to move at once and not wait for stragglers. His force now included 481 men of the 2nd Battalion; half of B Troop, 9th Parachute Field Company R. E. (sappers); and four 6-pounder anti-tank guns of the 1st Airlanding Anti-Tank Battery (with a fifth joining later).

Just as Frost's order went out to A Company in the vanguard, 'firing broke out afresh from their area'. But it did not delay the march, and when Frost reached A Company's old positions he found 'two lorries and three motor-cars in various stages of destruction, also an untidy little bunch of dead and wounded Germans'. They had been accounted for by A Company's No. 3 Platoon, commanded by Lieutenant Andrew 'Mac' McDermont, which had also captured 20 prisoners. Frost's only regret was that the vehicles, which would have been invaluable, were not captured intact.

With A Company in the lead, followed by HQ, C and B Companies, the 2nd Battalion began the march to the bridges down a small road that ran from the village of Heelsum to Oosterbeek, on the western outskirts of Arnhem. They passed through a 'dense undergrowth of gorse and birch, ideal cover for an ambush', but there was no time to spare for flank guards so they pressed on regardless.

They moved without incident for another couple of miles, collecting some prisoners that they passed back down the line. One of them told Frost that a company of SS troops had been in Arnhem that morning and were now thought to be covering the entrances to the town from the west. This prompted Frost to move up the column in a carrier to suggest to Tatham-Warter that he use Jeeps to move one of his platoons to Den Brink, a feature on the western edge of Arnhem, before returning to pick up the others. Tatham-Warter liked the sound of the plan, but before anything could be done 'the noise of firing broke out again from in front and the column ceased to move.'

According to Robin Vlasto, commanding No. 1 Platoon, the Jeeps did not arrive so they continued marching. As they approached a T-junction, they were fired on by Germans concealed in a wood. Ignoring the rifle bullets and mortar explosions, Jack Grayburn's No. 2 Platoon and McDermont's

No. 3 Platoon executed a textbook pincer attack, under the cover of smoke, and the enemy withdrew. Tatham-Warter was delighted.

After the rally had been sounded on the bugle, A Company moved off again with Vlasto's No. 1 Platoon back in the lead. Soon after Frost – who had hung back, trusting the 'thruster' Tatham-Warter to clear the way – was joined by Brigadier Lathbury who was pleased with the progress they were making. Elsewhere it was not going so well: the lead Jeeps of Gough's Reconnaissance Squadron had been badly shot up as they attempted to move down the railway embankment towards Arnhem and it was now down to the 2nd Battalion to secure the bridges. They could hear firing to the left, and Lathbury assumed it was the 3rd Battalion 'having a difficult time getting through'. Frost was to advance as quickly as he could, and Brigade Headquarters would follow him into the town.

Before long, A Company reached the little village of Heveadorp on the banks of the Lower Rhine, where they joined the main road that led to Arnhem through yet more woods. Unbeknown to Frost and his men, they had passed within a quarter of a mile of the still-working Heveadorp ferry. Divisional intelligence was aware of this ferry, and its ability to carry up to eight Jeeps per crossing, but had chosen not to secure it for emergency use. A vital opportunity to get troops onto the southern bank of the river had been lost.[3]

At around 6 p.m., having marched uninterrupted through the woods, A Company reached the outskirts of Oosterbeek, a village a mile to the west of Arnhem, where it was met by Dutch civilians 'delirious with joy'. They were lining the streets and offering trays of beer, milk and fruit; some ran up to embrace and kiss their liberators. Worried that his men were letting their guard down, Vlasto had to remind them to be wary of an ambush or snipers. They eventually stopped by some houses just before the railway bridge to drink some beer. Tatham-Warter was 'beaming and everyone [was] in excellent form'.[4]

Captain Tony Frank, Tatham-Warter's second-in-command (who had won a Military Cross on Sicily leading No. 1 Platoon), was struck by the 'incredible number of orange flowers or hand-kerchiefs' which 'suddenly appeared like magic'. He and the other officers did all they could to stop the locals from slowing down the column 'by pressing cakes, milk, etc' on the men.[5]

Further down the column, Major Dover was given permission by Frost to take C Company and some sappers off to the right flank to assault the railway bridge. It stood out clearly against the sky, and seemed to Dover very exposed as there was no cover by which to approach it.[6]

Lieutenant Peter Barry's No. 9 Platoon had been given the task of capturing the railway bridge, with No. 8 Platoon in close support. They passed through German flak positions in a brick kiln which had been heavily bombed by the RAF the day before. The remaining opposition was light and quickly overrun. Only as No. 9 Platoon reached the foot of the escarpment that led up to the railway track did it come under heavy fire from a machine gun and snipers on the far side of the river. Taking cover, Barry noticed a man dressed in black, wearing a German cap, run from the far end to the centre of the bridge, 'bend down and do something'. He ordered his Bren gunner to open fire, but the 'German ran off without being hit'.

Dover now appeared and ordered Barry to take a section forward and capture the north end of the bridge. Leaving the other two sections to provide fire support, Barry and nine men climbed up to the bridge under the cover of smoke. Dover thought it was a model attack and assumed that all was going well as their covering fire seemed to have silenced the opposition on the far bank.

Having reached the north end without difficulty, Barry told

his men they might as well carry on and capture the whole bridge. Only one man demurred, shaking his head as if Barry were a 'bloody fool', but he went anyway. To cover their advance, someone threw a smoke grenade. Unfortunately, the wind was in the wrong direction and most of it dispersed. They ran as fast as they could, their hobnailed boots making an awful clatter on the metal plates. Having gone about 50 yards, Barry ordered the men to get down. They were carrying a lot of equipment and needed to catch their breath.[7]

Watching from the road in Oosterbeek, Frost could see 'little figures' appear on the bridge. There was then a 'general surge forward' of the men in support, and Bren guns were set up on the embankment to deal with the Germans on the other side. His impression that the bridge had been captured intact was, however, a little premature.[8]

Barry and his forward section were still lying down when the metal plates in front of them 'heaved up in the air' and the centre of the bridge disappeared in a 'yellow flash and a tremendous explosion'. As the smoke and dust cleared, Major Dover could see that the centre span had collapsed into the river 'with the railway lines draping down like reeds into the water'.

Barry felt both disappointment and relief. By stopping they had saved their lives. No one had been injured in the explosion. Moments later he felt a sharp pain in his leg and looked back to ask his men if anyone was shooting. One said, 'No, it was a German bullet.'

A second hit him in the upper right arm, shattering the bone. The pain was excruciating.

From his position at Company HQ, Dover spotted Barry's men running back, dragging their commander with them. Out of wireless contact, he went forward with his batman 'to find out how badly the section had been hit and if there was any chance of crossing the river by other means than the bridge'.

As he reached the escarpment, a private scrambled down the embankment towards him. Before the soldier could deliver his message, he was shot and killed by a sniper. It was at this moment that Dover began to feel that fortune was not smiling on them 'although the sun was bright'.

Leaving the badly wounded Barry in the care of the company medic, Dover decided to move his men speedily to the main road and make for his second objective, the German Headquarters in the centre of town. Out of touch with Battalion HQ, C Company was on its own.[9]

The destruction of the bridge had ruined Frost's plan to move a company to the south bank of the river. The risk 'of dropping airborne troops on the far side of a large river obstacle when you actually require them on both sides' had not paid off. His only hope, now, was to head for the road bridge at speed and hope he could cross it before it was blown. But he was grimly aware of the difficulty of 'taking the big main bridge intact from one side only, if the other side was firmly defended'.

At the head of the column, meanwhile, the leading section of Robin Vlasto's No. 1 Platoon passed under a railway bridge at the Oosterbeek Laag Station and was rounding the next bend when it was attacked by a German armoured car with a 20mm cannon and machine gun. The two men on either side of Vlasto were hit: one killed and the other, Sergeant Bellinger, shot in the hand. While the platoon took cover, Tatham-Warter sent forward an anti-tank gun to engage the armoured car, but it had vanished.

Vlasto's platoon got going again, but soon came under machine-gun fire from the high ground of Den Brink, 500 yards to the left. Any attempt to move along the roads was met by fire from roving armoured cars, 'while anyone appearing on the railway line was hailed by machine-gun fire and sniping'. Tatham-Warter's solution was to try to work his company through the back gardens of houses lining the road. At the same time, Frost told Douglas Crawley to try to move B Company to the left under the cover of the railway embankment.[10]

It was around 7 p.m., and still light, when Major Crawley sent Lieutenant Peter Cane's No. 6 Platoon up the railway cutting. Unfortunately, the Germans had sited a machine gun to cover a bend in the railway, and this opened up as the platoon approached, killing Cane and two of his corporals. Also mortally wounded were two 21-year-old twins from Devon, Privates Claude and Tom Gronert, who had joined the army on the same day. The rest of B Company would continue to fight on the lower slopes of Den Brink until midnight. Only then was it able to disengage and resume its progress.[11]

By 7.30 p.m., A Company had reached the western town boundary near the St Elisabeth Hospital, 500 yards on from Oosterbeek Laag railway bridge. Apart from sniper fire and a brief encounter with the enemy at a road junction – leaving several dead and wounded Germans lying beside damaged cars and a white ambulance – there was little opposition. With Grayburn's No. 2 Platoon leading, the company moved via back gardens and side roads to the harbour where they found the pontoon bridge was missing its middle section, as expected, and deserted except for two guards who were captured.

They hurried on towards the road bridge and rallied under the ramp carrying the roadway. So far, so good: there was little sign of the enemy and the bridge was still intact. When Frost arrived, he seemed 'extremely happy, making cracks about everyone's nerves being jumpy'.

Tatham-Warter placed his Nos 1 and 3 Platoons in buildings on either side of the ramp, to secure the northern end, and sent Grayburn's platoon up the steps to the top of the embankment. There they took up positions beside the road, but did not interfere with the occasional German vehicle crossing the bridge.[12]

By this time, John Frost had selected a large corner house, overlooking the bridge, as his Battalion Headquarters. The owner, who spoke English, was 'not at all happy at the prospect of billeting soldiers of any sort'. The Germans had left, he told Frost, and he would much prefer the paratroopers 'to chase on after them'. Frost's response was that the Germans were still very much in evidence, and that he did not merely want billets, but 'to fortify the house in readiness for a battle'. Aghast at the prospect, the owner retired to the cellar, leaving Frost and his men to their own devices. He would have been appalled to see them tearing down his curtains, blinds and anything flammable, loopholing his walls, smashing his windows to reduce casualties from flying glass, and filling his baths and basins to provide a supply of water.

HQ Company took over a government building next door, with room to park the transport in a yard behind, and the Machine-gun and Mortar Platoons were in houses nearby, with the gun pits for the latter sited on a grass island in the centre of the road west of the bridge. Soon after, at around 8.45 p.m., the Brigade Headquarters Group arrived at the bridge in force, but without Lathbury who had gone to check on the 3rd Battalion's progress. Led by the brigade major, Tony Hibbert, the group included police, medics, signalmen, sappers, a platoon of Royal Army Service Corps, and Major Freddie Gough and a handful of his Reconnaissance Squadron in two Jeeps. Urquhart, meanwhile, had left Divisional Headquarters in a single jeep at around 5 p.m. to find Brigadier Lathbury and remind him that time was of the essence. Gough followed Urquhart, but never caught up with him because, by the time he reached Brigade Headquarters, the divisional commander had continued on to the 3rd Battalion in search of Lathbury. As in a French farce, nobody was where they should be.

Hibbert told Frost: 'Well the best thing we can do is that

you will command the bridge and I will hand over to you all my brigade staff that can be spared, apart from the signals who will be up in the attic of Brigade Headquarters. You can use the rest in a defensive role until the other battalions come up.'[13] This was wishful thinking as Lathbury's plan to advance on the bridge from three directions – thus reducing the ability of any one column to overcome local German opposition – began to unravel.

The attempts by elements of the 1st Parachute Brigade to reinforce Frost at the road bridge on 17 September would be blighted by confusion. According to Major Tony Deane-Drummond – who had escaped from Italian captivity in June 1942, crossing into Switzerland near Lake Lugano, and was later appointed deputy commander of the 1st Airborne Divisional Signals – the issue was the 'inadequacy of the wireless sets'. These were designed to communicate up to three miles and all their exercises and operations had worked on that basis. But at Arnhem the radios would have to cover the 8 miles to the bridge and 15 miles to Corps HQ at Nijmegen. Deane-Drummond's 'advice was that communications would be most unreliable, especially in view of the built-up nature of the ground north of the river but again this risk was accepted'. So 'it proved in practice and communications were not established satisfactorily until the Division was fighting within a small perimeter'.[14]

The radio sets that Deane-Drummond was referring to were the portable 68P sets, intended for speech over three miles, and generally used within an infantry battalion to control the companies, but also as a rear link from battalion to brigade or even, as in the case of the 1st Parachute Brigade, to division. The larger 22 sets were Jeep-mounted and had a range of five miles using rod aerials. They were used for the link between brigade and division, and as command sets by Urquhart and his brigadiers.

After landing by glider at around 1 p.m., Major-General Roy Urquhart headed for his tactical headquarters, sited in a wood near the landing zone, where he discovered that his signallers were having trouble contacting both his brigade commanders. The heavily wooded terrain and the presence of iron in the sandy soil were both affecting the radio signal. Urquhart later described the situation as: 'Shattering. One of the biggest shocks I had in my entire service. Not being able to talk to anyone.'

This was disingenuous. In reality, Deane-Drummond's boss, Lieutenant Colonel Tom Stevenson, had warned Urquhart before the campaign that communications were likely to be a problem. 'That the radios were proving "inadequate for the purpose" was broadly right,' wrote Louis Golden, Adjutant of the 1st Airborne Divisional Signals, in his memoir *Echoes from Arnhem*. 'What was wrong was the implication that previously they had been considered adequate for the demands which Operation Market was certain to make on them. They had not.'

Unable to communicate with his brigadiers, Urquhart set off in his Jeep around 5 p.m. to speak to them in person. He eventually caught up with Lathbury and the 3rd Battalion, at a junction on the Utrecht–Arnhem highway west of Oosterbeek, at dusk on 17 September. Together the two senior officers observed the fighting ahead, ducking occasionally to avoid mortar explosions. Urquhart was dissuaded from returning to Divisional HQ as this would have meant passing through terrain which was no longer in British hands. He decided, therefore, to remain with 'the brigade charged with the initial thrust to the Bridge and thereby usefully placed to give on-the-spot instructions'.

But he was unable to inform Divisional HQ of his whereabouts because his radio set was still not working properly. In failing light, Urquhart and Lathbury followed in the 3rd Battalion's footsteps until the leading company was engaged by Krafft's men near the Hartenstein Hotel on the outskirts of Oosterbeek. Soon after, Lathbury decided to halt the 3rd Battalion for the night, and continue the advance on the bridge in the morning.[15]

At around 9.30 p.m., though the signal was spasmodic, Hibbert was able to reach Lathbury on the brigade radio net and inform him that the 2nd Battalion and Brigade HQ, a total of around 600 men, were on the north end of the road bridge which was still intact. He then suggested that Lathbury send a battalion – or, at the very least, a company from each battalion – down the southern Lion route, which was still open, to reinforce the garrison at the bridge. Lathbury refused.

'We're in contact with the enemy,' he told Hibbert, 'and we're not very organised at the moment. The troops are too tired to move now. We'll make an attempt at first light.' He added that he and Major General Urquhart, then out of touch with divisional HQ, would remain with 3rd Battalion for the night.[16]

Lathbury later explained that he and Lieutenant Colonel John Fitch had decided that the 3rd Battalion, less its C Company (which had been sent along a parallel route in the hope of outflanking the German defenders), would 'take up an all-round defensive position' until the morning. Lathbury added: 'At last light on D-Day I was not worried about the situation. The enemy had certainly reacted quickly and were holding the two main roads from the West, Tiger and Leopard, but the 2nd Battalion were making good progress after overcoming early opposition. Owing to bad communications with the 1st Battalion I had not got a true picture of the scale of the opposition confronting them.'

He was unaware that Krafft's SS Panzergrenadiers were then in the process of falling back from Oosterbeek and linking up with elements of the 9th SS Panzer Division who were converging on Arnhem. What Lathbury certainly did know was that airborne soldiers had been trained to operate in the dark. Determined to regroup his scattered units, however, Lathbury chose to wait until 4.30 a.m. to resume the advance on the bridge.[17] It was, in Frost's estimation, a fatal miscalculation, as by that time the Germans had been given several hours to reinforce their blocking position. Though excellent soldiers, the Germans had 'one major weakness': they did not like fighting at night. Frost noted: 'Once darkness came the fire effect was greatly reduced, and then was the time to advance upon them, to bypass them, to do what one wanted. These precious hours were wasted.'[18]

33

'A very fine feat of arms'
– Arnhem, Holland, 17 September 1944

THE GERMAN UNIT THAT, more than any other, scuppered the 1st Parachute Brigade's plan to concentrate at the bridge was the 16th SS Panzergrenadier Reserve and Replacement Battalion, commanded by SS-Sturmbannführer Sepp Krafft. Tall with dark-blue eyes, Krafft had served on the Eastern Front with the security police before transferring to the Waffen-SS. The 16th, his first command, was comprised of two infantry and one heavy weapons companies: a total of 13 officers and 422 NCOs and men, many of them teenagers and only half-trained. Part of the battalion had been exercising in woods close to Wolfheze, a mile or two to the east of the landing zones, when Krafft received sketchy reports of an airborne assault. He at once despatched two patrols to gain more information, and ordered the 2nd Company to conduct a reconnaissance in force, while the 4th Company established a defence line in the vicinity of the Hotel Wolfheze. His remaining company – the 9th – was summoned from Arnhem to act as the battalion reserve.

At around the same time that one of Krafft's patrols was badly shot up by Frost's men, his 2nd Company emerged from woods beside landing zone 'S' and fired on four Horsas as they landed before falling back to join the 4th Company in its blocking position to the east of Wolfheze, astride the two main routes into Arnhem and the railway line. Deploying mortars, anti-tank guns and armoured cars, Krafft's men were able to hold up the 1st and 3rd Parachute Battalions until the early evening when their commander, fearing they might be encircled, ordered them to withdraw closer to Arnhem.[1]

During the early part of this crucial defensive action, Krafft was visited at his headquarters in the Hotel Wolfheze by Generalmajor Friedrich Kussin, the town commandant. After briefing Krafft on the various German counter-moves, Kussin set off back to Arnhem, ignoring advice that the main road might now be too dangerous. A few minutes later his Citroen staff car was intercepted by men from Fitch's 3rd Parachute Battalion. 'It appeared without warning,' recalled the platoon commander, 'and the front men of each of my leading sections, who were just behind the junction, opened up with Stens and rifles and riddled its exposed flank. It was all over in a flash. I saw a body leaning out of the door but pressed on, leaving it to someone else to sort out. I didn't know it was a general until after the war. Of course, it put my platoon on a high.'[2]

The counter-moves that Kussin had mentioned were being coordinated by SS-Obergruppenführer Wilhelm Bittrich, commanding II SS Panzer Corps, whose headquarters were at Doetinchem, 25 miles east of Arnhem. Receiving the first enemy situation reports at 1.30 p.m., Bittrich quickly realised that the road bridges at both Nijmegen and Arnhem were under threat. He therefore ordered Standartenführer Walter Harzer, commanding the 9th SS Panzer Division Hohenstaufen, to 'reconnoitre in the direction of Arnhem and Nijmegen'. He added: 'Quick action is imperative! The taking and securing of the Arnhem Bridge is of decisive importance.'

As Bittrich planned to give his other SS panzer division, the 10th Frundsberg under Brigadeführer Heinz Harmel, the responsibility for safeguarding Nijmegen, it was a mistake to mention that city to Harzer who then let his divisional reconnaissance battalion, under Viktor Gräbner, go charging off south on a wild goose chase. But the confusion was sorted out when Generalfeldmarschall Walter Model, commanding Army Group B, reached Bittrich's headquarters at 3 p.m, having fled his own command post in the Hotel Tafelberg in Oosterbeek convinced the British were trying to capture him. 'They almost got me,' he told Bittrich.

Once over his initial panic, Model issued a stream of orders: Harzer's Hohenstaufen would prevent the British airborne troops from taking Arnhem, while Harmel's Frundsberg would move towards Nijmegen to block the approach of Allied ground forces. The easiest way to do this, Model thought, was to set up blocking points at Nijmegen and on the road from there to Arnhem. Bittrich also wanted to blow up the road bridge over the Waal at Nijmegen. But Model insisted that both bridges were needed for a possible German counter-attack. At the same time, the Generalfeldmarschall asked his superiors to send all available reinforcements as a matter of urgency, including paratroopers, anti-tank and anti-aircraft units, and a panzer battalion of Mark VI 'Tiger' tanks.[3]

The units of the 9th SS Hohenstaufen that were rushed to Arnhem included an engineer company, a flak detachment, and battalions of pioneers, gunners and divisional recce troops. Until recently, Harzer had also commanded a panzer regiment and two panzergrenadier battalions; but the former was waiting for replacement tanks, while the latter were with a Kampfgruppe south of Eindhoven.[4]

Harzer's greatest concentration of armour – 30 half-tracks and 10 heavy armoured cars – was in Viktor Gräbner's reconnaissance battalion. By 5 p.m., while 30 vehicles prepared to move south over the Arnhem Bridge and set up a defensive position at Elst, half way down the road to Nijmegen, the remaining 10 were effectively blocking the northern 'Leopard' route into Arnhem. This forced Lieutenant Colonel David Dobie, commanding the 1st Parachute Battalion, to abandon his task of sealing off the north of the town, and instead move south to assist Frost. He was prevented from doing so, however, by the 9th SS Pioneer Battalion, commanded by Hauptsturmführer Hans Möller, which held the railway embankment east of Oosterbeek. 'With the coming of dawn,' wrote the melodramatic Möller, 'the dance began . . . It was a battle man against man – the "Red Devils" against the "Men in Black", elite against elite.'[5]

Ultimately, however, the fate of the British airborne troops at Arnhem would be decided by events further south where both American airborne divisions made largely unopposed landings between Eindhoven and Nijmegen on the 17th, and captured some first day objectives, including the vital road bridge over the River Maas at Grave. But many more bridges were destroyed or badly damaged by their German defenders, including four over the Maas–Waal Canal and, more importantly, the road bridge over the Wilhelmina Canal at Son, north of Eindhoven, which was blown before Major Dick Winters and the men of Easy Company, 506th Parachute Infantry Regiment, 101st Airborne Division – famously depicted in Stephen E. Ambrose's *Band of Brothers* – could secure it. An attempt to capture a separate crossing over the canal, a few miles to the west, was also unsuccessful.

Perhaps the greatest missed opportunity of the first day, however, was the failure by Major General James Gavin's 82nd Airborne Division to take possession of the road bridge over the River Waal at Nijmegen. Gavin's priority – as imposed by Browning – was to secure the Groesbeek Heights, and thereby protect XXX Corps' route of advance from a notional German counter-attack launched from the Reichswald Forest in Germany. Only once this was done, was Gavin prepared to order Colonel Roy E. Lindquist of the 508th Parachute Infantry Regiment to send a battalion into Nijmegen to assess the possibility of seizing the bridge. Lindquist botched the operation. Ignoring Gavin's instructions to approach the bridge along the riverbank, he sent his men straight up the main road where they were stopped in their tracks by recently arrived German reinforcements. Had they moved earlier, and with more stealth, they would have found the bridge defended by just 19 men from the 10th SS Frundsberg, a dozen more from a training battalion and a handful of local militia. Explosives were in place, but not wired up. Gavin's error would have serious consequences.[6]

Meanwhile, no sooner had the spearhead tanks of the British XXX Corps begun their advance into Holland at 2.35 p.m. on the 17th than nine were knocked out by anti-tank fire. Only after rocket-firing Typhoons, fighter-bombers and infantry had neutralised the German defenders, and an armoured bulldozer pushed the burning tanks off the road, could the column resume its advance. But thereafter XXX Corps encountered almost constant German opposition and, having expected to cover the 13 miles to Eindhoven 'within two to three hours', it had only managed the seven miles to Valkenswaard by nightfall.

Colonel Joe Vandeleur, commanding the Sherman tanks of the 3rd Irish Guards, was told by his brigadier 'to take [his] time getting to Eindhoven, that there was no hurry because the Son bridge had been blown, and [they] would have to wait for the bridging to be brought up'. The decision to halt was approved by the corps commander, Horrocks, who wrote later: 'In my opinion it was the act of an experienced commander to halt, rest his troops etc, while the bridge was being repaired.'

This is nonsense. Work on the Son bridge could only start

when the Guards Armoured Division got there with engineers capable of building a Bailey bridge. By halting at Valkenswaard, XXX Corps was putting the original schedule in jeopardy.

As if this were not bad enough, the entire Market Garden operation plan was found by the Germans in a glider that had crashed near Vught in central Holland. By evening, General-feldmarschall Model had the names of the formations involved, the bridge objectives, the location of the landing and drop zones, and the timing of the resupply lifts. Although not entirely convinced that the plan was genuine – flatteringly overestimating Allied competence – Model did at least alert all anti-aircraft units about the drops due to take place a few hours later.[7]

As dusk fell on 17 September, Lance Sergeant Bill Fulton led a seven-man section of MacDermont's No. 3 Platoon up the stairway that led to the northern ramp of the Arnhem road bridge. As he neared the top he heard German voices. Telling his men to keep quiet, he peeped over and saw, at a distance of just 15 yards, a truck filled with German soldiers.

He waited until the truck had moved off and then led his men along the right-hand side of the bridge. It was 'very dark, but you could see outlines'. Catching a few of the enemy hiding in small huts, he passed them back to the last man and told him to take them down the steps as prisoners. He and the others continued along the bridge until he could see, in the gloom, the muzzle of a rifle pointing at him. As he opened fire with his Sten gun, he was shot in the left thigh. He told his men to report that 'the bridge was well manned and would need more troops'. He then crawled behind an iron girder, and was later rescued by two medics.[8]

A second attempt to cross the bridge was made by Lieutenant Jack Grayburn's No. 2 Platoon. The plan was to move across the bridge in single file on either side, 'keeping close to the iron side of the bridge for camouflage'. The rest of the company would provide covering fire, as well as watch the northern approaches for an enemy counter-attack. As the success of the attack depended on stealth and surprise, Grayburn had got his men to blacken their faces, bind their boots with strips of material, and make sure there was no rattling equipment or weapons.

They had only gone a short distance, however, when German machine guns opened up at close range. Grayburn was shot in the shoulder, but 'continued to press forward with the greatest dash and bravery until casualties became so heavy that he was ordered to withdraw'. He directed the withdrawal personally, and was the last man to leave the bridge.

Grayburn and seven of his men had been hit by fire from a pillbox, sited near the junction of the ramp and the northern end of the bridge, and an armoured car nearby. Tatham-Warter had noticed the pillbox earlier and assumed that it was empty. He was wrong. 'The pillbox was almost alongside our forward defences in the houses by the bridge,' he noted, 'and the machine-gunner must have been a good soldier and certainly a brave man.'[9]

With another frontal attack out of the question, Tatham-Warter ordered Robin Vlasto's platoon and some sappers to 'mousehole' through some houses until they had a direct line of sight to the pillbox. Once in position, they opened fire with PIATs and a flame-thrower. 'Amid the noise of machine-gun fire,' wrote Frost, 'a succession of explosions, the crackling of burning ammunition and the thump of a cannon, came screams of agony and fear. A wooden building nearby was wreathed in flame and soon German soldiers came staggering towards our edge.'

With the whole of the north end of the bridge now in 2nd Battalion's hands, Frost was keen for A Company to push across and take the other side. But before they could begin their attack, a column of four German lorries approached from the other side of the bridge, seemingly unaware that the pillbox was out of action. The lorries were stopped in their tracks by a hail of fire from Tatham-Warter's men, and were themselves soon burning fiercely. More prisoners were taken, swelling the number in 2nd Battalion's hands to over 100. Keeping and feeding them would become, Frost realised, 'a fairly acute problem'.

A more immediate issue, however, was the fact that the fires on the bridge lit up the whole area like daylight and made it impossible for anyone to cross. Frost's solution was to find boats to ferry the brigade defence platoon and B Company to the south bank: while the former held a bridgehead, the latter would assault and capture the southern end of the road bridge. It came to nothing because no useable boats could be found and he was, in any event, out of radio contact with both B and C Companies.

Frost consoled himself with the knowledge that he held the most important end of the bridge from the perspective of the ground forces. As long as they reached him by the following day, and the bridge remained intact, all would be well. The possibility of the bridge being blown was, of course, a continual worry. The sappers had reassured him that the heat from the fires would have destroyed any fuses already laid from the bridge to the town, and that they had cut any cables they had found. But the same fires, not to mention the German presence on the south end, had prevented the sappers from removing any charges that might be there.[10]

Unable to complete their chief task, the 80 or so sappers of Captain Eric Mackay's A Troop, 1st Parachute Squadron, were ordered by Hibbert to go under the ramp and secure the east side of the bridge. Here, directly alongside the ramp, were four houses. The three closest to the river were the most important as the fourth was blanketed by trees. 'Whoever held these three houses held the bridge,' explained Mackay.[11]

Other reinforcements to reach the airborne perimeter at the bridge that first night included members of the 3rd Battalion's C Company, under Major 'Pongo' Lewis, who used the cover of the railway track to evade German forces and enter the town. Lewis got to the perimeter with 45 men, and it would have been more but for a last-minute clash with a German force that resulted in the death of a platoon commander and the capture of one and a half platoons.[12]

But there was still no sign of Victor Dover's C Company which, having decimated a party of enemy soldiers near St Elisabeth's Hospital, had been stopped by heavy machine-gun fire as it moved down the main thoroughfare of Arnhem in search of the German Headquarters. With no hope of forward progress, Dover ordered his tired and hungry men to take refuge in three large buildings on the north side of the street, about a mile from the bridge, where they set up all-round defensive positions.

That night, Dover briefly made radio contact with Doug Crawley whose B Company, delayed by the Den Brink action, had finally reached the pontoon bridge. Dover told Crawley that he was 'pinned down and would not be able to move until just before first light'; then he would double back and make his way with the Company to the towpath by the river and attempt to reach the bridge by that route. Dover's conversation with Crawley was the last time his wireless functioned, and the final contact he would have with the rest of the 2nd Battalion. From here on, C Company was on its own.[13]

By the end of his first day, Frost was feeling reasonably confident. The bulk of the brigade group of 2,000 men had been held up well short of their objectives, but he still had a mixed force of around 750 men to defend the north end of the road bridge. 'There was nothing more to be done for the present,' he wrote, 'but snatch what rest we could before the battle, which I knew would start in the morning.'

The rest of the night was 'fairly quiet' — bar the occasional exploding ammunition box and petrol tank on the bridge — and Frost took the opportunity to visit the men holding the perimeter, particularly A Company 'who were in great heart, as indeed they had every reason to be'. They had 'fought their way in for eight miles, through very close, difficult country, to capture their objective within seven hours of landing in Holland, accounting for 150 Germans and several vehicles en route'. It was, for Frost, 'a very fine feat of arms', not least because most of the prisoners were SS, 'fighting soldiers of great repute'.[14]

34

'It was little short of murder'
– Arnhem, Holland, 18 September 1944

A S DAWN BROKE ON 18 September, the second day of the Battle of Arnhem, John Frost and his men were standing to arms, tense and ready, squirrelled into buildings on both sides of the road bridge's northern ramp, and surrounded on all sides by the enemy. Their first visitors were a convoy of German trucks that drove slowly and unwittingly towards their defensive perimeter. Met by a stream of bullets, the drivers tried to accelerate or reverse the way they had come. But it was too late and, by the time they thought to surrender, few were still alive. The wounded were carried into Frost's aid post.[1]

One German casualty – shot in both legs – tried to crawl up a slope to safety. His slow and painful progress was watched by mortarman Private James Sims who was manning an observation post in a large building on the west side of the ramp known as the White House. After a superhuman effort, the German was just yards from safety, and about to clear the final obstacle, when he was shot in the head and killed by the man beside Sims. 'To me it was little short of murder,' wrote Sims, 'but to my companion, a Welshman, one of our best snipers, the German was a legitimate target. When I protested he looked at me as if I was simple.'[2]

Next came the cry that armoured cars were coming across the bridge from the south. For a brief moment, Frost hoped it might be the vanguard of Horrocks' XXX Corps. He quickly realised the truth when the leader of the column of armoured six-wheelers and half-tracks – 'obviously German and malignant' – nudged aside the still smouldering trucks and accelerated forwards. The armoured car hit one of the mines that Frost's men had scattered across the road, the explosion rocking the big beast but failing to stop it. It ran the gauntlet of airborne fire from an anti-tank gun, PIATs and small arms, and disappeared into the town, as did the next two. But the fourth armoured car was hit by an anti-tank shell, causing a road block, and six more were soon 'disabled and burning'.

From their vantage point to the east of the ramp, Eric Mackay's sappers added to the carnage by accounting for one half-track with a grenade, and shooting the driver of a second vehicle. One half-track tried to reverse and collided with the one behind. 'This caused a helluva traffic jam,' noted Mackay, 'and gave us the leverage we wanted. We just poured fire into them.'[3] Of the twenty vehicles from Viktor Gräbner's recon-naissance battalion that attempted to cross the bridge, twelve were knocked out and seventy men killed, including Gräbner himself.

Meanwhile Frost's men were being hit by German mortar and shell fire, and by infantry attacking from the north. It was bedlam. 'Behind each window and on every rooftop snipers and machine-gunners lay,' wrote Frost. 'To show ourselves for more than a second or two brought immediate attention and we were by no means untouched in this respect, as the call for stretch-er-bearers showed.' It was all hands to the pump as 'staff officers, signallers, batmen, drivers and clerks all lent a hand'. Incredibly, 'amid the din of continuous fire, and the crash of falling burning buildings', Frost heard laughter. Peering out of a window, he 'could just see Freddie Gough in action behind the twin K-guns★ mounted on his Jeep, grinning like a wicked uncle'.

After a couple of hours, the firing died away and Frost was able to take stock. Two men had been killed on the landing of the first floor and considerable damage done to the house. But it was impossible for him to get accurate news of casualties from the other headquarters – particularly A Company and Brigade – because the ubiquity of German snipers made any daylight movement between buildings extremely dangerous.

Even so, Frost was feeling pretty pleased with himself. It was largely thanks to his battalion that the important end of the bridge was still in Allied hands, and he was rather hoping that the 2nd Battalion alone 'would have the honour of welcoming the army into Arnhem'. He assumed that the rest of the brigade was on its way into Arnhem from the west, although he had received no confirmation. When Frost's signallers picked up a message from the leading elements of XXX Corps, there seemed a very real possibility that relief might take place that day. But as no location had been given, it was difficult to know exactly where the spearhead elements had got to.

During this pause, Frost's second-in-command, David Wallis, wrote a report of what had happened so far and sent it by homing pigeon back to London. Unwilling to take off at first, the pigeon was persuaded by some 'round abuse' from the regimental sergeant major.

As the day wore on, and the shelling, mortaring and

★ The Vickers K machine gun, gas operated and .303 calibre, was developed for use in aircraft, and later mounted in vehicles by the SAS and other special operations units. Its high rate of fire – up to 1,200 rounds a minute – meant it was often mistaken for the German MG-34 and MG-42 machine guns.

machine-gun fire from German positions on the north bank became almost continuous, Frost's signallers re-established a radio link to Major Doug Crawley and B Company. He was still near the pontoon bridge and wanted to know if he should stay there or join the bulk of the 2nd Battalion at the road bridge. 'Disengage and move towards us,' said Frost.

Crawley attempted to do so, but met stiff opposition en route, and one of his platoons was cut off in a side street half a mile short of the bridge. The next message was an encouraging one from the 1st Battalion which had reached the pontoon bridge but could not get any further. Could the force at the road bridge 'do anything to help'? Crawley offered to lead a strong fighting patrol in that direction, but had not gone far when he was recalled by Frost who had received 'a correction to the original message which now gave the position of the 1st Battalion as not far beyond the railway on the outskirts of the town'.[4]

Frost's men spent the rest of the 18th under almost constant shell and mortar fire, which gradually took its toll on the defenders' numbers. They were forced to beat off persistent attempts by enemy infantry to infiltrate their positions on either side of the bridge ramp. Close-quarter fighting used up much of the extra ammunition that had arrived the day before, forcing Frost to order his men to cease sniping to conserve bullets. This had two consequences: it allowed the Germans to improve their positions; and it convinced them that the British were losing heart, which could not have been further from the case.

Movement from one building to another by daylight was so dangerous that it was kept strictly to a minimum.[5] This did not prevent Frost from visiting all the positions to the west of the bridge during the 18th, including the White House which he reached at around 4 p.m., having exchanged fire with the enemy as he dashed across the road. Inside he found Lieutenant Jack Grayburn and the remnants of his No. 2 Platoon, and the Mortar OP manned by Lieutenant Woods and Private James Sims. Though suffering from a serious shoulder wound, Grayburn had refused to leave his men. 'His wounded arm was strapped up in a highly coloured sling improvised from a paisley shawl,' wrote Sims, 'which made a vivid splash of colour against his camouflage jacket. His voice was steady, his jaw set, but his eyes told of the pain which swept over him at intervals, during which he wandered in his speech.'

Frost appeared at the White House radiating confidence, according to Sims, and congratulated the officers and men on their brilliant defence. He also sent a man down to the river bank to see if any barges were still intact. Word came back the barges were a complete write-off. 'That's that, then,' said Frost. 'We'll stay where we are.'[6]

Back at Battalion HQ, Frost was relieved to hear that most of the Dutch civilians had scarpered during the night. They would be safer and spared the sight of their prized possessions 'lying pathetically scattered, broken and spoiled', and their houses turned into fortresses with windows shattered, furniture 'hastily built into barricades and all inflammable material got rid of as far as possible'.

As there was still no sign of Brigadier Lathbury, Tony Hibbert asked Frost to take over as acting brigadier 'so as to be able to direct relieving troops to their positions when they arrived'. Frost agreed, and moved into the larger government building next door, leaving his second-in-command, Major David Wallis, in charge of the battalion. At 6.30 p.m., Frost ordered the 1st and 3rd Battalions 'each to form a flying column with as much food, water and ammunition as they could carry to break through to the bridge by midnight'. Neither battalion – as we shall discover – was in a position to comply.

By nightfall, there was still no sign of relief or fresh ammunition. Once again, Frost visited as many outposts as he could, and found the men in high spirits. One told him: 'It's our most enjoyable battle. Let's always fight from houses.'

Their spirits were dampened by the news that acting battalion commander David Wallis had been killed as he investigated the loss to the Germans of two outlying positions. He was replaced by Digby Tatham-Warter who asked Frost if this was the worst fight he had been in.

'It's hard to say,' replied Frost. 'Some things are worse, others not so bad. We still have food and water. But we're dangerously low on ammunition.'

Like Frost, Tatham-Warter made regular visits to his outlying posts. On one occasion, Lieutenant Pat Barnett, the commander of the Brigade Defence Platoon, spotted Tatham-Warter holding an opened umbrella over his head, as if for protection. 'That thing won't do you much good!' shouted Barnett.

'Oh my goodness, Pat,' replied the major, with a look of exaggerated shock, 'what if it rains?'[7]

35

'Our numbers were dwindling fast'
– Arnhem, Holland, 18 September 1944

EARLIER THAT DAY, FOUR miles distant, Lieutenant Colonel David Dobie's 1st Parachute Battalion had begun its move into Arnhem, heading south-east before dawn towards the 'Tiger' route. But as the battalion approached the railway embankment at Oosterbeek it was engaged by a blocking line set up by SS-Obersturmbannführer Ludwig Spindler, the 9th Hohenstaufen's artillery commander. With seven men killed, two taken prisoner and others wounded, Dobie ordered a side-step to the right in search of the lower 'Lion' route. But more heavy resistance was encountered on the edge of Arnhem itself and by late afternoon, deciding that the battalion could go no further, Dobie ordered the men to take cover in houses close to St Elisabeth Hospital where they saw signs of the 3rd Parachute Battalion's earlier attempt to break through.

Some tried to take refuge in the hospital itself, but they were ordered out by doctors who were concerned that their presence was jeopardising the patients. 'There were bodies of our 3rd Battalion lying everywhere,' remembered one private. 'Officers and NCOs were running in and out of the houses trying to chivvy men along; some had stayed behind to comfort dead or dying comrades.'

Starting from its overnight position west of Oosterbeek, and a mile south of the 1st Battalion, Lieutenant Colonel Fitch's 3rd Battalion had been accompanied by Brigadier Lathbury and Major General Urquhart as far as the outskirts of Arnhem where its lead platoon paused at a riverside building known as the Rhine Pavilion. By then, German harassing fire had caused A Company and the support weapons – machine guns, mortars and anti-tank guns – to become detached from the rest of the column. When Fitch took stock, he realised he had with him only B Company, a few sappers, a single anti-tank gun and 'one major general who needed to get back, and one brigadier who wanted to go forward'.

He ordered his point platoon, Lieutenant Cleminson's No. 5, to pause while the rest of the battalion caught up. Had he not done so, some of the 3rd Battalion might have covered the remaining mile or so to the bridge. 'The Germans were certainly not in major strength yet,' remembered Cleminson, 'and I had only one serious casualty in my leading section so far that morning.'

But the missing men did not reappear and, in the meantime, German infantry and armoured cars kept Fitch and his men pinned down in houses between the main road and the river. At 4 p.m., Fitch ordered his men to try to reach the bridge by a route further away from the river. This meant heading north, through back gardens, to the smaller streets on the north side of the Utrechtseweg and west of St Elisabeth Hospital.[1]

It was during this move that Urquhart, Lathbury and the brigade intelligence officer, Captain Willie Taylor, became separated from the main group and, losing their bearings, began to head towards German positions. Lieutenant Cleminson ran to warn them and, before long, all four were running the gauntlet of German fire. Crossing one bullet-swept intersection, Lathbury was hit in the leg and back. The others dragged him to the safety of a nearby house where Urquhart shot an approaching German through a window with his .45 semi-automatic pistol. Aware that the capture of Urquhart, the divisional commander, would be a disaster for the operation, the wounded Lathbury urged the trio to leave him behind. They eventually did so, leaving by the back door and making their way down a narrow path to another house where an exceptionally brave couple, Mr and Mrs Anton Derksen, agreed to hide them in the attic.

Urquhart wanted to keep moving, but the others insisted it was too dangerous. The argument was ended by the arrival of a German self-propelled gun and infantry in the street outside. Escape was no longer an option. Urquhart and the others would remain in the attic, out of contact with divisional and brigade headquarters, until the following morning.[2]

Posterity has not been kind to the inexperienced Roy Urquhart. Airborne historian William F. Buckingham has accused him of making one bad decision after another. 'The problems began,' wrote Buckingham, 'with his endorsement of Lathbury's plan which . . . merely diffused and squandered 1st Parachute Brigade's combat power to no good effect. Urquhart's ill-judged interference with Gough effectively ended the Recce Squadron's *coup-de-main* effort before it began. His badly thought-out decision to leave his divisional HQ with no inkling of his intentions or destination and without a clearly defined chain of command, ultimately left 1st Airborne Division without leadership for the first 40 hours of the battle.'[3]

Another unit that attempted to link up with Frost at the bridge on 18 September was the missing C Company under Major Victor Dover. His plan was for the company to 'retrace its steps by way of the back-gardens of the houses . . . and make for the low road by the river'. But they were slowed by sniper fire and the 10-foot high walls that divided the gardens, and ambushed by machine guns and armoured cars as they tried to move down a narrow road that linked the main road and the railway line. As the company disintegrated, Dover and 25 men took up defensive positions in two houses on the main road. The rest 'were scattered on the far side of the street and out of sight'.

Bringing their armoured cars forward, the Germans fired 20mm shells at point blank range into the two houses, which quickly caught fire and filled with smoke. From across the road came the cries of wounded paratroopers calling for help. There was nothing Dover's men could do to help them and, under the circumstances, it is remarkable that they remained so steady. They would have fought on, but the situation was hopeless, and Dover knew it. He shouted: 'Cease firing!'

He wrote later: 'I had never seriously given a thought to the possibility of being taken prisoner and cannot describe what the first moments of capture are like, but every prisoner-of-war knows. The knowledge of failure and that there is to be no second chance is difficult to accept. I was conscious of the wounded about me, including Germans.'4

The closest any airborne reinforcements got to the bridge on 18 September was the small harbour near the dismantled pontoon crossing. Two small groups reached this area: a group of 3rd Battalion men led by Lieutenant John Dickson; and a separate force of 20 men under Major Tony Deane-Drummond, deputy commander of Divisional Signals, who had come forward from Divisional HQ, near the landing and drop zones, to try and improve radio communications by informing Brigade HQ of a change in frequency. Realising they were low on ammunition and could go no further, Deane-Drummond ordered his party to take up defensive positions in three houses with a commanding all-round view. That night they attempted to break out and link up with the 3rd Battalion. But none made it. Deane-Drummond and four men spent the next three days and nights hiding in the lavatory of a house the Germans had converted into a stronghold bristling with machine guns.[5]

During the morning of 18 September, Colonel Charles Mackenzie, the chief of staff, had become sufficiently concerned by Urquhart's continued absence from Divisional HQ to set off by Jeep to speak to 49-year-old Brigadier Philip 'Pip' Hicks, commanding the 1st Airlanding Brigade. A 'solid infantryman' from the Royal Warwickshire Regiment, Hicks had commanded his brigade in North Africa and ditched in the Mediterranean during Operation Ladbroke, in the disastrous airborne invasion of Sicily. The experience had 'shaken him more than he suspected', noted Urquhart, 'but he was still an excellent commander much loved by his men'.

Hicks and half his brigade – the 2nd South Staffords and 7th King's Own Scottish Borderers – had arrived in gliders on 17 September to guard the drop and landing zones for the second wave on the 18th. This would deliver the balance of his brigade and the 4th Parachute Brigade under John 'Shan' Hackett – a 'remarkable little man with a pugilist's nose, sharp alert eyes' and a 'vivid' personality – while Stanisław Sosabowski's 1st Polish Parachute Brigade was due to land south of the river a day later.

Finding Hicks on a dusty cart track near a wood, Mackenzie explained that Urquhart had been missing since the previous afternoon – feared killed, wounded or taken prisoner – and Lathbury was also incommunicado. This meant that Hicks would have to take over as acting divisional commander* and decide what to do about Frost's urgent need for reinforcements at the

---

* Before leaving his command post on the 17th, Urquhart had told his chief of staff, Colonel Charles Mackenzie, that if he was 'put out of the battle Lathbury should take command of the division with Hicks and Hackett succeeding in that order'. (Urquhart, *Arnhem*, p. 29)

bridge because, thus far, the 1st and 3rd Battalions had failed to link up with him.

It was unfortunate timing because Hicks's deputy had recently 'fallen to pieces – simply lost his nerve', and so another officer altogether had to be found to take over from Hicks as commander of the 1st Airlanding Brigade, while Hicks returned with Mackenzie to Divisional HQ where he found the situation 'somewhat confusing' with missing commanders, bad communications and a lack of clarity about which units were where. Only two things were certain: that the German reaction had been quick and violent and that the situation was immensely grave. 'It was,' admitted Hicks, 'one of the worst few hours I have ever spent in my life.'

Urged by Mackenzie, Hicks ordered one of his landing zone protection units, the 2nd South Staffs, 'to move off and assist the drive for the bridge'.[6] Though only at half-strength – the remaining portion was due to arrive later that day in the second lift – the battalion left its position north of the village of Wolfheze at 10.30 a.m. and moved towards Oosterbeek with the Jeeps and light armour in the lead, followed by the rifle platoons and the mortars. But the going was tough and, harassed by German fighter planes, snipers and machine guns, the 2nd South Staffs took around seven hours to cover the six miles to a point close to St Elisabeth Hospital on the outskirts of Arnhem where they joined the remnants of the 1st Parachute Battalion, under David Dobie. 'For some reason we halted here for the night,' recorded Private William Hewitt. 'This stop, I feel, was a mistake by our Commander, for whilst we lay all night at the roadside, the enemy was moving in more troops and armour between us and the bridge.'[7]

The halt did, however, give some of the troops from the second lift – the 4th Parachute Brigade and the balance of the 1st Airlanding Brigade – the opportunity to catch up. Delayed by low cloud and fog, they finally arrived at Ginkel Heath and the original landing zones, a couple of miles to the south, between 2 and 3 p.m. in the afternoon. The 127 planes and 261 gliders had to run the gauntlet of heavy German anti-aircraft fire as they approached the Arnhem area. Having jumped, the paratroopers were shot at by machine guns as they came in to land. 'Men were coming down dead in the harness,' recorded Major Blackwood of the 11th Parachute Battalion, 'and others were hit before they could extricate themselves.'[8]

The gliders were also shot at as they descended towards LZ-X, a mile west of Wolfheze. 'Gliders lay all over the place – many had come to grief and some were on fire, but the majority seemed to have come down OK,' noted Lance Corporal Jack Bird, a machine-gunner in the 2nd South Staffs' Support Company. 'Out we jumped and took up defensive positions around the glider whilst the kit was unloaded.'

Once on the ground, the 2nd South Staffs were sent after the rest of their battalion. Bird 'was struck by the colourful and picturesque appearance of the houses, which from the air had a doll's house look'. The Dutch welcomed them with cheers, offered them fruit and advised them on the direction the Germans had taken. All along the road were signs of the enemy's hasty retreat – 'kit and equipment all over the place'. The gruesome sights included 'a German staff car wrecked at a crossroad, the four occupants inside dead, one sprawled grotesquely out of the door which he must have flung open in an attempt to get out'. This was the corpse of Generalmajor Friedrich Kussin, Arnhem's town commandant, whose staff car had been ambushed on the 17th by the 3rd Battalion.

As Bird and the other reinforcements approached Arnhem, they were targeted by snipers and had to move 'warily'. They finally made contact with the tail of their battalion near the St Elisabeth Hospital at around midnight.[9]

★

The hospital, an imposing red-brick building run by nuns from a German religious order, had been staffed by the men of Lieutenant Colonel E. Townshend's 16th Parachute Field Ambulance since the first night of the battle. When the Germans arrived the following morning – led by the 9th SS Hohenstaufen's dental officer, a 'short and pompous' man with a shaven skull and 'angry stoat's eyes in a contemptuous face' – Townshend was told that all Allied personnel would have to leave apart from two surgical teams led by Major Cedric 'Shorty' Longland and Captain Lipmann 'Lippy' Kessel. Later that day, the dentist changed his mind and said that the surgical teams would have to go too.

Longland was operating on a patient when he was given the bad news. 'Normally gentle-mannered though dogged, the son of a rural parson, and with a fondness for medical research', he was also a veteran of the Sicily campaign and did not suffer fools. 'I've never heard such rot!' he told the interpreter. 'Tell your officer I protest most strongly.'

'I can't help that,' the interpreter responded.

'Please inform him,' said Langland, 'that we intend to go on operating whatever anyone may say. He can do as he pleases but we shall carry on.'

This infuriated the SS dentist who told the major that he and his men had to leave the hospital immediately as prisoners-of-war.

Langland simply repeated his intention, sounding if anything 'more casual than before'.

The dentist hesitated, unsure what to do. Eventually he gave in: the surgical teams could stay as long as they promised not to leave the theatre without permission. It was, remembered one of the British surgeons, 'Lippy' Kessel, a 29-year-old Jew born in Pretoria, South Africa, 'a moral as well as a practical victory'.

Kessel and Longland would eventually treat hundreds of wounded, British and German, as well as Dutch civilians caught in the cross-fire, while the battle raged outside. At one point, Kessel thought he saw through a window General Urquhart and a couple of aides 'edging past some houses'. A few minutes later, 'German patrols could be heard tramping and shouting through the corridors'. The surgeons carried on regardless.[10]

Brigadier 'Shan' Hackett, commanding the 4th Parachute Brigade, was met at the drop zone by Colonel Mackenzie who told him that Hicks had taken over the division. 'Look here, Charles,' said Hackett. 'I am senior to Hicks and should therefore assume command of the division.'

'I quite understand, sir,' replied Mackenzie. 'But the General did give me the order of succession and furthermore Brigadier Hicks has been here 24 hours and is much more familiar with the situation.'

Hackett was also unhappy to hear that he was about to lose one of his three battalions, the 11th, which Hicks had ordered into Arnhem to reinforce the 1st Parachute Brigade. Its second-in-command was the same Major Dickie Lonsdale who had commanded the 2nd Battalion's A Company in Sicily, winning a DSO in the process. Now, wounded in the hand by flak, he rejected the warning by the battalion doctor, Stewart Mawson, that he might suffer permanent damage without proper treatment. 'Stopping flapping around like a wet hen,' Lonsdale told him.

Trying to persuade him to take his wound seriously, wrote Mawson, was 'as useless as passing a bottle of milk around the sergeants' mess'.

Lonsdale's 11th Battalion eventually set off towards Arnhem at around 5 p.m., 'picking up *en route* our transport and anti-tank guns which had landed very successfully by glider', noted Major Blackwood. 'We had little opposition in this phase, bar snipers, and could appreciate the *Esquire* nude by Vargas, which some cheerful idiot had pinned to a tree with a couple of bayonets.'

The other two battalions, the 10th and 156th, were also slow to get moving, partly because of the 200 casualties inflicted in the air or on landing, a tenth of the brigade's strength. The confusion caused by Urquhart's absence had also played its part.[11]

Away to the south, Horrocks' XXX Corps was at least a day behind schedule, thanks to the halt at Valkenswaard, six miles south of Eindhoven, and equally slow progress on the 18th. Vandeleur's Shermans finally set off at 10 a.m. and, after another stop-start day, reached Eindhoven in the early evening where they were met by crowds of cheering civilians.

At Nijmegen, meanwhile, the arrival of odds-and-sods reinforcements from the 10th SS Frundsberg – collectively known as Kampfgruppe Reinhold – had sealed off the southern approaches to the bridge over the Waal. Major General Jim Gavin's main preoccupation that day was, in any case, not the capture of the bridge but the security of the landing zone where 454 gliders with the balance of his division and its 36 pack howitzers were due to land that afternoon. In the event, 385 gliders managed to land safely and only six howitzers were lost.

Meeting Gavin at 3.30 p.m., Lieutenant General 'Boy' Browning asked him what his plans were for the next 24 hours. Gavin said that his 'plan for the night of 18–19 September was to seize the bridge north of Nijmegen using one battalion of 504 [Regiment] and in conjunction with 508 [Regiment] envelop the bridgehead from the east and west'. At first Browning approved, 'but on giving it more thought, in view of the situation in the XXX Corps, he felt that the retention of the high ground south of Nijmegen was of greater importance, and directed that the primary mission should be to hold the high ground and retain its position west of the Maas-Waal Canal'.

Gavin had no option but to assemble his regimental commanders and issue an order for the defence of the Groesbeek Heights, to protect XXX Corps' advance from a possible German counter-attack from the great forest of Klever Reichswald to the east. It was another mystifying decision, and one that ignored the plain truth that only by securing the bridge over the Waal could XXX Corps have any chance of reaching Arnhem before Frost's perimeter was overwhelmed.[12]

36

'We were spellbound and speechless' – Arnhem, Holland, 19 September 1944

W ITH AMMUNITION AND FOOD running out, as the third day of the battle broke, Frost and the men at the bridge were pinning their hopes for Tuesday 19 September on the arrival of Sosabowski's Polish Parachute Brigade. Due to drop south of the bridge where the Germans were in force, the Poles' reception was bound to be hot. Frost was convinced that, amidst the confusion, his 'mobile storming party' would be able to get across the bridge to greet the newcomers on the far side. But the minutes ticked by and not a single Pole materialised. Nor did any of the other battalions in the division, at least four of whom were 'trying to batter their way in towards' the defenders at the bridge. The rest were 'stretched from Oosterbeek, the village outside Arnhem, to the area of the original landing'.

All day on 19 September, the Germans pummelled Frost's positions. Though every thrust by tanks, armoured cars and infantry was parried, the casualties kept mounting and, with medical supplies running out, Frost began to consider a temporary truce to evacuate the worst cases to the St Elisabeth Hospital.

At around midday Lance Sergeant Stan Halliwell, a sapper who had been captured that morning in a building east of the bridge, arrived at Brigade HQ under a flag of truce. He told

Frost that the German commander wished to meet him under the bridge at 3 p.m. to discuss the terms of the British surrender.

As far as the Germans were concerned, the British situation was hopeless. Frost felt differently, particularly when Halliwell informed him that the Germans themselves were 'most disheartened at their heavy losses'. Feeling that he only needed more ammunition to turn the tables on his SS opponents, he gave Halliwell a message to relay to the German commander: 'He can go to hell.'

When Halliwell explained that he had given the German officer his word of honour that he would return to captivity after delivering the message, Frost said it was up to him to decide. Halliwell opted to return, but changed his mind when he was targeted by machine-gun fire as he approached the German lines. He rejoined his unit, muttering: 'They can come and find me if they want me.'[1]

At this point in the battle, the fighting had become desperate. When three German Mark III panzers approached the house to the east of the bridge that was being held by Andrew McDermont's No. 3 Platoon, and started firing into the building, Captain Tony Frank ordered McDermont to evacuate his platoon while he and Private Robert Lygo, a PIAT gunner, engaged the tanks. Lygo fired four bombs and achieved three hits, knocking out one tank and forcing the others to withdraw. It was only thanks to Lygo's 'coolness and courage in the face of devastating fire that the Platoon was able to hold this house for so long', recorded his later citation for the Military Medal. 'Throughout these engagements he was isolated from the remainder of the Platoon and was acting entirely on his own initiative. On the second occasion he deliberately exposed himself to heavy fire in order to work his weapon forward to a position where he could get a more accurate shot.'[2]

Soon after, Digby Tatham-Warter strolled across from Battalion

HQ with his umbrella, 'quite unconcerned about any danger'. He was angry that McDermont's platoon had been ordered to withdraw, and wanted him to retake the house. Accordingly, McDermont got his platoon together – 15 to 20 men only – and 'they set off underneath the bridge, all very tired, just shrugging their shoulders and going back, but in no defeatist mood or anything like that'.

Leading from the front, McDermont and his batman, Private Archie McAuslan, re-entered the house by the back door and were half way up the staircase when three German soldiers appeared on the landing and shot them with machine pistols at point blank range. Jumping over the fallen bodies, the Germans tried to leave by the front door but were cut down by the rest of McDermont's men. Having retaken the house, the paratroopers tried to make McDermont and McAuslan comfortable by giving them morphine and placing them in easy chairs. They were later taken to the aid post at Brigade HQ where both died of their wounds.[3]

Towards evening, German fire had set ablaze all the buildings by the bridge, and the paratroopers were struggling to find alternative positions. Worse still, heavy tanks began to appear, 'incredibly menacing and sinister in the half-light, as their guns swung from target to target'. Frost recalled: 'Shells burst through our walls. The dust and settling debris following their explosions filled the passages and rooms. The acrid reek and smell of burning together with the noise bemused us.'

Battalion HQ was particularly badly hit, with Major Tatham-Warter and Father Egan – the first Army chaplain ever to earn his wings – among the minor casualties. The defenders responded with PIATs and an anti-tank gun, forcing most of the enemy armour to withdraw. But the last onslaught had left them drained, and in doubt whether they could hold out much longer. Frost climbed the stairs to the attic with Freddie Gough to watch the flames and discuss their next move should they be driven out by fire.

'What's worrying,' said Frost, 'is that if we take fire here, we can't fight it out to the last minute and then go and leave our wounded to be roasted. We'll have to leave them time to carry the bad cases up and out of it. The trouble is that I can't see where else we can go to. What do you think about going north?'

Gough thought it would be better to go 'westward towards the river bend', and they left it at that.

The night was 'fairly peaceful', with Frost prowling about from room to room, and snatching the occasional nap 'amongst the litter in one of the rooms'.[4]

Less than two miles away, still cooped up in the attic of 14 Zwarteweg in Arnhem, Major General Urquhart had spent the previous night (18/19 September) waiting for signs that the 1st Airlanding and 4th Parachute Brigades were attacking from the west. He kept asking himself: How far had XXX Corps advanced? Had the Americans succeeded at Grave and Nijmegen? Perhaps by now the 2nd Battalion had been given some help?

He woke from a fitful sleep to hear the wheeze of an engine as the German self-propelled gun on the street below started up, and drove off. Then his Dutch host appeared with the news that British soldiers were at the bottom of the road. Urquhart and his two companions rushed out, jettisoning a Sten gun in their haste, and met men from the South Staffords and the 11th Battalion. 'We've been sent by Brigadier Hicks to help the drive into the town,' an officer told Urquhart. 'Your HQ is now at the Hartenstein Hotel in Oosterbeek.'

As he admitted later, Urquhart probably should have remained where he was to coordinate the push into Arnhem. Instead he borrowed a Jeep and made for Oosterbeek at speed, accompanied by Taylor, but not Cleminson who hoped to rejoin the 3rd

Battalion. Feeling like 'an Aunt Sally on a rifle range' – as German sniper bullets pinged off the tarmac around them – he made it safely through to the hotel, to the surprise of Colonel Mackenzie: 'We had assumed, sir, that you had gone for good.'

The colonel then explained that Hicks had taken over the command, and modified the original plan. It was a 'disturbing picture', thought Urquhart, and urgently required the infusion of 'some overall direction into the separate moves to rejoin Frost'. When Hicks appeared, Urquhart told him that a senior officer was needed to co-ordinate the attacks by the four battalions then heading for the bridge. They picked Hicks's deputy, Colonel Hilaro Barlow, who set off in a Jeep with a wireless operator. They were never seen again.

The news that did arrive was far from encouraging. The South Staffords and elements of the 11th Battalion were 'in trouble on the main road about a mile from the bridge'; more enemy panzers were arriving in Arnhem; and XXX Corps had only reached the town of Graves, 20 miles away, meaning that Horrocks was 'already some 30 hours behind schedule' – and they still hadn't made it past Nijmegen.[5]

XXX Corps had linked up with the 82nd Airborne Division in woodland to the south of Nijmegen during the morning of the 19th. A few hours later, the Grenadier Guards Group and a battalion of the American 505th Parachute Infantry Regiment made a joint attack on the strongly fortified German bridgehead south of Nijmegen's road bridge. It was a heroic effort, but 'little progress was made'. Horrocks recalled: '[The enemy] set fire to every fifth building until some 500 houses were blazing fiercely. Into this hell plunged tanks, Guards and US paratroopers, but all to no avail. By midnight it was obvious that the bridges could not be captured by direct assault.'[6]

★

Meanwhile, the mixed force in Arnhem – the battered remnants of the 1st and 3rd Parachute Battalions, the 2nd South Staffords and the 11th Parachute Battalion – made a final attempt to reach the bridge – and relieve Frost – on 19 September. None got through. The South Staffords got as far as the Municipal Museum, 600 yards from their start point, before intense fire from mortars, assault guns and tanks stopped their advance. By late afternoon, it was all over. Apart from one company held back near the 11th Parachute Battalion's lines, the 2nd South Staffs had ceased to exist. Most were taken prisoner 'although some scattered groups and individuals managed to escape to the west'.[7]

Among the survivors was the machine-gunner Lance Corporal Bird who remembered hitching a lift on a Jeep, part of 'a long column of vehicles pulling out of Arnhem in the direction of Oosterbeek'. When the column was fired on, Bird continued on foot to Oosterbeek where a defensive perimeter was being formed around the Hartenstein Hotel. 'There,' he recalled, 'in a dugout on the bank of a stream in front of the old village church, I met up with some of my mob. I decided to "muck in" with them as I could not see any sign of my platoon.' Bird needed no encouragement to dig himself in: 'the deeper the better'.[8]

Urquhart had decided to concentrate his remaining force around the Hartenstein Hotel in Oosterbeek because, with the arrival of ever more German reinforcements, he feared that the division would be defeated in penny packets. As he put it: 'The Airlanding Brigade to the west and north-west was under severe attack; there were all the distant signs that Hackett was in some difficulty to the north, and in the town casualties mounted among the units making separate bids to break through. From every side we could hear the sound of battle.'

Having physically intervened to prevent a young officer and 20 men from fleeing in panic – and witnessed other signs of edginess, including 'indiscriminate shooting, unnecessary visits by the soldiers to the Hartenstein cellars', and an empty slit trench with a loaded Bren and a nest of grenades left deserted – Urquhart urged his commanders to keep strict discipline.

He had tried to request new supply dropping points, because the originals were in German hands, but the message had failed to get through. He and his men, as a result, were 'forced to witness the first act of the re-supply tragedy at Arnhem' as RAF crews braved violent and intense flak – only to make an unwitting present of their loads to the Germans. Urquhart's men did everything they could to prevent this: 'they waved, they paid out parachute material, they lit beacons'. But all to no avail.

One Dakota, though hit by flak and with its starboard wing aflame, kept descending to 900 feet. It seemed to Urquhart as if 'every anti-aircraft gun in the vicinity was sighted on the crippled aircraft'. Yet it flew on to the dropping zone and jettisoned its supplies, before coming round a second time. 'We were spellbound and speechless,' remembered Urquhart, 'and I daresay there is not a survivor of Arnhem who will ever forget, or want to forget, the courage we were privileged to witness in those terrible eight minutes . . . We saw the machine crashing in flames as one of its wings collapsed.'

Only later did Urquhart learn the name of the doomed pilot – Flight Lieutenant David 'Lummy' Lord of 271 Squadron – and that he had 'ordered his crew to abandon while making no effort to leave himself'. There was one survivor.

Of the 163 aircraft that attempted to drop supplies on 19 September, 13 were shot down and another 97 damaged. 'And despite our signals – yellow smoke, yellow triangles, scarf waving and the rest,' noted Urquhart, 'the best part of 390 tons of food and ammunition fell to the Germans.' Only a few canisters which fell off target were recovered by men of the RASC.

The misfortune continued as Polish troops came down in

gliders between the retreating men of the 10th Battalion and the Germans. In the confusion, 'which was not eased by the different gear worn by the Poles and their grey berets, identities were not established until some [Polish] lives had been lost' to friendly fire.[9]

During the 10th Battalion's withdrawal, 24-year-old Captain Lionel Queripel – from a distinguished line of army officers – repeatedly exposed himself to enemy fire as he rescued a wounded sergeant, repositioned his men, and knocked out two German machine-gun nests, recapturing a British anti-tank gun in the process. Later, despite wounds to his face and both arms, he remained in a vulnerable position, allowing his men to withdraw. He was killed soon after. When his body was recovered, it was buried with full military honours in Oosterbeek Cemetery. Like Lord, he was awarded a posthumous Victoria Cross for displaying 'the highest standard of gallantry under most difficult and trying circumstances', and for 'courage, leadership and devotion to duty' that 'were magnificent, and an inspiration to all'.[10]

37

'No living enemy had beaten us'
– Arnhem, Holland, 20 September 1944

B Y THE EARLY HOURS of Wednesday 20 September, the surviving remnants of the 1st Airborne had retreated to the makeshift fortress of Divisional HQ at Oosterbeek, apart from the 500 or so men of the 10th and 156th Battalions who were still outside, and Frost's battered force at the bridge. Urquhart received a signal from Corps HQ 'requesting a fresh dropping zone for the main force of Sosabowski's Polish Brigade', whose arrival had twice been postponed by bad weather. The only possible location now was south of the river, near Driel, and this was 'duly passed to Corps'.[1]

Dawn broke on 20 September with persistent rain and the heaviest German mortar bombardment yet, as the battle reached 'new levels of intensity'. Shrapnel peppered the defensive perimeter at Oosterbeek and the Hartenstein Hotel took a number of direct hits. Outside, noted Urquhart, 'lay the corpses of men still to be buried, smashed vehicles, shellpits and holes in the ground in which men hardened themselves for what was still to come'. They had dug slit trenches 'under the beech trees, and out among the laurel bushes; trees had been up-rooted and signal cables zig-zagged between the hotel and the strange building like a tower in the grounds [which was] artillery HQ'. Beyond this, in the hotel tennis courts, they had established a prisoner-of-war cage.

At 7.30 a.m., Urquhart's signallers managed to establish radio contact with Shan Hackett, whose 4th Parachute Brigade was fighting for its life to the north-west of Oosterbeek. When Urquhart ordered him to Divisional HQ, Hackett gave him a stern reality check. 'My entire brigade is engaged, attacked both frontally and on both flanks, and I've already had to alter my line of advance once. We have a certain number of tanks among us.' Getting to HQ would not be possible 'anytime soon'.

The news was utterly depressing for Urquhart. He knew from other sources that, except for the 2nd Battalion at the bridge, the 1st Parachute Brigade 'had to all intents and purposes been wiped out'. The South Staffords had 'ceased to exist as a unit', and the 11th Battalion had 'disintegrated'. This meant that 'whatever prospects there had been of reaching Frost at the Bridge were now gone'. Urquhart wrote: 'It was an awful conclusion to come to: it meant the abandonment of those men at the Bridge who had endured the most terrible battering. But with the weak force now left, I could no more hope to reinforce Frost than reach Berlin. Clearly the Germans now controlled every route into the town and Bridge. They were being strengthened almost hourly, and their [heavy Mark VI] Tiger tanks were causing havoc.'

He had fantasised about Hackett's brigade 'coming through the divisional area, reorganising, and then carrying out an offensive towards the bridge'. That was now impossible. He therefore ordered Hackett 'to forget the ultimate idea of pressing into the town, but to bring his brigade, or that part of it which survived, into position on the north-east side' of the divisional area. Urquhart's plan now was to hold on to a small bridgehead north of the Lower Rhine until XXX Corps caught up.

At 8 a.m., he was called to the phone. 'Hello, Sunray,' said a cheerful voice.

'Can you give me an inkling who you are?'

'It's the man who goes in for funny weapons.'

Urquhart knew plenty of airborne characters who were that way inclined. Which one was it? The caller tried again: 'The man who is always late for your "O" groups.'

It could only be Freddie Gough, commander of the 1st Airlanding Reconnaissance Squadron, and Frost's companion on the bridge. They had heard nothing from him since the first day of the battle. 'My goodness,' said Urquhart, 'I thought you were dead.'

Gough gave a quick resumé of what he had been up to, and the situation at the bridge where he and Frost's handful of men were still holding out.

'Please pass on my personal congratulations on a fine effort to everyone concerned,' said Urquhart. 'But I have to tell you the rest of the division is not in great shape. I'm afraid you can only hope for relief from the south. For the moment we can only try to preserve what we have left.'

'I understand, sir,' said Gough. 'It's pretty grim here. We'll do what we can.'

'I know you will. Best of luck.'[2]

The shelling at the bridge had begun soon after dawn, and by late morning most of the buildings on both sides of the ramp had been reduced to smouldering wrecks and their garrisons driven north.[3] The remnants of A Company, now led by the indomitable Lieutenant Jack Grayburn with his 'consuming hatred of Germans', took refuge in a vault under the bridge where they placed the wounded. The Germans sent in engineers with explosives to winkle them out. But they were driven off by a fighting patrol led by Grayburn who, though wounded again (this time in the back), refused to be evacuated. Finally, an enemy tank approached so close to the position that it became untenable.

Ordering his men to withdraw, he held the position until he was killed shortly afterwards, 'some said by a German flame thrower'.

Grayburn was awarded a posthumous Victoria Cross for the 'supreme gallantry and determination' with which he had led his men at Arnhem. 'Although in pain and weakened by wounds, short of food and without sleep,' noted his citation, 'his courage never flagged. There is no doubt that, had it not been for this officer's inspiring leadership and personal bravery, the Arnhem bridge could never have been held for this time.'[4]

Another officer who played his part was Captain Eric Mackay, commanding the sappers in the large U-shaped school on the east side of the ramp. After three days of almost constant combat and negligible sleep, Mackay's men were at the end of their tether, 'haggard and filthy, with bloodshot and red-rimmed eyes', and almost everyone wearing a field dressing. The stone stairs near Mackay's CP were 'sticky and slippery with blood', and just about the only clean items were the men's weapons.

Fortified with Benzedrine tablets, Mackay and his men spent the morning dashing from window to window, firing at the Germans. Eventually, with the roof on fire and the school filling with choking black smoke, Mackay ordered his men into the cellar. As they were coming downstairs, Corporal Joe Simpson realised he had left his captured Luger. 'I'm going back to get it,' he told the others.

'Leave it, you fool,' shouted Sapper Ron Emery. 'Let's get the hell out of here!'

Ignoring him, Simpson started back up the stairs. Moments later there was a crash from a tank round, causing part of the roof to cave in.

Eric Mackay came down the stairs. 'Where's Joe?' asked Emery.

'Don't go back up,' said Mackay. 'He's dead.' The tank round had removed the back of Simpson's head.

Down in the cellar, Mackay did a head count: he had 14 able-bodied men left, 31 wounded and 5 dead. It was time to evacuate. He ordered a lieutenant to lead the breakout to the north with six Bren gunners. Mackay and two men would remain behind as a rearguard, and the rest would act as stretcher-bearers.

When they had gathered on the ground floor, someone asked for a volunteer to go out first and cover them. Ron Emery raised his hand. He crept out with his Bren gun, scaled a wall and ran to the neighbouring building just as a machine gun opened up. He threw a phosphorus grenade and kept running. Turning the corner, he was confronted by a huge SS man with an MP-40 machine pistol. They stared at each other, until the German bolted. Emery shot him in the back.

Out of ammunition, he dropped the Bren and kept moving north, working his way through some back gardens. In one he tried to relieve a 'dead' paratrooper of his Sten gun. When the 'corpse' opened its eyes and protested, Emery shot back: 'It's not doing you much good lying there, boy!'

He and the paratrooper agreed to team up, but almost immediately, having scaled a few more walls, they were captured by a German patrol.

Mackay and the others, meanwhile, finding their route north blocked, headed east. It was the one direction the Germans would not expect them to take and, having lain up for the night, Mackay hoped to rejoin the main body north of the bridge.[5]

That, however, was wishful thinking. Grouped around the headquarters buildings, Frost and the remaining defenders were low on food, water and, above all, ammunition. Conditions in the cellar of Brigade HQ, where the hundreds of wounded were 'now lying crowded almost on top of each other, making it difficult for the doctors and orderlies to get round to attend them', were unsustainable. Frost now knew, as a result of Urquhart's contact with Gough, that no help would come from the rest of the division. All hopes now rested on relief from the south. But where was XXX Corps?[6]

The rebuff of the frontal attack by the Grenadier Guards and the US 505th Regiment on Nijmegen Bridge the day before had prompted 'Boy' Browning and Brian Horrocks to rethink. On the following day, 20 September, they would try to outflank the defenders by crossing the river 800 yards to the west. The 'appallingly difficult' task was given to the men of the US 504th Regiment, supported by the tanks of the Irish Guards and more than 100 artillery pieces. Shortly after midday on the 20th, having cleared the western suburbs of Nijmegen, they carried out 'one of the finest attacks of the war' by launching successive waves of assault boats across the swiftly running river.[7]

'It was a horrible, horrible sight,' recorded the onlooking Lieutenant Colonel Giles Vandeleur, who – like his cousin Lieutenant Colonel Joe Vandeleur – was there in command of a battalion of the Irish Guards. 'Boats were literally being blown out of the water. I could see huge geysers shooting up as the shells hit the water and the small-arms fire coming from the northern bank made the river look like some sort of seething cauldron.'

Though their assault boats were almost shot to pieces, the US soldiers kept paddling with rifle butts and helmets. Once on the far bank, the survivors attacked through a hail of fire, cursing and yelling at each other as they advanced. 'I felt,' wrote one, 'as if I could lick the whole German army.' Prisoners were shot out of hand in this mad dash for the road bridge. As they reached one end at dusk, tanks from the Guards Armoured Division began to cross from the other. It was a heroic achievement. Finally, Nijmegen Bridge had been taken.

But instead of pressing on to Arnhem, just 11 miles away, the leading tanks were ordered to halt until infantry support, fuel and ammunition had been brought forward. The surviving

American paratroopers were furious. Their battalion, and the engineers manning the boats, had lost 89 dead and 151 wounded. They had agreed to undertake the semi-suicidal crossing in daylight because they knew that every hour counted if the 1st Airborne Division at Arnhem were to be saved, and the final bridge captured.[8] For Horrocks, however, the imperative was to regroup. 'Another hurdle had been overcome,' he wrote later, 'and I went to bed a happy man – almost the last time, incidentally, that I was to do so in this battle.'

Assuming strong anti-tank defences along the high embankments that carried the road between Arnhem and Nijmegen, he wanted to wait for the arrival of the 43th Infantry Division which had been ordered up from the rear. By the time Horrocks resumed his advance on 21 September, it was too late to save Frost and his men.[9]

At Oosterbeek, persistent German shelling had forced Roy Urquhart to move his operations room into the cellars of the Hartenstein Hotel on the morning of the 20th. A table with maps was placed in the aisle running through the main wine cellar, manned by a duty officer. Urquhart's place was in the right-hand corner, between a blocked-up window grille and a wine rack. Next to him was an officer of the Phantom Reconnaissance Unit, with a direct wireless link back to the War Office.

Above the cellar, the hotel and its grounds were full of exhausted soldiers who had been living and sleeping in the same clothes since the landings. They stank of body odour and, as the two lavatories in the hotel were blocked, they had no option but to relieve themselves in the open. As this 'bitter day dragged on, with its numbing mortar and artillery attacks', recalled Urquhart, the fighting was fiercest on the position's western and eastern perimeters.

At 1.30 p.m., the remnants of the 4th Parachute Brigade's 10th

Battalion fought their way through to the perimeter, two days after landing. They were, remembered Urquhart, 'exhausted, filthy, and bleeding', but their 'discipline was immaculate'. Their commander, Lieutenant Colonel Ken Smyth, his right arm in a sling, reported: 'We have been heavily taken on, sir.' He had started with a force of 600. 'I have 60 men left.'

'What has happened to Hackett?' asked Urquhart.

'He'll be here as soon as they can disengage,' said Smyth. 'They were in rather a mess in the woods up there.'

Urquhart told Smyth to cover the crossroads at the north-east of the divisional area. Many of them would die there, including Smyth who was mortally wounded when a house collapsed.

Hackett eventually reached the western perimeter at 6.50 p.m. with just 70 officers and men, the survivors of his brigade HQ and the 156th Battalion, which had dropped with a combined strength of 711 officers and men. They had taken two days to reach a position to the north-west of Oosterbeek where, opposed by strong German forces, they were forced to withdraw south and then east into Urquhart's perimeter. The 156th was put into the line below the 10th Battalion, while Hackett set up his HQ in the wooded part of the hotel's grounds. Urquhart told him: 'Take a night's rest.'[10]

On the far side of the divisional area – the eastern perimeter, closest to Arnhem – the riflemen in 'Lonsdale Force' had been withdrawn that morning to the main defensive perimeter, leaving the South Staffords' machine-gunners and anti-tank guns to assist the 11th Battalion in the defence of a T-junction on the Benedendorpsweg, the main road running closest to the Rhine. Sergeant Jack Baskeyfield's two guns faced up the Acacialaan, a road that joined the Benedendorpsweg from the north, and covered any enemy approach from that direction. His right flank – to the east – was guarded by another anti-tank gun. Most of the paratroopers were posted in nearby houses.[11]

Soon after the departure of the riflemen, the Germans attacked Baskeyfield's position with infantry, tanks and self-propelled guns. Acting with 'coolness and daring', and with 'complete disregard for his own safety', the 21-year-old former butcher allowed the tanks to advance down the Acacialaan to within 100 yards of his guns before ordering his crews to fire. They eventually knocked out 'two Tiger tanks and at least one self-propelled gun', but the counter-fire killed and badly wounded the crews of both guns, and Baskeyfield himself was severely wounded in the leg. Despite this, he 'refused to be carried to the Regimental Aid Post and spent his time attending to his gun and shouting encouragement to his comrades in neighbouring trenches'.

After a short interval the Germans attacked 'with even greater ferocity than before, under cover of intense mortar and shell fire'. Manning one gun quite alone – loading, aiming and firing it, a task normally carried out by six men – Baskeyfield 'continued to fire round after round at the enemy until his gun was put out of action'. His persistence, according to his citation, 'was the main factor in keeping the enemy tanks at bay', and 'the fact that the surviving men in his vicinity were held together and kept in action was undoubtedly due to his magnificent example and outstanding courage'. Again and again, enemy attacks were beaten back, thanks to Baskeyfield.

Even after his gun was rendered useless, the badly wounded young sergeant would not withdraw from the fight. Instead he 'crawled, under intense fire, to another 6-pounder gun nearby, the crew of which had been killed, and proceeded to man it single-handed'. As he was about to engage a Stug III self-propelled gun – a 75mm cannon mounted on a tank chassis – another soldier 'crawled across the open ground to assist him but was killed almost at once'. Undeterred, Baskeyfield 'succeeded in firing two rounds at the self-propelled gun, scoring one direct hit which rendered it ineffective'. This extraordinarily brave man was about to fire a third shot when a shell from another tank exploded near his gun, killing him instantly.[12]

Shortly after Baskeyfield's death, with almost all the houses occupied by the paratroopers now ablaze, Major Lonsdale withdrew the survivors to the main perimeter. They were covered by fire from Baskeyfield's comrades in the support arms of the South Staffords. 'It was a near run thing,' noted the battalion war diary, 'as the last 6 pdr [six-pounder gun] passed the road junction . . . as a Tiger tank approached 25 yards away to the north.'[13]

Baskeyfield's body was buried in a temporary grave but never found after the war. For his quite astonishing act of courage and self-sacrifice, he was awarded a posthumous Victoria Cross, presented to his father by King George VI on 17 July 1945. The only non-officer to win the VC at Arnhem, his citation concludes: 'The superb gallantry of this N.C.O. is beyond praise. During the remaining days at Arnhem stories of his valour were a constant inspiration to all ranks. He spurned danger, ignored pain and, by his supreme fighting spirit, infected all who witnessed his conduct with the same aggressiveness and dogged devotion to duty which characterised his actions throughout.'[14]

Later that day, as German armour assaulted the eastern perimeter, Major Robert Cain of the South Staffords tried to stem the tide by firing PIAT shells over a house, mortar-like. When two tanks appeared round the side of the building, he fired at one and hit it. As he tried to fire a second shell, it exploded in the launcher. 'There was a flash and the major threw the PIAT in the air and fell backwards,' recalled a glider pilot. 'Everyone thought he had been hit by a shell from the tank exploding. He was lying with his hands over his eyes. His face was blackened and swollen. "I think I'm blinded," he said.'

Cain was stretchered to the aid station where, after a short rest, he regained his sight. He discharged himself and was back in the front line to meet an attack by Tiger tanks. Assisted by another soldier, he aimed and fired a 6-pounder gun, hitting a Tiger and bringing it to a halt. 'Reload!' he shouted.

'Can't, sir,' the soldier replied. 'Recoil mechanism's gone. She'll have to go to the workshops.'

Cain was the last of five men awarded the Victoria Cross for valour at Arnhem,* and the only one to survive the battle.[15]

Earlier that day, Frost had walked round his much-reduced defensive perimeter at the bridge, finding it fairly secure, but with some very weak points that could not withstand a determined assault. Shortly before noon, he was chatting to Doug Crawley, outside the latter's HQ, when a mortar bomb exploded with a savage crash. Frost was thrown several feet in the air, and landed face down, with severe pain in both legs from shrapnel wounds. Crawley had also been hit. Both officers began to crawl towards cover, and were dragged the last few yards by their men.

Frost was treated in the aid post by Jimmy Logan, the battalion doctor, who made light of his wounds and said that after a rest he 'should be able to carry on'. But the injuries were more serious than the doctor realised and, having gagged on a mouthful of whisky, Frost was carried down to the cellar on a stretcher to rest. 'I lay there rather dazed,' he recalled, 'hoping the worst of the pain would lessen. Several people came to see me, but I don't remember much. The news went from bad to worse. Digby was brought in to sit beside me for a while and he told me

---

* Among the many other lesser awards for men who had fought at Arnhem, or who escaped in the aftermath, were a CB (Companion of the Order of the Bath) for Roy Urquhart, a DSO (or Bar) for Shan Hackett, John Frost and Digby Tatham-Warter, a CBE for Philip Hicks, an MBE for Eric Mackay, an MC (or Bar) for Tony Deane-Drummond and Tony Hibbert, a US Silver Star for Tony Frank and a Military Medal for Bob Lygo.

about Jack Grayburn. Though hit several times he refused to leave his men and died in action with them.'

Given morphia to dull the pain, Frost drifted in and out of sleep. He woke in the evening to the sound of gunfire, as the Germans pounded the building. The doctors came to discuss evacuation in the event of fire. It would take at least an hour to move the wounded, they told Frost, and the decision could not be long delayed. When they returned to say the building was, in fact, now actually on fire, and something would have to be done fairly quickly, Frost sent for Freddie Gough and asked him to take all those able to fight – about 120 men – to a new position. Frost gave him his belt, pistol and compass, and they wished each other luck.

Accompanying Gough was Tony Hibbert, the brigade major. He recalled: 'We had by this time about 300 wounded in the cellars, but I still believed that XXX Corps would be coming up to the south bank within a matter of almost hours. And damn if we couldn't hear them! At 8 o'clock I realised that our little battle was finished. We just didn't have the ammunition. When the other side can run tanks right up to your front window with no chance of retaliating, there comes a moment when you can't go on.'

Later, Frost heard shouts from above: 'Don't shoot! Only wounded are here.'

German voices were in the passage outside, arranging for the removal of stretcher cases. Then it was Frost's turn. 'A German NCO rushed in,' he wrote, 'intimating that we must get out as soon as possible. With the help of one of the bomb-happy [i.e. shell-shocked] cases he dragged me up the stairs to the door. We had to move quickly outside to avoid burning debris from the house. I sat down among the stretcher-cases on the embankment leading to the bridge.'

All the buildings they had occupied were burning fiercely and, as he watched, the old Battalion Headquarters 'collapsed into a heap of smouldering rubble'. The whole scene was brilliantly lit up by the flames, and Germans and Britons worked together to bring the wounded out. Frost found his SS captors to be very polite and complimentary about the battle the paratroopers had fought. But it was no consolation. Frost and his men had done everything asked of them, and more, yet they had ended up in captivity. It was, he felt, 'shaming, like being a malefactor, no longer free'.

Nonetheless, he took an intense pride in what they had achieved. 'No living enemy had beaten us,' he wrote later. Instead they had been undone by a lack of ammunition, rest and positions from which to fight. No body of men, he felt, 'could have fought more courageously and tenaciously than the officers and men of the 1st Parachute Brigade at Arnhem Bridge'.[16]

38

'Get them out'
– Arnhem, Holland, 21–26 September 1944

T HE HEROIC DEFENCE OF the bridge finally came to an end when Freddie Gough's dwindling command was overrun in the early hours of Thursday 21 September. By then, more than half the 700 or so defenders had been killed or wounded, and most of the survivors captured. They had held the crossing for three days and four nights – much longer than the 48 hours planned – but it was not enough. Frost's 2nd Battalion, in particular, had paid the price for its obduracy. Of the 31 officers and 478 men who had landed at Arnhem, only 17 would avoid capture. The rest were killed, wounded and taken prisoner.* The battalion had ceased to exist.[1]

The battle, however, was not yet over. At 5.15 p.m. on the 21st, the parachutists of Sosabowski's 1st Polish Brigade were dropped at the rearranged zone south of the river, opposite Urquhart's perimeter. But the Heveadorp ferry there was no longer operating – the opportunity to make use of it having

---

* Among the fatalities were two rifle platoon commanders – Grayburn and McDermont – and the leader of the mortar platoon, Lieutenant Bryan Woods, who was badly wounded by mortar shrapnel towards the end of the battle and died in captivity.

been, bafflingly, missed – and they were forced to take up defensive positions in nearby Driel, on the south bank. That night, they made repeated efforts to cross the river and bolster the bridgehead – but only 250 made it over, and many more became casualties.

On Sunday, 24 September, the forward elements of XXX Corps' 43rd Division linked up with Sosabowski at Driel. On the other side of the river, a few miles to the north-east, the remnants of the 1st Airborne Division at Oosterbeek were out on their feet. They were under constant shell and mortar fire, weakened by persistent attacks from infantry, tanks and self-propelled guns, and the area they occupied was ever-diminishing. Earlier that day, the Germans had agreed to a truce so that the wounded could be taken to the St Elisabeth Hospital in Arnhem for treatment. For those left behind at the Hartenstein Hotel, the smell of decomposing corpses, unwashed bodies and make-shift latrines was almost unbearable.

Among the more serious casualties was Brigadier Shan Hackett who had been hit in the thigh and stomach by mortar shrapnel. When he arrived at the hospital, disguised as a 'Corporal Hayter' to fool the Germans, an SS doctor advised leaving him to die. 'That one's no good,' he told Lipmann Kessel, 'I wouldn't waste time on this.'

'Oh, I don't know,' responded Kessel. 'I think I'll have a go at this one.'

He operated immediately, and found no fewer than '12 rents' in Hackett's small intestine. Fortunately, Kessel was able to repair them and save the brigadier's life.★²

Also transported to the hospital, after spending five days with the other wounded at the Tafelburg Hotel in Oosterbeek, was

---

★ After a period of recuperation, Hackett escaped from the hospital with the help of the Dutch underground and eventually reached the safety of Allied lines.

Corporal Reg Curtis, the lanky veteran of North Africa and
Sicily, whose right leg had been shattered by mortar shrapnel
on 18 September. He found himself between two amputees and
asked them, in turn, how they were. One refused to answer; the
other turned slowly and said in a hoarse voice: 'Except for
shrapnel in my arm, a leg missing and a splitting headache – I'm
OK. I suppose I'm lucky to be alive.'[3]

That same day, Urquhart signalled Browning that, unless
'physical contact in some strength is made with us by early
25 September', it was unlikely they could hold out any longer.
'All ranks,' he wrote, 'are now completely exhausted as the result
of 8 days continuous effort. Lack of food and water and defi-
ciency in arms combined with high officer casualties has had its
effect. Even comparatively minor enemy offensive action may
cause complete disintegration. Should this become apparent all
will be told to break out rather than surrender. Controlled
movement from present position in face of enemy is out of the
question now. We have done our best and will continue to do
so as long as possible.'[4]

Brian Horrocks, commanding XXX Corps, still hoped to
reinforce Urquhart's bridgehead by attempting a major crossing
further downstream. But, General Dempsey, influenced by
Browning who was unwilling to sacrifice any more troops,
overruled him. 'No,' he told Horrocks. 'Get them out.'

That night, to facilitate the withdrawal, Horrocks sent the 4th
Dorsets across the river in boats in the vicinity of the now-
defunct Heveadorp Ferry. Only 240 of the 420-strong force
reached the far bank, and many more were killed or wounded
as they landed. A handful reached the airborne perimeter.

Urquhart and the remnants of his force were ferried across
the river after dark on 25 September, having left the badly
wounded in the care of the doctors and padres, and under the
cover of an artillery barrage. The operation was codenamed

'Berlin'. Taken to Browning's HQ, exhausted and wet, Urquhart reported: 'The division is nearly out now. I'm sorry we haven't been able to do what we set out to do.'

'You did all you could,' said Browning, as immaculately turned out as ever. 'Now you had better get some rest.'[5]

Of the 10,700 men who had been deployed on the north bank, only 1,741 officers and men of the 1st Airborne Division, 422 glider pilots and 160 members of the 1st Polish Parachute Brigade made it to safety. Accompanying them were 75 Dorsets, making 2,398 survivors in all.* The total casualties were 1,485 killed (or died of their wounds) and 6,525 – including wounded – taken prisoner. Dutch civilian deaths were 450, while a further 18,000 would die across Holland in the 'Hungry Winter' that followed. The official German casualty figures for the whole of the Market Garden area were 3,300, including 1,100 dead. But the best recent account of the battle from the German view thinks that is 'very much an underestimate, and, in fact, more than twice as many had died'. German casualties at Arnhem, alone, may have been between 3,500 and 4,000, and the same again elsewhere.

An SS corporal wrote: 'We had fought non-stop for 10 days

---

* They were followed over the Lower Rhine, in late October, by more than 120 members of the 1st Airborne Division who had either evaded the Germans or escaped from captivity, including Brigadier Lathbury, Majors Tony Hibbert and Tony Deane-Drummond (his second escape of the war), and Captain Tony Frank. The mass escape (codenamed Operation Pegasus) was assisted by the Dutch underground and the sappers of 43rd Division, and coordinated by Lieutenant Colonel David Dobie and Major Digby Tatham-Warter. 'Major Tatham-Warter,' noted his DSO citation, 'was largely responsible for the planning of a most brilliant and successful operation in which 130 armed men escaped through German lines and crossed the Rhone. For a month, behind the German lines, this officer moved about regardless of his personal safety and was an inspiration to all those who saw him.' (www.pegasusarchive.org/arnhem/tatham_warter.htm)

and nights. Coffee and Benzedrine had kept us awake. After it
was all over we were as exhausted as the British: we slept and
slept. All the Wehrmacht battalions that fought in Arnhem got
a special 10-day leave from Hitler. It was our last-ever victory.
But not the Waffen-SS. Himmler said we would get our holiday
after the Final Victory!'[6]

Operation Market Garden may have fallen at the final hurdle
– hence the title of Cornelius Ryan's bestselling history, *A Bridge
Too Far*, which Richard Attenborough made into the 1977 film
– but the ability of the 1st Airborne Division to hold Arnhem
bridge for as long as it did against a far more powerful enemy
was nothing short of astonishing. This was acknowledged by a
succession of senior officers. Brian Horrocks, for example, wrote
to Urquhart on 26 September to congratulate him and his men
on 'their tremendous achievement during the last eight days of
fighting'.

> I am afraid that your losses have been very heavy, but in your
> fighting north of the [Lower Rhine] you contained a large number
> of German reserves, and while your Parachute Brigade was
> holding the north end of the bridge at Arnhem, you prevented
> any reinforcements from moving down towards Nijmegen. This
> gave us just [enough] time to secure those vital bridges.
>
> There is no doubt that this may quite likely have a decisive
> influence on the war, and will, at any rate, I am certain, shorten
> the period of the war by several weeks.
>
> Well done 1st Airborne Division!

Miles Dempsey also praised Urquhart for the brilliant performance
of his division at Arnhem. 'From the moment that you came
under my command on September 17th,' he wrote, 'until the day
on which you were ordered to withdraw, you were fighting
ceaselessly against odds which increased as days went by. I want

all ranks in your splendid Division to know that this action of yours played a vital part in the whole Second Army Operation.'

Even Field Marshal Montgomery, who had invested so much personal capital in the operation, and was bitterly disappointed that it had come up short, allowed no trace of regret to permeate the letter he wrote to his protégé Urquhart before the latter's return to the UK on 28 September. Montgomery thanked him for everything the 1st Airborne Division had done for the 'Allied cause' at Arnhem, and for the 'magnificent fighting spirit' that Urquhart and his men had 'displayed in battle against great odds'. Failure would have 'gravely compromised' operations elsewhere. 'You did not fail,' wrote Montgomery, 'and all is well.'[7]

The final letter of praise was sent to Urquhart by General Dwight D. Eisenhower, the Supreme Allied Commander. 'Your officers and men were magnificent,' said Ike. 'Pressed from every side, without relief, reinforcement or respite, they inflicted such losses on the Nazi that his infantry dared not close with them. In an unremitting hail of steel from German snipers, machine guns, mortars, rockets, cannon of all calibers and self-propelled and tank artillery, they never flinched, never wavered. They held steadfastly.'

Eisenhower expressed his 'deep regret' that, so heavy had been the 1st Airborne Division's losses, Field Marshal Sir Alan Brooke, the Chief of the Imperial General Staff, feared it would 'probably not be possible to constitute [i.e. re-establish] it'. This was shocking for Urquhart to hear, after all his men had been through, and Ike's closing remark was little consolation. In this war, Eisenhower wrote, 'there has been no single performance by any unit that has more greatly inspired me or more highly excited my admiration, than the nine day action of your Division between September 17 and 26.'[8]

★

Everyone was full of praise for the bravery of the troops. But as the dust settled, the post-mortem began in earnest. How had such a massive operation gone so massively wrong? Roy Urquhart, in his official report of Operation Market, summed up the reasons as he saw them.

First, the distance to the objective from the landing and drop zones was 'much too great'. Second, it would have been possible to land some gliders close to the bridge for a *coup-de-main* attempt, and it had been a mistake not to try. Third, the handicap of landing the division in three lifts was one from which it never recovered, because it meant that only the 1st Parachute Brigade was available on the first day to capture the bridge. Fourth, not enough thought had been given to the unique problem of street fighting, and how best to keep moving down side roads and alleyways. Fifth, the intermittent nature of the wireless communications meant that effective command and control was impossible. Sixth, if additional units had reached the bridge, the defence 'would have been stronger and might have lasted longer'. Overall, however, taking into account the strength of the opposition and the 'time taken by XXX Corps', he doubted whether 'anything less than the whole division, plus the Polish Brigade, would have been able to hold the Bridge area until the arrival of the 2nd Army'.

In Urquhart's mind, therefore, his part of the plan could never have succeeded principally because XXX Corps took too long to reach him. His motivation for claiming this is obvious: it absolved him of any personal responsibility for the failure to hold the bridge. But despite being able to scapegoat XXX Corps, he was still left squirming to defend his decision to leave Divisional HQ within a few hours of landing.

'Normally at the start of the battle,' he wrote, 'there is little that a commander can do to influence affairs except to see for himself what is taking place. Often his very presence can be an encouragement to the troops and sometimes he can ginger up individuals or units who are not moving as quickly as they should. I did not visualise any major decision being required from me during the early stages – if the landings went well, which they did – but I thought that later it might be very difficult for me to get about because the battle would have been seriously joined and I would be busy.'

In retrospect, he realised that it 'might have been better' to have stayed with his HQ. Yet he could not have known that he would be 'pinned to the ground' and effectively hors de combat for some 36 hours. It was, he insisted, 'against one's nature and training to hang about at HQ'. In 9 cases out of 10, he was sure that a 'commander should get out and about once he is satisfied that the plan he has made is sound and that it has been satisfactorily launched'.

The other nails in the coffin of Operation Market were, in his view, the 'speed and efficiency of the German reaction' and the lack of close air support until late in the battle when a few 'low-flying rocket aircraft' appeared. Yet despite all the setbacks, wrote Urquhart, he and his men were able to fight on alone 'for much longer than any airborne division is designed to stay'.

He had no such praise for XXX Corps. He noted: 'I think it is possible that for once Horrocks's enthusiasm was not transmitted adequately to those who served under him, and it may be that some of his more junior officers and NCOs did not fully comprehend the problem and the importance of great speed. By and large, the impression is that they were "victory happy". They had advanced northwards very fast and had been well received by the liberated peoples, and they were now out of touch with the atmosphere of bullets and the battle . . . It took them a little time to attune themselves once more to the stern reality of tough fighting against the Germans.'

While giving the Guards Armoured Division and the US 82nd

Airborne Division due credit for their spectacular capture of
Nijmegen Bridge, Urquhart questioned the subsequent failure
to advance immediately cross-country to the Lower Rhine,
instead of following the main highway to Arnhem which – as
XXX Corps soon found out – was blocked at Elst. That might
have allowed a 'fairly strong force to reach the bank south of
our perimeter and to be ferried across'. By the time XXX Corps'
43rd Division, in the vanguard, arrived, it was too late.[9]

Urquhart concluded his official report with the words:

The operation was not 100 per cent successful and did not end
quite as we intended.

The losses were heavy but all ranks appreciate that the risks
involved were reasonable. There is no doubt that all would willingly undertake another operation under similar conditions in
the future.

We have no regrets.[10]

Of course, there *were* regrets. The one-sided fight in Holland
had destroyed Britain's original, and most experienced, airborne
formation. And yet, despite the fears of the Chief of the
Imperial General Staff, the 1st Airborne Division *was* rebuilt
around the Arnhem survivors, with the Polish Parachute
Brigade replacing the shattered 4th Parachute Brigade. It was
even slated for an operation to seize the Kiel Canal in the
spring of 1945. But that and other missions were cancelled,
and the division saw no more action for the rest of the war.
Instead, Urquhart took it to Norway in May 1945 to disarm
the large German garrison.

It was important work, but not the sudden game-changing
appearance behind enemy lines that the division had been
designed for. That role, much to the disappointment of Urquhart
and others, would be undertaken one last time by their great

rivals – and the formation that had performed miracles on D-Day – the 6th Airborne Division.

Horrocks responded to Urquhart's charge that his corps had 'been very slow in advancing' with a partial *mea culpa*. 'His criticisms are perfectly reasonable,' wrote Horrocks, 'when viewed from the airborne point of view. If I had been in his position, surrounded by the Germans, fighting desperately for eight days and always waiting for the 2nd Army which never arrived, I doubt whether I would have been half so reasonable. But if we were slow then the fault was mine because I was the commander.'

He had, he admitted, gone over the battle many times and wondered if there was anything more that he could have done. The 'sense of desperate urgency' was certainly there, 'and it was not for want of trying that we failed to arrive on time'. The one thing he might have done differently was use XXX Corps' 43rd Division on a 'different axis': instead of passing them through the Guards on the 22nd, he should have ordered its commander 'to carry out a left hook across the Lower Rhine much farther to the west [i.e. by moving cross-country] and so attack the Germans, who were engaged with the 1st Airborne Division, from behind'. The failure at Arnhem, he concluded – in yet another attempt to pass the buck – 'was primarily due to the astonishing recovery made by the German armed forces after their crippling defeat in Normandy'.

Even if XXX Corps had managed to get to Arnhem in time, and then advanced on to the North Sea, thus trapping German forces to the west, Horrocks doubted their ability to keep their supply lines open. 'Instead of XXX Corps fighting to relieve the 1st British Airborne Division,' wrote Horrocks, 'it would have been a case of the remainder of the 2nd Army struggling desperately to relieve XXX Corps cut off by the Germans north of Arnhem. Maybe in the long run we were lucky.'

Having done his best to muddy the waters, Horrocks attempted to answer the '64,000 dollar question': was Montgomery right to carry out the Arnhem operation, which meant advancing 60 to 70 miles into Holland? Would it not have been better if, after Brussels, 21st Army Group had turned north-west and cleared both sides of the Scheldt estuary to open the port of Antwerp? This, in turn, would have eased the supply issues that affected all the Allied armies on the continent.

On balance, Horrocks felt that Monty had been right to take the risk. The clearance of the Scheldt would have eased the supply problem, but it would not have shortened the war. Arnhem was designed to do just that and, on the information available, it had been a 'justified gamble'. Had the Germans not made 'one of the most remarkable military recoveries in history, it might well have succeeded'.[11]

Historians of the battle are divided over this question. In his 2018 *Arnhem: Battle for the Bridges, 1944*, Antony Beevor is adamant that it was a 'very bad plan from the start and right from the top'. The fundamental concept, he argues, 'defied military logic because it made no allowance for anything to go wrong, nor for the likely enemy reactions'. All the other deficiencies – such as bad radio communications and a lack of ground–air liaison – 'simply compounded the central problem'.[12]

William F. Buckingham is less damning. He sees it as a 'succession of needless errors', none 'fatal in itself', but collectively they tipped the balance. The lion's share of responsibility, in his view, lies with the 'airmen involved, whose decisions significantly tilted the odds against the airborne soldiers before they left the UK' by vetoing *coup-de-main* glider forces, choosing landing and drop zones too far from the targets, and restricting the number of lifts to one per day, thus providing just a single parachute brigade to secure the bridges at Arnhem on the first day. But it was then Browning's fault for approving the 'seriously flawed RAF plan', not to mention saddling the 1st Airborne Division with a 'totally inexperienced commander' in Roy Urquhart, and deliberately suppressing vital intelligence about the scale and the calibre of the likely German opposition. On the ground, too, Browning interfered with the 82nd Airborne's operations by insisting that the Nijmegen bridges be ignored in favour of the Groesbeek Heights. He did all this, Buckingham believes, out of personal ambition and incompetence, and paid the price when he was replaced as deputy commander of the First Allied Airborne Army by the infinitely better-qualified Lieutenant General 'Windy' Gale.

Others who failed in their duty, in Buckingham's view, were Horrocks (who 'failed to keep a close enough grip on his subordinate commanders'), Urquhart (who 'made a series of avoidable errors in the opening stages of the battle') and Lathbury (whose 'poorly thought out' plan for the advance into Arnhem 'needlessly dispersed the brigade's combat power precisely when it needed it most, in the first clashes with the still forming German defence'). Yet despite all the errors, Buckingham thinks – *pace* Beevor – that Operation Market Garden might still have achieved all its objectives. 'Had the German defence of the Nijmegen bridges been less stubborn,' writes Buckingham, 'and had the Guards Armoured [of XXX Corps] behaved with anything like the urgency the situation demanded, the link up could have been achieved before midnight on 20 September, only 24 hours late. The margin between success and failure was that narrow.'[13]

The last word on this epic battle should, however, come from the man who was given the division's toughest assignment: John Frost. 'People have grown so accustomed to talk about the failure at Arnhem,' wrote the legendary parachutist, 'that they do not notice that it was the delay at Nijmegen and the subsequent failures elsewhere that brought the operation to an end.' In other words, it was not doomed to failure and could have worked if everyone else had done what was expected of them.

It is both ironic and unfair that the most famous chapter in the wartime story of Britain's airborne force was ultimately a heroic failure. Frost claims he had never seen his men 'in better shape from the beginning to the bitter end'. Despite the chaos all around, there was 'a high degree of professionalism in an atmosphere of calmness' and, though men had to raise their voices to make themselves heard, there was no shouting or panic. 'People just did their job,' wrote Frost, 'had something to eat, a bit of a rest and then back to business.'[14]

But a litany of errors handicapped the 1st Airborne Division's task of capturing the Arnhem road bridge over the Lower Rhine. The plan was poor – drop and landing zones were only one side of the river and too far from the bridge; the division was delivered in three lifts, which meant that the force assigned to capture and secure the bridge on the first day was not strong enough; and intelligence that veteran SS panzer divisions were refitting in the area was, appallingly, ignored. On the ground, things went wrong – the weak radios were not up to the job; the decision-making by senior commanders, notably Lieutenant General Browning, Major General Urquhart and Brigadier Lathbury, was flawed; and XXX Corps, the ground force tasked with reaching Arnhem bridge within 48 hours, could have done with more dash.

And yet, in spite of all these blunders, the operation came perilously close to achieving all its objectives. On those grounds – and with the shortening of the war by several months at stake – it has to be seen, in the words of XXX Corps' commander Brian Horrocks, as a 'justified gamble'.[15]

The idea that the operation was not inherently doomed takes the sting out of the savage losses suffered by the 1st Airborne Division at Arnhem, whose fighting performance – particularly the 1st Parachute Brigade's defence of the bridge – was one of the finest, if not *the* finest, of the war. 'In the annals of the

British Army,' wrote Field Marshal Montgomery, 'there are many glorious deeds . . . But there can be few episodes more glorious than the epic of Arnhem, and those that follow after will find it hard to live up to the standards you have set . . . In years to come it will be a great thing for a man to be able to say: "I fought at Arnhem."'[16]

PART V

Zenith, 1945

39

Operation Varsity
– UK and Germany, March 1945

'**M**Y DEAR KATHLEEN,' WROTE Captain Alan Clements to his sister on 16 March 1945,

I thought I would take the opportunity of thanking you very much for your coming home while I was on leave. Buried in one of the Waverley novels★ I may not have seemed to have taken much notice of you but I appreciated it none the less . . .

I have made 2 parachute descents since I saw you, both cushy ones. In the first I was No 1, in the next No 8. In both cases I had a very heavy bag strapped to my leg. Conditions were ideal. Each time I rolled up my chute, lit a cigarette, and strolled over to the copse where the YMCA van is always in attendance . . .

I have been extremely busy recently rarely ceasing work before 10 o'clock at night. On the other hand it seems that I have the reverse experience of most soldiers. They start off their commissioned career, fresh and zealous, and become gradually bored, whereas as a [second lieutenant] I was far more fed up than I am as a captain with 5 years' service.

★ A hugely popular series of historical novels by Scottish author Sir Walter Scott (1771–1832).

Forbidden to give away operational secrets, Clements – then in the 6th Airborne Division – had included enough hints in this letter to convince his sister that he was preparing for another large-scale parachute drop.

The 1st Airborne Division, shattered by Arnhem, would never fight again. Instead, it was left to its sister division, the 6th, to learn from its mistakes before taking part in the last major airborne drop of the war. Clements had fought with both: his two previous bouts of active service had been as a platoon commander in the 1st Airborne Division's 1st Parachute Battalion in North Africa and Sicily (receiving a mention in despatches for good work at the Primosole Bridge). He would have dropped at Arnhem had he not, in early September 1944, accepted an offer from James Hill, his old battalion commander, to leave the 1st Battalion and join the staff of the 3rd Parachute Brigade, 6th Airborne Division, as Air Liaison Officer.

'I am sure you have done, as always, right,' wrote his bank manager father a few weeks after the switch. 'I think you deserved your comparatively easier time as ALO; I am sure you needed a change after your arduous campaigns . . . As I see it, you share in the feelings of those finer spirits to whom honour means more than wealth and self-sacrifice more than bodily comfort.'[1]

The father was trying to soothe his son's inevitable sense of guilt at having inadvertently avoided the destruction of his old battalion in Holland. Clements was, however, soon back in the firing line when his brigade, as part of the 6th Airborne Division, was rushed across the Channel to help stem the huge German counter-offensive in the Ardennes that was launched in mid-December 1944.

After the disappointment of Market Garden in September 1944, Ike Eisenhower had continued to pursue his 'Broad Front' strategy. In mid-October, Eisenhower, Montgomery and General Omar N. Bradley, commanding the 12th US Army Group, had agreed on the next phase of operations: the British would concentrate on securing the vulnerable salient in Holland, clearing the Channel coast and opening up the port of Antwerp; while the Americans advanced in the Saar and towards Cologne on the Rhine, the first step to securing the Ruhr.

This latter campaign involved pushing through the Hürtgen Forest, south of the Aachen, in a series of poorly executed battles against an obdurate foe that lasted for three months and cost the US First Army more than 30,000 casualties. General Patton's US Third Army had marginally more success in the Saar, attacking across a 60-mile front and eventually capturing Metz in mid-November. But, overall, Bradley's plan to 'smash through to the Rhine and encircle the Ruhr had failed'. He wrote: 'Between our front and the Rhine, a determined enemy held every foot of ground and would not yield. Each day the weather grew colder, our troops more miserable. We were mired in a war of ghastly attrition.'[2]

As the exhausted American troops were hunkering down for winter, the Germans struck back. In the early hours of 16 December 1944, they launched their last great offensive of the war against weakly held US positions in the Ardennes Forest, the site of their original Blitzkrieg success against the French in 1940. They enjoyed the same early breakthrough against the inexperienced American troops, who were taken completely by surprise, and either surrendered or fell back (thereby creating the famous bulge in the Allied line which gave the battle its more familiar name). But there the comparisons with 1940 end.

At the start of the war, German troops were attacking solely on the Western Front against two largely bankrupt armies: the French and the British. By late 1944 they were engaged on multiple fronts – on the Rhine, in Italy and in Poland – and against the combined might of the (rejuvenated) British and

Commonwealth, US and Soviet armies. The Allies enjoyed almost complete air superiority and a massive advantage in firepower, particularly tanks and artillery pieces. There was, as a result, no longer any realistic hope that a single offensive – however successful – could change the course of the war.

Hitler, naturally, did not agree and was prepared to gamble everything on an attack that would, he hoped, split the Western Allies, force the Canadians out of the war and the British into 'another Dunkirk'. It was 'an act of desperation', admitted one of Hitler's senior commanders, 'but we had to risk everything'.

Two panzer armies – the bulk of Germany's remaining armour – were assigned the task of reaching the Belgian port of Antwerp. Few of Hitler's generals believed this was possible, preferring a 'small solution' such as the envelopment of the US armies holding the Ardennes sector or reaching the River Meuse; others argued that the concentration of all German reserves in the west would leave the east vulnerable to the expected Russian offensive on the Vistula in Poland. But Hitler was adamant. 'In our current situation,' explained his operations chief, 'we cannot shrink from staking everything on one card.'

For the many ardent Nazis taking part, the objective was not ultimate victory but the phoenix-like rebirth of the nation (a concept made popular by the great Prussian military theorist Carl von Clausewitz). 'Fighting until the last moment,' claimed one, 'gives a people the moral strength to rise again. A people that throws in the sponge is finished for all time.'

Elite Waffen-SS formations were to be prominent in the attack: the panzer army spearheading the offensive contained no fewer than four SS panzer divisions, including the 9th Hohenstaufen that a few months earlier had decimated British airborne troops at Arnhem. They were given the pick of the best equipment and tanks, and would be responsible for numerous murders. They were not, however, the most effective soldiers. A senior commander later lamented that the non-SS panzer formations should have led the breakthrough, and not vice versa.

The initial success enjoyed by the German offensive was down to a number of factors: the element of surprise (not even middle-ranking German officers knew about the attack until the very last moment); a failure of intelligence; and the poor quality of many US troops facing the onslaught. 'The replacements,' complained one seasoned US soldier, 'both officers and men, are green. They don't know how to take care of themselves. They become casualties very fast sometimes . . . It is hard to get them worked in as members of the team.'

This enabled the Germans – attacking in a snowy landscape of 'thick woods, rocky gorges, small streams, few roads and saturated firebreak trails' – to make deep inroads into the US defences during the first few days of combat. But for every unit that capitulated without putting up a decent fight, another fought heroically, thus slowing down the German advance and buying time for reserves to plug the gap.[3]

Those reserves included the men of the 6th Airborne Division – commanded by Major General Eric Bols since 'Windy' Gale's promotion to deputy commander, First Allied Airborne Army, in early December – who were moved by train, sea and road over Christmas 1944 to defend the Meuse crossings between Dinant and Namur. By the time the 3rd and 5th Parachute Brigades were in position, the enemy advance had run out of steam. The Germans never got near the Meuse, let alone Antwerp, and the battle was effectively over by Christmas Day, though it took another month of hard fighting before the 'bulge' was flattened.

The 6th Airborne played its part – albeit in an infantry, rather than airborne, role – by advancing against the tip of the salient at the village of Bure, in Belgium, where the 5th Brigade's 13th Parachute Battalion sustained heavy casualties – including 68 killed – before the Germans withdrew.[4] Back in England, Alice Clements could only pray that her son would come through the battle unscathed. 'My darling Boy,' she wrote to Alan on 8 January 1945. 'We heard on the wireless last night that you are in action. You can guess how our thoughts are with you every moment of the day. We just can't imagine what it can be like in all this bitter cold. I say the Parachutist's Psalm★ for you . . . many times a day & the last thing before I fall asleep at night. I hope and pray this may prove to be the darkest hour before the dawn.'

Four days later, his mother wrote again, referring to a 'magnificent but to us terrible description of the 6th Airborne's attack on Bure' on the radio show *War Report*. 'Oh my darling,' she added, 'it is so terrible to think you are in all that . . . God bless and keep you.'

Her prayers for his salvation were answered when Alan and the rest of the 6th Airborne returned to the UK in late February, where he was able to steal home for a few days, to read and play chess. 'I expect you are very busy,' wrote his father when Clements was back at Brigade HQ, 'but not too much so I hope for a certain amount of leisure and reading. I am glad all is going well in the military sphere – surely the sky is lightening to wind'ard, and hope becomes once more a practical virtue and not a poet's dream!'[5]

It was wishful thinking. Three days later, Captain Clements as good as told his sister he was about to go back into action when he referred to practice jumps with heavy bags strapped to his leg, and working all hours. The operation – codenamed

---

★ There was no official 'Parachutist's Psalm', as Mrs Clements puts it, but she may have been referring to the eerily apt Psalm 91, part of which reads: 'He shall defend thee under his wings, and thou shalt be safe under his feathers: his faithfulness and truth shall be thy shield and buckler/Thou shall not be afraid of any terror by night: nor for the arrow that flieth by day.'

Varsity – was to drop two airborne divisions – the British 6th and American 17th – on the east bank of the River Rhine, north of Wesel. Their task was to seize bridges and other tactical features, and prevent German reinforcements from counter-attacking Field Marshal Montgomery's huge Anglo-American amphibious assault over the Rhine.

By March 1945, the strategic balance had tilted ever more in the Allies' favour. Defeating the Ardennes offensive had cost the western Allies 80,000 men, but Germany had lost more, along with hundreds of valuable tanks and aircraft that could not be replaced. In the east, meanwhile, the Soviets had launched their own offensive in January that, in less than a month, had moved the front line more than 300 miles from the River Vistula in Poland to the River Oder in eastern Germany, barely 50 miles from Berlin.

At a meeting with his army group commanders on 31 January, Eisenhower stressed how important it was to keep up the 'Broad Front' strategy with no weak links to prevent the Germans from making 'sudden powerful thrusts into our lines of communication'. Yet the main effort would be made by Montgomery's 21st Army Group in north-west Germany, reinforced by William Simpson's US Ninth Army. The ensuing advance was slow: Operation Veritable, an attack eastwards from Nijmegen through the Reichswald Forest, met stiff resistance from Germany's much smaller First Parachute Army; while Simpson's Operation Grenade, postponed by German flooding of the Roer Valley, made more rapid progress when it did get going on 23 February. Two weeks later, at a combined cost of 22,000 casualties, the two forces reached the west bank of the Rhine between the Dutch border and Koblenz.

Further south, Jacob Devers's US First Army captured the first bridge over the Rhine – the Ludendorff railway crossing at Remagen – with a remarkable display of daring and opportunism on 7 March. Patton's US Third Army seized its own bridgehead at Oppenheim on the 22nd. But Eisenhower still felt that the greater strategic opportunities lay in the plains of northern Germany, near Wesel, where Montgomery was meticulously planning his own leap over the Rhine.[6]

Like Market Garden, Montgomery's new offensive had separate ground and air components: Operation Plunder, the amphibious crossing of the Rhine; and Operation Varsity, the landing of paratroopers and glider-borne infantry in support on the east bank of the Rhine. There were, however, important differences that underlined the bitter lessons learned from Arnhem.

First, the drops would only begin *after* troops had got across the river, so the airborne forces would not again be marooned. Second, the airborne troops would be dropped in one wave as close to their objectives as possible. Third, the airborne troops would land within range of artillery support on the west bank of the Rhine, thus making the link-up with the advancing ground troops as easy as possible.

The one similarity with Market Garden was the decision to land the airborne troops by daylight. The risk of exposing the slow-flying gliders and transport aircraft to German flak was thought to be outweighed by the benefit of airborne troops being able to orientate themselves in daylight, assemble quickly, and locate and engage the enemy. Another compromise – forced by the limited Allied airlift capability – was the use of two airborne divisions instead of the original three (under the overall command of Major General Matthew Ridgway's US XVIII Airborne Corps). These two divisions would be the US 17th Airborne, which had never dropped but did have recent combat experience in the Ardennes; and the British 6th Airborne, which had overcome the disruption of a night jump to achieve all its main objectives with such distinction on D-Day.

The plan was to drop them east of Wesel in an area between the town and the River Issel, where they would seize wooded high ground known as the Diersfordter Forest, the town of Hamminkeln, and several bridges over the Issel. They would then be in a position to prevent German reinforcements from counter-attacking the amphibious bridgehead.[7]

Operation Plunder alone, noted the official US history, 'would rival D-Day in Normandy in terms not only of troops involved but also in build-up of supplies, transport, and special equipment, and in amount of supporting firepower, in complexity of deception plans, and in general elaboration'. It is not an exaggeration to say it was the 'most elaborate assault river crossing operation of all time'. The British, alone, stockpiled 60,000 tons of ammunition, 30,000 tons of engineer stores and 28,000 tons of other commodities. The US Ninth Army built up another 138,000 tons of supplies. The British had almost 3,500 artillery pieces, anti-tank and anti-aircraft guns, and rocket projectors; the Americans 2,070. The total number of troops involved was 250,000.

The opposition along the entire 22-mile zone of assault was estimated at 85,000, and many of those were second-rate *Volksturm* units made up of the young and the old. And that figure was probably an overestimate. The largest of the three corps that made up Germany's First Parachute Army, whose positions would be attacked, was only 12,000 strong. But while the German defenders lacked tanks and self-propelled guns, they had a reasonable complement of artillery and anti-aircraft guns, some of which had been withdrawn from Holland to deter an Allied airborne attack.[8]

To prepare the ground, thousands of Allied heavy bombers carried out a month-long campaign to destroy railway networks and bridges in north-west Germany, and prevent reinforcements from reaching the area. They also targeted German airfields, flak defences and other military installations. The combined tonnage of bombs dropped was more than 52,000.

At 3.30 p.m. on 23 March, Montgomery decided that the weather was favourable and the attack could begin. Hundreds of waiting units received the codewords: 'Two If By Sea.'

By 9 p.m. the shelling of German positions near Rees had reached a crescendo as assault waves of the British 51st (Highland) Division – part of Horrocks' XXX Corps in the British Second Army – entered the river and began to cross in their Buffalo amphibious vehicles. Within two and a half minutes, facing only light opposition, they had reached the far bank. In a matter of hours, British infantry had reached the outskirts of Rees. The German army group commander, Generaloberst Blaskowitz, responded by ordering one of his reserve formations, the 15th Panzergrenadier Division, to counterattack.

Meanwhile, the British 1st Commando Brigade had paddled across the river two miles west of Wesel and, after pausing to watch 200 RAF bombers drop 1,100 tons of explosives, advanced into the rubble-strewn city at midnight, though it was well into 24 March before they could declare it secure. Among the fatalities was the German divisional commander, Generalmajor Friedrich Deutsch.

The attacks continued through the night: both the 15th (Scottish) and the US 30th Infantry Divisions encountered little opposition as they crossed at 2 a.m., north and south of Wesel respectively; they were followed over, an hour later, by the US 79th Infantry Division on the right flank of the assault. By dawn, nine small bridgeheads had been secured on the eastern bank of the Rhine and casualties were relatively light. 'Plunder began more successfully than any of us dared hope,' wrote General Miles Dempsey, commanding the British Second Army. 'We had crossed the Rhine and so all the hard work had paid off.'[9]

The stage was now set for the arrival of the main players:

Captain Alan Clements and the other 5,000 men of the British 6th Airborne Division; and the 9,300 men of the larger US 17th Airborne Division. The combined force of more than 14,000 men made Varsity the largest airborne operation in history.

40

Jumping the Rhine
– Germany, 24–26 March 1945

A T 7 A.M. ON 24 March 1945, the first of 240 Dakota transport planes took off from airfields in East Anglia carrying the six battalions of the 3rd and 5th Parachute Brigades, 6th Airborne Division. They were followed into the air by 429 tugs – mostly Stirlings and Halifaxes – towing Horsa and Hamilcar gliders with Major General Eric Bols' Divisional HQ, the 6th Airlanding Brigade and supporting arms on board.

It was a beautiful clear day, remembered Nigel Poett, commander of the 5th Parachute Brigade, as he watched the majestic sight of 450 parachute aircraft passing below the glider stream over Belgium. 'As we approached the Rhine,' he wrote, 'we could see ahead the battlefield, covered by haze and the dust of the bombardment. At 1,000 feet we could see the area of the army administrative units and the supporting arms and artillery as we flew on.[1]

There were 540 Dakotas and 1,300 gliders in all, protected by almost 3,000 fighters. For James Hill, commander of the 3rd Parachute Brigade, the operation was a world apart – in 'skill, technique and planning' – from the 1st Battalion's primitive drop in North Africa in November 1942.[2]

Watching the huge air armada approach its target, from a nearby 'hill-top amid rolling downland', was British Prime

Minister Winston Churchill who had insisted on joining Montgomery's Tactical HQ the night before. 'It was full daylight,' wrote Churchill, 'before the subdued but intense roar and rumbling of swarms of aircraft stole upon us. After that in the course of half an hour over 2,000 aircraft streamed overhead in their formations.' Soon they returned at a different altitude, their parachutists dropped or their gliders released, and Churchill witnessed 'with a sense of tragedy aircraft in twos and threes coming back askew, asmoke, or even in flames'.[3]

At 9.52 a.m. – eight minutes ahead of schedule – the first parachutes appeared over zones to the west of Hamminkeln. Hill had asked the American pilots of the US IX Troop Carrier Command to drop the 2,200 men of his brigade 'in a clearing 1,000 by 800 yards in a heavily wooded area held by German parachute troops'. The drop took six minutes and was 'dead on target'.[4]

Hill's Brigade HQ and the 8th Battalion descended into a hail of small-arms fire from German troops dug into the edge of the Diersfordter Forest. 'During the artillery barrage,' remembered Panzergrenadier Rolf Siegel, 'we pressed ourselves into our trenches – they didn't seem quite deep enough then – only to re-emerge as the first aircraft arrived. By the time that we had set up the gun, parachutists were in the air. Within a few minutes there were hundreds of them, and many were collecting at various points. I am sure that we must have drawn attention to ourselves, because one group fell on us quickly.'

Firing an MG-42 machine gun, Siegel claimed to have shot up to 20 British parachutists before his post was overwhelmed. Wounded by grenade fragments, he was the only member of his team to survive.

Hill had told his men: 'Speed and initiative is the order of the day. Risks will be taken. The enemy will be attacked and destroyed wherever he is found.'[5]

They carried out his instructions to the letter, but many paid the price. They included Lieutenant Colonel Jeff Nicklin, commanding the 1st Canadian Parachute Battalion, whose parachute got tangled in the branches of a tall tree. As he hung there, desperately trying to free himself, he was riddled with bullets. Also killed during the drop, or soon after, was Captain Alan Clements, the bookish, chess-playing member of Hill's staff, and veteran of North Africa and Sicily, who, only eight days earlier, had told his sister how much he was enjoying life. The War Office telegram, with the news his family had been dreading since 1942, reached them on 5 April. Among the personal effects returned to his parents were a pipe, a fountain pen, a bone-handled penknife, a chess set, three volumes of poetry (Shelley, Tennyson and the *Oxford Book of English Verse*), and a history of England. Clements was 26 years old.[6]

The rest of the brigade fought on, with the 8th Battalion securing the drop zone by 11 a.m. and the other two battalions, the 9th and the 1st Canadian, occupying the western edge of the Diersfordter Forest. Major Fraser Eadie, who had taken command of the 1st Canadian, got the various companies on the move. 'By noon,' recalled Eadie, 'all companies had secured their objectives, but enemy fire that continually swept the east and south ends of the drop zone still had to be silenced. Our doctor, Captain Pat Costigan's medical crews really excelled in their rescue and evacuation of casualties through to our aid post, a somewhat battered church in the village. Those needing further major medical attention were moved to 224 Field Ambulance, who had set up an operating theatre in the priest's house across from the church. Corporal Fred Topham of the battalion medics displayed tremendous bravery in caring for and evacuating the wounded.'[7]

The 27-year-old Topham had worked in the gold mines at Kirkland Lake, Ontario, before enlisting in 1942 and then volunteering for parachute duty. A veteran of the fighting at Normandy and the Ardennes, he displayed 'gallantry of the highest order' during Operation Varsity. At 11 a.m., he went forward through intense fire to treat a badly wounded man in the open. As he worked, he was shot through the nose. Ignoring the 'severe bleeding and intense pain', he kept working on the casualty. Then he 'carried the wounded man steadily and slowly back through continuous fire to the shelter of the wood'.

During the next two hours, Topham refused to have his own wound treated until all the other casualties had been removed. When he was looked at, he persuaded the doctor not to evacuate him so that he could return to his company. As he headed that way, he came across a burning Bren gun carrier with wounded men inside. He was told by an officer there was nothing he could do: German mortar bombs were exploding, and some of the ammunition in the carrier had already ignited. But, unwilling to stand idly by while the men burned to death, Topham 'immediately went out alone in spite of the blasting ammunition and enemy fire, and rescued the three occupants of the carrier'.

One died soon after, but the other two were evacuated and owed their lives to Topham. For his 'outstanding bravery' and 'magnificent and selfless courage', he became the only member of the 6th Airborne Division to be awarded the Victoria Cross.[8]

A mile and a half to the north-east, the men of the 5th Parachute Brigade also faced heavy fire as they floated towards the ground. 'We had all been shot at on the way down,' remembered Nigel Poett, 'and, on the ground, there was considerable harassing fire. Men were struggling to get out of their parachutes and undo their kit bags, in which their weapons were carried. At the same time we were trying to recognise the landmarks to our various rendezvous.'[9]

With bullets crackling all around him, Private Ernie Elvin of the 7th Battalion slumped forward in his harness and pretended he was dead to fool the enemy. It worked because he reached the ground safely – albeit with a 'right old whack' – and quickly got organised. As he moved off, he spotted a group of dead men from the 12th Battalion, slumped around a gun. With not a mark on them, he assumed they had been killed by concussion.[10]

Sergeant Derek Glaister, also of the 7th Battalion, was shot in the left elbow as he landed close to a German 88mm anti-aircraft gun. After watching some of his colleagues land in trees where they were killed – a 'sickening sight' – he used his Sten gun to deter some approaching Germans. But as he tried to escape he was shot in the back by an officer and left for dead. Much later, he was put in a wheelbarrow by two captured airborne soldiers and taken to a German aid post.[11]

Lieutenant Philip Burkinshaw, meanwhile, of the 12th Battalion, another veteran of D-Day, had been given the job of taking out a battery of anti-aircraft guns that had 'wreaked havoc' on the slow-moving gliders. Using a classic 'Battle Drill' pincer attack, and masked by smoke, he and his No. 1 Platoon were able to capture the battery without loss. With the guns out of the way, he remembered, 'the situation became a little more relaxed, although B Company, particularly, had a tough task clearing the enemy out of numerous farm buildings'.[12]

Poett had lost a number of key members of his staff in the drop, including his brigade major, signals officer and chief administrative officer. He recalled: 'Just as the parachutists were reaching their RVs the glider element of the Brigade Group began to land in front of us and others to the south. These landings caused a considerable diversion of the fire away from us, but it was a tragic sight for us to see our gliders being hit and often blown up. The losses among the gliders were very heavy and only a small proportion of the anti-tank guns and vehicles carrying machine guns reached us. If a strong enemy counter-attack had come that afternoon we should have had a difficult time.' Fortunately, it did not.[13]

The last of 6th Airborne's three brigades – 6th Airlanding, commanded by Hugh Bellamy – began to land in gliders on zones to the north and east of Hamminkeln at 10.30 a.m. The brigade's task was to take the town and a number of bridges over the nearby River Issel.

In the last Horsa to take off from Birch airfield in Essex was young Private Denis Edwards of the 2nd Ox and Bucks who had fought with John Howard at Pegasus Bridge during the D-Day landings.* The glider's tow-rope had snapped on the ground, forcing its relegation to last place, but once in the air the tug pilot, Wing Commander Alex Blythe, flew a separate course so that he could regain his former position. As they approached the landing zone, a blizzard of shells and machine-gun bullets rose up to meet them. Edwards remembered rounds zipping through one side of the flimsy plywood fuselage and out the other side, though no one was hit. As they came in to land, 'an aileron, and the tail section were shot to pieces by shellfire'.

It was chiefly thanks to the skill of the glider pilot, Stan Jarvis, that the Horsa got down safely, and in precisely the right location. After fleeing the burning glider and taking cover, one of the soldiers told Jarvis: 'I know that we asked you to get us as close to the railway station as possible, but if you had landed any closer we would have been in the ruddy booking office.'[14]

---

* Another D-Day veteran – now a sergeant – refused to board his glider because he had a premonition that it was doomed. Arrested, stripped of his rank and later imprisoned, he did at least have the satisfaction of knowing he was right: the Horsa 'in which he would have travelled took a direct hit and was destroyed with no survivors'. (Edwards, *The Devil's Own Luck*, p. 179)

The battalion's task was to capture a railway bridge and a road bridge over the Issel river and then take a number of German defensive positions. But first they had to land safely. Major Tod Sweeney, another Pegasus veteran, recalled: 'The German anti-aircraft gunners had a marvellous target – big, slow-moving gliders going around looking for their objectives. It didn't matter too much exactly where I landed because mine was a headquarters glider. So we went zooming down, twisting and turning, but landed all right. We opened the door at the front, put the ramps down, got the Jeep out and then came under the most tremendous fire from a whole lot of steel helmets, which we could see on the side of a field by a half-made-up road.' It suddenly dawned on him that they had landed on the wrong side of the river, and were between the autobahn and the Issel 'with a Jeep and a trailer and five men and nothing else'.

Abandoning the vehicle, they made it across the river and linked up with a platoon of the Ox and Bucks, some of whom were badly wounded. After reporting to Battalion HQ, Sweeney discovered that they had achieved all their objectives, but at a fearful cost. They 'flew in 600 strong and had 110 killed in the landing', leaving the battalion's effective strength at under 300. 'The rest of the day,' noted Sweeney, 'was just a question of resisting attacks and sending out patrols. That night the Germans began a real assault, with tanks, and we had to blow the bridge over the Issel which we had seized that day to stop them coming across, which left only one of the bridges open.'[15]

The German armour was from the 116th Panzer Division, which also counter-attacked the Americans to the south. Its initial assault on the eastern end of the road bridge over the Issel, held by B Company of the 2nd Ox and Bucks, was beaten off. When it attacked a second time with heavy tanks, it was opposed by Lieutenant Hugh Clark's platoon. Clark asked his PIAT gunner if he could 'guarantee to hit the tank first shot'.

The response was non-committal, so 'in a moment of bravado' Clark grabbed the weapon, took aim and 'scored a hit with the first shot'. Fortunately, there was no reply as the tank was out of action. 'We heard the infantry scatter when the round hit,' noted Clark. 'I continued firing and scored four more hits.'

Having regrouped, the panzers attacked a third time with such violence that it seemed B Company was in danger of being overrun. When the news reached the brigade command post nearby, Hugh Bellamy ordered the destruction of the bridge. It was, he felt, preferable to allowing armour to cross the river and run amok in the brigade area. The bridge was blown at 2.35 a.m., and with it went the Germans' last opportunity to dislocate Operation Varsity. Clark was awarded the Military Cross.[16]

By the end of the first day, 24 March, the two airborne divisions had taken most of their objectives and managed to link up with each other and the 15th (Scottish) Infantry Division advancing from the Rhine, which meant the air resupply mission scheduled for the next day could be cancelled. The British airborne troops remained at their posts until the morning of 26 March when they were joined by the Churchill tanks of the 6th Independent Guards Brigade, before their breakout from the bridgehead two days later.

By then, the 6th Airborne had lost 1,344 of its original 4,976 men – including 238 killed – a casualty rate of 27 per cent. The US 17th Airborne's losses, by contrast, were 1,584 of 9,387 men – with 223 killed – a much lower attrition rate of just under 17 per cent. The vast majority of casualties were incurred on the first day of the operation, 24 March. Aerial losses, meanwhile, were surprisingly light: 55 transport planes and 16 gliders (just 3.8 per cent of the total) were destroyed; a further 339 planes were damaged.[17]

Why, then, had the losses incurred by the airborne divisions been relatively severe, and over such a short period? The US official historian questioned whether Operation Varsity had been either necessary or justified. 'In view of the weak condition of German units east of the Rhine and the particular vulnerability of airborne troops in and immediately following descent, some overbearing need for the special capability of airborne divisions would be required to justify their use. Although the objectives assigned the divisions were legitimate, they were objectives that ground troops alone under existing circumstances should have been able to take without undue difficulty and probably with considerably fewer casualties.'[18]

This is nonsense. The capture of the bridges over the Issel and the prevention of an effective German counter-attack undoubtedly assisted the ground forces in consolidating their bridgehead. The airborne forces also accounted for 1,000 German casualties and captured another 4,000, 'along with 90 major artillery pieces and many 20mm guns in multiple mountings and hundreds of machine guns'. All of these, noted Brigadier James Hill, could have been used 'to impede the deployment of the British and American armies across the Rhine'.[19]

Major General Matthew Ridgway, commanding the US XVIII Airborne Corps, noted in his report: 'The airborne drop was of such depth that all enemy artillery and rear defensive positions were included and destroyed, reducing in one day a position that might have taken many days by ground attack only.'[20]

So the lives of the Para Boys and Glider Lads were not lost in vain and, given their unique capability, Montgomery was right to use airborne forces in a well-planned operation that, as Hill put it, took 'advantage of lessons learned from the four previous operations'.[21]

Ridgway agreed, concluding his report:

(a) Concept and planning were sound and thorough, and execution flawless. The impact of the airborne divisions, at one blow, completely shattered the hostile defence, permitting prompt link-up with the assaulting 12 Corps, 1 Commando Brigade and Ninth Army to the south.

(b) The rapid deepening of the bridgehead materially increased the rapidity of bridging operations which, in turn, greatly increased the rate of build-up on the east bank, so essential to subsequent successes.

(c) The insistent drive of the Corps to the east and the rapid seizure of key terrain . . . were decisive contributions to this operation and to subsequent developments, as by it both British and United States armour were able to debouch into the North German plain at full strength and momentum.

(d) In planning and execution, the co-operation of participating air forces, both British and American, I consider completely satisfactory. There was no enemy air interception. The fighter-bombers, in their counter-flak role, were as effective as could be expected. The air supply by heavy bombers was timely and met a critical need. Troop delivery by IX Troop Carrier Command was on time, and with minor exceptions, in the correct areas.

(e) I wish particularly to record that throughout both planning and execution, the co-operation and actual assistance provided by the Commanders, Staff and troops of the British formations under which this Corps has served, which it commanded, or with which it was associated, left nothing to be desired.[22]

The First Allied Airborne Army's official report of Varsity was briefer, but just as complimentary. 'The operation,' it noted, 'was expertly planned and brilliantly executed by all concerned. It accomplished its mission with a minimum of loss both to personnel and aircraft.'[23]

In *Arnhem: Jumping the Rhine 1944 and 1945*, the best book on the subject, Lloyd Clark describes Operation Varsity as 'an outrageous success' and one that 'achieved everything that Montgomery hoped that it would'. Not only did it bring the end of the war in Europe 'one step closer', it also gave airborne forces a much-needed 'fillip in the wake of Market Garden'. Even though it was 'a conservative operation, conducted against a terminally weak enemy, its triumph was not a foregone conclusion', argued Clark. Any opposed crossing of the River Rhine is 'a great military examination, and Montgomery passed it'.

Winston Churchill, who witnessed the operation at first hand, summed up the mood of elation when he wrote in Montgomery's autograph book: 'The Rhine and all its fortresses lie behind. Once again they have been the hinge on which massive gates revolved. Once again they have proved that physical barriers are vain without the means and spirit to hold them. A beaten army, not long ago the master of Europe, retreats before its pursuers. The goal is not long to be denied to those who have come so far and fought so well under proud and faithful leaderships.'[24]

Operation Varsity, the landing of paratroopers and glider-borne infantry on the east bank of the Rhine to support an earlier amphibious crossing by ground troops, cost the British 6th Airborne Division more than a quarter of its men. Yet these heavy but far from crippling losses were a fraction of those suffered by the 1st Airborne Division at Arnhem. And, unlike the lives wasted in North Africa and Sicily to less tangible gain, Operation Varsity might conceivably have saved more lives than it cost, in helping to consolidate the Rhine bridgehead, and thus shorten the war by a few months. General Eisenhower called it 'the most successful airborne operation we carried out during the war'.[25]

Britain's airborne force had left the best until last, and in 1945 had reached its zenith.

41

Endgame

JUMPING THE RHINE IN March 1945 was the last major airborne operation of the war. Several more were planned, including Arena, the biggest of the lot, in which both British airborne divisions, plus four US airborne divisions and four air-transported US infantry divisions, were meant to establish a fortress area east of Paderborn, western Germany, towards which Omar Bradley's US 12th Army Group could advance. But it was cancelled by Eisenhower because the rapid advance of ground troops made it unnecessary.

Also called off were smaller American drops near the Black Forest, Cassel and the Eder River Dam; plans for the US 82nd and 101st Airborne Divisions to seize Berlin; and for the British 1st Airborne Division to land at Kiel and help liberate Denmark. Instead, as already noted, Roy Urquhart and the men of the 1st Airborne were sent to Norway after the German surrender on 7 May to maintain law and order, prevent sabotage and supervise the disarming of the huge German garrison of 350,000 men. This they achieved with relatively few casualties – though one officer and thirty-three men were killed, and one injured, in plane crashes – thanks to the co-operation of the German troops who, on the whole, 'were found to be orderly and still under the discipline of their officers'.

The best part of the operation was the enthusiastic reception the Norwegians gave to Urquhart and a small escort of 2nd South Staffords as they entered Oslo on 10 May, and later to the division as they participated in the ceremonies that welcomed HRH King Haakon VII back to Norway on 7 June. Before their departure at the end of the summer, men from the 1st Airborne were able to discover the truth about the fate of their comrades on Operation Freshman in 1942, arrange for their reburial with full military honours in Stavanger and Oslo, and take steps to bring some of the perpetrators to justice (see Chapter 12).[1]

In Burma, meanwhile, the last combat drop of the war was made by a composite Gurkha Parachute Battalion and supporting arms from Eric Down's 44th Indian Airborne Division* at Tawhai, near Rangoon, on 1 May 1945. The battalion's task – Operation Dracula – was to assist an amphibious assault on the Burmese capital by neutralising the Japanese defences at Elephant Point on the west bank of the River Rangoon. Preceded by Pathfinders, the main force took off in 38 Dakotas from Akyab airfield in western Burma and, despite light winds and rain, was dropped accurately over Tawhai, five miles from Elephant Point.

As the attack force closed in on the objective, it was mistakenly strafed by Allied aircraft and lost 15 killed and 30 wounded. It continued regardless and, as it began its assault, the lead company was fired on from the north by Japanese in three strongly held bunkers and some small boats. The boats were set on fire by rockets from Allied aircraft; the bunkers knocked out by small-arms fire and flame-throwers. The man chiefly responsible for neutralising the central bunker was Rifleman Manbahadur Gurung. Approaching to within 20 yards of the bunker 'over

---

* The 44th was still in the process of formation, training and reorganisation when it was ordered to provide a battalion of paratroopers to assist Operation Dracula.

completely open and bullet swept ground', he was spraying it with fire when the trigger on his flame-thrower jammed. Remaining where he was, in full view of all three bunkers, Gurung 'coolly remedied the stoppage and eventually successfully set the bunker on fire and silenced' the machine gun. For his 'coolness and personal disregard for danger at a critical juncture', he was awarded the Military Medal.

The attack cost the Gurkhas one officer and two men killed, and two wounded. The officer was 22-year-old Loretto-educated Lieutenant Robin Kynoch-Shand of the 153rd who had been awarded a Military Cross for escaping from Japanese captivity after the battle of Sangshak. The Japanese lost 37 men and 1 wounded POW. The following day, the paratroopers watched a convoy of ships take the 26th Indian Division up the river to Rangoon which it occupied without a fight.[2]

By coincidence, the last action of the war by Eric Bols's 6th Airborne Division was also on 1 May 1945 as it advanced 50 miles in daylight to capture the Hanseatic port of Wismar and become the first British formation to reach the Baltic. 'It was here,' remembered Nigel Poett, commanding the 5th Parachute Brigade, 'that we met the Russians. Fraternization was the order from higher command and we visited one another's headquarters and had a meal together. It was there that Monty came to our Divisional Headquarters to meet the Russian Commander, General Rokossovsky. Some of us were present at the meeting. Monty was very agreeable and complimentary about the Division.'[3] Since leaving the Rhine in late March, the 6th Airborne had carried out its instructions to 'maintain the speed of the advance at all costs' by fighting its way on foot across 300 miles of Germany, including forced crossings on both the River Weser and Elbe.

As the war in Europe drew to a close, plans were being drawn up for the recapture of Malaya from the Japanese – Operation

Zipper – on 31 August 1945. It required one airborne division and, as the 44th Indian was still not fully operational, the British 6th Airborne was earmarked. On 17 May – 10 days after VE Day – the division returned to England from Germany for some leave before its redeployment to the Far East. In the event, the plans for Zipper were altered and only the 5th Parachute Brigade was required for the capture of Singapore. It left for India by air and sea in July 1945 but never saw action because America's dropping of two atomic bombs on Hiroshima and Nagasaki, on 6 and 9 August respectively, prompted the Japanese government to surrender unconditionally on 14 August.

It had been the War Office's intention to retain the 1st Airborne Division as Imperial Strategic Reserve in the Middle East. But when the experienced 6th Airborne was no longer required in the Far East, it took on that role in the post-war British Army and the 1st Airborne – understrength, despite a drive to reconstitute it after Arnhem, and only partially trained – was disbanded on 15 November 1945.[4]

The 6th Airborne Division, deployed to Palestine as the Jewish insurgency against British rule intensified in late 1945, was tasked with internal security, helping to enforce curfews and search towns and rural settlements for arms and guerrillas. 'The Jews were determined to make Palestine their home,' noted Major John Waddy of the 9th Parachute Battalion, 'and if Britain got in their way they would fight us; indeed, many of their clandestine and even pseudo-official organisations had been preparing for it for some years . . . In between cordons and searches and curfews we were able to carry out some training but on the whole our true military life was fruitless for some two and a half years.'

In late 1947, as the British prepared to leave Palestine, the division was engaged by both Arab and Jewish forces fighting a civil war. The last of its troops were withdrawn from Haifa on

18 May 1948, a few days after Israeli independence. It had lost 58 killed and 236 wounded to enemy action. 'No one had any regrets,' wrote Waddy, who had been shot in the back and badly injured by a terrorist, 'at leaving the Holy Land.'[5]

On its return to the UK in 1948, the 6th Airborne Division was also disbanded as part of the reduction in the size of the post-war British Army. Henceforth, Britain's airborne capability would be confined to a single regular parachute brigade.

42

Aftermath

To witness with his own eyes the success of Operation Varsity was a moment of vindication for Winston Churchill. Almost five years earlier – in the dark days of June 1940, when Britain faced the Axis powers alone – he had almost singlehandedly willed Britain's airborne forces into being by demanding the 'development of parachute troops on a scale equal to 5,000' who could take the fight to the enemy.[1] It took years to get anything like that number, largely because the RAF, still fixated on strategic bombing, was unwilling to divert more than a few of its precious resources to the training and transporting of paratroopers and glider-borne troops who were mostly recruited from – and would remain part of – the British Army. But Churchill's unwavering fervour, and the single-minded determination of key pioneers like Louis Strange, John Rock, Eric Down, Richard 'Windy' Gale and Frederick 'Boy' Browning, meant that the size and scope of airborne operations became increasingly ambitious.

It was a long way for that raw band of volunteers who paraded at Perham Down on an overcast summer day in 1940 to have come. Handicapped during its early years by inter-service rivalry and a chronic lack of suitable aircraft and equipment, Britain's airborne force gradually expanded, learned from its mistakes and proved its worth in an impressive number of roles, from small-scale raids (Colossus, Biting and Freshman), and fighting like traditional infantry (North Africa and India), to its favoured option: dropping behind enemy lines to secure vital ground and infrastructure in conjunction with a ground offensive (Ladbroke, Fustian, Tonga, Market and Varsity).

It was in this final – and iconic – capacity that Britain's airborne force made its most significant contribution to Allied victory during D-Day in June 1944 and the Crossing of the Rhine in Operation Varsity, March 1945; but even at Arnhem in September 1944, where they ultimately came up short, their superhuman fighting spirit meant that a flawed operation very nearly succeeded in shortening the war. And it was by learning the lessons of Arnhem – notably the need to drop airborne troops in one wave and as close as possible to their objective, and their relief – that Operation Varsity's planners allowed the airborne soldiers to showcase what they could do.

Three years later, Winston Churchill (by then Leader of the Opposition) spoke at the unveiling of a combined memorial to the fallen of the Airborne Forces, the Commandos and the Submarine Branch of the Royal Navy. 'All were volunteers,' he said.

> Most were highly skilled and intensely trained. Losses were heavy and constant, but great numbers pressed forward to fill the gaps. Selection could be most strict where the task was forlorn. No units were so easy to recruit as those over which Death ruled with daily attention . . . We think of the Airborne Force and Special Air Service men who hurled themselves unflinching into the void – when we recall all this we may feel sure that nothing of which we have any knowledge or record has ever been done

by mortal men which surpasses the splendour and daring of their feat of arms.

Truly we may say of them as of the Light Brigade at Balaclava, 'When shall their glory fade?'[2]

Churchill was right: the glory of Britain's airborne troops did not fade. But their future use was uncertain. On 15 August 1945 – Victory over Japan Day – Field Marshal Sir Alan Brooke asked two of Britain's most successful wartime commanders, Field Marshals Sir Harold Alexander and Sir Bernard Montgomery, to assess the value of airborne forces.

Alexander's experience of airborne operations was limited to the campaigns in Sicily and the south of France (where the 2nd Independent Parachute Brigade had dropped near Fréjus on the coast and assisted the landing and rapid advance of the US Seventh Army). The different results in the two campaigns had, he noted, shown 'the strides that have already been made in ensuring the precision with which these operations can be carried out'.

As for the future, Alexander could see the value of attacking the enemy's 'open flank' by using airborne forces 'over the top'. He added: 'Apart from carrying troops tactically into battle, as parachutists and glider-borne units, the air can provide the most rapid means for switching our resources to any threatened point . . . There is, therefore, in the future Army, a need for airborne divisions to form the spearhead of airborne operations, while all formations must be trained to air movement, both as a means of providing the follow-up to the airborne assault and for rapid movement to any part of the world where British troops may be required.'

Montgomery, with direct experience of all the major airborne operations from 1943 to 1945, was even more effusive about the record and potential of such forces. From Sicily to the crossing of the Rhine, wrote Montgomery, they had proved to be a 'battle winning factor in deliberate operations'. In all these campaigns, even the disastrous Operation Market, 'the chief advantages which accrued from the employment of airborne troops were secured as a result of their descent from the air'. In other words, airborne troops should be used in an airborne manner.

Their value for Montgomery, however, was not merely material. The airborne threat could also be used to 'great advantage', as it was in June 1944 when it persuaded the Germans 'to retain major formations in the Pas de Calais area' after the initial landings in Normandy; and again in 1945 when it was used to 'inspire uncertainty and confusion in the enemy's mind and to upset his planning'.

There were some limitations to their use, chiefly weather, but Montgomery was convinced that scientific advances would make this factor 'less important in the future'.

Overall, he was passionately in favour of airborne forces. A nation without them, he wrote, would 'be severely handicapped and at a great disadvantage in future warfare'. There was no doubt in his mind that they would 'continue to have an important role in battle, and they definitely justify the expenditure of effort which they involve'.

His advice, however, was to simplify the organisation of airborne troops by doing away with airlanding brigades and concentrating instead on parachute brigades with a glider element for delivering heavy weapons. This was acted upon in early 1947 when the 6th Airborne Division's 6th Airlanding Brigade was replaced by the 1st Parachute Brigade. Ultimately, the glider as a military technology was doomed: the advent of the helicopter rendered it obsolete. On 31 August 1957, the Glider Pilot Regiment was disbanded and the new Army Air Corps was born.[3]

By the end of the Second World War, Britain's airborne force was riding high. Churchill's desperate gamble had paid off. But having come so far, so fast, and along an exponential learning curve – at a huge cost in men, materiel and, in some cases, reputations – the irony is that these crack troops would only be used in the way they were intended on one more occasion: the Suez Crisis of November 1956 when 668 men of the 3rd Parachute Battalion were dropped on El Gamil airfield at Port Said. That operation was a complete success and the airfield captured within 30 minutes at a cost of 4 men killed and 3 officers and 29 men wounded in the assault and subsequent fighting.[4]

Since Suez, and the advent of helicopters (which can deliver men and equipment to the battlefield much more safely and efficiently than either gliders or parachutes), British parachute battalions have only fought in their default role as assault light infantry. It is, of course, a role in which they excel, as demonstrated in Aden, Borneo, the Falklands, Sierra Leone, Iraq and Afghanistan, even if occasionally, as in the infamous 'Bloody Sunday' massacre of unarmed Irish civilians in Londonderry in 1972, the paratroopers' above-average aggression can have unhappy consequences.

Other nations, however, have carried out large-scale parachute drops since the Second World War: the Americans in North Korea in 1950 and 1951, Grenada in 1983, Panama in 1989, Afghanistan in 2001 and Iraq in 2003; the Pakistanis in Indian Punjab in 1965 and in their own Malakand region in 2009; the Indonesians during their occupation of East Timor in 1975; and the French in Vietnam in 1954 and Mali in 2013.

Britain could still deploy mass parachutists if it chose to. At the time of writing, the British Army retains an airborne capability in the form of four battalions of the Parachute Regiment: the 1st Battalion, which is permanently under the command of the Director Special Forces as part of the Special Forces Support Group (SFSG); and the 2nd, 3rd and 4th Battalions, which are the parachute infantry component of 16 Air Assault Brigade, a rapid reaction force which can deploy at a moment's notice by parachute, helicopter and air-landing transport plane anywhere in the world. 'Paratroopers,' explains the official British Army website, 'are trained to conduct a range of missions from prevention and pre-emption tasks, to complex, high intensity war fighting. Watchwords are professionalism, resilience, discipline, versatility, courage and self-reliance.'[5]

Britain's much respected Special Forces – the Special Air Service (SAS), Special Boat Service (SBS) and Special Reconnaissance Regiment (SRR) – are also parachute trained. They can execute jumps from as high as 30,000 feet using oxygen: both High Altitude, High Opening (HAHO), which is free falling for 8 to 10 seconds, deploying the parachute at around 25,000 feet before a gentle flight to the ground that can take up to 80 minutes, cover a distance of more than 20 miles, and allow teams to land silently inside enemy territory, without the noise of their aircraft alerting the opposition; and High Altitude, Low Opening (HALO), which involves jumping from the same height, but not deploying the parachute until 2,000 feet, thus allowing the team to land together, usually at night and even into water. Yet the innate vulnerability of airborne troops – who, by definition, are forced to fight at the outset without heavy weapons or close support – was exposed most recently by the costly attempt by helicopter-borne Russian airborne troops to capture Hostomel Airport near Kyiv in February 2022.

During the Second World War, the British Army learned through harsh experience that a successful airborne operation required certain pre-conditions: surprise, speed, reliable resupply, nearby ground support and air superiority. They are lessons that other nations would do well to heed.

Inserted behind enemy lines with only light weapons, unsupported by tanks and heavy artillery, airborne troops are and always were a singular breed. Field Marshal the Viscount Montgomery of Alamein, Commandant Colonel of the Parachute Regiment, put it best in his handwritten Foreword to Hilary St George Saunders's wartime history *The Red Beret*, published in 1950:

What manner of men are these who wear the maroon red beret?

They are firstly *all* volunteers, and are then toughened by hard physical training. As a result they have that infectious optimism and that offensive eagerness which comes from physical well-being.

They have 'jumped' from the air and by so doing have conquered fear.

Their duty lies in the van of the battle; they are proud of this honour and have never failed in any task.

They have the highest standards in all things, whether it be skill in battle or smartness in the execution of all peace time duties.

They have shown themselves to be as tenacious and determined in defence as they are courageous in attack.

They are, in fact, men apart – every man an Emperor.[6]

Postscript

W HAT BECAME OF THOSE airborne pioneers who survived?
The most senior, **Frederick 'Boy' Browning** (CB,
DSO) had not covered himself with glory during Operation
Market Garden, to say the least, yet he ended the war as a knight,
a lieutenant general and chief of staff to Admiral Lord Louis
Mountbatten, Supreme Allied Commander in South East Asia.
After a spell as military secretary at the War Office, he acted as
comptroller and treasurer to HRH Princess Elizabeth and, after
she became Queen, treasurer to her husband the Duke of
Edinburgh. He retired in 1959, after a suspected nervous breakdown, and died six years later following the partial amputation
of his left leg. 'Whatever the future of airborne forces may
be,' wrote Victor Dover in *The Sky Generals*, 'the insignia of
Bellerophon riding through the sky on the winged horse Pegasus
will always remain the symbol of those who wear the maroon
beret, and of the man who was its inspiration.'[1]

Undoubtedly the finest divisional commander was **Richard
'Windy' Gale** (CB, OBE, DSO, MC and Legion of Merit).
Having relinquished command of the 6th Airborne to Eric Bols
in late 1944, he helped to prepare Operation Varsity with Major
General Ridgway, and later took his 1st Airborne Corps HQ to

India where its plans to assist the liberation of Bangkok were cut short by the dropping of the atomic bombs. He commanded, in turn, the 1st Infantry Division in Palestine, all troops in Egypt and the Mediterranean, and the British Army of the Rhine. He also did a stint as director general of Military Training and was knighted. His final posting was as Deputy Supreme Allied Commander in Europe, with the rank of general. He died in 1982, at the age of 86. Dover wrote of him: 'The words of General Carl von Clausewitz seem appropriate to summarise General "Windy" Gale – "When personal courage is united to high intelligence, the command must naturally be nearest to perfect."'

It was the 1st Airborne Division's misfortune to be led during its biggest operations in 1943 and 1944 by two men who lacked Gale's judgement and experience: George Hopkinson and **Robert 'Roy' Urquhart** (CBE, DSO). Hopkinson paid the price of venturing too close to the front and was killed in 1943; Urquhart survived the bloodbath at Arnhem, but it was his last battle. After the division was disbanded in late 1945, he served as Director of the Territorial Army and the Cadet Force, and commanded the 16th Airborne Division (T.A.), the Lowland District and British Troops in Malaya during the Communist insurgency. In 1958, three years after retiring from the army, he published *Arnhem*, his account of the famous battle. He also acted as a military consultant for Richard Attenborough's 1977 feature film, *A Bridge Too Far*, in which he was played by actor Sean Connery. He died in 1988, at the age of 87.

Eric 'Dracula' Down (KBE, CB) never got to command airborne troops in action. Sent to India in early 1944 to raise the 44th (Indian) Airborne Division, he watched from the sidelines as his replacement Roy Urquhart presided over the destruction of the 1st Airborne Division at Arnhem. Although elements of the 44th saw combat, it was never committed as a complete formation. Down did, however, play a part in organising Chindit operations in Burma and jumped as an observer with the 2nd Independent Parachute Brigade in southern France. In late 1946, he commanded the 4th Infantry Division in Greece during the civil war, then all British troops and finally the British Military Mission which played a vital role in helping the Greek Army defeat the Communist insurgents. In 1952 he was promoted to lieutenant general and given the Southern Command. A year later he was knighted. He died in 1980 at the age of 78. A contemporary said of him, 'Not a good-looking officer, but devilish steady!'[2]

James Hill ended the war as military governor of Copenhagen with a chestful of medals that included the DSO and two Bars, Military Cross, Légion d'Honneur, Silver Star and the King Haakon VII Liberty Cross. He helped to establish the Parachute Regimental Association, but left the army as a brigadier and enjoyed a successful business career. He lived until the ripe age of 95, dying in 2006.[3]

Hill's colourful successor as boss of the 1st Parachute Battalion, **Alastair Pearson**, was awarded a DSO and three Bars,* as well as a Military Cross. Having relinquished command of the 8th Battalion in 1945 because of ill health, he returned to Glasgow to run his bakery. He later switched to farming, and remained an active member of the Territorial Army as commander of the 15th (Scottish Volunteer) Parachute Battalion and Chief of the Army Cadet Force in Scotland. After his death in 1995, at the age of 80, the then HRH the Prince of Wales, Colonel-in-Chief of the Parachute Regiment, described him as 'one of the greatest leaders of the Second World War . . . I doubt if any soldier has made a greater contribution to the Parachute Regiment than Alastair

---

* One of 16 officers to be awarded the equivalent of four DSOs, Pearson received his within the shortest time gap: two years.

Pearson. His exploits are legendary as must be indicated by the many decorations awarded to him in the field for outstanding leadership and conspicuous gallantry.'[4]

Like Hill and Pearson, **Geoffrey Pine-Coffin** (DSO and Bar, MC) fought with distinction in both the 1st and 6th Airborne Divisions: commanding the 3rd Battalion in North Africa; and the 7th Battalion in Normandy, the Ardennes and Germany. After the war he took the 7th Battalion to Palestine, and returned in 1947 to command the 1st Devons. He later became Colonel of the Parachute Regiment and Commandant of the Army Motor Transport School. He retired in 1958 and died 16 years later at the relatively young age of 65.[5]

John Frost (DSO and Bar, and MC), the legendary commander of the 2nd Parachute Battalion from 1942 until his capture at Arnhem in 1944, spent most of the rest of the war at Oflag IX-A/H at Spangenburg, near Kassel. He was receiving treatment for his chronic ankle wound at the POW hospital at Obermassfeldt in Thuringia when he was freed by spearhead units of Patton's US Third Army in March 1945. Having recovered his health, he commanded the 1st Airborne Division's Battle School in Norway, and later took the 2nd Battalion (now part of the 6th Airborne Division) to Palestine in 1946 where his wife Jean, serving with the division's YMCA unit, was struck in the stomach by a stray Jewish terrorist bullet but survived.

After a spell at the Staff College at Camberley, Frost served as the chief of staff (GSO1) of the 17th Gurkha Division in Malaya, commander of the 52nd (Lowland) Division, and boss of Malta Land Forces. He retired in 1968 with the rank of major general and, eight years later, acted as a military consultant on Attenborough's *A Bridge Too Far* (in which he was played by Anthony Hopkins). He was 'agreeably surprised' by the script and had only one 'adamant objection': that was to the scene where the Germans sent Sergeant Halliwell back to him with a request to meet the German commander, under a flag of truce, to discuss a surrender. Frost's actual response was: 'Tell them to go to hell.' In the script, however, Frost meets the German general and tells him he has 'no room for him or his soldiers as prisoners, and so he would have to continue fighting'. It was, noted Frost, 'magnificent cinema, but so divorced from reality that it was laughable'.

In the end, a 'very unsatisfactory and most unrealistic compromise was reached', in which one of Frost's officers sarcastically informed the Germans that they could not accept their surrender.[6]

In 1977, his initial qualms dispelled by Freddie Gough, Frost accepted the Dutch authorities' offer to rename the reconstructed Arnhem road bridge the John Frostbrug (John Frost Bridge). He saw it as a 'signal honour' for the whole battalion.

Three years later, he published a graphic and well-received memoir of his wartime service, *A Drop Too Many*. It was dedicated to 'every man in the Second Battalion of the Parachute Regiment: past, present, and in the future'. He died in 1993.[7]

After leaving the army with the rank of lieutenant colonel in 1948, **Terence Otway** (DSO) worked in colonial development in Africa, and in insurance, newspapers, import/export and leisure in the UK. Even before his retirement in 1979, he lobbied for the building of monuments to the Parachute Regiment in Normandy, and helped to improve war disability and widows' pensions. In 1997, he was present when the mayor of Merville-Franceville Plage unveiled a bronze bust in his honour in the grounds of the Merville Battery Museum. It depicted him as he was on D-Day, aged 28, during the assault on the battery. When he died in 2006, aged 92, his obituarist in *The Times* noted that, in the history of airborne forces, he would always be remembered for that astonishing feat.[8]

The same might have been said of **John Howard** (DSO, Croix de Guerre) for the daring capture of the bridges over the

Caen Canal and the Orne river by D Company of the 2nd Ox and Bucks Light Infantry. Like Otway, Howard would never command troops in battle again. In his case, a bad car accident in November 1944 left him with a fractured thigh and a broken pelvis, serious injuries that required multiple operations and a long convalescence. In 1946, after a spell as temporary commander of Alastair Pearson's 8th Parachute Battalion, he was invalided out of the British Army and joined the National Savings Office in Oxford. A 28-year career as a civil servant ended with his retirement as head of the Ministry for Agriculture and Fisheries for Cornwall and the Scilly Isles. 'I tried to put into my office work,' he remembered, 'the same conscientious attention to detail and leadership qualities that I had applied in the Army.'

In 1961, Howard was a technical advisor for the feature film about the D-Day landings, *The Longest Day*, based on the Cornelius Ryan book of the same name. His part was played by Richard Todd who, as a young 7th Parachute Battalion officer, had helped to repel the German counter-attacks. Later that decade, Howard met and became good friends with Hans von Luck, the commander of Panzergrenadier-Regiment 125 who had waited in vain for the order to counter-attack the airborne troops (and who, in 1989, would publish a detailed account of this and his other war service in *Panzer Commander*). Howard often lectured cadets in the UK and other NATO countries, and made regular trips to Pegasus Bridge on the D-Day anniversary and as a guest speaker. Eight years after Howard's death in 1999, at the age of 86, his daughter Penny arranged for the posthumous publication of his private papers, *The Pegasus Diaries*.[9]

Tony Deane-Drummond (DSO, OBE, MC and Bar), one of the 2nd Commando originals, ended the war with the rare distinction of having escaped twice from enemy captivity. At Arnhem, he tried to evade capture by swimming the Rhine, but was caught near the south bank when he stumbled into a German slit trench. Taken to a house on the outskirts of the town that was being used as a temporary prisoner-of-war 'cage', he met and exchanged stories with Freddie Gough and Tony Hibbert. Having all agreed that their best hope of escaping was while they were still in Holland, Deane-Drummond decided to hide in a wall-cupboard in the house until the Germans left. This ruse eventually worked, but only after he had spent an excruciating 13 days in the tiny cupboard – just 12 inches deep and 7 feet high – while the Germans used the room to interrogate Allied prisoners. 'I stood first on one leg, then the other,' he recalled. 'There was no room to sit down because the cupboard was too shallow. I managed to sleep all right, although occasionally my knees would suddenly give way and would drop forward against the door with a hammer-like noise.'

The interrogations he found fascinating. British soldiers were instructed to give only their name, rank and number. 'The Germans knew this, of course,' noted Deane-Drummond, 'but tried every guile to get more information. The usual trick was to pretend they were filling out a card for the Red Cross. They would then ask a series of innocuous questions until the prisoner was at ease, when a question of military importance would be tossed in. I was surprised that very few officers or men gave only their number, rank and name.'

Having finally escaped from the house on 5 October, Deane-Drummond contacted the Dutch resistance and was among the group of 130 airborne fugitives who, as part of Operation Pegasus, crossed the Lower Rhine and rejoined the Allies. He later commanded the 22nd Regiment, SAS, in Malaya and Oman (winning a DSO for the assault on the Jebel Akhdar in 1959), became the British gliding champion and wrote two memoirs, *Return Ticket* and *Arrow of Fortune*. He retired from the army with the rank of major general and died in 2012 at the age of 95.[10]

Deane-Drummond's fellow airborne pioneer, **Tony Hibbert**

(MC), also escaped captivity in Holland and, with Brigadier Lathbury and Major Tatham-Warter, helped to organise Operation Pegasus. But, soon after crossing the river, he broke both his legs in a vehicle accident as he was being driven to Nijmegen on the bonnet of a grossly overloaded Jeep. Discharged from hospital but still on crutches in April 1945, he joined T-Force – a joint US-British military mission to secure German scientific and industrial technology – and managed to enter Kiel and persuade Admiral Doenitz to surrender all German forces in Schleswig-Holstein and Denmark to the Allies. Invalided out of the army in 1947, he returned to the family drinks business and revived its fortunes by opening a chain of off-licences and selling canned soft drinks, managing along the way to introduce the ring-pull can to Britain. He died in 2014 at the age of 96.[11]

Of the other-rank survivors, **Reg Curtis** never recovered the use of his shattered right leg and it was amputated below the knee by a British doctor in Apeldoorn Hospital in Holland in November 1944. He was eventually moved to Stalag XIB prisoner-of-war camp in Lower Saxony where he remained until he was repatriated in the spring of 1945. By then his weight had dropped from its original 14 stone to just 8. After the war he married and started a landscape gardening business at Chestfield in Kent. He also wrote an account of his wartime service, *Churchill's Volunteer*, which was published in 1994. When he died in 2015, at the age of 95, his local newspaper described him as 'the last of the original paratroopers'.[12]

Denis Edwards was still only 20 years old when the war ended, one of only 40 of the original 180 members of D Company, 2nd Ox and Bucks Light Infantry, to survive the Normandy campaign. He went on to serve in the Ardennes, jump the Rhine (with Operation Varsity), and fight all the way to the Baltic. When he returned home without a scratch, someone commented: 'This man must have had the devil's own luck.'

Completing his service in the Parachute Regiment, Edwards returned to Kent and worked as an estate agent. He died in 2008, nine years after publishing his wartime memoir *The Devil's Own Luck: Pegasus Bridge to the Baltic 1944–45*. He concluded: 'We had to accept, with total conviction, that each and every one of us had a time to be born, a time to live and a time to die . . . Our job was simply to fight an enemy who threatened our homeland, and, hopefully, to avenge the deaths of our comrades, by killing a few more of the enemy before our own time was up and it was our turn to die.'[13]

Acknowledgements

The original plan for this book was to follow the fortunes of a single company of British paratroopers through the Second World War. But when my publisher Arabella Pike ran the idea past her father Hew, who had himself commanded 3 Para with distinction during the Falklands conflict, he asked: 'Why stop at a company? Why not tell the whole story of British Airborne from its creation in 1940 to its last major operation, the crossing of the Rhine, in March 1945?' I did not have a convincing answer, and *Sky Warriors* is the result.

Many people helped with the research and writing of this book. I would particularly like to thank my fellow historians Damien Lewis and Rob Lyman; Mike Beckett, author of *The Commando Compendium*; Paul Woodage of WW2TV; Captain Jonathan Astley, Chair of the Worcestershire Yeomanry Museum Trust; Christopher Jary, Chair of the Keep Military Museum Trust; James McKemey; Roger Sargologo; Teresa Bonfiglio; Jeremy Solel; Will Pike; and my daughters Tamar and Tashie who transcribed interviews with veterans. But my greatest debt of gratitude is to Iona McLaren, the former literary editor of the *Daily Telegraph*, who went through multiple drafts of the manuscript with a fine-tooth comb, suggesting cuts, rewrites and big picture perspective that have hugely improved the book. Her reward: a request from me to work her magic on my next history.

The research for this project was completed in multiple archives and thanks are due to the staffs of the Asian and African Collection of the British Library, the Imperial War Museum, the Liddell Hart Centre for Military Archives, the National Archives, the Imperial War Museum and the National Army Museum in London; the Durham University Archives; the Keep Military Museum, Winchester; the Mahn Centre for Archives and Special Collections, Ohio University Libraries; and the Worcestershire Yeomanry Museum.

Lastly, I'd like to thank my literary agent Caroline Michel; my publisher Arabella Pike and her excellent team at William Collins, notably Katherine Patrick, Sam Harding, Iain Hunt, Julian Humphries and Matt Clacher; and, last but not least, my wife Lou and daughters Nell, Tamar and Tashie, who can't quite believe that, thirty years after the first one was published, I've just finished my twentieth book.

Endnotes

INTRODUCTION

1. Evelyn Waugh, *Unconditional Surrender* (London: Chapman & Hall, 1961), Chapter V.
2. Michael Davie (ed.), *The Diaries of Evelyn Waugh* (London: Weidenfeld & Nicolson, 1976), p. 556.
3. William F. Buckingham, *Paras: The Birth of British Airborne Forces from Churchill's Raiders to 1st Parachute Brigade* (Stroud: Tempus, 2005), pp. 11–12; S. J. Anglim, 'Airborne Warfare Before 1940', https://www.paradata.org.uk/media/1378 [accessed 20 January 2022]
4. London, The National Archives (TNA), CAB 120/414, Churchill's memorandum to Ismay, 5 June 1940.
5. *Hansard* (Parliamentary Proceedings), House of Commons Debates, Volumes 360–2, 13 and 22 May, 4 Jand 26 June 1940.
6. John Howard and Penny Bates, *The Pegasus Diaries: The Private Papers of Major John Howard DSO* (Barnsley: Pen & Sword, 2006), pp. 2–22, 45, 53, 85–93.
7. John Golley, *The Big Drop: The Guns of Merville, June 1944* (London: Jane's, 1982), p. 58.

1 OPERATION COLOSSUS
– SOUTHERN ITALY, 10–12 FEBRUARY 1941

1. TNA, CAB 106/8, Operation Colossus, 'A narrative of the execution of the operation based on Information given by Lt. A. J. Deane-Drummond, Royal Signals', p. 1.

2. Anthony Deane-Drummond, *Arrows of Fortune* (London: Leo Cooper, 1992), pp. 17–18; 'A narrative of the execution of the operation based on Information given by Lt. A. J. Deane-Drummond, Royal Signals', pp. 2–3; Anthony Deane-Drummond, *Return Ticket* (London: The Popular Book Club, 1945), p. 29; https://www.paradata.org.uk/people/percy-p-clements [accessed 24 February 2022]; TNA, DEFE 2/152, 'Colossus', Report by Major Pritchard (from Sulmona POW Camp), 27 December 1941.
3. 'A narrative of the execution of the operation based on Information given by Lt. A. J. Deane-Drummond, Royal Signals', p. 3.
4. Deane-Drummond, *Return Ticket*, pp. 29–30; 'A narrative of the execution of the operation based on Information given by Lt. A. J. Deane-Drummond, Royal Signals', p. 3.
5. Deane-Drummond, *Arrows of Fortune*, p. 13.
6. https://www.paradata.org.uk/people/fortunato-picchi [accessed 18 February 2022]; TNA, DEFE 2/153, Enquiries regarding Pte P. Dumont, Major Macfie to Keyes, 29 September 1941.
7. Deane-Drummond, *Arrows of Fortune*, pp. 19–20.
8. Deane-Drummond, *Arrows of Fortune*, pp. 20–2; Deane-Drummond, *Return Ticket*, pp. 32–5.
9. TNA, DEFE 2/152, 'Colossus', Appendix X, Report on Pichi [*sic*] by Lt. A. J. Deane-Drummond, Royal Signals.
10. Deane-Drummond, *Arrows of Fortune*, pp. 22–4; Deane-Drummond, *Return Ticket*, pp. 35–40; 'A narrative of the execution of the operation based on Information given by Lt. A. J. Deane-Drummond, Royal Signals', p. 4.

2 'ARE YOU READY FOR THE FIGHT?'
– UK, JUNE–JULY 1940

1. 'Nominal Roll of No. 2 Commando as it was on the day it was formed', 22 June 1940, at http://gallery.commandoveterans.org/cdoGallery/v/units/2/2+cdo+nom+roll/Nominal+roll+of+the+first+2+Commando+later+11+SAS+Bn.jpg.html [accessed 19 January 2022]
2. TNA, WO 32/4723, Brig. O. M. Lund, Deputy Director of Military Operations (DDMO) to the Director of Recruiting and Organisation (DRO), War Office, 12 June 1940.
3. Chinnery, quoted in Max Arthur, *Men of the Red Beret: Airborne Forces 1940 to Today* (London: Century Hutchinson, 1990; repr. 1992), pp. 8–9.

4. TNA, CAB 120/414, Churchill's memorandum to Major General Hastings Ismay (Military Secretary to the Cabinet), 3 June 1940.

5. TNA, CAB 120/414, Churchill's memorandum to Ismay, 5 June 1940.

6. TNA, WO 32/4723, DRO to the GOC-in-Chief, Northern and Southern Commands, War Office, 9 June 1940.

7. Buckingham, *Paras:* pp. 62–4.

8. Buckingham, *Paras*, pp. 11–12; S. J. Anglim, 'Airborne Warfare Before 1940', https://www.paradata.org.uk/media/1378 [accessed 20 January 2022]

9. Buckingham, *Paras*, pp. 36–8.

10. Buckingham, *Paras*, pp. 20–21, 38–42; https://trove.nla.gov.au/newspaper/article/17267585/1188781 [accessed 30 January 2023]; https://theses.gla.ac.uk/1593/1/2001buckinghamphd.pdf [accessed 30 January 2023]

11. Buckingham, *Paras*, pp. 28–9, 42–4.

12. Buckingham, *Paras*, pp. 45–7.

13. Buckingham, *Paras*, pp. 52–6.

14. Buckingham, *Paras*, p. 70.

15. Winston Churchill, *The Second World War*, 6 vols (London: Cassell & Co., 1949–54), II, pp. 102–4; TNA, CAB 120/414, Churchill to Ismay, 5 June 1940.

16. Churchill, *The Second World War*, II, p. 127.

17. TNA, DEFE 2/791, Churchill to Ismay, 22 June 1940.

18. TNA, DEFE 2/791, Ismay to Churchill, 24 June 1940.

19. TNA, WO 32/4723, 'Record of a Meeting Held [at the War Office] at 12.0 Noon on 20th June 1940 to Consider the Organization of Irregular Forces'.

20. Buckingham, *Paras*, p. 76.

21. Buckingham, *Paras*, pp. 83–4; Jeremy Archer, 'From Dorset Yeoman to Distinguished Airman', at https://www.keepmilitarymuseum.org/info/from+dorset+yeoman+to+distinguished+airman+-+the+story+of+wing+commander+louis+strange [accessed 25 January 2022]

22. TNA, DEFE 2/791, Group Captain Bowman to Lieutenant General Bourne, 29 June 1940.

23. TNA, DEFE 2/791, Air Commodore Slessor to Lieutenant General Bourne, 4 July 1940.

24. TNA, DEFE 2/791, Bourne to Slessor, 5 July 1940.

3 'I'M AFRAID I'VE GOT SOME BAD NEWS'
– UK, JULY–SEPTEMBER 1940

1. Chinnery, quoted in Arthur, *Men of the Red Beret*, p. 9; TNA, WO 32/4723, 'Volunteers for Special Service', 30 June 1940.
2. TNA, WO 32/4723, 'Formation of Commandos and Irregular Troops', 25 June 1940; https://www.cheknews.ca/this-week-in-history-captain-george-paterson-a-remarkable-wwii-veteran-716796/ [accessed 10 February 2022]
3. 'Formation of Commandos and Irregular Troops', 25 June 1940.
4. Chinnery, quoted in Arthur, *Men of the Red Beret*, p. 9.
5. Buckingham, *Paras*, pp. 85–6; Major Peter Cleasby-Thompson, quoted in Arthur, *Men of the Red Beret*, p. xvi.
6. Buckingham, *Paras*, p. 89; Lieutenant Colonel T. B. H. Otway, *Airborne Forces of the Second World War, 1939–45* (London: HMSO, 1951; repr. 2021), p. 29.
7. Chinnery, quoted in Arthur, *Men of the Red Beret*, pp. 9–10.
8. Major Miles Whitlock, quoted in Arthur, *Men of the Red Beret*, pp. xvii–xviii.
9. Chinnery, quoted in Arthur, *Men of the Red Beret*, pp. 10–11.
10. TNA, DEFE 2/791, 'Present Situation in Respect of the Development of Parachute Troops' by Air Commodore Slessor, Air Staff Note, 12 August 1940.
11. TNA, DEFE 2/791, Jacob to Lieut. Col. A. H. Hornby, 14 August 1940.
12. TNA, DEFE 2/791, Wing Commander Knocker to Jacob, 23 August 1940.
13. Buckingham, *Paras*, pp. 102–4.
14. Buckingham, *Paras*, p. 107.
15. TNA, DEFE 2/791, Minutes of a Meetings held at the Air Mininstry at 3.30 p.m. on September 5th, 1940, to discuss the provision of Airborne Forces and a Note on the employment of Airborne Troops.

4 11TH SPECIAL AIR SERVICE BATTALION
– UK, JULY–DECEMBER 1940

1. Chinnery, quoted in Arthur, *Men of the Red Beret*, pp. 11–12.
2. Buckingham, *Paras* p. 108.
3. Chinnery, quoted in Arthur, *Men of the Red Beret*, p. 12; https://www.sallybosleysbadgeshop.com/shop.php?c=348#prettyPhoto[60529]/0/ [accessed 8 February 2022]

4. Cicely Paget-Bowman, quoted in Arthur, *Men of the Red Beret*, pp. 16–19.
5. Deane-Drummond, *Arrows of Fortune*, pp. 1–4.
6. https://www.pegasusarchive.org/arnhem/tony_hibbert.htm and https://www.paradata.org.uk/article/extended-biography-tony-hibbert [both accessed 15 February 2022]
7. Tony Hibbert, quoted in Arthur, *Men of the Red Beret*, pp. 1, 6.
8. Hibbert, quoted in Arthur, *Men of the Red Beret*, p. 2.
9. Paget-Bowman, quoted in Arthur, *Men of the Red Beret*, p. 18.
10. Hibbert, quoted in Arthur, *Men of the Red Beret*, p. 2.
11. https://www.paradata.org.uk/media/43 [accessed 15 February 2022]
12. Buckingham, *Paras*, pp. 118–19.
13. Buckingham, *Paras*, pp. 118–19.

5 'A PITY, A DAMNED PITY'
– UK AND MALTA, DECEMBER 1940–FEBRUARY 1941

1. TNA, DEFE 2/152, 'Colossus', General Notes, 1–5; TNA, CAB 106/8, Operation Colossus, 'A narrative of the execution of the operation based on Information given by Lt. A. J. Deane-Drummond, Royal Signals', p. 1.
2. TNA, DEFE 2/151, 'Colossus', Appendix I.
3. TNA, DEFE 2/152, 'Colossus', General Notes, 6–11.
4. Deane-Drummond, *Arrows of Fortune*, pp. 12–13; https://www.paradata.org.uk/people/trevor-ag-pritchard [accessed 17 February 2022]
5. Deane-Drummond, *Arrows of Fortune*, pp. 12–13.
6. https://www.paradata.org.uk/people/percy-p-clements [accessed 24 February 2022]
7. Deane-Drummond, *Arrows of Fortune*, pp. 12–13.
8. Chinnery, quoted in Arthur, *Men of the Red Beret*, p. 12.
9. Hibbert, quoted in Arthur, *Men of the Red Beret*, p. 4.
10. Deane-Drummond, quoted in Arthur, *Men of the Red Beret*, pp. 21–2; Deane-Drummond, *Return Ticket*, p. 17.
11. TNA, DEFE 2/152, 'Colossus', Training, 1–5.
12. TNA, DEFE 2/152, 'Colossus', General Notes, 18–24; Deane-Drummond, *Arrows of Fortune*, pp. 13–14.
13. Deane-Drummond, *Arrows of Fortune*, p. 14; TNA, DEFE 2/152, 'Colossus', Appendix III, Orders by DSO to Lt Deane-Drummond.
14. Deane-Drummond, *Arrows of Fortune*, p. 14; Deane-Drummond, *Return Ticket*, pp. 21–2.
15. TNA, DEFE 2/152, 'Colossus', Appendix II, Extraction from Operation Instruction.

16. Deane-Drummond, *Arrows of Fortune*, p. 15.
17. List of Clothing and Equipment used by X Troop during the Tragino Raid, www.paradata.org.uk/media/210 [accessed 24 February 2022]
18. TNA, DEFE 2/152, 'Colossus', Appendix I, Project 'T', 2 December 1941.
19. Deane-Drummond, *Arrows of Fortune*, pp. 15–16.

6 'VIVA CARABINIERI! VIVA DUCE!'
– ITALY, FEBRUARY 1941

1. Deane-Drummond, *Arrows of Fortune*, pp. 24–9; Deane-Drummond, *Return Ticket*, pp. 42–50.
2. TNA, DEFE 2/153, 'Colossus', Account of Escape by Sapper Alfred Parker R.E.; Deane-Drummond, *Return Ticket*, p. 50.
3. 'A narrative of the execution of the operation based on Information given by Lt. A. J. Deane-Drummond, Royal Signals', p. 4.
4. TNA, DEFE 2/153, 'Colossus', Keyes to Group Captain Harvey and Lieutenant Colonel Jackson, 9 June 1941.
5. TNA, DEFE 2/152, 'Colossus', Publicity 1–3; TNA, DEFE 2/153, 'Colossus', Major Macfie (DCO's Office) to Lieutenant Colonel Rock, 14 October 1941.
6. Major Macfie (DCO's Office) to Lieutenant Colonel Rock, 14 October 1941.
7. TNA, DEFE 2/153, 'Colossus', Air Chief Marshal Portal to Group Captain Harvey, 23 February 1941.
8. 'A narrative of the execution of the operation based on Information given by Lt. A. J. Deane-Drummond, Royal Signals', p. 5.
9. TNA, DEFE 2/152, Report on 'Colossus' Operation by Group Captain Harvey, 14 March 1941.
10. https://www.thegazette.co.uk/London/issue/35139/page/2212 [accessed 1 March 2022]
11. TNA, DEFE 2/153, Lieutenant Colonel Rock to Admiral Sir Roger Keyes, 16 June 1941.
12. https://www.paradata.org.uk/people/trevor-ag-pritchard [accessed 1 March 2022]

7 'A WHOLE YEAR HAS BEEN LOST'
– UK, JANUARY–JULY 1941

1. Buckingham, *Paras*, pp. 123–39.
2. TNA, CAB 120/262, Churchill to Ismay, 28 April 1941.

3. TNA, CAB 120/262, Churchill to Ismay, 27 May 1941.
4. Otway, *Airborne Forces*, pp. 27–8.
5. Buckingham, *Paras*, pp. 175–6.
6. Buckingham, *Paras*, p. 122.
7. Reg Curtis, *Churchill's Volunteer: A Parachute Corporal's Story* (London: Avon Books, 1994), pp. 6–69.
8. Buckingham, *Paras*, p. 138.
9. Curtis, *Churchill's Volunteer*, pp. 68–9.
10. https://www.pegasusarchive.org/eric_down.htm [accessed 4 March 2022]
11. Hibbert, in Arthur, *Men of the Red Beret*, p. 4.
12. https://www.pegasusarchive.org/eric_down.htm [accessed 4 March 2022]
13. Chinnery, in Arthur, *Men of the Red Beret*, pp. 12–13.
14. Hibbert, in Arthur, *Men of the Red Beret*, pp. 4–6,

8 A TALE OF TWO BRIGADES
– UK, SEPTEMBER–NOVEMBER 1941

1. https://www.pegasusarchive.org/normandy/richard_gale.htm [accessed 8 March 2022]
2. Otway, *Airborne Forces*, p. 34.
3. Buckingham, *Paras*, pp. 176–8.
4. Introduction by Brigadier S. J. L. Hill DSO MC, in Julian James, *A Fierce Quality: A biography of Brigadier Alastair Pearson* (London: Leo Cooper, 1989).
5. James, *A Fierce Quality*, Chapters 1–3.
6. TNA, WO 32/9778, Colonel G. W. Lambert to the C-in-C, Home Forces, 10 October 1941; Otway, *Airborne Forces*, pp. 37–8.
7. Bob Carruthers (ed.), *By Air to Battle: The Official History of the British Paratroops in World War II* (London: HMSO, 1945; repr. 2012), p. 28; Lambert to the C-in-C, Home Forces, 10 October 1941, Appendix A:
8. Buckingham, *Paras*, pp. 163–6; Otway, *Airborne Forces*, pp. 35–6.

9 MR DU MAURIER
– UK, OCTOBER 1941–FEBRUARY 1942

1. Otway, *Airborne Forces*, pp. 38–9.
2. Victor Dover, *The Sky Generals* (London: Cassell, 1981), pp. 38–43.
3. Brooke Diary, 22 October 1941, in Alex Danchev and Daniel Todman (eds), *War Diaries 1939–1945: Field Marshal Lord Alanbrooke* (London: Weidenfeld, 2001), p. 193.
4. Dover, *The Sky Generals*, p. 46.

5. Churchill, *The Second World War*, IV, p. 248.
6. TNA, DEFE 2/102, The Intelligence Aspect of the Bruneval Raid, 13 July 1942.
7. Major General John Frost, *A Drop Too Many: The Memoirs of World War II's Most Daring Parachute Commander* (London: Cassell & Co., 1980; repr. 1988), p. 46.
8. TNA, DEFE 2/100, Operation Biting, Appendix I, Airborne Division Operation Order No. 1, 11 February 1942.
9. Frost, *A Drop Too Many*, p. 46.
10. Frost, *A Drop Too Many*, pp. 1–27.
11. Frost, *A Drop Too Many*, pp. 27–39.
12. Victor Dover, *The Silken Canopy* (London: Cassell, 1979), pp. 21–2.
13. Frost, *A Drop Too Many*, p. 46.
14. TNA, DEFE 2/102, Request for model, 4 January 1942.
15. Frost, *A Drop Too Many*, pp. 41–2.
16. London, Imperial War Museum (IWM), Private Papers of Captain P. A. Young, 17/2/1, 'The Most Successful Raid of All'.
17. Max Hastings, *Finest Years: Churchill as Warlord 1940–1945* (London: HarperPress, 2009; repr. 2010), p. 239.
18. TNA, DEFE 2/100, Operation Biting, Air Operation Order.
19. Frost, *A Drop Too Many*, p. 47; Airborne Division Operation Order No. 1, 11 February 1942.

10 THE BRUNEVAL RAID
– UK AND FRANCE, FEBRUARY 1942

1. TNA, DEFE 2/101, Operation Biting, Appendix E.
2. Frost, *A Drop Too Many*, pp. 48–50; DEFE 2/101, Operation Biting, Appendix II, Personal Accounts: Major J. D. Frost.
3. Frost, *A Drop Too Many*, pp. 50–1; Operation Biting, Personal Accounts: Major J. D. Frost.
4. Young Papers, 'The Most Successful Raid of All'.
5. Operation Biting, Personal Accounts: Major J. D. Frost; TNA, DEFE 2/102, Statements from German RDF operator captured at Bruneval.
6. DEFE 2/101, Operation Biting, Appendix II, Personal Accounts: George Schmidt, POW.
7. Operation Biting, Personal Accounts: Major J. D. Frost.
8. Frost, *A Drop Too Many*, pp. 51–2; Operation Biting, Personal Accounts: Major J. D. Frost; DEFE 2/101, Operation Biting, Appendix II, Personal Accounts: Flight Sergeant C. W. F. Cox; DEFE 2/102, Operation Biting, Appendix I, Report of Flight Sergeant C. W. F. Cox.

9. IWM, Young Papers, 'The Most Successful Raid of All'.

10. DEFE 2/101, Operation Biting, Appendix II, Personal Accounts: 2nd Lt E. B. C. Charteris.

11. IWM, Young Papers, 'The Most Successful Raid of All'.

12. Frost, *A Drop Too Many*, pp. 53–5; Operation Biting, Personal Accounts: Major J. D. Frost, 2nd Lt E. B. C. Charteris and Flight Sergeant C. W. F. Cox; https://www.pegasusarchive.org/arnhem/john_timothy.htm [accessed 17 March 2022]

13. Frost, *A Drop Too Many*, pp. 57–8.

14. TNA, PREM 3/73, Operation Biting, Memo to the Prime Minister, 2 March 1942.

15. TNA, DEFE 2/102, Operation Biting, Air Scientific Intelligence Report No. 15, 13 July 1942.

16. George Millar, *The Bruneval Raid: Stealing Hitler's Radar* (London: Cassell & Co., 1974; repr. 2002), pp. 191–3.

17. Churchill, *The Second World War*, IV, p. 249.

18. Hastings, *Finest Years*, p. 239.

19. Frost, *A Drop Too Many*, pp. 58–9.

20. Frost, *A Drop Too Many*, p. 59.

21. TNA, DEFE 2/101, Operation Biting, Report by Major General Browning, 5 March 1942.

22. Millar, *The Bruneval Raid*, p. 184.

23. Report by Major General Browning, 5 March 1942.

24. Churchill, *The Second World War*, IV, p. 249; Frost, *A Drop Too Many*, p. 59.

11 'THIRSTING FOR ACTION'
– UK, MARCH–SEPTEMBER 1942

1. Otway, *Airborne Forces*, pp. 51–3.

2. IWM, Private Papers of Captain A. B. Clements, Box No. 67/343/1, Lieutenant Alan Clements to his granny, 29 April 1942.

3. Otway, *Airborne Forces*, pp. 51–3.

4. Frost, *A Drop Too Many*, pp. 62–4.

5. Robert Peatling, *Without Tradition: 2 Para 1941–1945* (Barnsley: Pen & Sword, 1994; repr. 2004), p. 53.

6. Otway, *Airborne Forces*, p. 59.

7. Peatling, *Without Tradition*, p. 53.

8. Otway, *Airborne Forces*, p. 54.

9. https://www.paradata.org.uk/media/43 [accessed 24 March 2022]

10. James, *A Fierce Quality*, Chapter 3.

11. Obituary of Brigadier Stanley James Hill DSO* MC in *The Times*, March 2006; James Hill in Arthur, *Men of the Red Beret*, p. 36.

12. Curtis, *Churchill's Volunteer*, p. 82.

13. Patrick Bishop, *Operation Jubilee: Dieppe 1942 – The Folly and the Sacrifice* (London: Viking, 2021), pp. 1–340.

14. Frost, *A Drop Too Many*, p. 62; Curtis, *Churchill's Volunteer*, pp. 87–8.

15. https://www.musicanet.org/robokopp/usa/comeands.htm [accessed 24 March 2022]

12 OPERATION FRESHMAN
– UK AND NORWAY, OCTOBER–DECEMBER 1942

1. TNA, DEFE 2/223, Operation Freshman, Summary of Operation.

2. TNA, DEFE 2/223, Operation Freshman, Minutes of a Meeting held at COHQ at 1100hrs on 14 October 1942.

3. TNA, DEFE 2/224, Airborne Division Operation Order for 'Freshman', 14 November 1942; TNA, AIR 39/45, Operation Freshman, No. 38 Wing RAF Operation Order, 16 November 1942.

4. TNA, DEFE 2/222, Operation Freshman, Briefing Notes on Escaping from Vermork to Sweden.

5. https://www.cwgc.org/our-work/news/a-brief-history-of-operation-freshman-and-the-stories-of-its-casualties/ [accessed 25 March 2022]

6. TNA, DEFE 2/223, Operation Freshman, Minutes of Meeting at COHQ on 26 October 1942.

7. Otway, *Airborne Forces*, pp. 70–1.

8. TNA, AIR 39/45, Operation Freshman, Report on 38 Wing Operation Order No. 5, 8 December 1942.

9. Claude Smith, *The History of the Glider Pilot Regiment* (London: Leo Cooper, 1992), p. 35.

10. Report on 38 Wing Operation Order No. 5, 8 December 1942.

11. TNA, DEFE 2/224, Operation Freshman, Appendix VII: Subsequent Intelligence, Summary of Statement made by SOE Agent, 15 January 1943; https://www.cwgc.org/our-work/news/a-brief-history-of-operation-freshman-and-the-stories-of-its-casualties/ [accessed 25 March 2022]

12. London, National Army Museum (NAM), 9203/218/111/1, Typescript translation of the 'Führer Befehl', Hitler's Commando Order of 18 October 1942.

13. https://www.paradata.org.uk/media/219 [accessed 30 March 2022]

14. TNA, DEFE 2/224, Operation Freshman, Translation of a report received from two Norwegians, Lieut. Col. J. S. Wilson to Col. R. A. R. Neville,

6 April 1943; https://www.cwgc.org/our-work/news/a-brief-history-of-operation-freshman-and-the-stories-of-its-casualties/ [accessed 25 March 2022]

15. https://www.eigersund.kommune.no/operation-freshman-execution-site.6541608-148494.html [accessed 12 December 2022]

16. Ray Mears, *The Real Heroes of Telemark* (London: BBC Books, 2003), pp. 84–94; https://forum.axishistory.com/viewtopic.php?f=6&t=41538&sid=396dad0508dfba058e76d0a1dc157342&start=15#google_vignette [accessed 26 March 2022]

17. TNA, DEFE 2/224, Operation Freshman, Lessons Learned, 6 May 1943.

18. Report on 38 Wing Operation Order No. 5, 8 December 1942.

13 'YOU WILL HEAR FROM ME ULTIMATELY' – NORTH AFRICA, NOVEMBER 1942

1. IWM, Clements Papers, Box No. 67/343/1, Lieutenant Alan Clements to his mother, 29 October 1942.

2. IWM, Clements Papers, Box No. 67/343/1, Lieut. Alan Clements to his mother, 29 October 1942; Reginald Clements to his son Alan, 25 November 1942.

3. Otway, *Airborne Forces*, pp. 61–2.

4. Curtis, *Churchill's Volunteer*, pp. 90–3.

5. Peatling, *Without Tradition*, p. 55.

6. Frost, *A Drop Too Many*, p. 66.

7. https://www.paradata.org.uk/people/r-geoffrey-pine-coffin [accessed 6 April 2022]

8. Otway, *Airborne Forces*, p. 75; Parker, *The Paras*, p. 44.

9. James Hill, in Arthur, *Men of the Red Beret*, p. 39; Otway, *Airborne Forces*, p. 75.

10. Curtis, *Churchill's Volunteer*, pp. 95–6.

11. Alastair Pearson, in Arthur, *Men of the Red Beret*, pp. 46–7.

12. James Hill, in Arthur, *Men of the Red Beret*, p. 41.

13. Report of 'S' Coy Column activities 17/18 Nov. 42 by Major P. Cleasby-Thompson, in https://www.paradata.org.uk/media/146 [accessed 7 April 2022]

14. Curtis, *Churchill's Volunteer*, p. 97.

15. Report of 'S' Coy Column activities 17/18 Nov. 42 by Major P. Cleasby-Thompson, in https://www.paradata.org.uk/media/146 [accessed 7 April 2022]

16. James Hill, in Arthur, *Men of the Red Beret*, pp. 42–4.

17. 'Gue Hill' by Lt S. Wandless, Appendix B, in https://www.paradata.org.uk/media/146 [accessed 16 April 2022]
18. James Hill, in Arthur, *Men of the Red Beret*, pp. 44–5; https://www.paradata.org.uk/article/soudia [accessed 16 April 2022]

14 PRIMUS IN CARTHAGO
– TUNISIA, NOVEMBER–DECEMBER 1942

1. Frost, *A Drop Too Many*, pp. 74–7; Lieut. Colonel J. D. Frost's report of the Depienne/Oudna operation, in Peatling, *Without Tradition*, p. 59.
2. Brigadier Dennis Rendell obituary, *The Times*, 21 October 2010; Frost, *A Drop Too Many*, p. 67.
3. 'Dennis Rendell recollects his disastrous Oudna experience', in Peatling, *Without Tradition*, pp. 75–6.
4. Frost, *A Drop Too Many*, pp. 78–80; Lieut. Colonel J. D. Frost's report of the Depienne/Oudna operation, in Peatling, *Without Tradition*, pp. 61–2.
5. 'Dennis Rendell recollects his disastrous Oudna experience', in Peatling, *Without Tradition*, pp. 76–7.
6. Frost, *A Drop Too Many*, pp. 67, 82–3.
7. Frost, *A Drop Too Many*, pp. 80–95; Lieut. Colonel J. D. Frost's report of the Depienne/Oudna operation, in Peatling, *Without Tradition*, pp. 66–9.
8. 'Dennis Rendell recollects his disastrous Oudna experience', in Peatling, *Without Tradition*, pp. 79–80.
9. Frost, *A Drop Too Many*, pp. 96–103; Lieut. Colonel J. D. Frost's report of the Depienne/Oudna operation, in Peatling, *Without Tradition*, pp. 69–71.
10. Otway, *Airborne Forces*, pp. 81–2.

15 PLUGGING THE GAPS
– TUNISIA, JANUARY–FEBRUARY 1943

1. TNA, WO 175/181, 1st Parachute Brigade War Diary, January 1943; Alastair Pearson, in Arthur, *Men of the Red Beret*, pp. 51–2.
2. Curtis, *Churchill's Volunteer*, pp. 111–13.
3. Pearson, in Arthur, *Men of the Red Beret*, p. 52; https://www.pegasusarchive.org/normandy/james_hill.htm [accessed 26 April 2022]
4. Ian W. Toll, *The Conquering Tide: War in the Pacific Islands 1942–1944* (New York: W. W. Norton & Co., 2015; repr. 2016), p. 187.
5. George McMillan, *The Old Breed: A History of the First Marine Division in World War II* (Washington: Infantry Journal Press, 1949), p. 137.

6. James Holland, *Together We Stand: North Africa, 1942–1943 – Turning the War in the West* (London: HarperCollins, 2005), pp. 511–19.
7. Otway, *Airborne Force*, p. 84.
8. IWM, Private Papers of A. B. Clements, Documents 5893, Box 67/343/1, 28 July 1944, 'The Battle of Djebel Mansour', pp. 2–8.
9. IWM, Private Papers of A. A. C. W. Brown, Documents 4625, Box 81/33/1, Typescript account of service with the 1st Parachute Battalion in North Africa.
10. IWM, Private Papers of A. B. Clements, Documents 5893, Box 67/343/1, 28 July 1944, 'The Battle of Djebel Mansour', pp. 2–8.

16 'WE LOST A LOT OF GRAND FELLOWS' – DJEBEL MANSOUR, 3–5 FEBRUARY 1943

1. Pearson, in Arthur, *Men of the Red Beret*, p. 54.
2. Clements, 'The Battle of Djebel Mansour', pp. 8–11.
3. Curtis, *Churchill's Volunteer*, pp. 120–1.
4. Pearson, in Arthur, *Men of the Red Beret*, pp. 54–5; Otway, *Airborne Forces*, p. 84; TNA, WO 175/181, 1st Parachute Brigade War Diary, February 1943.
5. Clements, 'The Battle of Djebel Mansour', pp. 11–13.
6. Pearson, in Arthur, *Men of the Red Beret*, pp. 55–6; 1st Parachute Brigade War Diary, February 1943.
7. 1st Parachute Brigade War Diary, February 1943.
8. Clements, 'The Battle of Djebel Mansour', pp. 14–20.
9. IWM, Private Papers of A. B. Clements, Documents 5893, Box 67/343/1, Letters from Mr Clements to his son Alan, 21 February and 28 March 1943.
10. Pearson, in Arthur, *Men of the Red Beret*, p. 56; Curtis, *Churchill's Volunteer*, p. 122; A. A. C. W. Brown, Typescript account of service with the 1st Parachute Battalion in North Africa.

17 'THEY HAVE PROVED THEIR MASTERY OVER THE ENEMY' – TUNISIA, FEBRUARY–MAY 1943

1. Frost, *A Drop Too Many*, pp. 113–16.
2. Holland, *Together We Stand*, pp. 588–9.
3. Frost, *A Drop Too Many*, p. 121.
4. Otway, *Airborne Forces*, p. 85.
5. Frost, *A Drop Too Many*, p. 134.
6. London, Liddell Hart Centre for Military Archives (LHCMA), Papers

of Lieutenant General Charles W. Allfrey, Box 3/1, Diary, 28 March 1943.

7. Frost, *A Drop Too Many*, pp. 156–65; Otway, *Airborne Forces*, pp. 86–7; Curtis, *Churchill's Volunteer*, p. 128.
8. Otway, *Airborne Forces*, p. 87.
9. https://www.paradata.org.uk/media/168 [accessed 16 May 2022]
10. https://www.paradata.org.uk/article/red-devils [accessed 16 May 2022]
11. Otway, *Airborne Forces*, pp. 87–8.
12. A. B. Austin, *Birth of an Army* (London: Victor Gollancz, 1943).
13. Carruthers (ed.), *By Air to Battle*, p. 79.
14. Frost, *A Drop Too Many*, p. 168.
15. Otway, *Airborne Forces*, pp. 81–2.

18 OPERATION LADBROKE
– SICILY, 9–10 JULY 1943

1. Churchill, *The Second World War*, V, p. 24.
2. Smith, *The History of the Glider Pilot Regiment*, pp. 42–3.
3. Otway, *Airborne Forces*, p. 97.
4. Otway, *Airborne Forces*, pp. 93–5.
5. Dover, *The Sky Generals*, pp. 67–71.
6. William F. Buckingham, *Arnhem 1944: A Reappraisal* (Stroud: Tempus, 2002), p. 17
7. TNA, CAB 106/688, 1st Air Landing Brigade Operation, p. 28.
8. Smith, *The History of the Glider Pilot Regiment*, pp. 55–7; Otway, *Airborne Forces*, p. 120.
9. Lloyd Clark, *Arnhem* (London, Headline, 2008; repr. 2009), p. 83.
10. https://www.pegasusarchive.org/sicily/george_chatterton.htm [accessed 24 May 2022]; Buckingham, *Arnhem 1944*, p. 18.
11. George Chatterton, *The Wings of Pegasus* (London: Macdonald, 1962; repr. 1982), pp. 40–2; https://www.pegasusarchive.org/sicily/george_chatterton.htm [accessed 24 May 2022]; Buckingham, *Arnhem 1944*, p. 18.
12. Smith, *The History of the Glider Pilot Regiment*, pp. 59–60; TNA, CAB 106/688, 1st Air Landing Brigade Operation, pp. 5–6.
13. http://ww2talk.com/index.php?threads/l-sgt-j-d-baskeyfield-2nd-airbourne-bn.58681/ [accessed 23 May 2022]
14. Clark, *Arnhem*, p. 87.
15. Buckingham, *Arnhem 1944*, p. 18.
16. Smith, *The History of the Glider Pilot Regiment*, pp. 61–2; Gilpin, quoted in Chatterton, *The Wings of Pegasus*, p. 83.

17. TNA, CAB 106/688, Sicily: 1st Air Landing Brigade Operation, p. 29.
18. Smith, *The History of the Glider Pilot Regiment*, pp. 61–2.
19. TNA, CAB 106/688, Sicily: 1st Air Landing Brigade Operation, pp. 29–31.
20. Staff Sergeant T. N. Moore, quoted in Arthur, *Men of the Red Beret*, pp. 125–9; Smith, *The History of the Glider Pilot Regiment*, pp. 63–4.
21. https://www.pegasusarchive.org/sicily/george_chatterton.htm [accessed 24 May 2022]; Chatterton, *The Wings of Pegasus*, pp. 71–5, 86–94; Smith, *The History of the Glider Pilot Regiment*, p. 62.
22. Dover, *The Sky Generals*, p. 75.
23. Buckingham, *Arnhem 1944*, p. 18.
24. TNA, CAB 106/688, Sicily: 1st Air Landing Brigade Operation, p. 33.

19 'I FLOATED DOWN LIKE A FAIRY QUEEN' – SICILY, 13–14 JULY 1943

1. IWM, Private Papers of J. A. Johnstone, Documents 7159, Box No: 77/173/1, 'Remembered with Advantages: A Personal Account of the Formation, Training and First Blooding of the 2nd Battalion, The Parachute Regiment', p. 1.
2. IWM Johnstone Papers, 'Winter of Discontent' and 'A Bridge Too Soon', pp. 1–44.
3. IWM, Johnstone Papers, 'Winter of Discontent' and 'A Bridge Too Soon', pp. 58–9.
4. Frost, *A Drop Too Many*, pp. 172–4.
5. IWM, Johnstone Papers, 'Winter of Discontent' and 'A Bridge Too Soon', pp. 59.
6. Frost, *A Drop Too Many*, pp. 176–7.
7. IWM, Johnstone Papers, 'Winter of Discontent' and 'A Bridge Too Soon', pp. 60–8.
8. Frost, *A Drop Too Many*, pp. 177–8.
9. TNA, CAB 106/689, Sicily: 1st Parachute Brigade Operation, p. 6.
10. Otway, *Airborne Forces*, p. 127.
11. Peatling, *Without Tradition*, p. 116.
12. Frost, *A Drop Too Many*, pp. 178–9.
13. Peatling, *Without Tradition*, p. 117–18.
14. Frost, *A Drop Too Many*, p. 180.
15. IWM, Johnstone Papers, 'Winter of Discontent' and 'A Bridge Too Soon', pp. 68–9.
16. Peatling, *Without Tradition*, p. 120.
17. Frost, *A Drop Too Many*, pp. 180–2.

20 'I'VE NO HESITATION IN SHOOTING HIM'
– SICILY, 13–17 JULY 1943

1. Pearson, quoted in Arthur, *Men of the Red Beret*, p. 119.
2. https://www.paradata.org.uk/article/personal-account-operation-fustian-captain-richard-bingley [accessed 31 May 2022]
3. Otway, *Airborne Forces*, p. 128.
4. https://www.paradata.org.uk/article/personal-account-operation-fustian-captain-richard-bingley [accessed 31 May 2022]
5. IWM, Clements Papers, Documents 5893, Box 67/343/1, Lieut. Alan Clements to his parents, 28 July 1943 (quoted in an article in the local press, 'They Landed by Moonlight').
6. https://www.paradata.org.uk/article/personal-account-operation-fustian-captain-richard-bingley [accessed 31 May 2022]
7. IWM, Clements Papers, Alan Clements to his parents, 28 July 1943.
8. TNA, CAB 106/689, Sicily: 1st Parachute Brigade Operation, p. 28.
9. Stainforth, quoted in Arthur, *Men of the Red Beret*, pp. 123–4.
10. TNA, CAB 106/689, Sicily: 1st Parachute Brigade Operation, pp. 28–9.
11. Curtis, *Churchill's Volunteer*, p. 144.
12. TNA, CAB 106/689, Sicily: 1st Parachute Brigade Operation, pp. 29–30.
13. Curtis, *Churchill's Volunteer*, p. 145; IWM, Clements Papers, Alan Clements to his parents, 28 July 1943; TNA, CAB 106/689, Sicily: 1st Parachute Brigade Operation, pp. 29–30.
14. Pearson, quoted in Arthur, *Men of the Red Beret*, p. 120.
15. Curtis, *Churchill's Volunteer*, pp. 146–8.
16. IWM, Clements Papers, Alan Clements to his parents, 28 July 1943.
17. https://www.paradata.org.uk/article/personal-account-operation-fustian-captain-richard-bingley [accessed 31 May 2022]
18. Frost, *A Drop Too Many*, pp. 183–4.
19. Pearson, quoted in Arthur, *Men of the Red Beret*, pp. 121–2.
20. Otway, *Airborne Forces*, p. 130.
21. TNA, CAB 106/689, Sicily: 1st Parachute Brigade Operation, pp. 31–33, 38.
22. TNA, CAB 106/691, Report on the Operations carried out by the 1st Airborne Division during the Invasion of Sicily (Operation Husky), Part 5: Lessons and Conclusions.
23. TNA, CAB 106/689, Sicily: 1st Parachute Brigade Operation, pp. 31–3, 38.
24. Frost, *A Drop Too Many*, pp. 185–7.
25. Frost, *A Drop Too Many*, p. 187; TNA, WO 373/3, Citation for the

Award of the MC to Captain Victor Dover, 15 August 1943; Dover, *The Silken Canopy*, pp. 52–68.

26. https://www.noonans.co.uk/auctions/archive/past-catalogues/494/catalogue/333716/ [accessed 6 June 2022]

27. https://www.paradata.org.uk/article/biography-sgt-neville-ashley-mm [accessed 6 June 2022]

28. https://www.pegasusarchive.org/sicily/john_bardwell.htm [accessed 13 June 2022]

29. Pearson, quoted in Arthur, *Men of the Red Beret*, pp. 122, 209–10.

21 'GET OVER THE SIDE!'
– APULIA, ITALY, SEPTEMBER–NOVEMBER 1943

1. Arthur, *Men of the Red Beret*, pp. 130–6.

2. Frost, *A Drop Too Many*, p. 189.

3. TNA, CAB 106/845, 'Operations of 1 Airborne Division in Apulia, September 9–October 1, 1943', p. 3.

4. Otway, *Airborne Forces*, pp. 132–3.

5. Hibbert, quoted in Arthur, *Men of the Red Beret*, p. 134.

6. Dover, *The Sky Generals*, pp. 82–3.

7. Frost, *A Drop Too Many*, p. 191.

8. https://www.pegasusarchive.org/arnhem/john_timothy.htm [accessed 13 June 2022]

9. Frost, *A Drop Too Many*, p. 190.

10. TNA, CAB 106/845, 1 Airborne Division in Italy, p. 10; Frost, *A Drop Too Many*, p. 192.

22 SHELDON'S CORNER AND SANGSHAK
– ASSAM, NORTH-EAST INDIA, 19–24 MARCH 1944

1. Harry Seaman, *The Battle at Sanghak: Prelude to Kohima* (London: Leo Cooper, 1989), p. 63.

2. Captain L. F. 'Dicky' Richards, HQ 50th Indian Parachute Brigade, quoted in Arthur, *Men of the Red Beret*, p. 145; 'Events Leading up to the Battles of Sheldon's Corner and Sangshak, March 1944', https://www.paradata.org.uk/media/355 [accessed 14 June 2022]; Seaman, *The Battle of Sangshak*, p. 2; Brigadier Paul Hopkinson's obituary, *Daily Telegraph*, undated, https://www.paradata.org.uk/media/11840 [accessed 14 June 2022]

3. 'Events Leading up to the Battles of Sheldon's Corner and Sangshak, March 1944'; Seaman, *The Battle at Sangshak*, pp. 15, 24; David Allison,

Fight Your Way Out: The Siege of Sangshak, India/Burma Border, 1944
(Barnsley: Pen & Sword Military, 2023), pp. 9–11.
4. Seaman, *The Battle at Sangshak*, pp. 63–5.
5. Paul Hopkinson and Captain L. F. 'Dicky' Richards, both quoted in
   Arthur, *Men of the Red Beret*, pp. 146–7, 155; Lieut. Col. Paul
   Hopkinson, 'Battle at Sangshak War Diary Report', pp. 1–2, https://
   www.paradata.org.uk/media/1466 [accessed 23 June 2022]
6. Seaman, *The Battle at Sangshak*, p. 77.
7. Eric Nield, *With Pegasus in India: The Story of 153 Gurkha Parachute
   Battalion* (Singapore: J. Birch & Co.,1970), p. 63; Captain F. G. 'Eric'
   Neild, quoted in Arthur, *Men of the Red Beret*, p. 163.
8. Richards, quoted in Arthur, *Men of the Red Beret*, pp. 148–9.
9. Hopkinson, quoted in Arthur, *Men of the Red Beret*, pp. 156–7; Seaman,
   The Battle of Sangshak, pp. 85–6.

23 'FIGHT YOUR WAY OUT'
– ASSAM, NORTH-EAST INDIA, 24–31 MARCH 1944

1. Seaman, *The Battle at Sangshak*, pp. 88–9.
2. Hopkinson, quoted in Arthur, *Men of the Red Beret*, pp. 159–60.
3. Richards, quoted in Arthur, *Men of the Red Beret*, p. 151.
4. Hopkinson, quoted in Arthur, *Men of the Red Beret*, pp. 160.
5. Seaman, *The Battle at Sangshak*, pp. 92–103; Richards, quoted in Arthur,
   Men of the Red Beret, pp. 151–2.
6. Seaman, *The Battle at Sangshak*, pp. 103–4; Hopkinson, in Arthur, *Men
   of the Red Beret*, p. 161; Neild, *With Pegasus in India*, pp. 65–6.
7. Butchard and Richards, in Arthur, *Men of the Red Beret*, pp. 154,
   166–70; Seaman, *The Battle at Sangshak*, pp. 115–17.
8. Seaman, *The Battle at Sangshak*, pp. 117–22; Allison, *Fight Your Way
   Out*, pp. 154–5.
9. Durham University Archives (DUA), Louis Allen Papers, GB 33 ALN,
   Brigadier (Retd) M. R. J. Hope Thomson to the Managing Director,
   J. R. Dent & Son Ltd, 4 March 1986.
10. Richards, in Arthur, *Men of the Red Beret*, p. 154.
11. Hopkinson, in Arthur, *Men of the Red Beret*, p. 162; Hopkinson, 'Battle
    at Sangshak War Diary Report', pp. 9–10 https://www.paradata.org.uk/
    media/1466 [accessed 23 June 2022]
12. Field Marshal Viscount Slim, *Retreat into Victory* (London: Cassell, 1956;
    repr. 1986), pp. 344–5.
13. Frank McLynn, *The Burma Campaign: Disaster into Triumph, 1942–1945*
    (London: Bodley Head, 2010), pp. 298–9.

14. Slim, *Retreat into Victory*, p. 345.
15. London, British Library (BL), Asian and African Collection (AAC), Victor Brookes, 'Games & War', pp. 5–6.
16. TNA, CAB 101/206, The Formation of 44th Indian Division.
17. https://www.paradata.org.uk/people/maxwell-rj-hope [accessed 24 June 2022]
18. BL, AAC, Victor Brookes, 'Games & War', p. 6.

24 'THE SPEARHEAD OF THE INVASION' – DORSET AND NORMANDY, 5 JUNE 1944

1. Howard, *The Pegasus Diaries,* pp. 113–14.
2. Howard, *The Pegasus Diaries*, pp. 110, 114–17; Denis Edwards, *The Devil's Own Luck: Pegasus Bridge to the Baltic 1944–45* (Barnsley: Pen & Sword, 1999; repr. 2016), pp. 34–5.
3. Edwards, *The Devil's Own Luck: Pegasus Bridge to the Baltic 1944–45* (Barnsley: Pen & Sword, 1999; repr. 2016), p. 19.
4. Private Walter Parr, in https://www.iwm.org.uk/collections/item/object/80011311 [accessed 7 July 2022]
5. Howard, *The Pegasus Diaries*, pp. 2–22, 45, 53, 85–93; Stephen E. Ambrose, *Pegasus Bridge: D-Day – The Daring British Airborne Raid* (London: Simon & Schuster, 1985; repr. 2016), pp. 55, 213–18.
6. TNA, AIR 37/553, 38 Group Operation Order No. 500.
7. Topographical Report on Bridges by the Brigade Major, 6th Airlanding Brigade, 17 May 1944, in Ambrose, *Pegasus Bridge*, pp. 69–73.
8. Howard, *The Pegasus Diaries*, pp. 93–4; Ambrose, *Pegasus Bridge*, pp. 73, 215–16.
9. Lieutenant Tod Sweeney, in Arthur, *Men of the Red Beret*, p. 187.
10. Howard, *The Pegasus Diaries*, pp. 94–9, 101.
11. Edwards, *The Devil's Own Luck*, p. 33.

25 'HAM AND JAM!' – NORMANDY, D-DAY, 6 JUNE 1944

1. Howard, *The Pegasus Diaries*, pp. 119–21; Edwards, *The Devil's Own Luck*, p. 40–1.
2. Athens, Ohio University Libraries (OUL), Mahn Center for Archives and Special Collections (MCASC), Cornelius Ryan Collection of World War II Papers, Box 21, No. 5, Interview of William James Gray.
3. Private Walter Parr, in https://www.iwm.org.uk/collections/item/object/80011311 [accessed 7 July 2022]

4. Edwards, *The Devil's Own Luck*, p. 43.
5. OUL, MCASC, Ryan Collection, Interview of William James Gray.
6. Howard, *The Pegasus Diaries*, pp. 121–2; Ambrose, *Pegasus Bridge*, p. 216.
7. Howard, *The Pegasus Diaries*, p. 122.
8. https://www.pegasusarchive.org/normandy/tony_hooper.htm [accessed 8 July 2022]
9. Sweeney, in Arthur, *Men of the Red Beret*, pp. 189–90.
10. Staff Sergeant Roy Howard, in Arthur, *Men of the Red Beret*, pp. 175–8.
11. Sweeney, in Arthur, *Men of the Red Beret*, pp. 189–90; Howard, *The Pegasus Diaries*, pp. 122–3.

26 'BLIMEY, WE'VE 'AD IT NOW!'
– NORMANDY, 6 JUNE 1944

1. Howard, *The Pegasus Diaries*, pp. 193–6; Nigel Poett, *Pure Poett: The Autobiography of General Sir Nigel Poett* (London: Leo Cooper, 1991), pp. 64–7.
2. Ambrose, *Pegasus Bridge*, pp. 122–4; Howard, *The Pegasus Diaries*, pp. 196–7.
3. Edwards, *The Devil's Own Luck*, pp. 44–5.
4. Private Walter Parr, in https://www.iwm.org.uk/collections/item/object/80011311 [accessed 7 July 2022]
5. Howard, *The Pegasus Diaries*, p. 127; Werner Kortenhaus, *The Combat History of the 21st Panzer Division* (2007; repr. and translated 2014), p. 91.
6. OUL, MCASC, Ryan Collection, Interview of William James Gray.
7. Ambrose, *Pegasus Bridge*, pp. 106–7, 129.
8. Howard, *The Pegasus Diaries*, p. 128; Edwards, *The Devil's Own Luck*, p. 45; Kortenhaus, *The Combat History of the 21st Panzer Division*, p. 91.
9. https://www.pegasusarchive.org/normandy/geoffrey_pine_coffin.htm [accessed 8 July 2022]
10. Major R. J. N. Bartlett, 'Parachute Operations "D" Day', *The Oxfordshire and Buckinghamshire Light Infantry Quarterly Journal*, 17/5 (November 1944), p. 41.
11. www.pegasusarchive.org/normandy/john.butler.htm [accessed 26 July 2022]
12. Howard, *The Pegasus Diaries*, p. 129; War Diary of Lieutenant Colonel R. G. Pine-Coffin in IWM, Private Papers of H. J. Butler, Documents 17891.
13. https://www.pegasusarchive.org/normandy/richard_todd.htm [accessed 8 July 2022]

27 'ABOUT BLOODY TIME!'
– NORMANDY, 6 JUNE 1944

1. Hans von Luck, *Panzer Commander: The Memoirs of Colonel Hans von Luck* (New York: 1989; repr. 1991), pp. 171–3.
2. Kortenhaus, *The Combat History of the 21st Panzer Division*, pp. 50–8.
3. Von Luck, *Panzer Commander*, pp. 173–4; Ambrose, *Pegasus Bridge*, pp. 4–5, 137–41.
4. Kortenhaus, *The Combat History of the 21st Panzer Division*, pp. 91–2.
5. Parry, *The Parachuting Parson*, pp. 31–3.
6. https://www.pegasusarchive.org/normandy/richard_todd.htm [accessed 8 July 2022]
7. https://www.pegasusarchive.org/normandy/geoffrey_pine_coffin.htm [accessed 8 July 2022]
8. https://www.pegasusarchive.org/normandy/richard_todd.htm [accessed 8 July 2022]
9. https://www.dungannonwardead.com/persondepth.asp?cas_id=1141 [accessed 27 July 2022]
10. Kortenhaus, *The Combat History of the 21st Panzer Division*, p. 92.
11. Edwards, *The Devil's Own Luck*, pp. 54–5.
12. https://www.pegasusarchive.org/normandy/geoffrey_pine_coffin.htm [accessed 8 July 2022]
13. Lord Lovat, *March Past: A Memoir* (London: Weidenfeld & Nicolson, 1948), p. 321.
14. https://www.pegasusarchive.org/normandy/richard_todd.htm [accessed 8 July 2022]; https://www.pegasusarchive.org/normandy/geoffrey_pine_coffin.htm [accessed 8 July 2022]; Lovat, *March Past*, p. 322.
15. Howard, *The Pegasus Diaries*, p. 137; Lovat, *March Past*, pp. 322–3.
16. Howard, *The Pegasus Diaries*, p. 137.
17. https://www.pegasusarchive.org/normandy/geoffrey_pine_coffin.htm [accessed 8 July 2022; Howard, *The Pegasus Diaries*, p. 130.
18. https://www.pegasusarchive.org/normandy/richard_todd.htm [accessed 8 July 2022]
19. https://www.pegasusarchive.org/normandy/geoffrey_pine_coffin.htm [accessed 8 July 2022]
20. Howard, *The Pegasus Diaries*, pp. 138–44.
21. TNA, WO 106/4315, 6 Airborne Division: Immediate Report No. 2, 11 June 1944.
22. Smith, *The History of the Glider Pilot Regiment*, p. 97.
23. Von Luck, *Panzer Commander*, p. 175.

28 'GRADE A STINKER OF A JOB!'
– DORSET AND NORMANDY, APRIL TO JUNE 1944

1. John Golley, *The Big Drop: The Guns of Merville, June 1944* (London: Jane's, 1982), pp. 15–20, 32–3; https://www.pegasusarchive.org/normandy/terence_otway.htm [accessed 2 August 2022]; TNA, WO 106/4315, 6th Airborne Division: Immediate Report No. 19 (Merville Battery), 18 June 1944.
2. https://www.pegasusarchive.org/normandy/terence_otway.htm [accessed 2 August 2022]
3. Golley, *The Big Drop*, pp. 16–19.
4. Hill, in Arthur, *Men of the Red Beret*, pp. 198 and 200.
5. https://www.pegasusarchive.org/normandy/terence_otway.htm [accessed 2 August 2022]; Golley, *The Big Drop*, pp. 46–8.
6. https://www.pegasusarchive.org/normandy/terence_otway.htm [accessed 2 August 2022]
7. Golley, *The Big Drop*, pp. 71–2.
8. Garry Johnson and Christopher Dunphie, *Brightly Shone the Dawn: Some Experiences of the Invasion of Normandy* (London: Frederick Warne, 1980), pp. 44–9; https://www.pegasusarchive.org/normandy/allen_parry.htm [accessed 10 August 2022]
9. https://www.pegasusarchive.org/normandy/terence_otway.htm [accessed 2 August 2022]; Golley, *The Big Drop*, pp. 58–9.
10. TNA, WO 106/4315, 6th Airborne Division: Immediate Report No. 19 (Merville Battery), 18 June 1944.
11. TNA, WO 106/4315, 6th Airborne Division: Immediate Report No. 19 (Merville Battery), 18 June 1944; Golley, *The Big Drop*, p. 73.
12. https://www.pegasusarchive.org/normandy/terence_otway.htm [accessed 2 August 2022]; TNA, WO 106/4315, 6th Airborne Division: Immediate Report No. 19 (Merville Battery), 18 June 1944.
13. https://www.pegasusarchive.org/normandy/terence_otway.htm [accessed 2 August 2022]; TNA, WO 106/4315, 6th Airborne Division: Immediate Report No. 19 (Merville Battery), 18 June 1944; Golley, *The Big Drop*, pp. 107–8.

29 'GET IN! GET IN!'
– NORMANDY, 6 JUNE 1944

1. CSM Sid Knight, in Arthur, *Men of the Red Beret*, p. 220.
2. Golley, *The Big Drop*, pp. 90–2; https://www.pegasusarchive.org/normandy/terence_otway.htm [accessed 2 August 2022.]

3. Alan Jefferson, *Assault on the Guns of Merville* (London: John Murray, 1987), pp. 111–13.
4. https://www.pegasusarchive.org/normandy/allen_parry.htm [accessed 10 August 2022]
5. Knight, in Arthur, *Men of the Red Beret*, p. 221.
6. Golley, *The Big Drop*, pp. 90–2; https://www.pegasusarchive.org/normandy/terence_otway.htm [accessed 2 August 2022.]
7. https://www.pegasusarchive.org/normandy/terence_otway.htm [accessed 2 August 2022]; TNA, WO 106/4315, 6th Airborne Division: Immediate Report No. 19 (Merville Battery), 18 June 1944; Golley, *The Big Drop*, pp. 132–6.
8. OUL, MCASC, Ryan Collection, Box 21, Folder 9, Interview of Padre John Gwinnett; https://www.pegasusarchive.org/normandy/allen_parry.htm [accessed 10 August 2022]; TNA, WO 106/4315, 6th Airborne Division: Immediate Report No. 19 (Merville Battery), 18 June 1944.
9. Golley, *The Big Drop*, p. 156.
10. TNA, WO 106/4315, 6th Airborne Division: Immediate Report No. 19 (Merville Battery), 18 June 1944.
11. https://www.pegasusarchive.org/normandy/terence_otway.htm [accessed 2 August 2022]; Golley, *The Big Drop*, pp. 157–9; Obituary of Lieutenant Colonel Terence Otway, *Daily Telegraph*, 25 July 2006.
12. Otway, *Airborne Forces*, p. 180.
13. Jefferson, *Assault on the Guns of Merville*, pp. 142–57.
14. Otway, *Airborne Forces*, pp, 188–91, 197–200.

30 'IT WILL BE SOME BLOOD BATH' – LINCOLNSHIRE, UK, SEPTEMBER 1944

1. OUL, MCASC, Ryan Collection, Box 111, Folder 7: Robin Vlasto.
2. Lieut. Gen. Sir Brian Horrocks, *A Full Life* (London: Collins, 1960), p. 205.
3. Clark, *Arnhem*, pp. 10–14.
4. Saul David, *Military Blunders* (London: Robinson, 1997), p. 115.
5. Antony Beevor, *Arnhem: The Battle for the Bridges, 1944* (London: Viking, 2018; repr. 2019), p. 7.
6. OUL, MCASC, Ryan Collection: Robin Vlasto.
7. Clark, *Arnhem*, p. 24.
8. OUL, MCASC, Ryan Collection: Robin Vlasto.
9. Beevor, *Arnhem*, pp. 28–33; Cornelius Ryan, *A Bridge Too Far* (London: Hamish Hamilton, 1974; repr. 1975), p. 79.

10. John Baynes, *Urquhart of Arnhem: The Life of Major-General RE Urquhart* (London: Brassey's, 1993), pp. 69–70.

11. Frost, *A Drop Too Many*, pp. 194–5.

12. Stephen Orme, 'The 3Cs: How important were shortcomings in Command, Control and Communication in the destruction of the 1st Airborne Division at Arnhem in September 1944' (unpublished Master's dissertation, University of Buckingham, 2016), p. 24; Major-General R. E. Urquhart, *Arnhem* (London: Cassell & Co., 1958), 15.

13. Baynes, *Urquhart of Arnhem*, p. 72.

14. Dover, *The Sky Generals*, pp 127–9.

15. Otway, *Airborne Forces*, pp. 262–5; Beevor, *Arnhem*, p. 55; Orme, 'The 3Cs', p. 53.

16. Captain Eddie Newbury, in Beevor, *Arnhem*, p. 64.

17. Christopher Jary, *They Couldn't Have Done Better: The Story of the Dorset Regiment In War and Peace 1939–67* (London: Simper Fidelis Publications, 2014; repr. 2017), p. 194.

18. OUL, MCASC, Ryan Collection, Box 108, Folder 6: Major Brian Urquhart; Jary, *They Couldn't Have Done Better*, pp. 194–6.

31 'BLIZZARD OF SILK'
– LINCOLNSHIRE, UK, 15–17 SEPTEMBER 1944

1. Frost, *A Drop Too Many*, pp. 198–9.

2. TNA, WO 219/5137, Operation 'Market': Story of 1 Parachute Brigade; and 1 Parachute Brigade Opeartion Order No. 1; Urquhart, *Arnhem*, pp. 10, 13; Buckingham, *Arnhem*, p. 197.

3. Frost, *A Drop Too Many*, pp. 199–200.

4. Orme, 'The 3Cs', p. 52.

5. Frost, *A Drop Too Many*, pp. 201–2.

6. www.pegasusarchive.org/arnhem/tatham_warter.htm [accessed 31 August 2022]; Dover, *The Silken Canopy*, p. 85.

7. Dover, *The Silken Canopy*, pp. 80–1.

8. OUL, MCASC, Ryan Collection: Robin Vlasto.

9. OUL, MCASC, Ryan Collection: Robin Vlasto; Frost, *A Drop Too Many*, p. 203.

10. Dover, *The Silken Canopy*, p. 81; Frost, *A Drop Too Many*, p. 204.

11. James Sims, *Arnhem Spearhead: A Private Soldier's Story* (London: IWM, 1978; repr. 1980), pp 33–51.

12. Frost, *A Drop Too Many*, pp. 204–5.

13. Dover, *The Silken Canopy*, p. 82.

14. Beevor, *Arnhem*, p. 77; Chatterton, *The Wings of Pegasus*, p. 174.

15. Buckingham, *Arnhem*, p. 86.
16. Frost, *A Drop Too Many*, p. 207.
17. Sims, *Arnhem Spearhead*, pp. 55–6.
18. Dover, *The Silken Canopy*, p. 84.

32 'YOU MADE IT THIS TIME, DICKY' – HOLLAND, 17 SEPTEMBER 1944

1. Frost, *A Drop Too Many*, pp. 207–8; Account of the 2nd Battalion's Operations at Arnhem 17th September 1944 by Major Tatham-Warter, www.pegasusarchive.org/arnhem/tatham_warter.htm [accessed 31 August 2022]
2. Dover, *The Silken Canopy*, pp. 84–5.
3. Frost, *A Drop Too Many*, pp. 208–10; Middlebrook, *Arnhem*, pp. 143–5; OUL, MCASC, Ryan Collection: Robin Vlasto.
4. OUL, MCASC, Ryan Collection: Robin Vlasto.
5. Frank, in Middlebrook, *Arnhem*, pp. 145–6.
6. Dover, *The Silken Canopy*, p. 87.
7. Lieut. Peter Barry, in Middlebrook, *Arnhem*, p. 147.
8. Frost, *A Drop Too Many*, p. 211.
9. Lieut. Peter Barry, in Middlebrook, *Arnhem*, pp. 147–8; Dover, *The Silken Canopy*, pp. 89–91.
10. Frost, *A Drop Too Many*, p. 212; Lieut. Robin Vlasto Diary.
11. Middlebrook, *Arnhem*, pp. 149–50.
12. OUL, MCASC, Ryan Collection: Robin Vlasto; Middlebrook, *Arnhem*, pp. 152–3.
13. Frost, *A Drop Too Many*, p. 216; Major Hibbert interview, Media/55, in www.paradata.org.uk/people/tony-hibbert [accessed 9 September 2021]; Beevor, *Arnhem*, p. 126.
14. Deane-Drummond, *Return Ticket*, p. 170.
15. Orme, 'The 3Cs', pp. 67–77; Middlebrook, *Arnhem*, pp. 126–9; Urquhart, *Arnhem*, pp. 45–6.
16. Major Hibbert interview, Media/56, in www.paradata.org.uk/people/tony-hibbert [accessed 12 September 2021]
17. Orme, 'The 3Cs', pp. 82–3.
18. Frost, *A Drop Too Many*, pp. 257–8.

33 'A VERY FINE FEAT OF ARMS'
– ARNHEM, HOLLAND, 17 SEPTEMBER 1944

1. Beevor, *Arnhem*, pp. 71–2, 93–5; Robert Kershaw, *It Never Snows in September: The German View of Market-Garden and the Battle of Arnhem, September 1944* (London: The Crowood Press, 1990; repr. 2008), pp. 81–2.
2. Middlebrook, *Arnhem*, pp. 131.
3. Beevor, *Arnhem*, pp. 106–8.
4. Beevor, *Arnhem*, p. 95.
5. Beevor, *Arnhem*, p. 131; Kershaw, *It Never Snows in September*, pp. 106–7.
6. Beevor, *Arnhem*, pp. 114, 123–4
7. Beevor, *Arnhem*, pp 88–90, 154: Horrocks, *A Full Life*, pp. 211–13.
8. Fulton, in Middlebrook, *Arnhem*, pp. 156–7.
9. Tatham-Warter, in Middlebrook, Arnhem, pp. 157–8; Lieut. Jack Grayburn's VC citation, www.pegasusarchive.org/arnhem/jack_grayburn [accessed 12 September 2021]
10. Frost, *A Drop Too Many*, pp. 217–18.
11. OUL, MCASC, Cornelius Ryan Collection of WWII papers, Box 110, Folder 55: Eric M. Mackay.
12. Middlebrook, *Arnhem*, pp. 159–60.
13. Dover, *The Silken Canopy*, pp. 91–7.
14. Frost, A Drop Too Many, pp. 218–19.

34 'IT WAS LITTLE SHORT OF MURDER'
– ARNHEM, HOLLAND, 18 SEPTEMBER 1944

1. Frost, *A Drop Too Many*, p. 219.
2. Sims, *Arnhem Spearhead*, pp. 82–3.
3. OUL, MCASC, Ryan Collection: Eric M. Mackay.
4. Frost, *A Drop Too Many*, pp. 219–23.
5. Frost, *A Drop Too Many*, pp. 222.
6. Sims, *Arnhem Spearhead*, pp. 90–1.
7. Frost, *A Drop Too Many*, pp. 223–5; Hibbert, in Arthur, *Men of the Red Beret*, p. 297; http://www.pegasusarchive.org/arnhem/tatham_warter. htm [accessed 30 September 2022]

35 'OUR NUMBERS WERE DWINDLING FAST'
– ARNHEM, HOLLAND, 18 SEPTEMBER 1944

1. Middlebrook, *Arnhem*, pp. 167–83.
2. Urquhart, *Arnhem*, pp. 62–4.

3. Buckingham, *Arnhem 1944*, p. 111.
4. Dover, *The Silken Canopy*, pp. 97–104.
5. Deane-Drummond, *Return Ticket*, pp. 175–9.
6. Urquhart, *Arnhem*, pp. 60–1; Beevor, *Arnhem*, pp. 142–3.
7. http://www.pegasusarchive.org/arnhem/william_hewitt.htm [accessed 30 September 2022]
8. Beevor, *Arnhem*, pp. 147–9.
9. http://www.pegasusarchive.org/arnhem/jack_bird.htm [accessed 30 September 2022]
10. Lipmann Kessel, *Surgeon At Arms* (London, 1958; repr. 1974), pp. 23–5.
11. Beevor, *Arnhem*, pp. 150–2.
12. Beevor, *Arnhem*, pp. 162–9.

36 'WE WERE SPELLBOUND AND SPEECHLESS' – ARNHEM, HOLLAND, 19 SEPTEMBER 1944

1. Frost, *A Drop Too Many*, pp. 225–7; OUL, MCASC, Cornelius Ryan Collection of World War II Papers, Box 110, Folder 46: Stanley Halliwell.
2. https://www.paradata.org.uk/people/robert-lygo [accessed 30 September 2022]
3. http://ww2talk.com/index.php?threads/lieutenant-andrew-mcdermont.72044/ [accessed 30 September 2022]; https://www.pegasusarchive.org./sicily/tony_frank.htm [accessed 3 October 2022]
4. Frost, *A Drop Too Many*, pp. 227–8.
5. Urquhart, *Arnhem*, pp. 80–5.
6. Horrocks, *A Full Life*, p. 218.
7. Buckingham, *Arnhem 1944*, p. 154.
8. http://www.pegasusarchive.org/arnhem/jack_bird.htm [accessed 30 September 2022]
9. Urquhart, *Arnhem*, pp. 86–91.
10. http://www.vconline.org.uk/lionel-e-queripel-vc/4587953689.html [accessed 30 September 2022]

37 'NO LIVING ENEMY HAD BEATEN US' – ARNHEM, HOLLAND, 20 SEPTEMBER 1944

1. Urquhart, *Arnhem*, pp. 101–2.
2. Urquhart, *Arnhem*, pp. 103–5.
3. Frost, *A Drop Too Many*, p. 229.
4. OUL, MCASC, Ryan Collection: Robin Vlasto; Citation for

Lieutenant Jack Grayburn's Victoria Cross, *The London Gazette* 23 January 1945.

5. OUL, MCASC, Cornelius Ryan Collection of WWII papers, Box 110, Folder 55: Eric M. Mackay; and Box 110, Folder 41: Ronald Emery.

6. Frost, *A Drop Too Many*, p. 229.

7. Horrocks, *A Full Life*, pp. 218–19.

8. Beevor, *Arnhem*, pp. 208–19.

9. Horrocks, *A Full Life*, pp. 220–1.

10. Urquhart, *Arnhem*, pp. 105–10.

11. http://www.pegasusarchive.org/arnhem/john_baskeyfield.htm [accessed 3 October 2022]

12. John Daniel Baskeyfield VC, in *The Victoria Cross and the George Cross: The Complete History*, 3 vols (London: Methuen, 2013), III, p. 584.

13. War Diary of the 2nd South Staffords, Airborne Forces Archive, https://paradata.org.uk/media/3941?mediaSection=Post-combat%20 reports&mediaitem=82281 [accessed 3 October 2022]

14. Baskeyfield, in *The Victoria Cross and the George Cross*, III, p. 584.

15. Beevor, *Arnhem*, p. 244.

16. Frost, *A Drop Too Many*, pp. 229–31; www.pegasusarchive.org/arnhem/tony_hibbert.htm [accessed 3 October 2022]

38 'GET THEM OUT'
– ARNHEM, HOLLAND, 21–26 SEPTEMBER 1944

1. Peatling, *Without Tradition*, p. 142.

2. Urquhart, *Arnhem*, p. 159; Kessel, *Surgeon at War*, p. 13.

3. Curtis, *Churchill's Volunteer*, p. 185.

4. TNA, WO 219/5137, 1st Airborne Division Report on Operation Market, Part IV.

5. Horrocks, *A Full Life*, pp. 229–30; Urquhart, *Arnhem*, pp. 161, 179–80; Jary, *They Couldn't Have Done Better*, pp. 238–42.

6. Clark, *Arnhem*, p. 234; Kershaw, *It Never Snows in September*, p. 377.

7. TNA, WO 219/5137, 1st Airborne Division Report on Operation Market, Part IV.

8. Urquhart, *Arnhem*, pp. 197–8.

9. Urquhart, *Arnhem*, pp. 198–204.

10. Urquhart, *Arnhem*, pp. 204–5.

11. Horrocks, *A Full Life*, pp. 230–2.

12. Beevor, *Arnhem*, pp. 36, 365.

13. Buckingham, *Arnhem 1944*, p. 200.

14. Frost, *A Drop Too Many*, p. 259.
15. Horrocks, *A Full Life*, pp. 230–2.
16. TNA, WO 219/5137, 1st Airborne Division Report on Operation Market, Part IV.

39 OPERATION VARSITY
– UK AND GERMANY, MARCH 1945

1. IWM, Private Papers of Captain A. B. Clements, Box No. 67/343/1, Captain Alan Clements to his sister, 16 March 1945; and Reginald Clements to his son Alan, 28 September 1944.
2. Clark, *Arnhem*, pp. 241–5.
3. Antony Beevor, *Ardennes 1944: Hitler's Last Gamble* (London: Viking, 2015).
4. Arthur, *Men of the Red Beret*, pp. 401–7.
5. IWM, Private Papers of Captain A. B. Clements, Box No. 67/343/1.
6. Clark, *Arnhem*, pp. 256–66; Hastings, *All Hell Let Loose*, pp. 610–11.
7. Matthew J. Seelinger, 'Operation Varsity: The Last Airborne Deployment of World War II', *On Point*, 10/3 (December 2004), 9–17.
8. Charles B. MacDonald, *US Army in World War II: European Theater of Operations – The Last Offensive* (Washington DC: Office of the Chief of Military History, 1973), Chapter XIV.
9. MacDonald, *The Last Offensive*, Chapter XIV; Clark, *Arnhem*, pp. 269–297; TNA, WO 218/214, 'FAAA Narrative of Operation Varsity, 24 March 1945', pp. 1–6.

40 JUMPING THE RHINE
– GERMANY, 24–26 MARCH 1945

1. Poett, *Pure Poett*, pp. 82–3.
2. Hill, in Arthur, *Men of the Red Beret*, pp. 409–10.
3. Churchill, *The Second World War*, VI, pp. 360–2.
4. Hill, in Arthur, *Men of the Red Beret*, pp. 409–10.
5. Clark, *Arnhem*, pp. 307–10.
6. IWM, Private Papers of Captain A. B. Clements, Box No. 67/343/1.
7. Eadie, in Arthur, *Men of the Red Beret*, p. 429.
8. *The London Gazette*, 31 July 1945, p. 3965.
9. Poett, *Pure Poett*, p. 84.
10. Elvin, in Arthur, *Men of the Red Beret*, p. 419.
11. Glaister, in Arthur, *Men of the Red Beret*, pp. 422–4.
12. Philip L. Burkinshaw, *Alarms and Excursions* (privately published, 1991), p. 45.

13. Poett, *Pure Poett*, p. 84.
14. Edwards, *The Devil's Own Luck*, pp. 179–82.
15. Sweeney, in Arthur, *Men of the Red Beret*, pp. 413–16.
16. Clark, *Arnhem*, pp. 326–8.
17. TNA, WO 218/214, 'FAAA Narrative of Operation Varsity, 24 March 1945', pp. 9–10.
18. MacDonald, *The Last Offensive*, Chapter XIV.
19. Hill, in Arthur, *Men of the Red Beret*, p. 410.
20. Otway, *Airborne Forces*, p. 315.
21. Hill, in Arthur, *Men of the Red Beret*, p. 410.
22. Otway, *Airborne Forces*, p. 315.
23. TNA, WO 218/214, 'FAAA Narrative of Operation Varsity, 24 March 1945', p. 12.
24. Clark, *Arnhem*, pp. 329–30.
25. Dwight D. Eisenhower, *Crusade in Europe* (New York: Doubleday, 1948; repr. 1997), p. 390.

41 ENDGAME

1. Otway, *Airborne Forces*, pp. 323–8.
2. Otway, *Airborne Forces*, pp. 381–3; WO 373/41, Rifleman Manbahadur Gurung's citation for the Military Medal; Allison, *Fight Your Way Out*, pp. 147–9.
3. Poett, *Pure Poett*, p. 86.
4. Otway, *Airborne Forces*, pp. 314, 329–30.
5. Waddy, in Arthur, *Men of the Red Beret*, pp. 339–40.

42 AFTERMATH

1. TNA, CAB 120/414, Churchill's memorandum to Ismay, 5 June 1940.
2. Otway, *Airborne Forces*, p. 389.
3. Otway, *Airborne Forces*, Appendix P: The Value of Airborne Forces, pp. 446–50; Chatterton, *The Wings of Pegasus*, pp. 222–35.
4. https://www.paradata.org.uk/article/last-drop-action [accessed 28 January 2023]
5. https://www.army.mod.uk/who-we-are/corps-regiments-and-units/infantry/parachute-regiment/ [accessed 25 May 2023]
6. https://www.paradata.org.uk/media/986 [accessed 25 May 2023]

ENDNOTES

POSTSCRIPT

1. Dover, *The Sky Generals*, pp. 150–4.
2. https://www.pegasusarchive.org/eric_down.htm [accessed 17 October 2022]; Dover, *The Sky Generals*, p. 182.
3. https://www.pegasusarchive.org/normandy/james_hill.htm [accessed 17 October 2022]
4. https://www.pegasusarchive.org/normandy/alastair_pearson.htm [accessed 17 October 2022]
5. https://www.paradata.org.uk/people/r-geoffrey-pine-coffin [accessed 20 October 2022]
6. https://www.pegasusarchive.org/sicily/john_frost.htm [accessed 17 October 2022]; Frost, *A Drop Too Many*, pp. 248–57.
7. Frost, *A Drop Too Many*, p. xvi.
8. Obituary of Lieutenant Colonel Terence Otway, *The Times*, 27 July 2006.
9. Howard, *The Pegasus Diaries*, pp. 190–3.
10. Deane-Drummond, *Arrow of Fortune*, pp. 108–13; https://www.paradata.org.uk/people/anthony-j-deane-drummond [accessed 20 October 2022]
11. https://www.pegasusarchive.org/arnhem/tony_hibbert.htm [accessed 20 October 2022]
12. Curtis, *Churchill's Volunteer*, pp. 192–215; https://www.kentonline.co.uk/canterbury/news/last-original-paratrooper-dies-aged-91646/ [accessed 20 October 2022]
13. Edwards, *The Devil's Own Luck*, pp. 195–7.

Bibliography

Primary Sources, Unpublished

Asian and African Collection, British Library (BL), London
Victor Brookes, 'Games & War'

Durham University Archives (DUA), Durham
Louis Allen Papers

Imperial War Museum Archives (IWM), London
Private Papers of H. J. Butler
Private Papers of A. A. A. C. Brown
Private Papers of Captain A. B. Clements
Private Papers of J. A. Johnstone
Private Papers of Captain P. A. Young

Liddell Hart Centre for Military Archives (LHCMA), London
Papers of Lieutenant General Charles W. Allfrey

Mahn Centre for Archives and Special Collections, Ohio University Libraries (OUL), Athens
Cornelius Ryan Collection of World War II Papers

The National Archives (TNA), Kew, London
AIR 37/553 – Operation Tonga: Airborne Plan
AIR 39/45 – Operation Freshman
CAB 101/206 – The Formation of 44th Indian Division

CAB 106/8 – Operation Colossus

CAB 106/688–91 – Operation Husky: 1st Airborne Division

CAB 106/845 – Italy: 1st Airborne Division

CAB 120/262 – Airborne Forces

CAB 120/414 – Combined Operations: General

DEFE 2/100–102 – Operation Biting

DEFE 2/151–153 – Operation Colossus

DEFE 2/222–4 – Operation Freshman

DEFE 2/791 – Provision of Airborne Forces

PREM 3/73 – Operation Biting

WO 32/9778 – Airborne Forces: policy and requirements

WO 32/4723 – Parachute Regiment: Formation

WO 106/4315 – Operation Neptune: 6th Airborne Division

WO 175/181 – 1st Parachute Brigade War Diary: November 1942–June 1943

WO 218/214 – Operation Varsity: 1st Allied Air Army

WO 219/5137 – Operation Market: 1st Airborne Division

WO 373/3 – Citation for the award of MC to Captain Victor Dover

WO 373/41 – Rifleman Manbahadur Surung's citation for the Military Medal

The National Army Museum (NAM), London

9203/281/111/1 – Typescript translation of the 'Führer Befehl', Hitler's Commando Order of 18 October 1942

Primary Sources, Published

Published Documents, Diaries, Letters and Memoirs

Alanbrooke, Field Marshal Lord, *War Diaries: 1939–1945*, ed. by Alex Danchev and Daniel Todman (London: Weidenfeld, 2001)

Bartlett, Major R. J. N., 'Parachute Operations "D" Day', *The Oxfordshire and Buckinghamshire Light Infantry Quarterly Journal*, 17/5 (November 1944)

Burkinshaw, Philip L., *Alarms and Excursions* (privately published, 1991)

Chatterton, George, *The Wings of Pegasus* (London: Macdonald, 1962; repr. 1982)

Churchill, Winston, *The Second World War*, 6 vols (London: Cassell & Co., 1944–54)

Curtis, Reg, *Churchill's Volunteer: A Parachute Corporal's Story* (London: Avon Books, 1994)

Deane-Drummond, Anthony, *Arrows of Fortune* (London: Leo Cooper, 1992)

Deane-Drummond, Anthony, *Return Ticket* (London: The Popular Book Club, 1945)

Dover, Victor, *The Silken Canopy* (London: Cassell, 1979)

Edwards, Denis, *The Devil's Own Luck: Pegasus Bridge to the Baltic 1944–45* (Barnsley: Pen & Sword, 1999; repr. 2016)

Eisenhower, Dwight D., *Crusade in Europe* (New York: Doubleday, 1948; repr. 1997)

Frost, John, *A Drop Too Many: The Memoirs of World War II's Most Daring Parachute Commander* (London: Cassell & Co., 1980; repr. 1988)

Hansard (Parliamentary Proceedings), House of Commons Debates, Volumes 360–2

Horrocks, Lieutenant General Sir Brian, *A Full Life* (London: Collins, 1960)

Howard, John, and Penny Bates, *The Pegasus Diaries: The Private Papers of Major John Howard DSO* (Barnsley: Pen & Sword, 2006)

Kessel, Lipmann, *Surgeon At Arms* (London, 1958; repr. 1974)

Lovat, Lord, *March Past: A Memoir* (London: Weidenfeld & Nicolson, 1948)

Luck, Hans von, *Panzer Commander: The Memoirs of Colonel Hans von Luck* (New York: 1989; repr. 1991)

Nield, Eric, *With Pegasus in India: The Story of 153 Gurkha Parachute Battalion* (Singapore, J. Birch & Co., 1970)

Poett, Nigel, *Pure Poett: The Autobiography of General Sir Nigel Poett* (London: Leo Cooper, 1991)

Seaman, Harry, *The Battle at Sanghak: Prelude to Kohima* (London: Leo Cooper, 1989)

Sims, James, *Arnhem Spearhead: A Private Soldier's Story* (London: IWM, 1978; repr. 1980)

Slim, Field Marshal Viscount, *Retreat into Victory* (London: Cassell, 1956; repr. 1986)

Urquhart, Major General R. E., *Arnhem* (London: Cassel & Co., 1958)

Waugh, Evelyn, *The Diaries of Evelyn Waugh* (London: Weidenfeld & Nicolson, 1976), ed. by Michael Davie

Waugh, Evelyn, *Unconditional Surrender* (London: Chapman & Hall, 1961)

Newspapers and Journals
Daily Telegraph
London Gazette
The Times

Secondary Sources

Books and Articles

Allison, *Fight Your Way Out: The Siege of Sangshak, India/Burma Border, 1944* (Barnsley: Pen & Sword Military, 2023)

Ambrose, Stephen E., *Pegasus Bridge: D-Day – The Daring British Airborne Raid* (London: Simon & Schuster, 1985; repr. 2016)

Arthur, Max, *Men of the Red Beret: Airborne Forces 1940 to Today* (London: Century Hutchinson, 1990; repr. 1992)

Atkinson, Rick, *An Army at Dawn: The War in North Africa, 1942–1943* (London: Little, Brown, 2003)

Austin, A. B., *Birth of an Army* (London: Victor Gollancz, 1943)

Baynes, John, *Urquhart of Arnhem: The Life of Major-General RE Urquhart* (London: Brassey's, 1993)

Beevor, Antony, *Ardennes 1944: Hitler's Last Gamble* (London: Viking, 2015)

——, *Arnhem: The Battle for the Bridges, 1944* (London: Viking, 2018)

Bishop, Patrick, *Operation Jubilee: Dieppe 1942 – The Folly and the Sacrifice* (London: Viking, 2021)

Buckingham, William F., *Arnhem 1944: A Reappraisal* (Stroud: Tempus, 2002)

——, *Paras: The Birth of British Airborne Forces from Churchill's Raiders to 1st Parachute Brigade* (Stroud: Tempus, 2005)

Carruthers, Bob (ed.), *By Air to Battle: The Official History of the British Paratroops in World War II* (London: HMSO, 1945; repr. 2012)

Clark, Lloyd, *Arnhem: Jumping the Rhine 1944 and 1945* (London, Headline, 2008; repr. 2009)

David, Saul, *Military Blunders* (London: Robinson, 1997)

Dover, Victor, *The Sky Generals* (London: Cassell, 1981)

Golley, John, *The Big Drop: The Guns of Merville, June 1944* (London: Jane's, 1982)

Hastings, Max, *Finest Years: Churchill as Warlord 1940–1945* (London: HarperPress, 2009; repr. 2010)

Holland, James, *Together We Stand: North Africa, 1942–1943 – Turning the War in the West* (London: HarperCollins, 2005)

Jary, Christopher, *They Couldn't Have Done Better: The Story of the Dorset Regiment in War and Peace 1939–67* (London: Simper Fidelis Publications, 2014; repr. 2017)

Jefferson, Alan, *Assault on the Guns of Merville* (London: John Murray, 1987)

Johnson, Garry, and Christopher Dunphie, *Brightly Shone the Dawn: Some Experiences of the Invasion of Normandy* (London: Frederick Warne, 1980)

Kershaw, Robert, *It Never Snows in September: The German View of*

Market-Garden and the Battle of Arnhem, September 1944 (London: The Crowood Press, 1990; repr. 2008)

Kortenhaus, Werner, *The Combat History of the 21st Panzer Division* (2007; repr. and translated 2014)

Lewis, Jon E. (ed.), *Voices from D-Day: Eyewitness Accounts of the Battle for Normandy* (London: Robinson, 1994)

MacDonald, Charles B., *US Army in World War II: European Theater of Operations – The Last Offensive* (Washington DC: Office of the Chief of Military History, 1973)

McLynn, Frank, *The Burma Campaign: Disaster into Triumph, 1942–1945* (London: Bodley Head, 2010)

McMillan, George, *The Old Breed: A History of the First Marine Division in World War II* (Washington: Infantry Journal Press, 1949),

Mears, Ray, *The Real Heroes of Telemark* (London: BBC Books, 2003)

Middlebrook, Martin, *Arnhem 1944: The Airborne Battle* (London: Viking, 1994)

Millar, George, *The Bruneval Raid: Stealing Hitler's Radar* (London: Cassel & Co., 1974; repr. 2002)

Norton, G. G., *The Red Devils: From Bruneval to the Falklands* (London: Leo Cooper, 1971)

Otway, Lieutenant Colonel T. B. H., *Airborne Forces of the Second World War, 1939–45* (London: HMSO, 1951; repr. 2021)

Payne, Roger, *Paras: Voices of the British Airborne Forces in the Second World War* (Stroud: Amberley, 2014)

Peatling, Robert, *Without Tradition: 2 Para 1941–1945* (Barnsley: Pen & Sword, 1994; repr. 2004)

Ryan, Cornelius, *A Bridge Too Far* (London: Hamish Hamilton, 1974; repr. 1975),

Seelinger, Matthew J., 'Operation Varsity: The Last Airborne Deployment of World War II', *On Point*, 10/3 (December 2004),

Smith, Claude, *The History of the Glider Pilot Regiment* (London: Leo Cooper, 1992)

The Victoria Cross and the George Cross: The Complete History, 3 vols (London: Methuen, 2013)

Toll, Ian W., *The Conquering Tide: War in the Pacific Islands 1942–1944* (New York: W. W. Norton & Co., 2015; repr. 2016)

Academic Theses

Buckingham, William Frederick, 'The establishment and initial development of a British airborne force, June 1940–January 1942' (unpublished PhD thesis, University of Glasgow, 2001)

Orme, Stephen, 'The 3Cs: How important were shortcomings in Command, Control and Communication in the destruction of the 1st Airborne Division at Arnhem in September 1944' (unpublished Master's dissertation, University of Buckingham, 2016)

Websites

Anglim, S. J., 'Airborne Warfare Before 1940', https://www.paradata.org.uk/media/1378 [accessed 20 January 2022]

Archer, Jeremy, 'From Dorset Yeoman to Distinguished Airman', at https://www.keepmilitarymuseum.org/info/from+dorset+yeoman+to+distinguished+airman+-+the+story+of+wing+commander+louis+strange [accessed 25 January 2022]

Brigadier Paul Hopkinson's obituary, *Daily Telegraph*, undated, https://www.paradata.org.uk/media/11840 [accessed 14 June 2022]

'Events Leading up to the Battles of Sheldon's Corner and Sangshak, March 1944', https://www.paradata.org.uk/media/355 [accessed 14 June 2022]

Lieut. Col. Paul Hopkinson, 'Battle at Sangshak War Diary Report', pp. 1–2 https://www.paradata.org.uk/media/1466 [accessed 23 June 2022]

List of Clothing and Equipment used by X Troop during the Tragino Raid, www.paradata.org.uk/media/210 [accessed 24 February 2022]

Major Hibbert interview, Media/55, in www.paradata.org.uk/people/tony-hibbert [accessed 9 September 2021]

'Nominal Roll of No. 2 Commando as it was on the day it was formed', 22 June 1940, at http://gallery.commandoveterans.org/cdoGallery/v/units/2/2+cdo+nom+roll/Nominal+roll+of+the+first+2+Commando+later+11+SAS+Bn.jpg.html [accessed 19 January 2022]

Private Walter Parr, in https://www.iwm.org.uk/collections/item/object/80011311 [accessed 7 July 2022]

War Diary of the 2nd South Staffords, Airborne Forces Archive, https://paradata.org.uk/media/3941?mediaSection=Post-combat%20reports&mediaitem=82281 [accessed 3 October 2022]

https://www.dungannonwardead.com/persondepth.asp?cas_id=1141 [accessed 27 July 2022]

https://www.kentonline.co.uk/canterbury/news/last-original-paratrooper-dies-aged-91646/ [accessed 20 October 2022]

https://www.noonans.co.uk/auctions/archive/past-catalogues/494/catalogue/333716/ [accessed 6 June 2022]

https://www.paradata.org.uk/article/biography-sgt-neville-ashley-mm [accessed 6 June 2022]

https://www.paradata.org.uk/article/last-drop-action [accessed 28 January 2023] https://www.paradata.org.uk/article/red-devils [accessed 16 May 2022]

https://www.paradata.org.uk/article/personal-account-operation-fustian-captain-richard-bingley [accessed 31 May 2022]

https://www.paradata.org.uk/article/soudia [accessed 16 April 2022]

https://www.paradata.org.uk/media/43 [accessed 15 February 2022]

https://www.paradata.org.uk/media/168 [accessed 16 May 2022]

https://www.paradata.org.uk/media/219 [accessed 30 March 2022]

https://www.paradata.org.uk/people/maxwell-rj-hope [accessed 24 June 2022]

https://www.paradata.org.uk/people/robert-lygo [accessed 30 September 2022]

https://www.paradata.org.uk/people/trevor-ag-pritchard [accessed 17 February 2022]

https://www.paradata.org.uk/people/percy-p-clements [accessed 24 February 2022]

https://www.paradata.org.uk/people/fortunato-picchi [accessed 18 February 2022]

https://www.paradata.org.uk/people/r-geoffrey-pine-coffin [accessed 6 April 2022]

https://www.paradata.org.uk/media/43 [accessed 24 March 2022]

https://www.paradata.org.uk/media/146 [accessed 7 April 2022]

https://www.pegasusarchive.org/arnhem/jack_bird.htm [accessed 30 September 2022]

https://www.pegasusarchive.org/arnhem/jack_grayburn.htm [accessed 12 September 2021]

https://www.pegasusarchive.org/arnhem/john_baskeyfield.htm [accessed 30 September 2022]

https://www.pegasusarchive.org/arnhem/john_timothy.htm [accessed 17 March 2022]

https://www.pegasusarchive.org/arnhem/tatham_warter.htm [accessed 31 August 2022]

https://www.pegasusarchive.org/arnhem/tony_hibbert.htm [accessed 20 October 2022]

https://www.pegasusarchive.org/arnhem/tony_hibbert.htm [accessed 15 February 2022]

https://www.pegasusarchive.org/arnhem/william_hewitt.htm [accessed 30 September 2022]

https://www.pegasusarchive.org/eric_down.htm [accessed 4 March 2022]

https://www.pegasusarchive.org/sicily/george_chatterton.htm [accessed 24 May 2022]

https://www.pegasusarchive.org/sicily/john_bardwell.htm [accessed 13 June 2022] https://www.pegasusarchive.org/sicily/john_frost.htm [accessed 17 October 2022];

https://www.pegasusarchive.org./sicily/tony_frank.htm [accessed 3 October 2022]

https://www.pegasusarchive.org/normandy/allen_parry.htm [accessed 10 August 2022]

https://www.pegasusarchive.org/normandy/geoffrey_pine_coffin.htm [accessed 8 July 2022]

https://www.pegasusarchive.org/normandy/james_hill.htm [accessed 26 April 2022]

https://www.pegasusaarchive.org/normandy/john.butler.htm [accessed 26 July 2022]

https://www.pegasusarchive.org/normandy/richard_gale.htm [accessed 8 March 2022]

https://www.pegasusarchive.org/normandy/richard_todd.htm [accessed 8 July 2022]

https://www.pegasusarchive.org/normandy/terence_otway.htm [accessed 2 August 2022]

https://www.paradata.org.uk/article/extended-biography-tony-hibbert [accessed 15 February 2022]

https://www.pegasusarchive.org/normandy/tony_hooper.htm [accessed 8 July 2022]

https://trove.nla.gov.au/newspaper/article/17267585/1188781 [accessed 30 January 2023]

https://www.sallybosleysbadgeshop.com/shop. php?c=348#prettyPhoto[60529]/0/ [accessed 8 February 2022]

https://www.thegazette.co.uk/London/issue/35139/page/2212 [accessed 1 March 2022]

http://www.vconline.org.uk/lionel-e-queripel-vc/4587953689.html [accessed 30 September 2022]

https://www.musicanet.org/robokopp/usa/comeands.htm [accessed 24 March 2022]

https://www.cwgc.org/our-work/news/a-brief-history-of-operation-freshman-and-the-stories-of-its-casualties/ [accessed 25 March 2022]

https://www.eigersund.kommune.no/operation-freshman-execution-site.6541608-148494.html [accessed 12 December 2022]

https://forum.axishistory.com/viewtopic.php?f=6&t=41538&sid=396dad0508dfba058e76d0a1dc157342&start=15#google_vignette [accessed 26 March 2022]

http://ww2talk.com/index.php?threads/lieutenant-andrew-mcdermont.72044/ [accessed 30 September 2022]

Index

INDEX

SKY WARRIORS

senior German commanders 319; help to rescue wounded from Hartenstein Hotel 428; parachute capability 27–8; resistance at Arnhem 369, 370–1, 372, 374, 375, 378, 381–4, 385, 387, 390, 391–2, 393–4; response to Normandy airborne landings 297–8, 304–14, 317; *see also* named Operations
Gestapo 131, 132, 133
Geyr von Schweppenburg, General der Panzertruppe Leo 306
Gillett, Richard 249
Ginestra aqueduct 10–14
Ginkel Heath 403
Giraud, General Henri 149
Glaister, Sergeant Derek 460
Glider Pilot Regiment (GPR): disbanded 476; formation 87 and note; Norwegian campaign 125, 127, 128, 129; Sicilian campaign 194–5, 197–201; use of Denison smock 329n
glider pilots 4–5, 89
Glider Training School 87
glider-born brigade *see* 1st Airlanding Brigade
Godbold, Corporal 292
Goddard, Group Captain R.V. 42
Golden, Louis, *Echoes from Arnhem* 378
Golley, John, *The Big Drop* 339
Gondrée Café, Caen Canal 281, 288, 297, 303
Gondrée, Georges 281, 315
Goodwin, Lieutenant Colonel J.A. 238
Göring, Reichsmarschall Hermann 27
Gough, Major Freddie 485, 487; briefed on Operation plan 359; description of 358–9, 393, 417–18; Operation Market Garden 371, 376, 393, 410–11, 417–18, 427, 429
GQ Parachute Company 38
Gräbner, SS-Hauptsturmführer Viktor 383, 392
Grant, Flight Lieutenant Tommy 201
Grave 345, 412
Gray, Private Bill 287–8, 298
Grayburn, Lieutenant Jack: death of 429n; eats a hearty breakfast 362; Operation Market Garden 368, 370–1, 375, 386–7, 418–19, 427, 429n; posthumously awarded Victoria Cross 419; wounded 387, 394–5, 418
Graydon, Captain 254

Great War (1914-18) 25, 31, 80–1, 83n, 89
Greenhalgh, Lance Corporal Fred 288
Greenway, Captain the Honourable Paul 330
Grieve, Sergeant 112
Grigg, Sir John 3
Grini concentration camp 132
Groesbeek Heights 406–7
Gronert, Private Claude 375
Gronert, Private Tom 375
Guadalcanal 168
Gué Hill, Tunisia 147–9, 167
Guest, Sergeant 172
Gurkhas 244n, 247, 251, 258, 262, 469–70
Gurung, Manbahadur, Rifleman 469–70
Gwinnett, John (battalion padre) 338

Haakon VII of Norway 469
Hackett, Brigadier 'Shan': awarded DSO (or Bar) 426n; escapes after recuperation from wounds 430 and note; Operation Market Garden 405, 413, 417, 423, 430
Haggie, Dr 167
Haining, Lieutenant General Robert 41, 42–3
Halliwell, Lance Sergeant Stan 408–9, 484–5
Hamminkeln 453, 461
Hardwick Hall Camp, Derbyshire 74, 80–4, 93
Harmel, Brigadeführer Heinz 382–3
Harold, Company Sergeant Major Bill 327
Harries, Jack 5
Hartenstein Hotel, Oosterbeek 378, 411, 413–14, 416–21, 422–3, 423, 428, 430
Harvey, Group Captain 65, 67–9
Harzer, Standartenführer Walter 382, 383
Haugland, Knut 124n
Haydon, Major General Charles 124
Heathrow 86
Helberg, Claus 124n
Helleland, Norway 133
Heroes of Telemark (film, 1965) 134n
Heveadorp Ferry 371, 429–30, 431
Hewitt, Private William 402
Hibbert, Captain Tony 487; awarded MC (or Bar) 426n; comment on Major Down 77–8, 79, 118; Italian campaign 240; joins No.2 Commando 50 and note; and Operation Colossus 56;

542

Torch 141; post-war life and death
483–4; as second-in-command of 1st
Parachute Battalion 118, 119; Sicilian
campaign 220–1, 224, 226, 228–30;
Tunisian campaign 165–6, 167, 176,
177, 178–80, 182–3, 188; walks and
talks with Monty 235–6
Pegasus Bridge (1944) 4, 288n, 315, 317,
461, 486
Pepin, A.R. 48
Perham Down, (Hants) 473; Cambrai
Barracks at 21; parade at 21–2, 29;
training at 33, 34
Pescopagano 18
Pétain, Marshal Philippe 144
Phoney War (1939-40) 83
Picchi, Fortunato (Private Pierre Dupont
pseud) 15, 19–20, 62–3, 66 and note,
67
Pickard, Wing Commander Charles 99,
104, 107
Picture Post 84
Pierse, Air Marshal Sir Richard 41
Pim, Richard 111
Pine-Coffin, Major Geoffrey 'Wooden
Box' 117, 293, 315; arrival in
Normandy 300, 301 and note; back-
ground and description 142; and
Operation Torch 142; post-war life
and death 484; report on fighting
around Caen Canal bridge 309, 316;
response to German attacks 311, 312;
return to US 222n; rewarded for
D-Day work 318; Tunisian campaign
186, 188
Platts, Gus 237–8
Poett, Brigadier Nigel 291–2, 295–6, 314,
459, 460–1; congratulated on
achieving D-Day objectives 341; frat-
ernizes with the Russioans 470
Point 7378 (Battle of Sangshak, 1944)
257–8, 259, 261, 262
Polish 1st Independent Parachute Brigade
345, 350, 355, 401, 408, 416, 429, 432,
435, 437
Ponte Grande, Sicily 193, 196, 201,
206–7, 209, 210
Pool, Lieutenant 318
Port Sunlight, Merseyside 127
Portal, Air Chief Marshal Sir Charles
67–8, 109–10, 115
Porteous, Peter 50n

Poulsson, Jens-Anton 124n
Pound, Sir Dudley 64
Priday, Captain Brian 279; description of
276; error in landing 289–90, 291,
300, 316–17; expected to supported
Howard 283; given command of D
Company 317; Orne bridge 271, 282,
289–90; reunited with D Company
317
Primosole Bridge, Sicily 4, 210, 211, 216,
220–7, 446
Prince of Wales (battleship) 96
Prins Albert (cross-Channel ferry) 107
prisoner-of-war camps 67, 70n, 164, 192,
488
prisoners-of-war (POWs) 131, 132, 241–2,
470, 484
Pritchard, Major Trevor 'Tag': confirm's
blowing up of aqueduct 67; description of 54–5; escape plan 14n–15n;
given gallantry medal 69–70 and note;
Operation Colossus 11, 13, 54, 57, 58;
sends message to Keyes 67; walk to
'freedom' and humiliating surrender
15–20, 61–4

Queripel, Captain Lionel 415
Quilter, Raymond 38 and n, 47

radar 90–2, 95–6, 101, 102–3, 110–11, 113,
119, 338
Radcliffe, Willoughby 187
RAF Bomber Command 91, 194
RAF Elementary Flying Training School
87
RAF Harwell, Oxfordshire 327, 329
RAF Manston, Kent 31
RAF Mildenhall, Suffolk 57
RAF Netheravon, Wiltshire 114–15
RAF No.38 Wing 114, 128, 135, 194
RAF Ringway, Manchester 46, 56, 245;
Central Landing School (CLS) (later
Central Landing Establishment [CLE])
at 31, 33, 54, 65, 69, 71; Churchill's
visit to 72; death at 37–8; lack of suit-
able aircraft 40–1; No.3 Advanced
Training Course 75; parachute training
at 35–8, 74, 75, 81–2; relocation of
No.1 Glider Training School to
Thame 86
RAF St Eval, Cornwall 142
Rangoon 469, 470